RAASAY

The Island and Its People

by
NORMA MACLEOD

First published in 2002 by
Birlinn Limited
West Newington House
10 Newington Road
Edinburgh
EH9 1QS

www.birlinn.co.uk

Copyright © Norma MacLeod 2002
Colour illustrations copyright © Anne and Andrew Gillies, Raasay

The right of Norma MacLeod to be identified as the author
of this work has been asserted by her in accordance
with the Copyright, Designs and Patents Act 1988

All rights reserved. No part of this publication may be reproduced,
stored, or transmitted in any form, or by any means, electronic,
mechanical or photocopying, without the express
written permission of the publisher.

ISBN 1 84158 235 2

British Library Cataloguing-in-Publication Data
A catalogue record for this book is available from the British Library

The publisher acknowledges subsidy from the

towards the publication of this book

Designed and typeset by Carnegie Publishing Ltd, Lancaster
Printed and bound by Creative Print and Design, Ebbw Vale, Wales

Contents

	Acknowledgements	v
	Abbreviations	vi
	MacLeods of Raasay – Revised Genealogy	vii
	Map of Raasay	viii
	Introduction	1

Part I The History of Raasay

1	The History of Raasay to *c*.1500	7
2	The History of Raasay, *c*.1450–1630s	19
3	The History of Raasay, 1630s–1750	44
4	The History of Raasay, *c*.1750–*c*.1800	59
5	The History of Raasay, *c*.1800–1846	75
6	The History of Raasay, 1846–1872	95
7	The History of Raasay, 1872–1900	118
8	The History of Raasay, 1900–*c*.1950	158
9	Epilogue	173

Part II Genealogy

10	Genealogy of the MacLeods of Raasay	187
11	Genealogy of the MacLeods of Gairloch	220

Appendices

1	Ancient Ruins Still Survive	231
2	Songs of Raasay	243
3	Some Place-Names of Raasay and Rona	257
4	Document Sources	266
5	List of Lairds/Owners of Raasay and Rona	273

Charts

Kings of Man/MacLeods/Lords of the Isles	275
MacLeods of Lewis	276
MacLeods of Raasay, based on Alexander MacKenzie 1889	277
MacLeods of Raasay, based on Alick Morrison 1974	278
Gaelic/English Equivalents Equivalents	279

Maps

Map of Scotland/Ireland/England	280
Map of West Coast of Scotland	281
Map of Raasay, Rona and East Coast of Skye	282
Selected Bibliography	283
Index	285

Acknowledgements

My interest in the history of Raasay was sparked by my father, Norrie Gillies, talking about the place and its people. His keen interest in my findings kept me looking for more. The late Dr Alasdair MacLean, Aird Bhearnasdail encouraged me to believe that I could write a book. Without his advice, based on his extensive knowledge of the North West of Scotland, I would not have attempted to do so.

Many others have helped me with information and to source documents. I would like to thank various Government Departments, and their staff, for their help:

- Dualchas, Skye and Lochalsh Area Museums and Heritage Service, the Highland Council, Portree – Mary Carmichael and Nancy Gatz.
- Highland Council's Libraries – Morna MacLaren and David McClymont at Portree: Mr A. MacLeod, Genealogist, Inverness and Mr R. Stewart, Archivist, Inverness.
- SEERAD, Scottish Executive Environment and Rural Affairs Department, Portree (formerly DAFS).

Thanks also to Mary Gillies and Charlie MacLeod, both originally from Raasay, and to Mr D. R. MacDonald: Morag MacLeod: Roger Miket: Mr W. D. H. Sellar and Martin Wildgoose for their specialist knowledge. Any errors are my own. I am most grateful to Anne and Andrew Gillies, Raasay. Their patience, over a long period, in dealing with my frequent requests for help is much appreciated.

Over the years many other people have also answered my many questions. To each of you my sincere thanks.

This book is all the richer for the photographs that are included in it. Many thanks to all those people who allowed their photos to be used.

Norma MacLeod
September 2002

Abbreviations

BoAS	Board of Agriculture for Scotland
DAFS	Department of Agriculture & Fisheries for Scotland
GSS	Gaelic Schools Society
HIDB	Highlands & Islands Development Board
HIES	Highlands & Islands Emigration Society
HLL	Highland Land League
OPR	Old Parish Register
OSA	Old Statistical Account
SHS	Scottish History Society
SLC	Scottish Land Court
SSPCK	Scottish Society for the Propagation of Christian Knowledge
TGSI	Transactions of the Gaelic Society of Inverness
b	born
bro	brother
c	circa (about)
d	died
dau	daughter
nk	not known
unm	unmarried
=	married
?	uncertain
[ ]	used for explanation, usually within a quotation.

Money

shilling: 20s. = £1 [1s. = 5 pence]
d. penny: 12*d.* = 1s.

MacLeods of Raasay – Revised Genealogy

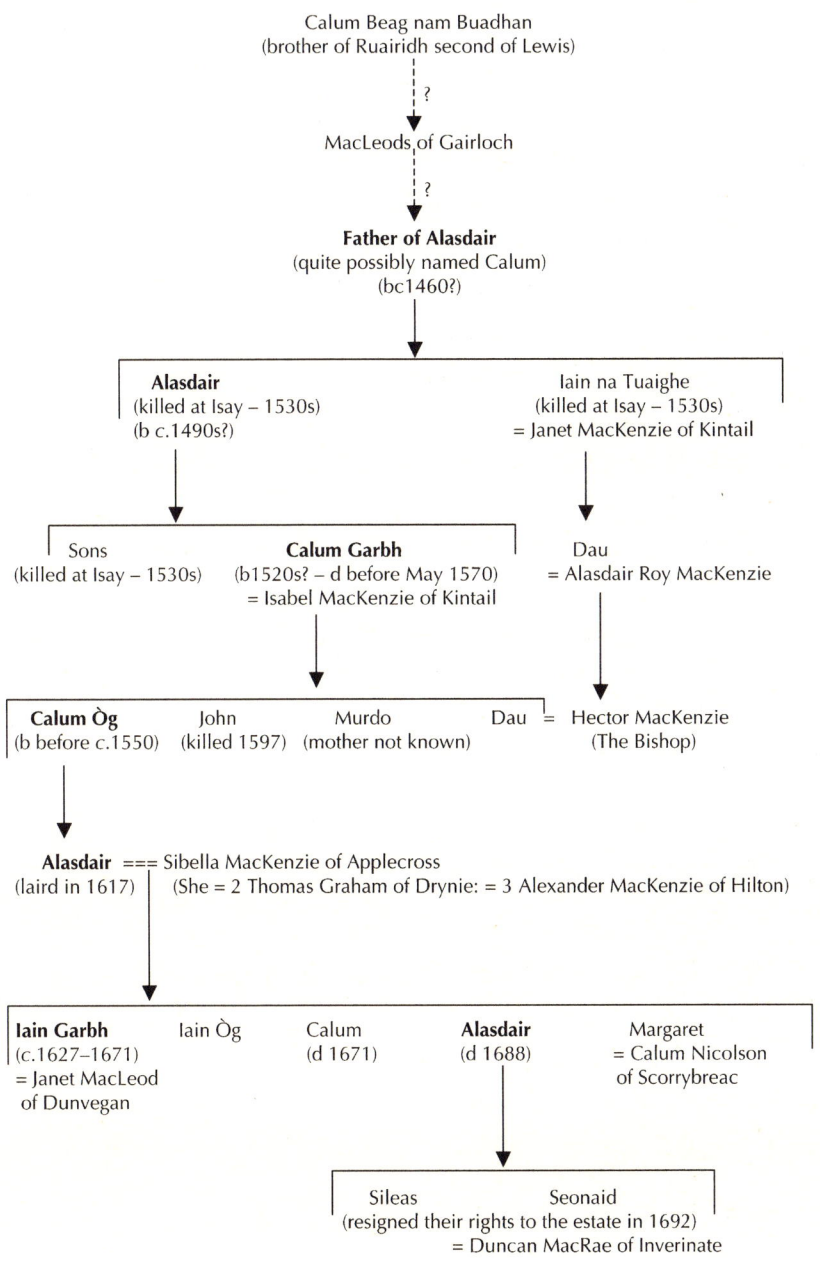

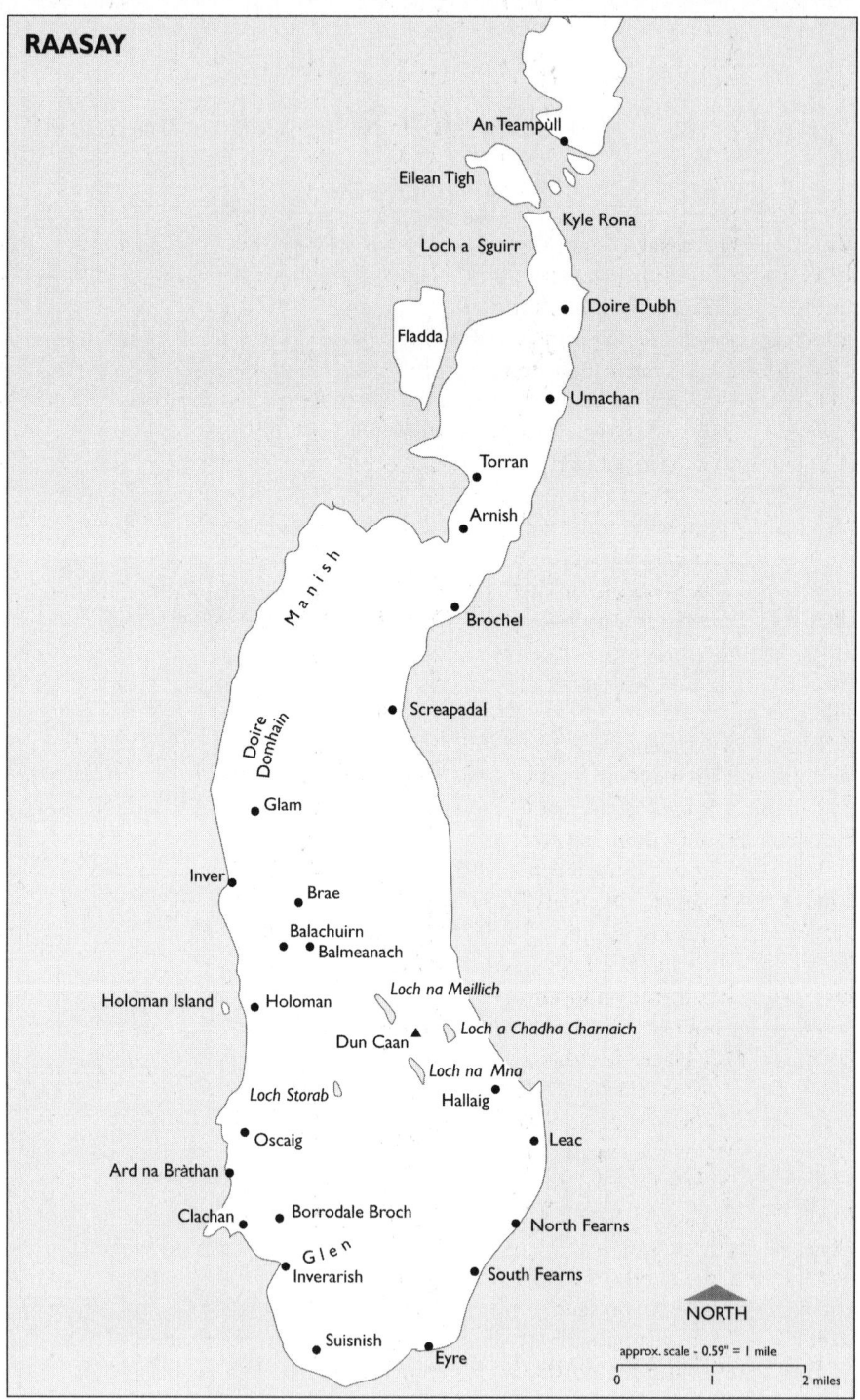

Introduction

The island of Raasay is one of a group of islands lying off the east coast of Skye. Running roughly north to south, it stretches for about thirteen miles and, over much of its length, is three miles wide. A part of the parish of Portree, it is separated from the main part of the parish by the Sound of Raasay. The distinctive flat top of Dun Caan was formed from a basalt plug. Rising to 1456 feet, it is Raasay's highest hill and can be seen for miles around. The volcanic ridge, north from Dun Caan, is above 800 feet over most of its length. Along the east coast of the island, a series of cliffs and precipices fall steeply to the sea. The rugged coastline is one of the many areas on the island that affords spectacular views. Most of the population, now about 180, live in the south west of the island where the land is fertile and lower.

Access to the island is by car ferry from Sconser, Skye, at the mouth of Loch Sligachan. The modern roll-on roll-off ferry can carry up to twelve cars on each fifteen-minute crossing. During the height of the summer there are ten such crossings each day, with six in winter, allowing easy access for locals and visitors alike.

The variety of geological formations found on the island creates a diversity of landscapes and habitats for plant and animal life. Raasay is thus a favourite destination for geologists, botanists and bird-watchers as well as those looking for the tranquillity and the scenery.

The ferry lands beside Suisnish Pier, built by William Baird & Co. early last century to exploit the deposits of iron-ore. The remains of some of these works can be seen around the pier. To the right, the road leads to Eyre, a crofting township at the south of the island. To the left, it first reaches the village of Inverarish, where the shop and post office are found. Two terraces of miners' houses were built here by Bairds during their short spell on the island. The older houses of Mill Place sit closer to the shore.

Further north is Clachan. Archaeological evidence indicates that this area was occupied even before it became a significant site for the early Church in the Isles about the end of the twelfth century. The area around Clachan has the largest concentration of historical and archaeological sites on the island. In the churchyard is St Moluag's Chapel. The Battery, close to the Old Pier, was built about 1809, when there was fear of a French invasion. Raasay House was the main home of the MacLeods of Raasay from the late seventeenth to the mid-nineteenth century. Part of the present building dates from about 1750. Part of the farm steading dates from the early nineteenth century.

The road continues north, past the townships of Oscaig, Balachuirn and Balmeanach, Brae and Glam. To the north west of the present-day Glam Steading is the site of the old township of Glam, where Bonnie Prince Charlie hid for two days in 1746, while government troops scoured the north west of Scotland in search of him. The green, fertile and wooded landscape of the south end has now been replaced by open, heathery moorland with rocky outcrops and small lochs, based on Torridonian sandstone.

The road crosses from the west coast of Raasay to Brochel on the north-east coast. The MacLeods of Raasay occupied Brochel Castle until the second half of the seventeenth century. From Brochel to Arnish is 'Calum's Road'. Calum MacLeod of Arnish took ten years to build this road, after which it was tarred by the regional council, allowing vehicular traffic to go to Arnish from 1976.

North of 'the neck' of Raasay at Tairbeart, are found some of the oldest rocks in Britain, Lewisian gneiss. Worn down by erosion and ice, the hummocky surface has areas of peat formed in the hollows. There are many small lochs here, typical of this surface. This area, and the island of Rona to the north, carried very few people until the first half of the nineteenth century, when the MacLeods of Raasay began clearing the population from the south end. From the late 1850s until the 1920s, the bulk of the population lived on north Raasay, in the townships of Umachan, Doire Dubh and Kyle Rona, on Fladda and on Rona itself.

Rona is roughly four miles long and two miles wide. The small township of Doire na Guaille is in the south end. Dry Harbour was the main settlement. Some people lived in Big Harbour and the northern township of Braig.

Off the north-west coast of Raasay is the island of Fladda. Today it has only holiday homes. Off the northern tip of Raasay is the small island of Eilean Taigh, which, although occupied in the past, is now deserted.

Traditionally, the bulk of the population of Raasay lived on the east coast in the townships of Fearns, Hallaig, Screapadal and Brochel. The road from Inverarish goes only as far as Fearns. A track reaches Hallaig, but the route from there to Brochel along the coast is only for the fit and adventurous.

The story of Raasay is complex. The island was, and indeed still is, affected by people and events far beyond its shores. The history of the island is inextricably linked to its owners, both past and present.

This book is an attempt to bring together the many strands, scattered through various publications and other documents, of Raasay's story. Equally important is the unrecorded information, passed down through many generations, of people and times past. While researching for this publication, conflicting accounts of people and events have been found. Many of the events and dates, previously accepted, cannot be reconciled with known and authenticated information. It has thus been necessary to undertake a reassessment of the history of Raasay, involving research of original documents where possible.

This book, therefore, is one person's interpretation, based on the balance of probability and the information found to date. As far as possible, particularly where there is a conflict of opinion, sources have been given. New information will continue to be found that will shed more light on Raasay's history.

The book is in two parts – the first gives the history of Raasay, and the second the genealogy of the MacLeods of Raasay, with some information about the

MacLeods of Lewis and the MacLeods of Gairloch. The second part, therefore, gives more detail about the people and the relationships mentioned in part one.

The genealogy of the MacLeods of Raasay during the eighteenth and nineteenth centuries is far from certain. Again, it is hoped that further research here will lead to better understanding.

Unfortunately pressure of time has made it impossible to present more than an outline of the history of the twentieth century. Certainly, it is too soon to attempt to cover the last fifty years, but in the fullness of time, as more documents become available, this will become a more realistic proposition.

Part I

The History of Raasay

I

The History of Raasay to c.1500

There is no doubt that Raasay has been occupied for many millennia before recorded history. All the evidence for occupation and settlement before about AD 1500 has come from archaeological surveys of the area.[1] Raasay has had the benefit of such surveys since the early 1990s, each concentrating on different areas of the island, and each producing new evidence. The extent of each of these surveys has depended on available funding, and so evidence to date is patchy. This work is ongoing and in the fullness of time will permit a far more comprehensive assessment of the island's pre-history.

Mesolithic Period (8000–3000 BC)

By far the oldest site found to date lies on the north west tip of Raasay at Loch a' Sguirr. Here, there is a substantial rock shelter with a large platform above the sea cliff. Radiocarbon dating indicates that it was occupied about 7600 BC, just after the end of the last Ice Age. Bone and stone tools were found on the site. There were two types of stone tool found, some of flint-stone that probably came from the Staffin area of Skye and some of bloodstone from the Island of Rhum.

The people of that time were hunter-gatherers, and may have used such shelters in winter. Another site on Raasay, at Clachan Bay, has produced tools of a similar period. This site is now in the inter-tidal zone, covered by a layer of peat. The period immediately following the Ice Age saw large fluctuations in land and sea levels, caused by a combination of ice melt, resulting in a rise in sea level, and the land rising when the weight of ice came off it.

A survey carried out in 2001 identified twenty-one caves on the island, many of them between Hallaig and Screapadal, all having shell middens indicating occupation at some time. Although these middens have an upper layer of relatively recent date, older evidence may be found below that. Further work has yet to be carried out on these sites.

Raasay is not alone in producing evidence for these, our earliest settlers. Along the neighbouring coastlines, recent work has revealed a wealth of evidence which would appear to indicate a large number of mobile communities exploiting the wealth of natural resources in a remarkable variety of ways.

Neolithic Period (3200–2200 BC)

The neolithic period is characterised by the transition from predominantly hunter-gatherers to a more settled society, cultivating cereals and with domesticated animals. While the discovery of a polished stone axe-head from Arnish, and possibly the standing stone at Church Wood, show that the island was settled, little is otherwise known of life here at this time.

Bronze Age (2200–700 BC)

Technologically the introduction of at first copper, then later bronze-working, gave its name to a long period in which many other changes also took place. Archaeology shows the transition in burial practices from multiple to single burials, sometimes in stone 'chests' or cists. It is the discovery of the large capstone, often through recent agricultural working, which can betray their presence, as in the case of those at Eyre, Brae and Torran.

The one at Eyre, about eighty metres north of the lighthouse, is typical. The cist now stands alone, as the body of the cairn has long since disappeared. On the north side of the mound, two stones are set on edge, and may be the remains of the kerb that would have surrounded it.

Local tradition has woven a colourful story around this cairn, and the man said to be buried in it: some invaders landed on the beach at Eyre, but were met by local people who turned them back. The invaders managed to board their boat, and tried to get off the shore to make their escape. A local man got hold of their painter (the rope, whatever kind of rope they had at that time, at the bow of the boat). He held on and dug his heels in. When someone on board the boat cut the rope, he fell backwards and was so badly injured that he died soon afterwards and was buried at Eyre.

Below the mission house at Torran is a ring cairn, a burial site with a ring of stones around it. The Brae site is known as Storab's Grave. Here only the cist remains. In local tradition, Storab is said to have been a Dane or Viking who has left his mark elsewhere on Raasay – in Loch Storab in the hills to the south-west of Dun Caan, and in the Storab Burn, which runs north-west to the sea at Inver. Tradition has it that Storab was on an island in the loch. He was being pursued, but whether by locals or outsiders is not known. He leapt from the island to the shore and made off, running towards Inver, but a marksman, with a bow and arrow, managed to kill him very close to the spot where he was buried.

Iron Age (700 BC–c. AD 550)

Understandably, more evidence relating to this period has been found than for earlier times. Perhaps the most obvious – certainly the largest before decay set in – is the ruin of the Broch which stands in Borrodale Wood to the west of the Free Church. Brochs are essentially fortified dwellings, known to have been built between around 500 BC and AD 200. With a distribution throughout northern and western Scotland, their construction from massive, unmortared stone blocks has resulted in some spectacular survivals. At Glenelg, on the mainland opposite Skye for example, stand the towering remains of Dun Troddan and Dun Telve. Complete with their deep entrances, narrow, curving passageways and stairs winding within the walls across spacious, corbelled cells, they are testimony to one of the most striking types of structure in Britain before the arrival of the Romans.

Brochs formed but one element in the Middle Iron-Age built landscape. Another was the round house. Its steeply pitched roof was supported on low stone walls and timber uprights within. Today they are identifiable only as hut-circles from the surviving residue of walling. More than ten have been found in Raasay around the iron ore mine, along the 'Burma Road' area and in the Glen area, suggesting that the people of the time were making use of these deposits. Quite possibly more are, as yet, undiscovered in that area. Others have been found on the island in various places, such as Brochel Wood and Torran.

In the area of Brochel Castle there is the possibility of another type of structure, known to have been built, during but not solely, in the Iron Age – a dun. Duns are small, fortified enclosures occupying defensive positions such as promontories or hilltops.

Souterrains are narrow underground passageways, thought to have been built during the Iron Age for the cool storage of produce. At least two have been identified on Raasay. There is one at Clachan and one behind Suisnish House. The one at Clachan was visited by Johnson and Boswell during their stay on the island in 1773, but it subsequently became a dumping ground for rubbish. With the assistance of the local historical society, in the spring of 1990 the dump was removed to reveal a long deep cleft in the natural rock, 14 metres long by 1.5 metres high, capped with massive stone slabs. It is now open once again to visitors. It is known as Uamh na Raimh, the Cave of Oars.

One explanation for this name is that in 1746, when government forces were searching for Bonnie Prince Charlie, boats on Raasay were being destroyed or taken away. It is said that the oars from the confiscated boats were taken to the souterrain and kept there under guard. Johnson, although he refers to it as the 'oar-cave', believed that it had been used as such in the days of 'piratical expeditions'.[2] Quite reasonably, he questions how hiding the oars could possibly have been of benefit. It is strange that he was not given the explanation above, if indeed that had been the case.

People at this time lived in single farms. Their houses were dispersed, probably about one-quarter mile apart, and so were unlike the cluster settlements of today.

Early Christian (sixth century–tenth century)

EARLY CHRISTIAN SETTLERS IN THE NORTH WEST OF SCOTLAND

By about AD 500 a colony of Scotti, from the kingdom of Dàl Riata, an Irish kingdom in what is now County Antrim in the north-east of Ireland, had become sufficiently established here for their rulers to move from Ireland to the west coast of Scotland. The name, Dàl Riata, was also transferred across the water, and the two parts were ruled from Scotland. Their area extended from the Mull of Kintyre to Ardnamurchan and the southern Hebrides. About AD 843, Kenneth, son of Alpin, who was already King of the Scots of Dàl Riata, also became King of the Picts, and their centres of power moved from their original western homeland into the previously Pictish centres further east.

In AD 565 St Columba came from Ireland and founded the monastic community on Iona. That community gave leadership to a group of similar monasteries in Scotland and Ireland. Iona came to be considered the spiritual capital of the Scots, shown by the fact that their kings were buried there until 1097.

Although there was no resident bishop on Iona in Columba's time, a 'shadowy line' of bishops is traced there from about the early eighth century until 966. By this time, however, the leadership of the group of monasteries in Scotland and Ireland, loyal to the name of Columba, had passed from Iona to Kells, County Meath in Ireland.[3] During the late tenth and early eleventh century the Earls of Orkney ruled the western isles of Scotland, and ecclesiastically the area may have been attached to the diocese of Orkney for a time.

THE VIKINGS

The end of the eighth century saw a new wave of people coming to the west coast of Scotland. From Scandinavia, the Vikings came, initially as raiders. Their advanced ship design and knowledge of navigation allowed the Vikings to dominate the seaways. Scandinavia, sometimes referred to as Lochlainn, covered a large area including present-day Norway, Sweden and Denmark. The Vikings who raided and settled in the north west of Scotland were from Norway, while those who raided the east coast of England, about the same time, were from Denmark. This gave rise to a tendency, in the eighteenth and nineteenth centuries, to attribute anything old to 'the Danes'.

From Orkney and Shetland, known to the Vikings as the Nordreys, they moved south, through the islands of the west coast of Scotland, the Sudreys. In AD 795 Skye was pillaged and devastated. Within one hundred years, raiding had given way to settlement, and integration of the Viking and Gaelic cultures. During the ninth century the Western Islands of Scotland were known within the Gaelic world as Innse Gall, the Islands of the Foreigners. Two thirds of the place-names of Trotternish in Skye are of Scandinavian origin. From about AD 850 at the latest, these Viking settlers adopted Christianity.

From settlement came trade, and Dublin became a major Viking trading centre. It is of great significance that Skye and Raasay lie on the route between the Viking homeland in Norway and the major trading centre of Dublin. The discovery of hoards of silver in Skye, such as at Storr Lochs, indicates that wealth was coming into this area.

During this early period, the only evidence of Viking influence and settlement on Raasay is found in place-names. The name 'Raasay' is believed to be Norse. It is thought to mean 'Roe Deer Island', the ending -ey or -ay being Old Norse for 'island'. Rona may mean 'Seal Island'. In the past, Rona was sometimes spelt 'Ronay'. It should be remembered, however, that prior to standardised spelling, no great importance was attached to the spelling of place-names (or indeed of personal names).

Other names on Raasay also give evidence of Norse influence. The ending -dal or its English form -dale is found here in Borrodale, Screapadal and the old township of Ramisdal in the Glen area. Tarbert, or in Gaelic Tairbeart, is found south-west of Arnish, and describes perfectly the narrowest part of the island.

The name is derived from 'tairm-bert' – 'an over-bringing'. In some places, such a narrow point was useful, as the Viking longships could be dragged overland to the sea on the other side.

On a hill above the inner end of Loch Braig on Rona, there is an old burial place. There are two names for this place. One tradition names it Uaigh Nighean Righ Lochlainn, the Grave of the Daughter of the King of Denmark. The story tells that the daughter of the King of Denmark had eloped with a Greek prince. Her father and his men were chasing after the couple, and caught up with them on Rona. The prince was slain and a grave dug for him. The princess leapt in beside him and the two were buried together.

Another tradition names it Leac Chlann Greige, the Tombstone of the Children of Greece. In this tradition there are said to be two or three brothers and a princess buried under the stone, all of them Greek. This story appears to be based on the Irish/Celtic story of Deirdre. There are variants of this story here and there in many places all over the Highlands.

SYMBOL STONES ON RAASAY

At some time point within the long time-span, c.500–1200 AD, symbol stones were carved. There are two found on Raasay. On the rock face beside the old landing place, on the south side of the Battery at Clachan, is the very worn outline of a foliate cross. This cross is copied on another stone that now stands by the roadside near the north entrance to Raasay House. On this stone, below the cross is a tuning fork symbol, which in turn lies above a crescent and V rod symbol. This stone is not in its original position. It was possibly found in 1824, when the road from Raasay House to the landing place was being made and moved to its present position.

Although these symbols are on the same face of the stone as the cross, it is believed that they were pre-Christian. That the cross appears above them on this stone may indicate the continued use of these Pictish symbols after the people of the area became Christian. It is thought that because both appear together on the same stone, the symbols had some non-religious meaning. It has been speculated that they indicated rank, or designated the owner of the land on which they stood. It is also possible that they related to marriage, and the joining of two houses. However, their actual purpose remains uncertain.

Medieval (eleventh century–fifteenth century)

Raasay and Rona were clearly sites of importance to the early Church in the Isles. This is shown, not only by the chapel, dedicated to St Moluag at Clachan, but also by the sites on Rona and at Torran.

The chapel of St Moluag was a subsidiary church of the cathedral church on St Columba's Isle in Snizort, from where the canons objected to the appointment of a Bishop of the Isles in 1331. In 1433 Bishop Angus had secured papal approval to transfer his cathedral church from Snizort elsewhere, although this planned move may never have taken place.

Church land in Snizort, amounting to three merklands, and the whole of

Raasay and Rona, amounting to eight merklands, was held by the Bishop of the Isles until the Act of Annexation in 1587. This Act transferred ownership of all Church lands and their revenues to the Scottish Crown as part of the reformation of the Church.

These two separate pieces of land, a total of eleven merklands, were held during the sixteenth century by the MacLeods of Raasay, initially as 'feeholders and tenants of the Bishop of the Isles' and, after the 1587 Act, from the Crown. A Crown charter of 1596 to the MacLeods of Raasay states that these lands had been the 'benefice of the churches and chapels of the parishes of Kilmoluag in Raasay and Snizort in Trotternish'. The charter further states that the MacLeods had held these lands 'since time immemorial'.

KINGS OF MAN AND THE ISLES – BISHOPRIC OF THE ISLES
About 1079, Godred Crovan, who also ruled Dublin for a time, took over the Isle of Man. In time he and his dynasty took control of the western seaboard of Scotland, from the Butt of Lewis to the Isle of Man. Following Magnus Barelegs' expedition of 1098, the Kings of Man and the Isles held the area under the superiority of the Kings of Norway.

Olaf the Red had become King of the Isles by 1114. He supported a bishop, based on Skye, rather than Iona. This bishop, named Wimund, had been consecrated at York, and was regarded, at least in York, as covering the Isles in general. It may be that even at this early date, there was a connection with the church of Snizort at Skeabost. Although the name of only one bishop on Skye is known, there may well have been a line of bishops based there.

There were also other ecclesiastical centres within the kingdom of the Isles, and in 1134 King Olaf arranged that there should, in future, be only one bishop for his whole kingdom. He granted the right of election of a bishop to the monks of Furness Abbey in Lancashire. Until this time they had had no connection with the Isles. The next two Kings of Man confirmed these rights on Furness. The bishops were consecrated by the Archbishop of York. Although the diocese of the Isles had been subordinated to the Archbishop of Trondheim in Norway by 1153, it appears that three of the four bishops before 1198 were consecrated at York.

The Norwegian Kings of Man had undisputed control over the area until, in 1156, Somerled challenged Godfrey the Black. The kingdom was then divided, Godfrey and his descendants retaining Man and the northern isles of Skye, Lewis and Harris, while Somerled and his descendants were in possession of the southern Hebrides. Although the kingdom of the Isles was then politically divided, there is no reason to suppose that there was more than one office of bishop for the whole area.

The sons of Godfrey the Black, Ragnall and Olaf the Black, were married to two sisters. When the Bishop of the Isles objected to Olaf's marriage, he dismissed his wife, and married instead Christina, daughter of Farquhar, Earl of Ross. The story is told by W. D. H. Sellar:

> Ragnall's wife took considerable offence at this insult to her sister and sent letters secretly in Ragnall's name to their son Godfrey Donn (the Brown) in Skye, directing him to seize and kill Olaf. Godfrey collected some men and

set off for Lewis. Olaf, however, narrowly escaped and fled to his father-in-law the Earl of Ross. The vicecomes [sometimes called the sheriff] of Skye, Paul son of Balki, described as 'a vigorous and powerful man throughout the kingdom of the Isles' wished no part in the murder of Olaf. He too fled to the earl of Ross where he entered into an alliance with Olaf ...

Olaf and Paul came secretly to Skye and learnt that Godfrey was staying with only a few men 'on a certain island called the isle of St Columba'. Under cover of night they dragged five ships from the nearest shore of the sea and encircled the island. When Godfrey and his men awoke in the morning, they were amazed to see that they were surrounded. Although outnumbered they put up a brave resistance but were eventually defeated. Olaf and Paul put to death everyone they found outside the bounds of the church. Godfrey Donn himself was seized, blinded and castrated ... Despite his injuries, Godfrey remained active.[4]

This happened in 1223, on Eilean Chaluim Chille, St Columba's Isle, in Kilmuir, Skye. Godfrey Donn was King of the Hebrides in 1230, after which he and Olaf the Black agreed on the division of the area. The northern Hebrides of Skye, Lewis and Harris were Godfrey's share. Although Raasay is not mentioned, it may be assumed that it was considered as a satellite island of Skye.

The earldom of Ross had been created about 1223, and was based in Central and Easter Ross. The area known today as Wester Ross, from Kintail to Loch Broom, was then part of north Argyll. The first Earl of Ross was Farquhar mac an t-Sagairt, son of the priest. He was born in Ross, probably the son of a priest at Tain, the main religious centre in north-east Ross. The Earl of Ross then began his bid to take over north Argyll.

The Bishops of the Isles continued to be elected by the monks of Furness Abbey. By 1231 the bishop had begun to build his cathedral at Peel, off the coast of the Isle of Man, but no chapter of dean and canons was set up there. There was a complication in that the sons of Somerled held the central part of the kingdom, including Iona, and also, for a time, used the title King of the Isles (*Rex Insularum*). The right of patronage of the bishop became a matter of politics, as both Kings of the Isles – those of Man, and those of Somerled's sons – sought to influence the appointment of the bishops. Some of the candidates for the bishopric were therefore probably rivals.

Godfrey Donn and his descendants held Skye (probably including Raasay), Lewis and Harris until 1262, when William, Earl of Ross, attacked Skye in a direct challenge against them. In 1266 the Treaty of Perth finally ceded the Isle of Man and the Western Isles to the Scottish Crown. The Earl of Ross then had control of all the islands north of Ardnamurchan Point, including Skye.

When the Isles were transferred to Scottish control, the appointment of the bishop fell to the Scottish government. Although the first bishop probably lived on the Isle of Man, the second and third were buried at Rothesay, on the island of Bute, where they may well have had their seat. This may reflect the Scottish king's desire to strengthen his influence in the area of the Firth of Clyde rather than elsewhere in the Isles.

In 1331 'the canons of Snizort and the clergy of Skye' objected to the bishop appointed by King Robert I, and sent a deputation to the Archbishop of Trondheim, seeking his confirmation for their preferred choice. This was not successful, however, and another Scot secured the position. Professor Watt gives more information about these canons and clergy of Skye:

> We do not know who these canons of Snizort were. But in the normal usage of the church at that time 'canons' in this context would mean members of a formally constituted collegiate body of clergy, each with a separately defined income, and responsible as a body for maintaining the services of their church in person or by deputy. And 'the clergy of Skye' would normally mean the clergy dispersed in parish benefices who would meet from time to time in synod, perhaps under the archdeacon of the whole diocese. In that the canons concerned themselves on this occasion with electing a bishop, their church can fairly be described as a cathedral of the diocese – note that I do not say *the* cathedral, for there is no suggestion that at this stage that the diocese of the Isles had been split up. But it was not uncommon for a diocese to have two churches whose clergy (whether secular or regular clergy) formed a double cathedral chapter e.g. Bath and Wells, Coventry and Lichfield, and Dublin with two rival cathedral chapters within the same city. It seems to me likely that the early-fourteenth-century community or collegium of canons at Snizort may well have had a continuity of existence since the time when there had been a separate bishop of Skye in the early twelfth century; but that they aroused themselves to making a duplicate episcopal election (and so to creating documentation that survives today) only when they felt that Scottish royal interference in the appointment of a bishop of the Isles was going too far.

Church affairs became even more complicated in the 1330s, when the English king took over the administration of the Isle of Man. At least two Manxmen, rather than Scots, were appointed as Bishops of the Isles, in 1349 and 1374. A further complication arose when the western church as a whole became split during the Great Schism of 1378–1419. During that time, Scotland adhered to the pope at Avignon, while the English government adhered to the pope at Rome. Professor Watt explains

> During this difficult period each pope appointed a succession of bishops of the Isles, with one series of bishops loyal to England and presumably resident on Man, and the other series loyal to Scotland and resident somewhere in Scotland. This latter place may well have been Snizort, even if this cannot be proved. What we do know is that as a result of these years of schism, it was agreed by the unified papacy after 1419 that there should in future continue to be two separate dioceses, Sodor and Man in England, and the Isles in Scotland. In 1426 the man appointed by Pope Martin V to the Scottish diocese was Angus, a son of Donald Lord of the Isles. He it was who in 1433 secured papal approval of a plan to 'transfer his cathedral church from Suusperdy [generally accepted as being Snizort] with the consent of all those whose interest

it is, to some honest place within the diocese, and to create in the said church twelve canonries and as many prebends'. We know little of Bishop Angus' success with his plans, except that two canonries with prebends (i.e. fixed endowed incomes) can be identified at Strath on Skye in 1450 and Kingarth on Bute in 1463. There is no evidence that the bishop's plan for a move was ever put into effect. The Scottish government in 1498 was to suggest to the pope that Iona Abbey should be erected as the cathedral of the bishop of the Isles 'until the principal kirk on the Isle of Man should be recovered from the English'; but of course there was never any likelihood of the old united diocese of the Isles being recreated, and there is no evidence in any official document to prove that the plan to move the bishop's cathedral to Iona was ever implemented.

The Earls of Ross continued to control the islands north of Ardnamurchan Point, on behalf of the Scottish crown. About 1402, Donald MacDonald, second Lord of the Isles claimed the earldom of Ross on behalf of his wife. Eventually, the Lords of the Isles were recognised as Earls of Ross also, and took control of the lands of the earldom, particularly on the west coast. The Scottish Crown and Parliament were never at ease with one man being in control of such a large area, and their relationship with the lordship from then on was not an easy one. From about 1475 the lordship was bitterly divided by an internal power struggle. By 1493 the Scottish Parliament was convinced that John, fourth Lord of the Isles, was no longer able to control the area and that order must be restored. To that end parliament declared that John was forfeited and deprived him of his lands and his title. He was thus forced to make a 'voluntary resignation' and surrender the lordship.

EARLY CHURCH SITES ON RAASAY AND RONA

In the latter part of the twelfth or early thirteenth century a very substantial chapel was built on Raasay. It was dedicated to St Moluag. He had been the Bishop of Lismore, where he died in AD 592. Lismore is an island just north of Oban, at the mouth of Loch Linnhe. Like Columba, Moluag was an Irish missionary. The name of the site, Kilmoluag, takes its name from the chapel. Today the village is known as Clachan, the Gaelic name for a kirk-town or the village around a church.

Medieval sculptured slabs, or part of such slabs, have been found within the general area of the churchyard and burial ground. Raasay Heritage Trust now holds a fragment of one such sculptured stone that was found in the churchyard. These stones may have been brought to Raasay from places further south, such as Iona itself. It is known that many such stones were 'recycled' in this way. Their presence here indicates that this was an important site, and that the people living here then held a high position in their society.

Writing about 1695, Martin Martin refers to other structures. He says

> They preserve the memory of the deceased ladies of the place by erecting a little pyramid of stone for each of them, with the lady's name. These pyramids are by them called crosses; several of them are built of stone and lime, and

have three steps of gradual ascent to them. There are eight such crosses about the village ...

Samuel Johnson, who carried a copy of Martin's book with him on his travels, makes mention of this passage. He says

> It is told by Martin, that at the death of the Lady of the Island, it has been here the custom to erect a cross. This we found not to be true. The stones that stand about the chapel at a small distance, some of which perhaps have crosses cut upon them, are believed to have been not funeral monuments, but the ancient boundaries of the sanctuary or consecrated ground.

Boswell elaborates on this by saying

> The eight crosses which Martin mentions as pyramids for deceased ladies have gone in a semi-circular line comprehending [surrounding] the chapel. They have been real crosses and have marked out the boundaries of the sacred territory within which an asylum was to be had. The one which we observed upon our landing was the one which made the first point of the semi-circle. There are – [this is left blank] remaining, and they have ended at an opposite point on the west.

Two structures have been found, both having a large base of squared stone, with a second and possibly third step on top. One is near the gate on the summit of the Battery and the second on a steep slope behind St Moluag's chapel. Although neither their date nor their function is known, they would appear to be the crosses described by Martin Martin and Johnson and Boswell.

The burial ground surrounds the chapel. Like all old burial grounds, this one was originally circular, as far as the ground would permit. In Victorian times it was squared. Gravestones, flat slabs with no marks or inscriptions, have been found in the area that is now a part of the farmhouse garden. The last burial on this site was in the 1990s, although the 'New Cemetery' on the hill above the Orchard came into use about 1885.

Over the centuries the ground level within the old graveyard has risen substantially as it was necessary to re-use the graves. This was done after a period of about twenty years. Probably as a result of the re-use of the grave, some large bones were uncovered and put in the window of the church. The large bones belonged to Faobairne MacCuidhein. This giant of a man was a MacKay. Long ago the MacKays were called Clann 'ic Cuidhein, an older form of the name. Faobairne MacCuidhein lived in Eyre and seems to have been the strong man of the island. It is said that when he was in his prime, he was down in the Manish township where they were killing cattle 'for the pot'. When they were finished, Faobairne MacCuidhein took seven quarters (one cow and three-quarters of a second beast) and went off with them to Eyre. It is said that the bone of his thumb, knuckle to the first joint, was 4.5 inches long. Johnson and Boswell's party was shown a bone from the heel, and Dr Murdo MacLeod of Eyre, Snizort, said that the foot must have been 27 inches long.

In 1773 Johnson and Boswell commented on the chapel, which was by then roofless and ruinous. Although the chapel had a good deal of earth inside it, there were several gravestones on the floor, but without any legible inscriptions. The burying place of the MacGilleChaluim, the MacLeods of Raasay, was on the south side of the chapel, and south of that was another smaller one for another family. A little to the east of it was the burying place of yet another family of the MacLeods. Above the door on the east end was a small bust or image of the Virgin Mary, carved on a stone, making it part of the wall.[5]

Beside St Moluag's Church is a newer nineteenth century memorial chapel. It was built by John, the last of the MacLeod lairds, in memory of his daughter, Mary Julia Hastings MacLeod, who died, in 1839, aged three.

At the south end of Rona is a place called An Teampùll, where there is a small ruined chapel of rubble and shell-lime construction. The building is believed to date to the late twelfth or early thirteenth century, as does St Moluag's Chapel at Clachan. No archaeological survey of Rona has yet been carried out. When Rona was populated in the nineteenth century the Graham family of Doire-na Guaille and Kyle Rona used it as a burial ground. Theirs is the sole grave marker in the small cemetery, and as such underlines the scarcity of the historical record for the countless generations of Rona and north Raasay families interred here.

The name Torran has some ecclesiastical significance. This is borne out by the fact that there is an old burial site there. By the end of the nineteenth century, only children of north end families were buried there. Adults were buried in the graveyard at Clachan. Although no evidence of a chapel has been found at Torran, the name and the presence of a burial ground points to an association with the church.

On Raasay there is a very strong tradition that the island was held by the MacSweens before it was taken over by the MacLeods. It is said that these MacSweens were related to the MacSweens of Roag, near Dunvegan. No written record has been found of the MacSweens' presence on Raasay. The last MacSween to hold Raasay was Iain Mòr MacSuain, 'a great warrior and a good man'.

Because Raasay at that time was Church land, it could be surmised that the MacSweens were either tenants or office bearers of the Church. They appear to have held a recognised position of significance. On St Columba's Isle in Snizort there is a large sculpted stone showing a warrior with helmet and armour, holding a sword. In one corner of this stone are the initials IMS, RMS and IMS, one below the other. It is believed that these initials refer to three generations of the MacSweens. The initials may have been added to the stone, indicating that it had been re-used.

Some traditions say that Iain Mòr MacSuain granted his lands to his foster son, a MacLeod, while others refute this, suggesting that the MacLeods took over Raasay by force. The possibility of the gift of fosterage cannot be discounted, as such gifts were not uncommon at the time. However, this explanation may have become current at some later date if it was not known then how ownership came about. The Crown charter of 1596 certainly indicates that the MacLeods had previously held Raasay officially from the Church.

Brochel Castle stands on the north east coast of Raasay and is now in a ruinous condition. The style of building suggests construction during the fifteenth century.

Although some traditions relate that the MacSweens built it, others attribute it to the MacLeods. The castle appears to have had two phases of construction, suggesting that it had been enlarged at some time. It is therefore possible that both traditions are true. Did the MacSweens build it, and the MacLeods extend it?

There is another possibility. Could there have been a time when both the MacSweens and the MacLeods lived on Raasay together? Perhaps the MacSweens had their main residence around the Clachan area, while the MacLeods were in the north of the island at Brochel Castle.

Notes

1. Surveys of Raasay have been carried out by Martin Wildgoose, The Association of Certified Field Archaeologists from Glasgow University and The Centre for Field Archaeology from Edinburgh University. Copies of these reports are held at Dualchas, Skye and Lochalsh Area Museums and Heritage Service, the Highland Council, Portree.
2. R. Sharpe, *Raasay: Documents and Sources* (1978), p. 46.
3. D. E. R. Watt, 'Bishops in the Isles before 1203, in *The Innes Review*, vol. 45, no. 2 (1994), pp. 102–5. Information about the Bishops of the Isles and the church at St Columba's Isle at Skeabost comes from this and correspondence held by Dualchas, Skye and Lochalsh Area Museums and Heritage Service, the Highland Council, Portree.
4. W. D. H. Sellar, 'The Ancestry of the MacLeods Reconsidered', in *TGSI*, vol. LX, pp. 235–6.
5. R. Sharpe, *Raasay: Documents and Sources* (1978), p. 54.

2

The History of Raasay, c.1450–1630s

EARLY MACLEOD LAIRDS OF RAASAY

The MacLeod lairds of Raasay were known as the MacGilleChaluim. There is documentary evidence of their presence on the island from the sixteenth century. A Crown charter granted to Calum MacLeod of Raasay in 1596 states that his great-grandfather and his 'predecessors since time immemorial' had held Raasay from the Bishop of the Isles. Calum's great-grandfather, possibly also named Calum, may have been born about 1460. It is therefore quite likely that the MacLeod lairds held Raasay for a large part of the fifteenth century.

The MacLeods of Raasay were, most likely, descended from the MacLeods of Gairloch. There would have been close association between Raasay and Gairloch families. Evidence of this may be found in the place-name Laimrig Chloinn mhic Ailein, the Landing Place of the Clan or Children of Allan, on the east coast of Raasay between Brochel and Kyle Rona. This natural jetty or landing place was ideally situated for contact between the MacLeods at Brochel and their relatives in Gairloch.

At that time, and indeed for many centuries after, the sea was the 'motorway'. It was the custom of the times that other lairds, going elsewhere, would stop off and spend some time on the island.

A history of the MacLeans of Boreray, North Uist, tells of such a visit.[1] On his way to the MacDonald lands in Uist, Hugh MacDonald called on the Raasay laird. In the MacDonald retinue was Neil Bàn MacLean, Hugh MacDonald's foster brother. Hugh MacDonald and the Laird of Raasay engaged in a gambling game, similar to chess. At length, the Raasay laird had won North Uist from MacDonald, and knew that MacDonald did not have the money to buy it back. However, Neil MacLean paid gold and silver to buy it back for MacDonald, probably knowing that he would be well rewarded for doing so. Indeed he was, as he received a verbal lease for the island of Boreray as well as other land in North Uist. The date of this verbal lease is taken to be about 1460.

The Raasay laird is named as MacLeod in this account and later Crown charter evidence suggests that it may well be correct.

The MacLeods lived in Brochel Castle until about the mid-seventeenth century. Although there may already have been a building on the site, tradition says that the MacLeods were responsible for further building. There is a very detailed story told of how they came by the money to finance this undertaking.[2]

One day, when the MacLeods were hunting on Glamaig, Skye, a favourite dog was lost. The following day the laird and his Gille Mòr (his right-hand man) eventually found the dog aboard a large birlinn at anchor in Loch Sligachan. When he attempted to retrieve the dog, the Gille Mòr was seized by the crew.

Being a strong man, he soon had them overboard. When a youth on the boat tried to take the dog below decks, he too was flung aside.

It was later learned that the birlinn belonged to the Laird of Craignish, south of Oban, and that the youth, his son, had been mortally injured. Some time after, at a gathering in Dunvegan Castle, the Laird of Craignish promised a purse of gold to anyone who could tell him who had killed his son. The Gille Mòr admitted that it had been his fault, but explained that it had been a dreadful accident. He was given the gold and, with MacGilleChaluim, left very soon after. Because his conscience would not let him keep the gold, he gave it to MacGilleChaluim who used it to build Brochel Castle.

The building work at Brochel would have involved a large number of skilled craftsmen and labourers. Probably some were local men. Such activity, then as today, would have caused some excitement and an air of anticipation among those living on the island and the surrounding area. Necessary materials for the building work that were not near to hand, and many of the workmen, would have come in by sea. The ruins of this castle still stand as testimony to the skill of those who designed and built it.

While the story of the financing of the castle may seem somewhat far fetched, there may indeed be some truth behind it as there was another link between the Campbells of Craignish and the MacLeods of Raasay. A history of the Campbells tells that Marion Campbell of Craignish married 'Gillicallum MacLeod of Raasay, second son to the laird of MacLeod'.[3] They met, we are told, on the shore near Craignish when 'Gillicallum MacLeod … with his birlinn happened to be in these parts'. Their marriage probably took place some time before 1510. The identity of Marion's husband is uncertain.

Although mention of this marriage is not found in any of the MacLeod histories, it is given in those of the Campbells. Prior to her marriage with one of the MacLeods, Marion had been living with the Laird of Ardkinglass, also a Campbell, as his concubine and had by him at least three sons. It is said that because of their relationship, through Marion, there was a close friendship between the Campbells of Craignish, the Campbells of Ardkinglass and the MacLeods of Raasay. Her husband was the second son of the Laird of Raasay at that time. Iain Garbh, Laird of Raasay about the middle of the seventeenth century, is said to be directly descended from Marion. The story says that he was her 'great-grandson or fourth from her'.

In 1518 the Laird of Raasay joined his chief, MacLeod of Lewis, in a raid on Ardnamurchan against the MacIan branch of the MacDonalds.[4] MacIan was 'killed by the Laird of Raasay'. This information comes from a history of the MacDonalds that was written sometime after 1628, that is just over one hundred years after the events it records. In historical terms, that is fairly recent, so it may be assumed that the information is reasonably accurate. The laird in question is unnamed. It is said that he was the 'weakest and least powerful of all the Island Lairds'. This has been interpreted, by some, as an indication that he had just taken over the Raasay estate, and was young. It is more likely, however, to reflect the fact that because Raasay was a relatively small island, the laird was unable to raise as many fighting men as other chiefs.

An expedition, such as that to Ardnamurchan would have been by sea. As well as seamen to man the boats, a retinue of fighting men and servants would have accompanied the laird. That the Laird of Raasay took part in the raid in 1518 indicates a degree of stability, both economically and politically, on the island at that time. Fighting men were supported by the general population of the estate as part of the chief's retinue and did not take part in the day-to-day agricultural work.

Which Raasay laird accompanied his chief, MacLeod of Lewis, to Ardnamurchan in 1518? Alexander MacKenzie maintains that the laird in 1518 was Calum Garbh, but the Calum Garbh described by him was born after 1500 and would not have been old enough to be the laird.[5]

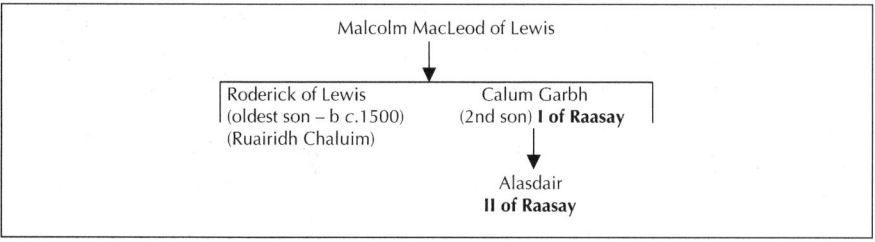

Figure 2/1. MacLeods of Raasay, as given by Alexander MacKenzie.

Perhaps the most likely candidate for leadership of the expedition to Ardnamurchan is Alasdair, who may have been born about 1490. However, depending on the accuracy of the estimated dates of birth, it is possible that the laird in 1518 was Alasdair's father (possibly named Calum).

Although the MacLeods had taken over the island and estate of Raasay, the people living there would not all have been MacLeods. Surnames as such did not come into common usage until much later, but very few, if any, estates would have had people of only one surname living on them. There are many possible reasons for

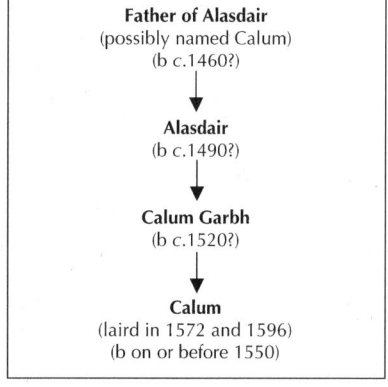

Figure 2/2. MacLeods of Raasay, as found in Crown charters.

people with surnames, other than that of the laird, living on an estate. One of the most obvious reasons would be that even when an estate was taken over by another clan, many people would remain living on it. This would not necessarily be the cause of any problems, as generally, then as in later times, people looked for stability, both economically and politically. The new laird would be likely to cultivate the trust and loyalty of the leading men already established on the estate. By doing so, he would enhance his own position, minimising the risk of a 'takeover bid'. On Raasay, some MacSweens, relatives of the previous tenants, would still be found. Another reason might be that a man had specific skills that were of benefit to the laird and the estate. Some of the skilled workmen, who came to Raasay to build the castle at Brochel, may have settled on the island. There were other skills also that would be in demand, such as blacksmiths, swordsmen, seamen, boatbuilders and so on. Yet another reason for a different surname to occur is that when the laird married it was often the case that some members of her clan moved with the bride to her new home, where they were given land. Old surnames were often lost when families adopted the surname of the chief, as an indication of loyalty and for protection. Tracing how various surnames came to be in an area can reveal a great deal about its past history.

Very few names of the people of this early period in history have come down to us. Although those most often recorded were the lairds, it cannot be assumed that everyone whose name we know was a laird. On Raasay, as elsewhere, the men of the laird's retinue were significant. They were usually relatives. In written histories of Raasay the name Iain na Tuaighe, John of the Axe, occurs. Correctly or otherwise, previous histories of the MacLeods attribute many marriages to this man, as a result of which he has been accused of causing later disasters that befell both the MacLeods of Lewis and the MacLeods of Raasay. It is said that Iain na Tuaighe 'ran off with' the wife of his uncle, the chief of the MacLeods of Lewis. This, it has been claimed, caused the downfall of the MacLeods of Lewis. It is also claimed that a massacre of the MacLeods of Raasay and Gairloch was somehow the result of this marriage. These points are discussed in full later and also in Part II. In all probability, Iain na Tuaighe was a brother of Alasdair.

Little is known of Alasdair, but a Crown charter of 1596 confirms the name of one of his sons, Calum Garbh. He was probably born about 1520 or shortly after.

RAASAY AND THE CHURCH

In 1526 a new vicar was appointed to the churches of Snizort and Raasay, confirming the link between Raasay and Snizort, through the Church. The vicar was Donald Monro. His father, Alexander, had lands near the Cromarty Firth, and his uncles held positions in the Church on the east coast of Scotland, under the bishopric of Aberdeen. His mother, Janet, was a daughter of Farquhar MacLean of Dochgarroch.

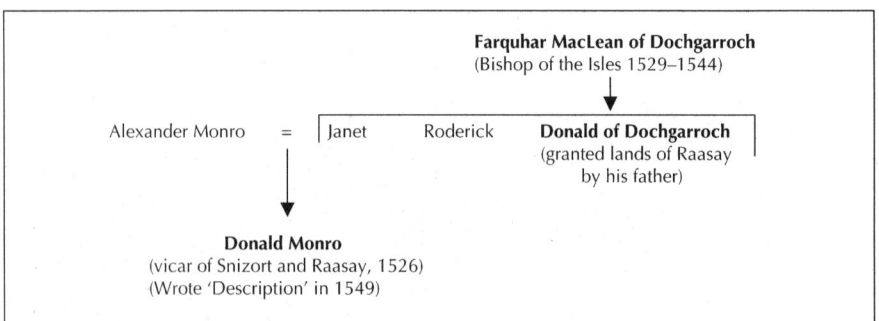

Figure 2/3. Relationship between Donald Munro and the MacLeans of Dochgarroch.

Farquhar MacLean of Dochgarroch, grandfather of Donald Monro, was appointed Bishop of the Isles in 1529.[6] At that time the bishopric was not financially well off, and in 1533 Bishop Farquhar took action against 'MacNeill the Laird of Barra' and 'MacGillechallum callit of Raasay' for non-payment of dues.[7] It is unclear what dues the bishop was trying to collect. It may have been the teinds, one tenth part of the produce of the land, that were payable to the Church, or it may have been unpaid rent if, as seems likely, the MacLeods were official tenants of the Church.

However, it is clear from the wording of the prosecution, that the bishop was not willing to concede that MacLeod had any right to be the Laird of Raasay. Bishop Farquhar had plans for the Church lands of Raasay and Snizort himself, and MacLeod being in possession did not help these plans. In 1544 Farquhar MacLean resigned from the position of bishop, in favour of his son, Roderick, having first received a 'precept of legitimation', allowing his heirs to succeed to his property.[8] He granted the lands of Raasay and Snizort, part of the bishop's heritage, to his son, Donald MacLean of Dochgarroch. MacLeod of Raasay was in possession, however, as tenant of the Church, although he may well not have been paying the rent.

THE MACLEODS OF LEWIS

The 1520s and 1530s were unsettled times for the MacLeods of Lewis. Possibly because of that, there were repercussions which affected the families of both Gairloch and Raasay. Malcolm MacLeod of Lewis had been granted a Crown charter for his lands in 1511. The estate of Lewis had been forfeited by the Crown in 1506 because Torcall, Malcolm's older brother, had supported Donald Dubh MacDonald's bid to revive the Lordship of the Isles. In 1511 the king returned the estate to the MacLeods, but specifically excluded Torcall and his heirs from the succession. It is believed that Malcolm held the estate until his death, although no date is known for that. After his death it appears that John, a son of Torcall, held the estate until his death in the early 1530s although he was not recognised by the Crown. It was not until the early 1530s, therefore, that Ruairidh Chaluim, son of Malcolm, took over the administration of Lewis and the chieftainship of the MacLeods.

Although the history and genealogy of the MacLeods of Lewis is not yet fully

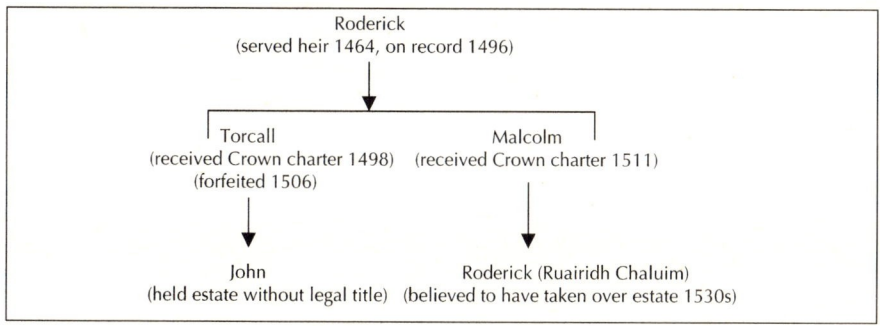

Figure 2/4. The MacLeods of Lewis.

understood, it is clear that, from as far back as the 1460s, there was internal conflict over the estate between the many families of MacLeods living on Lewis.

THE MASSACRE AT ISAY

This massacre is discussed fully in Part II, where charts showing relationships can also be found. In the early 1530s a terrible massacre was perpetrated on the island of Isay, off Waternish Skye, which dealt a severe blow to the families of both Raasay and Gairloch. The man responsible for this massacre was a Ruairidh MacLeod from Lewis. Although some authors maintain that Ruairidh MacLeod was of the Gairloch branch, this is most unlikely. The place chosen – Isay – was owned by the MacLeods of Lewis. It has been claimed that the massacre at Isay took place about 1568, but this too is inconsistent with later evidence. The earlier date makes it much less likely that the perpetrator was from the Gairloch branch.

It is not entirely clear who Ruairidh MacLeod from Lewis was. He may have been Ruairidh Chaluim. Indeed a history of the MacKenzies of Kintail strongly suggests this. He may, however, have been another Ruairidh MacLeod, as the name appears to have been very common among the MacLeods in Lewis.

Whoever he was, Ruairidh invited all the leading members of the MacLeods of both Raasay and Gairloch to a feast on Isay. He told them that he had important business which he wished to discuss. After they had feasted well, Ruairidh went into another room and invited each one to come to him separately. As each man entered the room he was killed. The reason for this massacre, as given in the MacKenzie history, is that Ruairidh of Lewis wanted to open up the succession of both Gairloch and Raasay for his nephew, Ruairidh mac Allan of Gairloch, who was at that time 'a young man'.

Many people were killed at Isay, among them Alasdair MacLeod of Raasay and his brother, Iain na Tuaighe. All but one of Alasdair's sons were killed. Allan MacLeod of Gairloch had been married twice. Ruairidh mac Allan was a son of the second marriage, to a MacLeod of Lewis. All Allan's sons by his first wife were killed.

The only one of the Raasay and Gairloch MacLeods to escape the massacre at Isay was Calum Garbh, son of Alasdair MacLeod. He was just nine at the time and was being fostered away from home. Fostering was then a common practice. In part it served to cement bonds of friendship between the families involved but it also served, as in this case, to protect the child.

When news of the massacre became known, a Raasay man named Donald M'Neil, Donald, son of Neil, who was loyal to the murdered laird, took young Calum Garbh to the Laird of Calder, who kept him safely until he came of age. The Laird of Calder (Cawdor) was, at that time, a Campbell. No doubt Donald M'Neil was a MacLeod, probably related in some way to the laird. The MacKenzie history says that Ruairidh mac Allan, of the Gairloch family, took over Raasay. One may assume that he did so under the instruction and the supervision of his uncle in Lewis.

When Calum Garbh came of age, probably in the 1540s, Donald M'Neil took him home to Raasay but kept him hidden, waiting until the time was right. With the help of the keeper of Brochel Castle, and being informed by him that Ruairidh mac Allan was then away, Donald M'Neil entered the castle and took control of it by murdering the guards. He then sent for Calum Garbh who was duly pronounced Laird of Raasay. Celebrations, in the usual form of feasting and entertainment, would have continued for some time after the restoration of the rightful heir to his estate.

Dean Donald Monro, who had been appointed vicar of Snizort and Raasay in 1526, wrote a 'Description of the Western Isles of Scotland' in 1549. His description, written for the Church, highlights that which was important to the Church. Because the original text can be difficult to read, it is followed here by a version in more modern English. Donald Monro says

> Twa mile of sea fra this Ile of Scalpay foirsaid northwart lyis ane Ile callit Raarsay seven mile lang from the south to the north, lyand but ane mile of sea from Trouternes, twa mile of breid, with pairt of birkin woods, mony deir, pairt of profitable land, inhabite and manurit; with twa castellis, to wit, the castell of Kilmaluok and the castell of Brerkdill; with two fair orcheartis at the saidis twa castellis; with ane paroche kirk callit Kilmaluok; ane roche cuntrie, but all full of frie stanes and gude querrellis, gude for fisching, perteining to Mcgillechallum of Raarsay be the sword, and all to the Bischop of the Iles in heritage. This Mcgillichallum sould obey Mccloyd of Leozus.
>
> At the north end of this foirsaid Ile of Raarsay be ane half mile of sea fra it lyis ane Ile callit Ronay, mair nor ane mile lang, full of wood and hedder, with a heavin for hieland Galeis in the middis of it. And the said heavin is quiet for fostering of thieves, ruggaris and reevaris till await upon the pailing and spuilzeing of poor mens geir, perteining to Mcgillichallum of Raarsay be force and to the Bischop of the Iles be heritage.[9]

❧❦❧

> Two miles of sea from the Isle of Scalpay, aforesaid, northwards lies an Isle called Raasay – seven miles long from the south to the north, lying but one mile of sea from Trotternish – two miles broad, with part birch woods, many deer, part of profitable land, inhabited and manured; with two castles, to wit, the castle of Kilmoluag and the castle of Brochel; with two fair orchards at the said two castles; with one parish church called Kilmoluag; a rocky country, but all full of freestone and good quarries, good for fishing – pertaining to MacGilleChaluim of Raasay by the sword and all to the Bishop of the Isles in heritage. This MacGilleChaluim should obey MacLeod of Lewis.
>
> At the north end of this aforesaid Isle of Raasay by one half mile of sea from it lies an Isle called Rona, more than one mile long, full of wood and heather, with a haven for Highland galleys in the middle of it. And the said haven is quiet for fostering thieves, robbers and reivers to wait upon the damaging and uplifting of poor men's gear – pertaining to MacGilleChaluim of Raasay by force and to the Bishop of the Isles by heritage.

This description is important, because it is the earliest on record with reference to the Scottish islands. From the Raasay perspective, it is interesting, as much for the detail that is omitted as for that which is given. Donald Monro reiterates the point that Raasay and Rona belonged to 'the Bishop of the Isles in heritage'. By that time, no doubt, his uncle, Donald MacLean of Dochgarroch, had been granted these lands by Bishop Farquhar, but was unable to take possession. It is also of interest that in the section of his description dealing with Skye the church at Snizort is not even named, although Donald Monro himself had been vicar there, and would therefore have known of its previous significance to the bishopric.

The description of Raasay and Rona gives information about those islands. There was good agricultural land on Raasay that was being worked profitably. The island had fairly extensive birch woods. The remnants of these today can be seen on the east of the island. The 'fair orchards' at the castles would have been more akin to gardens rather than orchards in the modern sense.

Monro says that there were castles at Brochel and Clachan, each having a garden. The castle at Brochel, clearly built for defensive purposes, was the principal seat of the MacLeods of Raasay until about the middle of the seventeenth century. However, the agricultural land in the south and west of the island would have been just as important, arguably more so, than the land around Brochel. Control of this land would have been every bit as important to the estate as the north end of the island. Sometime between 1577 and 1595 a survey of the islands was compiled, giving details of revenue and fighting power for the government. This makes no mention of the 'castle' at Clachan.[10] It may therefore be assumed that the building with a garden, probably within the grounds of the present mansion house garden, was not built for defence. Because it is mentioned by Monro, it could perhaps be assumed that it was of more solid construction than the other houses on the island at that time.

A survey of the garden of Raasay House has found evidence of a cobbled yard below the present ground level. More work has yet to be done on this site, and it will be interesting to see what is found in this area after further archaeological work.

It is not known today where the freestone quarries were, but later descriptions also mention them. It is quite possible that there were many outcrops of suitable rock all over the island. They were clearly significant, even at that time.

Hunting was a favourite pastime of the lairds, and Raasay had 'many deer'. The good fishing was also noted.

Rona, to the north of Raasay, was full of wood and heather. Today there are virtually no trees on Rona. The harbour was suitable for Highland galleys. Not all harbours were. One of the coves in the harbour is known as Port nan Robairean, the Harbour of Thieves, confirming Monro's 'thieves, ruggaris and reevaris'. Although the MacLeods held Rona, by force or otherwise, it is unlikely that they made a great deal of use of it in the early period, except perhaps for hunting. Any stock grazed there would have to be defended, as it would have been a great temptation for those so inclined to raid and take away beasts that were in the charge of only a few stockmen. Thus it became a haven for broken men. These people were unattached to a clan, for whatever reason, and had to resort to piracy and the like to stay alive. Rona, wooded and essentially unused, would have been the kind of place where they would be, for the most part, undisturbed.

THE NORTH-WEST HIGHLANDS IN THE FIRST HALF OF THE SIXTEENTH CENTURY

The sixteenth century was one of unsettled times in the north-west. This was due in part to the power vacuum left after the fall of the Lordship of the Isles, and the continuing attempts to revive it. Many areas were being fought over and 'held by the sword'. Although major clan chiefs of this period are in the main shadowy figures of whom we now have only an occasional glimpse, they held great power and their political dealings were aimed at increasing that power. This is true in particular of the MacLeods of Lewis. Their situation, on the outer edge of the kingdom of Scotland, kept them largely out of the reach of king and government. They were a law unto themselves. If it was to their advantage, they were happy to become involved in disputes other than their own.

Ruairidh Chaluim became chief of the MacLeods of Lewis about 1532. This happened after agreement had been reached with Donald Gorm of Sleat. His wife was a daughter of John, who had held Lewis without legal title until his death. Under this agreement Ruairidh undertook to assist Donald Gorm in driving the MacLeods of Dunvegan out of Trotternish, and also in helping him in his bid to re-establish the Lordship of the Isles and the Earldom of Ross. In May 1539 Ruairidh joined Donald Gorm and invaded Trotternish. Then, taking advantage of MacKenzie's absence from home, they raided Kinlochewe and Kintail. During this latter raid, Donald Gorm was killed at Eilean Donan Castle by an arrow shot from its walls.

Ruairidh Chaluim was also politically active much further from home. In 1545 he was one of seventeen barons and members of the Council of the Isles who were attempting to bring the Isles, and a great part of the mainland of Scotland, under the superiority of the English king. In August of that year they were at Knockfergus in Ireland with a force of 4 000 men and 180 galleys. There they took an oath of allegiance to the King of England. However, by the end of that month the Regent Arran and Lords of the Privy Council of Scotland had again taken control. Those involved in the uprising were given the opportunity to go to them and arrange their affairs. On that occasion they were reconciled, but Ruairidh was in trouble again in 1547 when he refused to join the Regent Arran at the Battle of Pinkie.

It is not known what, if any, part the MacLeods of Raasay and Gairloch took in these dealings. It is worth remembering that at this time the major clan chiefs of the north-west Highlands were powerful people who would not hesitate to become involved in affairs far outwith their own area, if by doing so they could possibly gain by it. The Crown and Privy Council were virtually powerless to stop them. They used forfeiture of estates and commissions of fire and sword against either individuals or clans, essentially using other clans to control those out of line. This inevitably led to even more raiding and feuding and general lawlessness in the region. No details exist about raids against Raasay during this period, although some may have taken place.

CALUM GARBH MACLEOD OF RAASAY

Sometime in the 1540s Calum Garbh took control of Raasay and the estate. His name, Calum the Brawny, suggests that he was a strong, well-developed, probably good-looking man. Perhaps a character not to be meddled with lightly! He would have been the laird when Donald Monro wrote his 'Description'.

There is a story that, probably in the late 1540s or early 1550s, the MacLeans of Dochgarroch decided to try to enforce their rights to the island.[11] One fine evening in late autumn, a party of armed men landed on the east side of Raasay, just as it began to get dark. They intended to reach Brochel Castle and take the people of Raasay unawares. It so happened that the Gille Mòr (the laird's right-hand man) had been out hunting and was making his way home, when he realised that someone was following him. When he accosted the man, he recognised his accent as being from the eastern Highlands. The Gille Mòr was on his guard. He knew of the problems the laird was having with the Bishop of the Isles and the MacLeans. When the man asked the way to Brochel, he replied that he was going in that direction and would show him. Although the Gille Mòr tried to find out more, the stranger would tell him nothing. The Gille Mòr became even more suspicious when he became aware that a large body of men was following them.

He knew that in front of them in the hillside was a large chasm, about four feet wide and of great depth, and he also knew exactly where it was. When they came to it, the Gille Mòr leaped over it, but his companion dropped into it without a sound. Those following also fell in, and the Gille Mòr continued home where he reported what had happened. The following day, the laird called on his men and they went with ropes to rescue those invaders who were still alive. They were tended on Raasay until they were able to go home. Some, who were not able to do so, settled on Raasay and have descendants on the island to this day.

Although there is no documentary evidence to support the theory, there may have been at least one Cummings man in the band of raiders, who remained on Raasay with the MacLeans. The MacLeans of Dochgarroch were a branch of the Clann Theàrlaich, based around Urquhart Castle. There are known to have been marriages between the MacLeans and a family of Cummings who had the farm of Dulshangie in the same area.[12] It is certainly true that, in the early part of the nineteenth century, the only Cummings found in Skye parishes were either on Raasay or in the parish of Snizort. The names James and William were also common to both the Raasay/Snizort families and the Dulshangie family.

Calum Garbh married Isobel MacKenzie. Although the date of this marriage is not known, it may have taken place in the late 1540s. Isobel was a daughter of Kenneth MacKenzie of Kintail, known as Coinneach na Cuirc, Kenneth of the Whittle.[13] Although Isobel is described as a 'natural daughter', she held her place in society as the daughter of the chief. Marriage agreements, at that time, were used to strengthen ties between clans.

The older Celtic laws of marriage were still widely followed then, and indeed into the next century. The ancient Irish/Celtic law of marriage allowed for polygamy, taking of concubines and divorce. Many types of union were recognised, some lasting, some temporary. As well as a first or chief wife, a man could have a second wife. Various types of concubine, inferior to a second wife, were also recognised. The children of most of these unions would be regarded as legitimate for the purpose of succession. Divorce was a recognised institution and available to both parties on a number of grounds.

All this, of course, was clean contrary to the teaching of the Church. Official Vatican records show that it was often considered politic and desirable to present relationships resulting from Celtic secular marriage in canon law guise. An official dispensation to marry, long after the event, and the official legitimation of a son and heir did not mean that the marriage was not already considered valid or the son legitimate within the context of Gaelic society.[14]

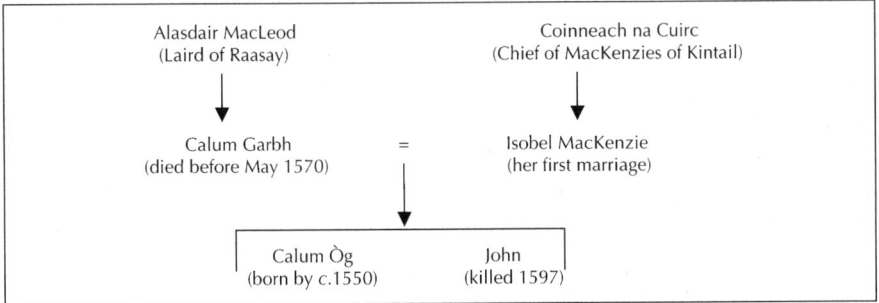

Figure 2/5. Calum Garbh MacLeod and Isobel MacKenzie.

That Calum Garbh was able to contract a marriage of this status shows that he held a good position within that society. He may also have received a valuable dowry along with his wife. The backing of a powerful clan, such as the MacKenzies of Kintail, would have stood the Raasay laird, and consequently the people of the island, in good stead.

The kinship between the MacLeods of Raasay and those of Lewis is not known. The memory of an atrocity, such as at Isay, would be long remembered. It is more than likely, however, that there were different factions of MacLeods in Lewis and it is quite possible that members of the Raasay and Gairloch family had contact with some of them. In spite of the internal power struggle within the MacLeods of Lewis, they were still a very powerful clan at this time. Because the relationship between the MacLeods of Raasay and Gairloch and Lewis was a blood tie, it may be assumed that any friendship with any of the factions of Lewis would have been of benefit to the MacLeods of Raasay.

Calum Garbh and Isobel had at least two sons. They were Calum Òg and John. Calum Garbh had died before May 1570, by which time Isobel MacKenzie had married her second husband, James MacKintosh of Stroine.[15] It is not known how long before 1570 Calum Garbh died, but he was succeeded as Laird of Raasay by his son, Calum Òg.

DISPUTED SUCCESSION OF THE MACLEODS OF LEWIS

About this time, the MacLeods of Lewis were very much engaged in a dispute over succession, which centred on the paternity of Torcall MacLeod, known as Torcall Conanach. His mother was Janet MacKenzie, and Torcall had been brought up by her people in Strathconon, hence his name. Janet's second husband, Ruairidh Chaluim, chief of the MacLeods of Lewis, claimed that he was not the father of Torcall. The MacKenzies, naturally, backed Torcall's claim. This dispute raged until the end of the century, resulting ultimately in the downfall of the MacLeods of Lewis.

Ruairidh Chaluim had, in 1541, married Barbara Stewart, of the Royal Stewart family. Their son, Torcall, was known as Torcall Oighre, Torcall the Heir. In 1563, Mary, Queen of Scots wrote to Torcall. In this letter she asked him not to become engaged in marriage without her previous consent because he was of Stewart blood. However, Torcall Oighre and his men were drowned, possibly about Christmas 1566. One tradition says that they were crossing from Lewis to spend Christmas with MacDonald in Trotternish, while another suggests that a storm drove the boat to the west of Assynt, into Eddrachillis Bay. There, it is said, Torcall and his men were murdered by a Donald Bayne, who had recently seized the lands of Assynt from the MacLeods. Whatever the true story, Torcall Oighre died in 1566. It was then that the dispute as to the succession of the Lewis estate assumed great importance.

As a result of this dispute, a Crown charter was granted in 1572.[16] Torcall Conanach is named as the 'son and heir apparent of Roderick MacLeod of Lewis' in the lands of Lewis. If Torcall had no legitimate sons, his heir was to be 'Calum, son of Calum Garbh MacLeod of Raasay and his heirs'.

Ruairidh Chaluim also had five 'natural' sons. Some backed their father while others backed Torcall Conanach. There is no concrete evidence as to which side the MacLeods of Raasay took in this dispute. Their relationship with the MacKenzies of Kintail might suggest that they sided with Torcall Conanach. This appears to be backed up by the evidence of the Crown charter of 1572.

RAASAY'S DEALINGS WITH THE BISHOP OF THE ISLES AND THE CROWN

In 1580 John, Bishop of the Isles, was again taking action against several island chiefs, among them 'Gilleschallum M'Gilleschallum of Rasay'.[17] It is not recorded whether this prosecution was any more successful than that of 1533, by Bishop Farquhar MacLean.

It appears that the Laird of Raasay should have been paying the bishop sixteen merks yearly. It must, therefore, have been a great irritation to the bishop that a survey of the island, carried out some time between 1577 and 1595, stated that the Laird of Raasay collected five hundred merks from the estate annually, presumably from leases or rentals. It may be noted that the estate rental given here, amounting to £333 6s. 8d, is higher than the figure given by Johnson and Boswell in 1773. Then, it was said, the laird received £250–300 annually.

A few years later MacLeod of Raasay appears to have been charged with 'molesting people engaged in the northern fisheries'.[18] The Crown used the fisheries around the coast as a source of revenue. The exclusive rights to inshore fishing had been granted, for a fee, to the royal burghs. It is quite understandable that, like many others around the coasts, Calum Òg may have tried to extract payments from these fishermen. Such demands, in the form of shore dues or part of the catch, would have seemed reasonable to west coast lairds, but were a source of continual complaint from the fishermen to the authorities during the sixteenth century. The result was that, often, those harassing the fishermen were denounced as rebels by the king or privy council, and had to wait some time before being allowed to make their peace with the authorities.

THE RAID ON CAITHNESS

Harassing fishermen was not the only possible reason for being denounced as a rebel by the privy council. Increasingly, clan or personal feuds gave rise to one or other party going to Edinburgh to put his case, and the other being denounced as a rebel, or having a 'Commission of Fire and Sword' brought against him. Following some disagreement, the Earl of Sutherland obtained a commission of fire and sword against the Earl of Caithness.[19] In February 1588 he was joined by a number of other clan chiefs and their men. Among them were Calum Òg, Laird of Raasay and his brother, John. When this large force entered Caithness, the people fled in alarm. Many were killed. Livestock and other goods were taken. This became known as Latha na Creach Mhor or the Day of the Great Spoil. Although the town of Wick was burnt, the church was saved. In the church was a lead case with the ashes of the heart of the previous Earl of Caithness. It is said that John MacLeod threw the ashes to the wind.

The authorities had for decades now been trying to gain some control over the north-west of Scotland, largely in an effort to increase the royal revenues. Many lairds and chiefs had been denounced as rebels or had commissions of fire and sword raised against them. MacLeod of Raasay is known to have been involved in reiving (cattle raiding or seaborne piracy, including molesting those engaged in fishing in the area) and refusing to pay his dues to the bishop. After a time most of those so denounced made their peace with the king, and all was well until the next time. In 1593, 'M'Gillecallum of Raarsay' was included in a general pardon for many lairds who had been outlawed for such conduct.

CROWN CHARTER TO THE MACLEODS OF RAASAY, 1596

The first Crown charter to the MacLeods of Raasay was granted to Calum Òg by James VI in 1596. It was dated 20th July 1596 at Falkland.[20]

> The King has granted as fee farm to Calum MacGilleCalum, son and apparent heir of Calum Mac Alasdair MacGilleCalum of Raasay, his heirs and assignees whatsoever – the lands of Raasay, namely [townships are named], extending to 8 merklands of old extent, besides the lands of Eyre in Trotternish [townships are named], extending to 3 merklands, the total 11 merklands of old extent, together with the fortalices, mills, woods, teinds, etc. advowson [the right of presentation to a church living held by a vicar] of the churches and chapels of the parishes of Kilmoluag in Raasay and Snizort in Trotternish (occupied by the said elder Calum and his tenants) in the diocese of the Isles, Invernessshire. They have belonged to the said elder Calum, his father, grandfather and predecessors since time immemorial, feeholders and tenants of the bishop of the Isles. The lands came to the King by the Act of Annexation ...

The cost of issuing this charter was two hundred merks. Today this would probably come under the heading 'legal fees'.

This charter gives a great deal of information. It confirms that the lands of Raasay and Snizort had belonged to the Church, for the purpose of giving the Church officials a living, and that they went together as a 'package'. The Act of Annexation, passed in 1587, transferred ownership of Church lands and their revenues to the crown as part of the reformation of the Church, which had by then been ongoing for decades. Although 1560 is often taken as the date of the Reformation, attempts to reform the Church began before that. Because no previous Crown charter for this land had been issued, it was necessary for this one to give more detail than usual about the recipient, Calum Òg. As well as naming him, the charter also names his father, Calum (Garbh), and his grandfather, Alasdair MacGilleChaluim. It is unclear from the wording whether or not Alasdair's father was named Calum.

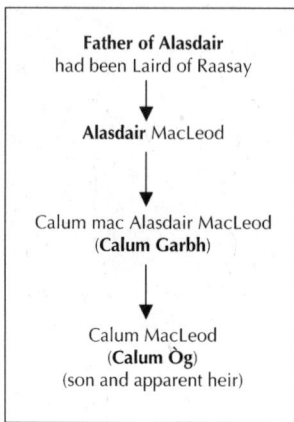

Figure 2/6. Raasay lairds from charter of 1596.

It was usual that when a landowner, who had held his lands from the Crown, died, his heir had to prove his right to inherit the said lands. This was done by means of a 'Retour', also known as 'Service of Heirs'. Because the MacLeods had not, until now, held their lands from the Crown, there had been no retours concerning their lands. The granting of this charter, however, had to rectify that. Therefore Calum Òg is named as 'apparent heir' of his father, Calum Garbh.

The charter further states that the lands had been held by Calum Garbh's 'grandfather and his predecessors since time immemorial'. Even allowing for the possibility that there could be some exaggeration in this statement, it confirms the theory discussed earlier that Alasdair was not the first of the MacLeods to hold these lands. Earlier lairds are not named, possibly because they were not direct ancestors of Alasdair's father. It may be that before his father, a brother, cousin or some other relative held Raasay. Perhaps that is why there has been no record found of the MacSweens – they had gone before written histories. The existence of even Scottish Crown and parliamentary records in this early period are sparse. If the MacSweens had held the lands from the Church, as seems probable, there is virtually no hope of finding any record of them, as there are no records of the Synod of Argyll and the Isles before 1638.[21]

The charter of 1596 also gives a list of the townships of Raasay at that time. They are given as Claichane (Clachan), Oscaig, Inverweig (Inver), Claim (Glam), Madniso (Manish), Brewquhill (Brochel), Awirnis with the islands of Pladda and Ronehae (Arnish with the islands of Fladda and Rona), Screbiddill (Screapadal), Hallaig, Auldali, Livast, Nefuernyn (Fearns), Laggan, Atthro, Satir (Achadh Satir ? – the Field of Satir), Ire (Eyre), Suisnis (Suisnish), Inverarois (Inverarish) Toradoill (Borrodale) and Ramsdall (Ramisdal).

This list begins at Clachan, possibly because of the presence of the Church there. That in itself may have given Clachan an equal, or even greater, importance than Brochel. It then proceeds up the west side of the island to the north end. The township of Arnish has both the islands of Fladda and Rona, which would confirm the belief that they were not occupied at this time, although they may have been used for grazing. The list then continues down the east side of the island to Hallaig. Two townships, Auldali and Livast, are named between Hallaig and Fearns. It is not known where they were.

After Fearns, the list goes inland, most likely following the line of the present road, and names Laggan, Atthro and Satir. Laggan may be Lac, meaning a hollow, which is below the south ridge on the way into Fearns from the Glen. Although two townships, Atthro and Satir, are named here, a later list names only one as Achositore. This is probably a mis-spelling of the Gaelic *Achadh Satir*, the Field of Satir. Satir was in the Glen area, past the mine workings from the sheep pen to the top of the hill into Fearns. The list then continues along the coast from Eyre, round to Inverarish. It then follows the river (or burn) up the glen. It may therefore be assumed that Ramisdal was on the west side of the glen, while Satir was closer to Fearns on the east side.

HOW THE PEOPLE LIVED

The clan chief, or laird, was considered to be the guardian, not the owner, of the land. Farms, tacks and tenancies were held by verbal agreement. Rent was in the form of foodstuffs, such as grain, butter, cheese, sheep and poultry, and other services and conditions, known as 'casualties'. Specific items and amounts varied. The land had to produce enough food to feed the population and provide for the chief and hierarchy of the clan. Food produced over and above that required for subsistence was available for bartering. This surplus could be used to gain, for example, a favourable marriage settlement.

People lived in townships worked on the run-rig system. A head dyke, often built of turf, enclosed the arable land close to the houses. Beyond this was common land used for grazing. Part of the tenancy agreement was the right to cut peats and wood for fuel, use heather for ropes, take turf or thatch for the houses and all the other things that were necessary at the time.

Forests were more extensive then than now, and because of their importance they were carefully managed. Although the birlinns and large boats may have been built elsewhere, small boats would have been built locally, although not necessarily on Raasay itself. Wood was also used for many other purposes, such as housing and farming implements. For Raasay, at this time, as in later centuries, it was another commodity that could be exchanged or bartered. It has already been mentioned that food surpluses could also be so used, as could Raasay's extensive supplies of freestone for building and millstones.

The most usual crops were corn and grass. In some places there were also oats and bere/barley. The domestic animals were cattle, sheep, poultry and some horses. Cattle and sheep were much smaller than the breeds of today. The arable land was fertilised with livestock manure and seaweed. The livestock were wintered within the head dyke and put out to the common grazing after the crops were planted in the spring. Herd-boys were responsible for ensuring that they did not stray, either into the growing crops, or beyond their own common grazing. Each township would have been self-sufficient.

Townships were let either to one tenant or to multiple tenants, often referred to as joint tenancies. Each person had a fixed share, not necessarily equal. The run-rig system had intermixed strips of arable land. These strips were divided between the tenants every year, each working his own strips separately. Although this was divided on a year to year basis, it does not imply that there was any great movement of people or any feeling of insecurity on their part. Townships were not a static entity. As population grew or declined, land could be taken into cultivation or left fallow.

The population of Raasay at this time, in view of later figures, could perhaps be guessed at somewhere between three and five hundred. The MacLeods held a good social position. In the 1580s and 1590s they had men available to make raids. We know of those to Caithness and to Torridon. Fighting men were generally not required to take part in the day-to-day farming work. They formed part of the chief's retinue, and were supported by the clan. At this time, Raasay must have been far removed from subsistence agriculture.

The people on Raasay during the sixteenth century made their living by working the land. Although the MacLeods are known to have taken part in raids on other areas, no record has come down to us of attacks on Raasay. They had the backing of the MacKenzies of Kintail, a powerful clan at that time. Society was built around the clan, or the general population of the estate. All the people, from the highest to the lowest, were working towards the same goals. What was good for the chief and his retinue was also good for the people, in both social and economic terms.

Raasay at this time was by no means an isolated little 'island kingdom'. The estate was in two parts. The three merkland in Snizort stretched from Eyre, Snizort over the hill to the east side of Trotternish, taking in the areas of Totaroam and Rigg. The sea was the link between these two parts of the estate.

So far, little has been said about the sea, in relation to the lives of the people. It is important to remember that the sea played an important part in their lives. Like their Viking ancestors, they were good seamen and used the sea much as we use motorways today. Good boats, boatbuilders and repairers, and seamen were very important. The whole of the west coast was their neighbourhood. Trips to Lewis, Ardnamurchan, Gairloch, Torridon and Caithness were no problem. An added advantage was that when they arrived at their destination, whether for feasting or raiding, their men were fresh. They had not had to march for days to get to wherever they were going.

This 'motorway on their doorstep' also allowed socialising. People called in as they were passing. Raasay was very well placed for that type of contact, and the people, as well as the lairds, would have been well informed about events far afield because of it. Lairds did not go anywhere on their own, even for social visits. Their retinue of principal men, some fighting men, seamen and servants would always accompany them.

It was the custom of the times that sons of the chiefs were often fostered with another family. In part this was for the safety of the child, but it also acted to cement bonds of friendship between the two families. It has already been shown that Calum Garbh survived the massacre at Isay in the early 1530s because he was being fostered away from home. As with all these old customs, it was governed by rules, well understood and closely observed by all parties concerned.

John MacLeod, brother of Calum Òg, had been fostered in the house of Bayne of Tulloch, near Bonar Bridge on the Dornoch Firth. As a gift of fosterage, Bayne had promised John the lands of Torridon. Such a gift was not uncommon. However, Bayne, by then an old man, left the lands of Torridon to his own son, Alasdair. For several years, John MacLeod did what he could to get those lands, which he firmly believed should be his. His strategy took the form of raids on the lands in question, during which livestock were taken away, crops burned and much trouble caused. The lands of Torridon were not far from Kintail, and even closer to Gairloch and Applecross, where branches of the MacKenzies lived. Although the MacKenzies may not have helped John, they did nothing to stop him. His mother, after all, was Isobel MacKenzie.

On numerous occasions Alasdair Bayne complained to the authorities and John MacLeod, when he did not appear to answer the charges, was declared a rebel. In 1595 John MacKenzie, minister of Urray near Dingwall, was also denounced as a rebel for not appearing to answer the charge of aiding and abetting John by allowing him into his house. As the minister was still in his post in 1601, it can be assumed that no further action was taken against him. However, the charges continued to be brought against John.

In 1597, shortly before the Candlemas market at Conon, John was again denounced as a rebel, and Alasdair Bayne and his men came to the market well prepared and armed.[22] With them were some Munros. John did not know of the charges against him and went to the market as usual. Alasdair Bayne struck him without warning and John fell dead. A MacKenzie man, who was standing nearby, asked who had dared to spill MacKenzie blood in such a base manner. He had no sooner spoken than he too was killed. It has been said that these two men were among the best swordsmen of their day in the north of Scotland.

The war cry of the MacKenzie went up, and the Baynes and Munros fled, hotly pursued by MacKenzies and, no doubt, some of the MacLeods. The Baynes no doubt later regretted the conduct of their leader, as they lost many men that day.

THE DEMISE OF THE MACLEODS OF LEWIS

As the sixteenth century drew to a close, times were becoming more difficult. John MacLeod, brother of the Laird of Raasay was killed in 1597. This was not a good year for the MacLeods of Lewis either. Their blood ties with the MacLeods of Raasay meant that although little is known of their dealings, it may be assumed that there was some contact between these two branches of the clan. The MacLeods of Lewis had been involved in the bitter dispute over succession during the second half of the sixteenth century. It is not known when Ruairidh Chaluim, chief of Lewis, died but it was probably in the late 1580s or early 1590s. Despite

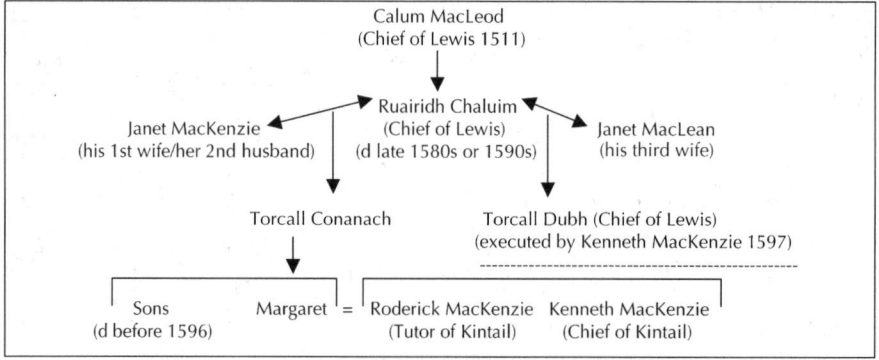

Figure 2/7. MacLeods of Lewis at the end of the sixteenth century.

the charter of 1572, Torcall Conanach did not succeed him. Another of Ruairidh Chaluim's sons, Torcall Dubh, became chief.

Because both of Torcall Conanach's sons had died before 1596, his son-in-law, Roderick MacKenzie, claimed the lands of Lewis on behalf of his wife. Roderick MacKenzie, later known as the Tutor of Kintail, was the brother of Kenneth, then chief of the MacKenzies of Kintail. Kenneth, later Lord Kintail, had been trying for many years to acquire the lands of Lewis for himself. Torcall Dubh and his men were captured and taken to Ullapool, and word was sent to Kenneth MacKenzie informing him of this.

> Lord Kintail sent an order to execute Torcal Dubh MacLeod with his whole company, which order was no sooner received but was as soon put in execution without Doome or Law, only one gentleman of the house and family of Raasay made his escape. This was done in the month of July 1597 and at the very moment of his execution there was an extraordinary great earthquake which much astonished the malefactors, though hardened with cruelty and mischief.[23]

Thus the chief of the MacLeods of Lewis was killed. Although the above account mentions a gentleman of the Raasay family, it is not clear how involved they had been with events in Lewis. It is quite possibly there was some involvement, although there are few specific references to Raasay people.

In 1598 King James VI granted a charter of Lewis, for a fee, to a company of gentlemen known as the Fife Adventurers. The MacLeods naturally resisted this takeover of the estate. By playing both ends against the middle, Kenneth MacKenzie of Kintail was able to buy the estate from the Fife Adventurers in 1608. By then they were so discouraged that they were more than willing to sell up and leave.

Torcall Dubh of Lewis married a daughter of Norman MacLeod, chief of Dunvegan. She was thus a sister of Sir Ruairidh Mòr of Dunvegan. Torcall Dubh and his wife had three sons – Ruairidh, William and Torcall. Ruairidh attended Glasgow University. William was possibly the 'Gillielmus MacClaudius' who graduated from there in 1622, the same year as he witnessed the signature of his uncle, Ruairidh Mòr.[24] Torcall was brought up at Dunvegan.

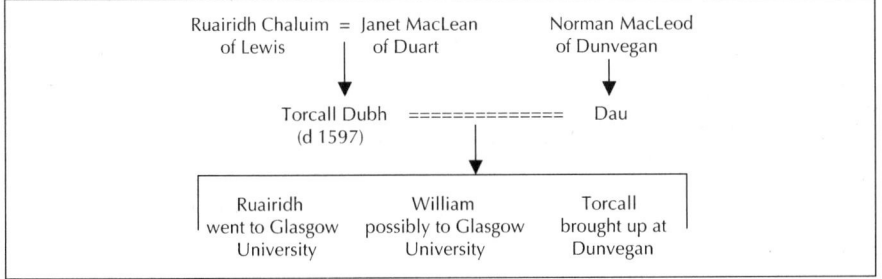

Figure 2/8. Torcall Dubh of Lewis.

The late Somhairle MacLean gave an interesting addition to this story. He began by saying that there were five MacLeod families in Raasay who were not connected, as far as was known, on the male MacLeod side. Somhairle continued

> Some years ago, I asked the late Ewen MacLeod, Eóghainn Thorcuil Chalum mhic Thormaid which of the families he was. His reply was 'Chan ann a mhuinntir Ratharsair a bha sinne idir; s ann a thàinig sinne á Leódhas o Thorcuil Dubh a chaidh a chrochadh. (It is not of the people of Raasay we were at all. We came from Lewis, from Torcuil Dubh, who was hanged.) [25]

So at least one of Torcall Dubh's descendants settled in Raasay. This may not, however, have happened immediately. A daughter of Sir Ruairidh Mòr of Dunvegan married Iain Garbh who became Laird of Raasay about the middle of the seventeenth century. The Lady of Raasay was therefore a first cousin of Torcall Dubh's children.

The problems between the MacLeods of Lewis and the MacKenzies of Kintail may have placed Calum Òg of Raasay in a difficult position. He was a first cousin of Kenneth MacKenzie of Kintail and of Roderick MacKenzie, son-in-law of Torcall Conanach, both of whom had designs on the lands of Lewis. Arguably, based on the 1572 charter, Calum Òg himself had a claim to the Lewis lands, as heir of Torcall Conanach.

Perhaps because Calum Òg did not wish to antagonise either the MacKenzies or the MacLeods of Lewis, in 1608, he resigned superiority of the lands of Raasay to Andrew, Bishop of the Isles.[26] He did this knowing that the bishop would

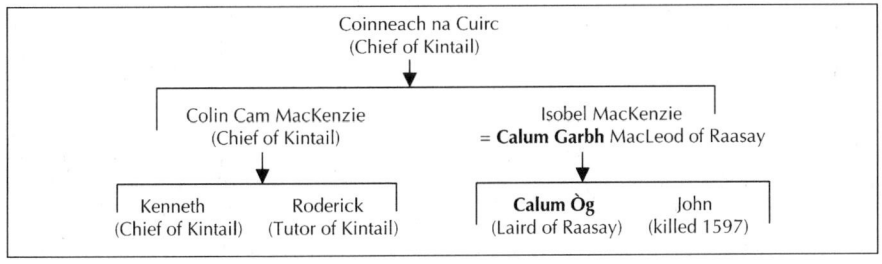

Figure 2/9. Relationship between the MacLeods of Raasay and the chiefs of Kintail.

then pass superiority of Raasay to Kenneth MacKenzie of Kintail. A Crown charter by King James VI, in June 1610, confirmed this.

> The King has confirmed the charter of Andrew, Bishop of the Isles, by which, since Calum MacGillichaluim of Raasay, in fulfilment of a certain contract, resigns his lands in favour of Kenneth MacKenzie of Kintail with the consent of the Dean and Chapter of the Isles, he (the Bishop) ratified the grant to the said Kenneth ...[27]

It is not clear why this resignation was either necessary or desirable. Calum Òg did not resign ownership of the lands, merely superiority. Possibly, in spite of the Crown charter of 1596 in his favour, the MacLeans of Dochgarroch were still claiming ownership. It may be that by resigning superiority to the bishop, in favour of MacKenzie of Kintail, Calum Òg was giving himself the protection of the MacKenzies, without openly favouring them over either the MacLeods of Lewis or the MacLeans of Dochgarroch.

THE MACLEODS OF RAASAY/THE MACLEODS OF GAIRLOCH/ THE MACKENZIES OF KINTAIL

Although very little is known of the MacLeods of Gairloch during the sixteenth century, it would appear that they were still in possession of at least part of the lands of Gairloch. The histories, previously given, of this branch of the MacLeods suggest that they were in a state of constant war with the MacKenzies of Kintail.

A feud, lasting many years, between the MacKenzies of Kintail and the MacDonalds of Glengarry was not settled until after the death of Lord Kenneth of Kintail in 1611. An incident took place during this feud which shows that the MacKenzies and the MacLeods of Gairloch were acting together. Kenneth MacKenzie sent Alexander MacKenzie of Achiltie and John Holmach, a son of Ruairidh mac Allan of Gairloch, to 'view the coast'. They went in John Holmach's eight-oared boat, taking with them sixteen gentlemen and eight 'scallag moires'. It has already been seen that the MacLeods of Raasay and the MacKenzies were on good terms with each other. This incident shows that the MacLeods of Gairloch were not in the state of perpetual war with the MacKenzies, as other histories would have us believe.

The name John Holmach is of interest. Holm or Tulm derives from the Old Norse *holmr*. Today, in Gaelic, it means a round hillock, but in the past it was used to describe any feature that stood out, such as a hill on flat ground. It may

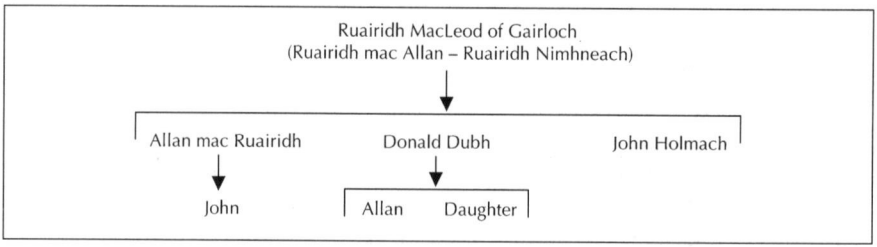

Figure 2/10. The MacLeods of Gairloch

be significant that on the west coast of Raasay lies Holoman Island, and on the east coast of Skye, just south of Berreraig Bay, lies Holm Island. The island is a large lump of rock, sitting just to the south of the old boundary between Portree parish and that part of the parish of Snizort that belonged to the MacLeods of Raasay. Quite possibly these two 'Holms' were used in the past as marks or guides for people moving back and forth across the sound between the two parts of the estate. John Holmach may have been fostered by someone living near one of those features, or he himself may have lived near one of them at some time. Descendants of John Holmach are known by the surname Tolmie.[28]

Evidence from the privy council records that, prior to January 1609, some MacLeods were involved in a raid against 'Donald Mac Alastair Roy in Dibaig'. This is most likely Diabaig, in the Gairloch area. Although the reasons for the raid are not known, the names of the MacLeods who took part are of interest. They were 'Allan Mac Donald Dubh Mhic Rory' of Culnacnoc in Trotternish, 'Murdo Mac Gillechallum, brother of Gillecallum Raasay, Laird of Raasay, Gillechallum Mac Rory Mhic Leoid' in Lewis and also from Lewis 'Norman Mac Ghillechallum Mhoir and Rory Mac Ghillechallum Mhoir, his brother'.[29]

Allan (son of Donald Dubh), who was living in Trotternish, was one of the Gairloch MacLeods, a nephew of John Holmach. Murdo was Calum Òg's brother, from Raasay. The others were of the Lewis MacLeods. That they were together on one raid suggests that they may well have been otherwise working together, not necessarily only on raids. Raids did not just happen. Each one had its reasons. Whether these reasons were just or not depended on one's point of view.

Clearly some of the MacLeods of Gairloch were living on Skye at this time, but not necessarily on MacLeod of Raasay land. Culnacnoc is just north of the Lealt river, which formed the boundary between the parish of Snizort (MacLeod of Raasay land) and the parish of Kilmuir. Today, the Lealt river forms the boundary between the parishes of Portree and Stenscholl (created in 1833 when the parish of Kilmuir was divided). It is said that Murdo, half brother of Calum Òg, was the ancestor of the MacLeods of Marrishadder in Trotternish.

Although the sequence of events leading up to 1610 are extremely blurred, Alexander MacKenzie states that about then there was a battle at Loch an Fhéidh in Glen Torridon, where the MacKenzies of Gairloch inflicted a defeat on the MacLeods of Gairloch. The chief of that branch at the time, John mac Allan mac Ruairidh, was taken prisoner, while his uncle, John Holmach mac Ruairidh, escaped.

THE SEA FIGHT AT CLACHAN

It is said that in August 1611,[30] Murdo MacKenzie, son of MacKenzie of Gairloch and Alasdair Bayne, heir apparent of Tulloch, left the mainland and set sail with their men in a boat loaded with wine and provisions. There are two possible reasons for the trip. One possibility is that MacKenzie wanted to secure the hand in marriage of the only daughter of Donald Dubh mac Ruairidh MacLeod of Gairloch. As John mac Allan mac Ruairidh was a prisoner and John Holmach mac Ruairidh was in exile, she was the direct heir to the estates of Gairloch.

This was the tradition in Gairloch. The other possible reason for the trip was to find and apprehend John Holmach mac Ruairidh.

For some reason, whether by accident or design, the boat went into Clachan Bay in Raasay, and dropped anchor within sight of the MacLeod's residence there. 'Young MacGilleChallum' of Raasay learned that Murdo MacKenzie was aboard and discussed matters with 'MacGilleChallum Mòr MacDhomhnuill Mhic Neill', who persuaded him to visit the ship as a friend and somehow secure MacKenzie, who could then be exchanged for their prisoner, 'John MacAllan Mhic Rory'. Young Raasay, with MacGilleChaluim Mòr and some of their men, went aboard and were offered food and wine. All aboard ate and drank to excess, except four of the Gairloch men who were not too happy about this turn of events. Eventually, Bayne and most of the Gairloch men retired below decks to sleep off the effects of the drink, leaving MacKenzie and the Raasay men alone.

MacLeod laid hold of MacKenzie, declaring that he was his prisoner, but was pushed aside by the latter. The Raasay men drew their dirks, and as MacKenzie stepped back to draw his sword, his foot struck the gunwale of the ship and he fell into the sea. The MacLeods on the shore, seeing the commotion on board, launched their small boats. Seeing MacKenzie making for the Skye shore, they pelted him with stones or oars and he drowned. Meantime, aboard the galley, although those who had retired drunk did not put up much resistance, the four who had abstained certainly did. All the Raasay men aboard the galley were killed.

The height of the galley sides gave them an advantage over the small boats. They cut away the anchor, and hoisting sail for home, managed to reach the safety of Gairloch. Three of these men are said to have lived to a good age.

There has been considerable debate in previous histories of the MacLeods about which member of the Raasay family was killed in this fight. Some maintain that it was Calum Garbh, while others believe that it was Calum Òg. At least part of the confusion stems from the fact that Alexander MacKenzie believed that Calum Garbh was born about 1560 and did not become laird until the early 1580s. This was not the case, and because Calum Garbh had already died before 1570, it could not have been him who was killed. Calum Òg was laird by 1572 when the Crown charter in favour of Torcall Conanach of Lewis named him as such. By 1611 he would have been at least sixty years of age.

An account from the history of the MacKenzies[31] says that the man killed was 'Gillichallum Oig, Laird of Rasay', and that 'he was made against his will by Gillichallum moire m'Donald mhic Neil to go to the ship' to take MacKenzie prisoner.

Because Calum Òg's mother was Isabel MacKenzie, this account might be assumed to be accurate. It was written about 1667 and, by reason of that early date, may hold more weight than later histories. One might ask whether an experienced chief would do anything 'against his will' as described in the MacKenzie history. Could it have been a son of Calum Òg who was killed? Could 'Gillichallum Oig' mean 'Young MacLeod of Raasay', referring to the heir apparent. The eldest son of a laird was often referred to in that manner. However, the evidence of both the MacKenzie history and Sir Robert Gordon, who wrote *A Genealogical History of the Earldom of Sutherland*, published in 1813, indicated that it was Calum Òg who was killed.

RAASAY AFTER 1611

The name of Calum Òg's wife is not given in any of the histories. Neither is the date of their marriage. Although there is no record of another laird before 1617, Mr Sellar has indicated that there were sometimes long gaps between the death of a laird and a following 'service of heir'.[32]

On 27 April 1617 Alasdair MacLeod of Raasay delivered to Lord Colin, Earl of Seaforth, an 'Inventory of Writs and Evidents'. Because the Earl of Seaforth held the feudal superiority of the Raasay estate, this inventory may have been necessary for Alasdair to prove to him that he should succeed his father, Calum Òg, as Laird of Raasay. It is said that Alasdair was served heir to his father on 18 February 1617. Some accounts maintain that Alasdair did not come of age until 1617. This is unlikely, as his father was born about 1550. Therefore, if it was Calum Òg who died during the sea-fight at Clachan, it may be that the date given for that fight was too early. Perhaps it should be dated closer to 1617.

The 'Inventory of Writs and Evidents' may also have been the cause of some confusion for earlier writers. In describing the various charters, the inventory appears to describe people as alive or dead at the time it was written in 1617. However, some have taken this to describe the position at the time of the particular charter.

Some MacLeans of the Dochgarroch family and possibly some Cummings had probably already settled on Raasay. By now, another branch of the family, the MacLeans of Duart, held the island of Scalpay, just to the south of Raasay. They were related to the Dochgarroch branch, and also to Torcall Dubh's mother. Other members of this branch of the MacLeans, the Clann Theàrlaich, were known to be working with Donald Gorm of Sleat about 1615. The MacLeans, therefore, had a significant presence in the area.

Alasdair MacLeod married Isobel MacKenzie from Applecross.[33] Some writers refer to her as Sibella. She was the daughter of Ruairidh MacKenzie of Applecross, a branch of the MacKenzies of Kintail. Although no date is given for this marriage it had certainly taken place by the 1620s and possibly before that.

Although, as yet, they were having little effect on Raasay people, changes were affecting the region. The Statutes of Iona had been drawn up in 1609, and revised in 1616, and gave a clear indication that the king and privy council had begun their efforts to enforce the laws of Scotland in the north-west. This new regime did not affect Raasay people directly, but the MacLeods and the people of Raasay were in close contact with many who were affected. The two major landowners in Skye, the MacLeods of Dunvegan and the MacDonalds of Sleat, as well as the Earls of Seaforth of Lewis and Kintail were now obliged to go to Edinburgh each year and to have their children educated in the Lowlands.

In 1628 a meeting, attended by the Earl of Seaforth, MacLeod of Dunvegan, MacDonald of Sleat, MacKinnon of Strath, the Captain of Clanranald and Alasdair MacLeod of Raasay was held at Duntulm. They all signed a contract, agreeing that none of their people would hunt in any deer forest without a written licence from their superior, which would be shown to the forester. This makes clear both that they were willing to comply with the Statutes of Iona, at least as far as hunting was concerned, and that they could police their own estates.

Calum Òg had received a Crown charter for the Raasay estate in 1596. In 1608 he resigned superiority, but not ownership, to the Bishop of the Isles, knowing that superiority would pass to the MacKenzies of Kintail, later the Earls of Seaforth. Farquhar MacLean of Dochgarroch, when he was Bishop of the Isles, 1529–44, was granted the legal right to pass on the estate of Raasay to his son and heir, Donald MacLean of Dochgarroch. This he did, but although Donald tried to obtain possession, he was unsuccessful. Having once received legal title, the MacLeans of Dochgarroch did not give up their claim on Raasay.

In 1631 their legal title to the Raasay estate was confirmed by an Instrument of Sasine[34] in favour of Alexander MacLean of Dochgarroch as heir to his father, Donald. It is interesting that one of the witnesses to this sasine was John MacLeod of Raasay.[35] This suggests that the MacLeods may not have been unduly perturbed by the MacLean ownership. However, the MacLeans were not, at any time, able to take possession of Raasay. Although the witness was John MacLeod of Raasay, he was not the laird.

As required, prior to the issuing of the sasine, a retour was necessary. This retour, dated 1630, names the townships of Raasay as Clachan, Oistage (Oscaig), Innerwig (Inver), Clam (Glam), Maenes (Manish), Browkill (Brochel), Awoynes cum insula Phladda (Arnish with the Island of Fladda), Ronaha (Rona), Skrebidell (Screapadal), Helleg et Larg (Hallaig and ?), Lebost, Naseiring (Fearns), Lagan (Lac?), Achositore (Achadh Satir – the Field of Satir ?), Ire (Eyre), Swysnes (Suisnish), Inneraros (Inverarish), Borradaill (Borrodale), and Ramisdill (Ramisdal).

Comparison with the previous list, given in the Crown charter of 1596, shows that the townships of the west side are the same as far as Arnish. In 1596, because Fladda and Rona went with Arnish, it was assumed that they were grazing lands for that township. This time, however, Rona is mentioned as a separate entity, suggesting that, by then, some people were living on it. Perhaps Monro's 'ruggaris and reevaris' had gone and Rona had become a more integral part of the estate. As in the list of 1596, two townships are named between Hallaig and Fearns. In 1596 they were Auldali and Livast, now they are Larg and Lebost. One of them may be Leac. As with the earlier list, this one goes inland from Fearns naming Laggan and Achositore (named as two townships in 1596), before proceeding round the south end to Eyre and finishing up at Ramisdal in the Glen area. Thus the lists are essentially the same.

Notes

1. H. H. MacKenzie, *The MacLeans of Boreray* (1946), p. 1.
2. R. Miket and D. L. Roberts, *The Mediaeval Castles of Skye and Lochalsh* (1990), p. 18.
3. 'The Manuscript History of Craignish', Miscellany of the Scottish History Society, *SHS*, 3rd series, vol. IV, p. 232.

4. H. MacDonald, 'History of the MacDonalds', written after 1628, *SHS*, Highland Papers, vol. 1, ed. J. R. N. MacPhail, p. 58.
5. A. MacKenzie, *History of the MacLeods* (1889), pp. 340–97, where all references to Alexander MacKenzie can be found.
6. N. M. Bristol, *Warriors and Priests: The History of the Clan MacLean* (1995), p. 110.
7. R. Sharpe, *Raasay: Documents and Sources* (1978), p. 65.
8. N. M. Bristol, *Warriors and Priests: The History of the Clan MacLean* (1995), p. 118.
9. D. Monro, 'Description of the Western Isles of Scotland 1549' *Monro's Western Isles of Scotland*, ed. R. W. Munro (1961), p. 70.
10. R. Sharpe, *Raasay: Documents and Sources* (1978), pp. 32–3.
11. J. G. MacKay, 'Social Life in Skye from Legend and Story', *TGSI*, vol. XXIX, pp. 349–50.
12. W. MacKay, *Urquhart and Glenmoriston: Olden Times in a Highland Parish* (1893), p. 514.
13. J. MacKenzie, 'Genealogie of Surname of M'Kenzie', written *c*.1667, *SHS*, Highland Papers, vol. 2, ed. J. R. N. MacPhail (1916), p. 33 (so called 'for his notable dexterity in engraving' according to Lord Cromartie).
14. W. D. H. Sellar, 'Marriage, Divorce and Concubinage in Gaelic Scotland', *TGSI*, vol. LI, pp. 464–93.
15. *MacKintosh Muniments*, p. 32.
16. R. Sharpe, *Raasay: Documents and Sources* (1978), pp. 67–8.
17. R. Sharpe, *Raasay: Documents and Sources* (1978), pp. 65–6.
18. R. Sharpe, *Raasay: a Study in Island History* (1977), p. 40.
19. A. MacKenzie, *History of the MacLeods* (1889), pp. 351–2.
20. R. Sharpe, *Raasay: Documents and Sources* (1978), p. 73.
21. Rev. M. MacAulay, *Aspects of the Religious History of Lewis* (Inverness), p. 1.
22. J. MacKenzie, 'Genealogie of Surname of M'Kenzie *c*.1667', *SHS*, Highland Papers, vol. 2, ed. J. R. N. MacPhail (1916), p. 35.
23. 'The Ewill Trowbles of the Lewes', *SHS*, Highland Papers, vol. 2, ed. J. R. N. MacPhail (1916), p. 269.
24. I. F. Grant, *History of the Clan MacLeod 1959* (1981 edition), pp. 239–40.
25. Dr S. MacLean, 'Some Raasay Traditions', *TGSI*, vol. XLIX, p. 383.
26. W. Fraser, *The Earls of Cromartie*, vol. 2 (1876), p. 502.
27. R. Sharpe, *Raasay: Documents and Sources* (1978), pp. 74–5.
28. H. H. Mackenzie, *The MacKenzies of Ballone* (1941), pp. 76–7.
29. A. MacKenzie, *History of the MacKenzies* (1879), p. 191.
30. A. MacKenzie, *History of the MacLeods* (1889), 363–5; A. Nicolson, *History of Skye* (1930, revised and ed. Dr A. MacLean 1995), pp. 296–7; Sir Robert Gordon of Gordonstoun, Baronet, *A Genealogical History of the Earldom of Sutherland* (1813), pp. 276–8.
31. J. MacKenzie, op. cit., p. 52.
32. Mr W. D. H. Sellar is an authority on the history of north-western Scotland in the medieval period.
33. 'The MacKenzies', *SHS*, Genealogical Collections, vol. 1, ed. J. T. Clark (1900), p. 99.
34. A legal term meaning the act of handing over ownership of feudal property.
35. (An Associate of the Family), *History of the Clan Tarlach O'Bui* (1864), p. 79.

3

The History of Raasay, 1630s–1750

RAASAY IN THE MID SEVENTEENTH CENTURY

According to the written histories of the MacLeods, they had lost the lands of Gairloch by the second decade of the seventeenth century, but they still held the Raasay estate, including the lands in Snizort, Skye. The MacLeods of Lewis had by then, or shortly after, been forced to give up their fight for Lewis, which was held by the MacKenzies of Kintail, who also had the feudal superiority of Raasay. The MacLeans of Dochgarroch, in spite of having a sasine in their favour in 1631, did not have Raasay, although some may have been living on the island. There is every reason to suppose that some members of all three branches of the MacLeods were not only in contact but also working with each other. Some members of the MacLeods of Lewis and of Gairloch were now living either on Raasay or in Trotternish, Skye.

The MacLeods of Raasay had, very successfully, managed to steer a course through a very difficult period in their history and were now about to enter into less turbulent times.

Alasdair MacLeod had become Laird of Raasay in 1617. The date of his marriage to Sibella (or Isabella), a daughter of Roderick MacKenzie of Applecross, is not known.

Probably about the middle of the seventeenth century, Margaret, daughter of Alasdair and Sibella, married Calum, a son of Donald, the Nicolson Chief of Scorrybreac. Scorrybreac is just to the north of Portree. Many journeys would have been made, back and forth across the Sound, in preparation for the marriage. This would have been a time of feasting and celebration for the island. Songs were composed to celebrate the marriage, and in praise of both these houses.

Such songs have been passed down through the generations. Many, of course, have now been lost, but one has been noted down gives a tantalising glimpse of life then.[1] It speaks of the 'big wide house' with the 'spacious hall' that Margaret

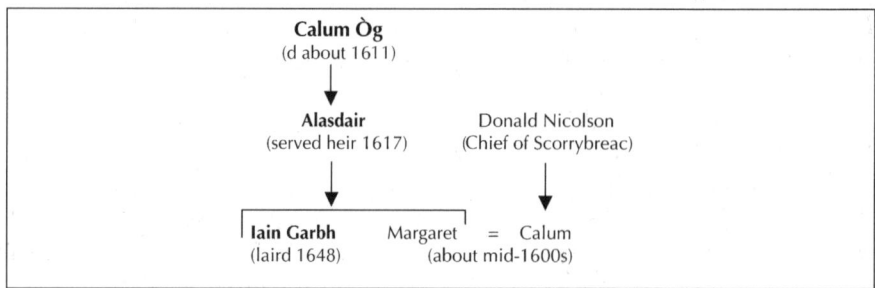

Figure 3/1. MacLeods of Raasay and Nicolsons of Scorrybreac.

was going to in Scorrybreac. It had a 'smooth, swept floor', such that 'an apple would roll up and down on it'. A pig and a cow were being prepared for the feast. Wine would be drunk from 'brown cups with lovely lips', and from 'cold, sliver cups'. There would be 'drink as strong as comes from Holland'. They would eat off 'pewter dishes and plates'.

Clearly this describes the type of residence of the lairds and chiefs, but it is obvious that Raasay and Skye then, three and a half centuries ago, were not inward looking, insular places. It confirms that the lairds, chiefs and consequently the people were in contact with, and knew about areas far away from their own part of Scotland. Only Holland is mentioned here, but there was contact with other countries of Europe and, of course, with Ireland.

IAIN GARBH, LAIRD OF RAASAY

By 1650 Alasdair MacLeod had died and his son, Iain Garbh, was the Laird of Raasay. He is said to have been the last of the MacLeods of Raasay to use Brochel Castle. He married Janet MacLeod, a daughter of Ruairidh Mòr of Dunvegan. This marriage would have been the cause of even greater feasting and celebration than that of his sister. Iain Garbh, whether or not he was the Laird of Raasay at the time of his marriage, was at least the heir apparent, and the MacLeods of Dunvegan were a very significant clan. A marriage of this status confirms both the circumstances and the aspirations of the MacLeods of Raasay. Iain Garbh was a strong, good-looking man, well liked and respected by all who knew him.

A sister of Ruairidh Mòr had married Torcall Dubh of Lewis. It may have been because of their relationship with Iain Garbh's wife that descendants of Torcall Dubh settled on Raasay.

Before Easter, in 1671 it is said, Iain Garbh and sixteen of his men, including his brother Calum, went to Lewis to attend the christening of a child of the Earl of Seaforth. After the feasting they left Lewis in their birlinn to return to Raasay, but all were drowned. This was a devastating blow for Raasay, and indeed for everyone who knew the laird. It seemed impossible that a man of his stature should be drowned while sailing his own birlinn. These being superstitious times, the story spread that witchcraft had played a part.[2]

It is said that MacDonald of Duntulm was not happy about a part of the Raasay estate dividing his lands in Trotternish. He could do nothing about it, but was all the more irritated when he heard that Iain Garbh had said that one day he would possess even more. MacDonald's foster mother had also been the foster mother of Iain Garbh. She was reputed to have the gift of witchcraft. MacDonald now sent for her and told her that she could have a piece of land that she had often asked for, if she would sink the Raasay birlinn on its return journey. She agreed.

A tub was filled with water, into which she placed an eggshell. When the boat was sighted approaching the Skye coast, she climbed up the *slabhruidh* (a chain for hanging pots over the fire). Her daughter was given a stick with which she was to stir the water in the tub, slowly at first, then more quickly, first to the right, then to the left. This raised a commotion in the tub. People watching the galley from the shore saw that it was suddenly in distress. All at once the wind, which until then had been blowing from the south, now blew also from the north, and the galley was caught in the eddy between the two. Some of the onlookers declared that they saw a black cat ascend the mast, and that Iain Garbh was seen aiming a blow at it with his battle axe. The galley laboured heavily, and suddenly plunged down head foremost. So perished the brave and fearless Iain Garbh and his crew, on a beautiful day, within sight of a number of people on the shore who could not believe what they were seeing.

Immediately after, an immense wave rushed onto the shore, carrying with it a huge body of sand, which formed a great bank called to this day Mol Stamhain, Staffin Beach. A *mol* is a shingly beach of worn stones or pebbles. Local people said that on the anniversary of the loss of Iain Garbh, the incoming tide made a terrific roar on the *mol*, which could be heard for miles around.

The woman lost no time in applying for the reward, but MacDonald refused. She vowed vengeance, but he threatened to have her burnt as a witch. One day, some time later, when she was fishing at Rudha nam Bràithrean, Brothers' Point, south of Staffin, her sister, who lived on Harris, was also fishing from a rock just south of Scalpay. Their lines became entangled in the middle of the Minch. The one was as stubborn as the other, and the battle raged as each one pulled and better pulled. At last, the one from Harris proved the stronger, and her sister was pulled into the sea and drowned, not far from the spot where she herself had drowned Iain Garbh.

Iain Garbh's brother, Alasdair, told James Fraser, minister of Wardlaw (now Kirkhill, Inverness), about the accident.[3] He said that 'after a rant of drinking on the shore' they set off from Lewis in a strong gale of north wind. Perhaps they had too much sail and no ballast, or perhaps the seamen could not manage the strong Dutch canvas sail, but the boat was overwhelmed and the men drowned in view of the coast. None of them was ever found. Only some pieces of the birlinn and one or two greyhounds were cast up on the shore.

Many laments were composed for Iain Garbh. Màiri nighean Alasdair Ruaidh, the famous bardess, composed one, and there is a tradition in Raasay that one of his sisters composed one each Friday for a year after his death. Pàdraig Mòr MacCrimmon, of the famous MacCrimmon pipers of Dunvegan, composed the *piobaireachd* 'Cumha Iain Ghairbh Mhic Ghille-Chaluim', 'Lament for Iain Garbh MacGilleChaluim'.

Although it has been said that Iain Garbh drowned at Easter 1671, this may not be so. It is known that the Laird of Raasay was in debt to Iain Breac MacLeod of Dunvegan in 1680.[4] The Laird of Raasay is named, at that time, as 'John MacLeod of Raasay'. The date of the drowning has come from the Wardlaw Manuscript, but although that gives details about many events, very few dates are given. It can probably be assumed that this debt was what might be termed today a 'cash flow problem' rather than a serious financial problem. The cash-based economy was something that these lairds were just getting used to. MacLeod of Dunvegan would have had his own debts to meet, probably making it necessary for him to chase up his debtors.

Iain Garbh's youngest brother, Alasdair, now became Laird of Raasay. Little

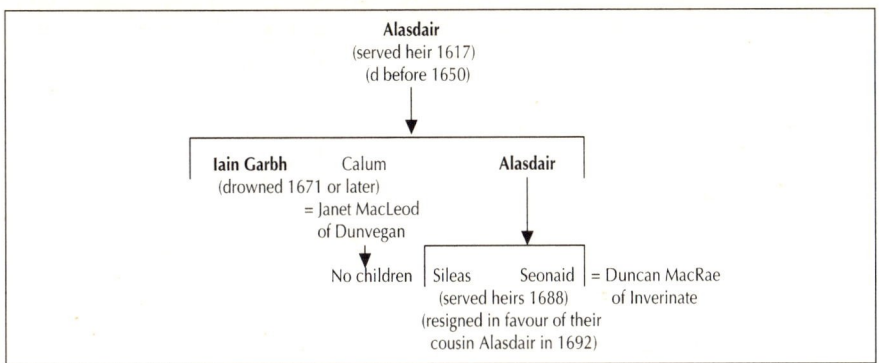

Figure 3/2. MacLeods of Raasay after Iain Garbh.

is known of him, but he appears to have died by 1688 when his daughters, Sileas and Seonaid (usually translated as Giles or Julia, and Janet), became his 'joint heirs of line conquest and provision'. Although the laws of Scotland allowed Alasdair's daughters to inherit the estate, the people of Raasay thought otherwise.

It was important for the estate to have a strong leader. The sense of clan identity was very strong. Clan (in Gaelic *clann* meaning children or descendants) does not necessarily mean people of the same surname, but people who lived on the estate, the 'people of Raasay'. Seonaid was married to Donnchadh nam Piòs, Duncan MacRae of Inverinate, near Kyle of Lochalsh. Sileas was unmarried. It followed, therefore, that if these ladies were allowed to inherit Raasay, it would in a very short time pass to Seonaid's eldest son and become an addition to the MacRae estate of Inverinate. The MacLeod identity that had been so strong and powerful in the days of Iain Garbh would then have to change dramatically, and take second place to Inverinate. It can be readily understood that the people of Raasay, as well as the leading men of the island, opposed this vigorously. There followed a legal dispute over the succession. At length, in 1692, Sileas and Seonaid resigned their rights to their cousin, Alasdair. The MacRaes of Inverinate, it is said, were none too happy about this turn of events.

THE RETOUR OF 1688

The retour that named Sileas and Seonaid as heirs also named the townships of Raasay at that time. They were Kilmiluach (Clachan), Ausach (Oscaig), Balliechurne (Balachuirn), Balliemeanoch (Balmeanach), Invervig (Inver), Glam, Moisnes (Manish), Crochill cum pertinentiis de Sciepadeall (Brochel with Screapadal), Hallag (Hallaig), Leaghk (Leac), Kamorick, Lieboast, Slagadine, Slachro, Fearne (Fearns), Stair (Satir), Ire (Eyre), Shuashnesmore (Suishnish Mòr), Shuashnesbeg (Suishnish Beag), Inneraross (Inverarish), Broradell (Borrodale), Glen, and Kylehan: with the two islands called Rona and Fladda.

There has been an obvious increase in the number of farms or townships over the fifty plus years. Balachuirn and Balmeanach appear for the first time. Screapadal appears to be counted along with Brochel. Between Hallaig and Fearns there are now five townships named. It is possible that errors have crept into the list or these may have been small townships that were later considered to be part of either Fearns or Hallaig. It may well be, however, that this area was now more densely populated than in the past. Satir is again listed after Fearns, but before Eyre. Suisnish is now divided. Ramisdal now appears to be known as Glen. Arnish is not named, but it must be assumed that it would be included with the area called Kylehan. Rona and Fladda are now both named as separate entities.

In part, the reason for these additions will be due to natural population increase. The generally troubled times of the previous century had given way, increasingly, to more peaceful times. Raasay had been, as far as we know, peaceful and prosperous during Iain Garbh's time, so it was natural that the population would increase. Another reason for new farms being created during the seventeenth century was the growing effectiveness of the measures by the king and parliament to bring this region under their control. The Statutes of Iona in 1609 were the first step towards this goal. Raasay, although essentially unaffected, was nonetheless in close and constant contact with others who were directly involved.

There were many changes during the seventeenth century as the hierarchy of the major clans and their chiefs had been forced into contact with Lowland ideas and customs. This required cash money. The barter and exchange system that had operated in the north-west was no longer enough. Goods, mainly cattle, were sold at Lowland markets. Expensive clothes, furnishings and other goods, were now being bought there. The effects were being felt, even in Raasay. By then, not only would the laird be dealing in cattle to raise cash to buy goods, but his relatives and the other leading men of the island would be doing the same. The ordinary tenants would, initially, have seen little change. They would have paid their rent in livestock and produce, as they had always done, but now their landlord set this against a cash value. The cattle of the tenants would have been sent to market along with his own beasts.

As well as the livestock, the other goods and casualties that had formed part of the rental agreement were also given a monetary value. The Statutes of Iona had supposedly abolished these, on the grounds that they were oppressive. They continued, however, but under different names. In 1692, Alasdair MacLeod of Raasay granted lands in liferent to his wife, Florence, including the 'hereyeld' horses.[5] This gave Florence the best horse of any deceased tenant, as well as the rents for that land during her lifetime.

During the sixteenth century, the people of Raasay had supported the laird and his fighting men as part of their tenancy or leasing agreements. These men worked, and fought, for the good of the people, socially and politically. A strong leader gave stability to the estate. Good marriage contracts and the fostering of children cemented bonds between clans, again giving stability to the area. Now the tenants, although they still paid their rent in livestock or produce, found that it had a monetary value. That money was spent outwith the area in which it was produced and was therefore of no direct benefit to the people of the estate. This shift in values was the beginning of the end of the clan system.

The leading men of Raasay, previously the fighting men of the laird's retinue, now had to support themselves. These men, many of them relatives of the chief, were leased farms (called tacks) by the laird, for which they paid rent, either in cash or in kind. They did not usually work the land themselves, however, but allowed cottars to build their houses close by. In exchange for a small plot of land and grazing for a cow, these cottars worked the farm for the tacksman. They were usually given a day or so off per week to work their own land. Sometimes the tacksman let part of his tack under tenancy agreements. This would have led directly to an increase both in the number of townships on Raasay and also to an increase in population. Men did not get married unless, or until, they had the means to support their wives and families. By getting land on which to build their houses and grow some crops and a job labouring for the tacksman, they had the means to do so. This increase in the number of townships or tacks is clear in the 1688 retour.

Raasay people were notable seamen. Any fishing carried out by local people in the north-west would have been for home consumption only. Drying, due to lack of salt for curing, was the method used to preserve the fish. Seals, as well as fish, were sometimes caught. They were used for meat, skins for ropes, and oil.

There was, however, another reason why local people could not fully utilise this natural asset in the seas around them. The Scottish Crown had sold the commercial fishing rights to the seas around Scotland. The deep sea fishing, mainly for herring, had been sold to the Dutch, and inshore fishing was the exclusive right of the royal burghs. Official records show that there were many complaints by the fishermen, about local harassment. Local lairds were in the habit of charging for dues for anchorages, as well as demanding money for each last (twelve barrels) of fish caught. The charges and demands varied from area to area. In this respect, it may be assumed, the Raasay laird was no different from others in the area.

RAASAY DURING THE LATE SEVENTEENTH AND EARLY EIGHTEENTH CENTURY

About 1695 Martin Martin, a member of the Martins of Bealach in Trotternish, Skye, wrote a 'Description of the Western Isles of Scotland'. Martin was at one time governor to Donald MacDonald, younger of Sleat, and afterwards to young MacLeod of Dunvegan. Raasay, he tells us, is better suited to pasture than cultivation. There were woods in all quarters of it. On the east side of the island was a great quantity of petrified substance, of which very fine lime was made. A quarry of good stone was also on the east side. On the west side were many caves, used by several families in summer when they moved there for grazing their animals and for fishing. He mentions the forts on the island. The one in the south end is Dun Caan, said to be from one Canne, cousin to the King of Denmark. That in the north end is an artificial fort, three storeys high, called Castle Vreokle. The seat of the laird is at Clachan which was 'adorned with a little tower, and lesser houses, and an orchard with several sorts of berries and pot herbs'.

The year 1707 saw the union of the parliaments of Scotland and England. This opened up the English markets and, as a consequence, the price of cattle rose. Like landowners on Skye, the MacLeods of Raasay would have taken advantage of this, and sent droves to the markets at Crieff or Falkirk. From the beginning of the century there were two annual fairs in Portree. The balance of the economy was moving fairly swiftly now from the barter system to that of a market economy. However, this was less true for the small tenant than for the landlord and tacksmen.

Population continued to grow, but there was, as yet, no problem of land shortage. About this time, the system of 'soumming' was introduced, to determine the number of livestock that could be kept by each township.[6] Later evidence suggests, however, that although soumming was required in other areas there was no such pressure on Raasay, and tenants could keep as many beasts as they wished. Many tenants had about ten sheep as well as some cattle and poultry. In summer, after the crops were planted, and peats cut for fuel, the cattle would be taken away from the townships to their summer pastures. On Raasay, this would have been to the islands of Rona and Fladda, as well as into the hills. There was no shortage of labour. Sons and daughters of tenants, who were not yet able to set up as tenants themselves, were employed as servants, often agricultural servants, by small tenants as well as tacksmen and the laird.

It has been noted that Alasdair MacLeod of Raasay was married to Florence. In all other histories and genealogies of the Lairds of Raasay Alasdair's wife is said to be Catherine, a daughter of Sir Norman MacLeod of Bernera. Catherine was thus a granddaughter of Sir Ruairidh Mòr of Dunvegan and also of Sir James MacDonald of Sleat. As was the case with Iain Garbh, this too was a marriage

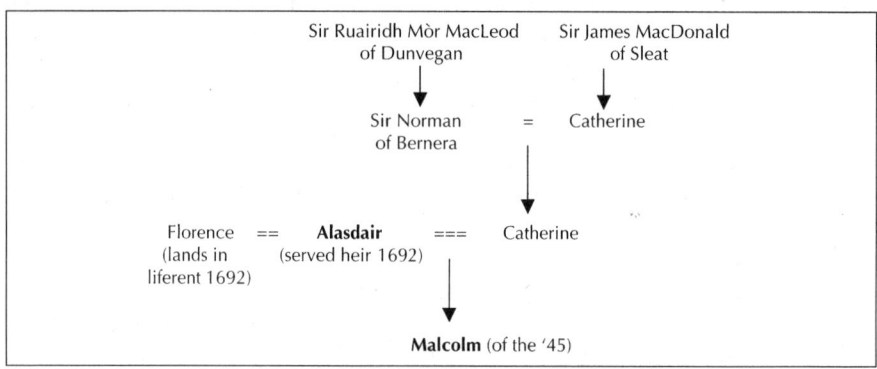

Figure 3/4. Malcolm MacLeod of Raasay (Malcolm of the '45).

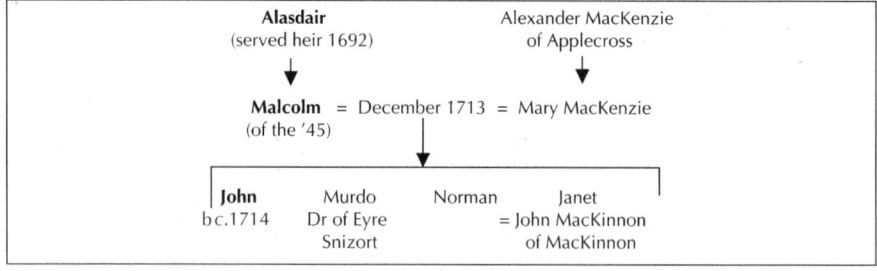

Figure 3/5. Malcolm MacLeod's first marriage.

of status and significance. Alasdair and Catharine had at least one son. He was Malcolm, later known as Malcolm of the '45.

In December 1713, Malcolm MacLeod married Mary MacKenzie of Applecross. In due course, their family was John, Murdo, Norman and Janet.

Although raiding and feuding was now generally a thing of the past, the sense of identity was still very much alive. Competition, in the form of sports, was an enjoyable pastime. The story is told that a Raasay team went to Applecross for a shinty match. For some reason, when the match was due to start the Raasay team was a player short. A man from Applecross, a MacBeath, agreed to play with the Raasay team, who eventually won the game. When it was over, MacBeath said to the Raasay laird, 'Well, after what I have done, I don't need to go back among my own people'. MacLeod replied, 'That's all right. Come back to Raasay with me and I'll give you a place there.' So, he did that. MacBeath was a blacksmith. He was given a place up near Dun Caan called to this day Peighinn a' Ghobhainn, Pennylands of the Smith. From that time, in appreciation of the laird's generosity towards him, MacBeath took the name MacLeod. His descendants, Alasdair Mòr, Charles and Roderick, were living in Arnish at the end of the nineteenth century.

It is not known when Alasdair MacLeod died, but his son, Malcolm, succeeded him. This man was Malcolm of the '45. Malcolm was laird by 1726, when there is a record of his dealing with merchants on the mainland. In September that year, he owed Bailie John Steuart of Inverness £6, a modest amount compared to that owed by others from Skye. Also in 1726, Malcolm and his wife, Mary MacKenzie, mortgaged lands in Rona and Screapadal, possibly to finance major building work on their house at Clachan.

In 1726 the large parish of Snizort, which included the island of Raasay, was divided and the parish of Portree created. Raasay fell within the new parish of Portree. But the Skye part of the Raasay estate remained in the parish of Snizort, stretching over the hill to the east coast of Trotternish between Portree and Kilmuir.

RAASAY'S PART IN THE 1745 REBELLION
The MacLeods of Raasay were keen supporters of the Stuart claim to the throne of Scotland. When the news came that Charles Edward Stuart, known also as Bonnie Prince Charlie or the Young Pretender, had landed in Scotland, Malcolm MacLeod began making plans to join him. He realised, however, that there would be great risks involved, not least that he could be ruined financially and lose his estates should the rising fail. He therefore transferred his entire estate to his oldest son, John, sometimes referred to as 'Rona' or 'Young Raasay'.

Malcolm, Laird of Raasay, and his cousin, Malcolm MacLeod of Eyre (Raasay), met with Alexander MacDonald of Sleat and MacDonald of Kingsburgh at Sconser. News reached them there of the victory at the Battle of Prestonpans. It was proposed that MacLeod of Raasay, with 100 men, should join up with MacDonald of Sleat, who could raise about 900 men, and that this considerable force would then be at the disposal of the Stuarts. Detailed arrangements were made. However, the following morning MacDonald of Sleat received letters from

President Forbes of Culloden and MacLeod of Dunvegan, both men urging him not to join the rebel forces. MacDonald changed his mind and did not join the prince's army.

Despite this, MacLeod of Raasay did join the rebel army in which he held the rank of colonel. With him was his second son, Murdo, who was a surgeon, and Malcolm MacLeod of Eyre, who was a captain. They were joined by his cousin, Donald MacLeod of Bernera, Harris, who is remembered as the 'Old Trojan of Bernera'.

It is not necessary here to detail the story of the '45, except as it relates directly to Raasay. There have been many books published giving full details of the campaign.

> The MacLeods of Raasay marched to Perth and formed part of the Jacobite army that remained in Scotland while the Prince marched into England, joining the army at Stirling in January 1746. At the Battle of Falkirk they fought alongside Glengarry's regiment and were with that regiment also at Culloden where Raasay's son Dr Murdo was wounded. The men fled back to Skye after the battle and a dozen or so were taken prisoner and five transported. Raasay was never captured or forfeit.[7]

At the Battle of Falkirk, the MacLeods of Raasay and Bernera were attached to one of the two Glengarry battalions in the first line. It is estimated that they had about 150 men. They were also in the first line at Culloden with about 120 men. On this occasion, they do not appear to have been attached to any other regiment. There are accounts regarding the payments received by those who, with their men, supported the prince. Colonel MacLeod of Raasay received, amongst other payments, £24 17s. 0d. for officers and men for a period of seven days.

About mid-March 1746, Lord Loudoun, on the government side, came to Skye with 800 troops to keep an eye on the area. He sent some men over to Raasay to collect and take away all the boats. MacDonald of Sleat persuaded him to leave a small boat for John's use, and Malcolm of Eyre was able to hide another. Loudoun left some soldiers on Raasay but they did little harm, apart from disarming a few men who had drifted home early from the prince's army. Various boats were also prowling around the west coast, looking for rebels and information. One of those, commanded by Captain Hay, visited Rona, where his men slaughtered cattle and plundered some villages in the north end of Raasay.

The Battle of Culloden took place on 16 April 1746, after which the government stepped up its efforts to find and capture Prince Charlie and anyone who had helped him. Malcolm MacLeod of Raasay went into hiding in Knoydart, but Captain Malcolm of Eyre and Dr Murdo, who had been wounded, came back home.

In the middle of May, Captain Ferguson of the *Furnace* came to Raasay. Lieutenant Dalrymple was sent ashore with his men. All the houses on Raasay, including the mansion house, were burnt. Only the windows of the mansion house were saved. The troops also found the furniture and silverware that had been hidden in a nearby cave. In all, 300 houses were destroyed.

Dalrymple then divided his men into three groups. They marched over the island, one along each shore and one over the hill. A lot of livestock (cattle, horses, sheep and goats) were killed and left dead on the spot. Unarmed, and without boats in which to escape, the people could do nothing to defend themselves.

On 28 June, Prince Charles and Flora MacDonald crossed to Skye from North Uist. John MacLeod, Young Raasay, was then staying with his wife's people in Totaroam, to the north of Portree, as his house on Raasay had been destroyed. Word was sent to him that Charles was in the area. John relayed this news to his father in Knoydart. It was decided that, for the present, Raasay was a safer hiding place than Skye.

Because a Portree crew could not be trusted to take Charles to Raasay, John and Murdo, with the help of some women, dragged an old leaky boat over boggy ground and down the steep incline, from the Storr Lochs to the shore, probably at Holm. From there the brothers, with the help of a small boy, rowed over to Raasay. In Raasay they met with Malcolm of Eyre, who tried to discourage John from taking any further part in the affair. He would not be put off, however. Malcolm, whose own boat had been hidden, arranged for two men, John MacKenzie and Donald MacFriar, to row for them, and they set off from Raasay with John and Murdo on the evening of 30 June. They landed about half a mile north of Portree. Malcolm and Donald MacFriar went to MacNab's Inn in Portree (now the Royal Hotel) and left word of their whereabouts. They then returned to the boat to await Charles.

The prince met them on the shore very early the following morning, and they left for Raasay. Landing about daybreak, they made for a small shepherd's hut at Glam. The township of Glam was to the north-west of the present day Glam Steading. Charles, Malcolm and Murdo settled down to rest, while the two boatmen were posted as lookouts. During the two days they spent on Raasay, John was able to bring them provisions. No one came to Raasay while Charles was on the island, but people were very suspicious of a tobacco vendor who had arrived some time before that. Although he had long since sold his tobacco, he did not leave the island. On one occasion he came close to the hut. The MacLeods would have shot him, but Charles disagreed. John MacKenzie, who was acting sentinel at the door, overheard the discussion. He remarked in Gaelic, 'Well, well; he must be shot; you are the king, but we are the parliament, and will do what we choose.' Seeing the others smile, Charles asked for a translation. On getting it, he laughed aloud and said John was a clever fellow. The tobacco vendor paid no attention to the hut, and was allowed to go on his way unmolested. It was later learned that he too was a fugitive from Culloden.

Charles was very uneasy on Raasay, it being a small island. Malcolm of Eyre offered to take him to Lochbroom, where he was expecting a French ship to arrive soon, but the long sea crossing in a small boat was so dangerous that the offer was declined. He wanted to go back to Trotternish, but the MacLeods knew that there were many government troops there. The men, who two days earlier had taken him over to Raasay, now took Charles back to Skye, landing at Nicolson's Rock near Scorrybreac. There, Charles sent John to look for information, and Murdo to Camustinavaig to wait for him, so that neither would know where he was going next.

Malcolm was then persuaded to guide him through Skye to the MacKinnon lands of Strath, as they were loyal supporters of the Stuart cause. Malcolm took the Prince to his brother-in-law, John MacKinnon in Elgol.

After arrangements had been made, Charles and Malcolm smoked a pipe together. Malcolm was then given the pipe, a silver stock buckle and ten guineas (under protest) along with a note of thanks for Dr Murdo MacLeod, who was waiting at Camustinavaig. Prince Charles then set off with the MacKinnons by boat for the mainland. Malcolm watched them for a time and then made his way back to Raasay. News of the prince's visit to the area had already become public knowledge, as had the identities of those who had helped him.

Eight men now went into hiding on Rona, including John (Young Raasay) and Dr Murdo. One and a half thousand government troops were by now searching the north end of Skye, and General Campbell and a Captain Scott came to Rona. There their soldiers lashed two men, one of whom died of his wounds. All that is known of the other is his name – Malcolm MacLeod. The troops also ravished a blind girl and then moved onto Raasay to continue the search. At this stage they knew that Prince Charles had come to the area, and to capture him was very much their main objective.

Malcolm of Eyre, whose house had been destroyed in a previous raid, was now hiding on the island with his servant, Donald Nicolson. They went to 'the top of the island' for a good view of what was going on, but ran into forty redcoats, who shot at them. Malcolm got away, but Donald Nicolson was caught. The redcoats were desperate to know who had escaped, but Donald, although he was severely tortured and left for dead, gave no information.

Malcolm now got another servant, John Roy Montgomery, who knew of a place where they would not be found. There they stayed for two days and nights without food or water. They then risked going to see Murdo MacLeod of Brae, Malcolm's uncle, where John's sister was a servant. That night, because of heavy rain, they stayed in a nearby barn, but MacLeod of Talisker and his men surprised them in the early morning. Again they were shot at, but managed to escape. They made their way back to John's safe place, taking with them a small boy who might otherwise have given them away. Again the redcoats were desperate to know where they were going. Some soldiers ravished two local girls, Christina Montgomery and Marion MacLeod.

This was the worst time of all for the people of Raasay, who knew nothing and so could not have given information to the troops even if they had wanted to. Many more cattle were slaughtered, and the people were robbed of everything, in some cases even the clothes on their backs.

MacLeod of Talisker was now based on Skye, but was making daily visits to Raasay with his men. He now swore that all remaining livestock would be ferried off the island unless Malcolm was found.

Meantime, the boy had been pleading with Malcolm to be allowed to go. On the third day, after swearing that he would tell nothing, he went for food and news, but was captured. When threatened with hanging, he told where the fugitives were, and so they were captured.

Malcolm was taken, first to Portree, and then by sloop, commanded by Captain

Ferguson, to London, where he remained a prisoner until July 1747. He returned to Scotland in a poste chaise, along with Flora MacDonald, who had taken the prince over the sea to Skye, disguised as her maid. Malcolm MacLeod of Eyre may later have held the tack of Brae on Raasay. It is as Captain Malcolm of Brae that he is more generally known.

From then, mid July, until the Independent Companies were disbanded in mid September the people of Raasay were subjected to intermittent harassment.

John MacLeod, Young Raasay, estimated that in all 280 cattle, 700 sheep and less than twenty horses were destroyed, as well as thirty-two boats. Over 300 houses were also destroyed along with furniture and other belongings. These losses for the people, calculated as if they were selling between themselves, was above 24000 merks Scots, plus two years' crops. John calculated his personal loss at above £1500 sterling. He said that there were eighty to ninety families in Raasay. A tenant with three or four cows was thought to be able to pay his rent, but some had only had that much, and it was now taken from them.

Of those Raasay people who took part in the rebellion, Colonel Malcolm MacLeod, Laird of Raasay, was pardoned. Captain Malcolm MacLeod of Eyre (Raasay), later possibly of Brae, was taken prisoner, but later pardoned and released without even being questioned. Dr Murdo MacLeod, later of Eyre (Skye) was wounded at Culloden, but pardoned. Donald MacFriar was pardoned. There were also other prisoners from Raasay. Those who were flogged were Malcolm MacLeod Rona, Donald Nicolson and John Montgomery, servants of Malcolm of Eyre. Those who were transported were Angus MacDonald, tailor, Neil MacLeod and Angus MacQueen. There is also mention of a Sergeant John MacKenzie.

The above account has been compiled from information given at the time by those who took part. It must therefore be taken as essentially true, although there are some discrepancies, possibly due to a tendency to exaggerate losses. John MacLeod says that there were between eighty and ninety families on Raasay, but he also says that over 300 houses were destroyed.

Although the Raasay estate was not forfeited, the population of Raasay now had to begin the difficult task of re-building, not only their homes and their stock, but also their lives. That they were able to do so shows great resolve and strength of character.

The late Dr Alasdair MacLean, Aird Bernisdale, an authority on the people and events of the rebellion, believed that the accounts given of MacLeod of Talisker's treatment of Raasay, and in particular his treatment of Captain Malcolm of Eyre, were exaggerated. The two were friends. After the rebellion, MacLeod of Talisker is known to have been negotiating for a commission in one of the regiments of the army of the Netherlands, which was essentially a British organisation. A report such as Malcolm gave about MacLeod of Talisker's devotion to duty as a company commander could only help his career prospects at that time.[8] Indeed, MacLeod of Talisker was one of the many guests in Raasay House, enjoying John MacLeod's hospitality during Johnson and Boswell's visit in 1773.

The Earl of Loudoun, who had been actively engaged on the government side during the rebellion, died in 1782. His cousin, James Muir Campbell, the fifth earl, succeeded him. There was evidently no grudge held against the family by the MacLeods of Raasay. In fact they must have kept in contact, as Flora, eldest daughter of John of Raasay, married the fifth earl in Edinburgh in 1777.

It is possible that descendants of the Donald Nicolson, servant of Malcolm MacLeod of Eyre, may have emigrated to Australia. A paper was found in the family bible of a relative of Mr W. B. Clarke from Australia. So far Mr Clarke has been unable to establish how the people mentioned in it relate to his own family.

The paper was written some time after 1888 and traces back through the generations to a Donald Nicolson. One of Donald's descendants lived in Sleat, Skye, and two of Donald's great-grandsons emigrated to Australia. The paper states that Donald Nicolson helped Prince Charles in 1746. Signed by Angus Nicholson, it says

> It was my great-grand-father who took Prince Charles Stuart out of McKinnons House in Strathaird on the Isle of Skye. The house was surrounded by English soldiers and officers, and put him on board the French ship. At the same time there was thirty thousand pounds reward for his head dead or alive.

The name Donald is not uncommon among the Nicolsons, and this may not have been the Donald Nicolson, servant of Malcolm MacLeod of Eyre, whom the redcoats caught on Raasay. However, the number of people who had personal contact with Prince Charles would have been kept to an absolute minimum to reduce, as far as possible, the risk of word getting out as to his whereabouts. It is possible that Donald Nicolson, mentioned in the paper from Australia, was the same Donald Nicolson, servant of Malcolm MacLeod of Eyre, Raasay. If so, he may well have been with Malcolm and the prince on their journey from Raasay to Strathaird. It has already been mentioned that, in earlier centuries, lairds and tacksmen usually had servants with them. This would still have been the norm at this time.

Although the account talks of English soldiers and officers, many of the Highland clans, such as the MacLeods of Skye, were active on the government side. This rebellion was not, as it is often portrayed, a case of Scotland (or even Highland Scotland) against the English.

The above is just one example of information coming back 'home' from abroad that can be added to information available here. There is a great deal of family information, handed down by emigrants, that could help to shed light on the history of our area over the last two to three hundred years.

THE IMMEDIATE AFTERMATH OF THE 1745 REBELLION

The decision by Malcolm MacLeod to support the Stuart cause in 1745 was not a good one for the island or the people. Of the 100 men who 'went out' with the laird, it is said that fourteen were killed. Considering the slaughter committed at Culloden, perhaps the Raasay contingent escaped lightly. For the people of Raasay, however, 1746 was a terrible year. From April to September, they were harassed by the presence of government soldiers, in their distinctive red coats.

Clachan Bay and the Battery from Borrodale, showing the Old Landing Place close to the boathouse. (Anne Gillies)

Top Barn in snow. Boswell described the original Heather Barn in 1773. It burnt down in 1856 and was rebuilt on the same site. (Anne Gillies)

East Suisnish, showing the pier and the mine buildings, taken from the ferry. The five buildings in a row are the kiln bases. (Anne Gillies)

The ruin of the house at Brae that belonged to Eachainn Iain Eachainn, Hector MacLeod. Nearby is Storab's Grave. It was from Brae that Captain Malcolm wrote his account of the 1745 rebellion. Portree Bay can be seen across the Sound of Raasay. (Anne Gillies)

Lazy beds above Hallaig. (Anne Gillies)

The east coast looking north from Hallaig. (Anne Gillies)

Inside North Raasay Sheep Stock Club's fank at Glam. Originally part of the Hill Farm created by the Woods in 1878 but abandoned soon after. (Gail Martin)

Left. Ruins at Hallaig. (Anne Gillies)

Bottom left. Creagan Beaga and Sgurr nan Gillean. (Anne Gillies)

Bottm right. Ratharsair Bheag Waterfall and Norman Gillies, a great-great-grandson of both Iain Raghnaill and Tormod Dhòmhnaill. (Anne Gillies)

James Gillies and Hugh MacKay gathering the Manish sheep near Loch na Bruithne (Loch of the Talking). (Anne Gillies)

Ploughing at Mill Park with West Suisnish behind, including Churchton house and Suisnish House in the trees. (Anne Gillies)

Ruins at Manish, looking towards the Storr. Holm Island can be seen against the Skye coast. (Anne Gillies)

Taigh an Achaidh and the fank at Kyle Rona with John William, Andrew and James Gillies. (Anne Gillies)

The Island of Fladda with the fank in the foreground. (Anne Gillies)

The last gathering on Fladda, 27 August 1998, before the sheep were cleared to make way for trees, with John 'the Caley' Nicolson, Charlie Cumming and Andrew Gillies. (Anne Gillies)

From Balmeanach looking across Loch Eadar da Bhaile to Balachuirn. (Anne Gillies)

Harvesting the North Bay field, showing the Old Pier and the Battery. (Anne Gillies)

The occasional visits by Captain Ferguson on the *Furnace* and other government troops based outwith the Highlands were possibly even more disruptive than the visits by MacLeod of Talisker and his men. The troops trampled over the island, disturbing people and animals, and damaging crops. Destruction of crops and taking away livestock had been the main tactic in the days of raiding and feuding in the sixteenth century, but the Statutes of Iona in the early seventeenth century had, over the intervening 150 years, largely eradicated that practice. The disruption caused was undoubtedly a serious setback for the people. By the end of the year, when the disturbance was over, everyone had the difficult task of putting things in order, not to mention the difficulties of getting through the period until the new crops could be harvested the following year.

Raasay, like the rest of the region, had undergone profound change in the course of the previous 150 years. The laird's retinue of relatives and principal men were now 'gentlemen farmers' or tacksmen. The people living on the estate, who had in the past fought alongside the laird and farmed the land to support everyone, were now the tenants and cottars of the landowner.

The crushing of the '45 Rebellion is often assumed to have been the beginning of the end of the clan system. It may however be viewed as the end of a process that had started with the Statutes of Iona in 1609, when the government began their attempts to bring the Highlands under central control. The major landowners had been forced into contact with the Lowlands at that time, and were now trading freely outwith their own area. The Battle of Culloden, and more particularly its aftermath, had once and for all stamped central authority on the region.

Although it was known that Malcolm MacLeod, Dr Murdo and Captain Malcolm of Eyre had taken part in the rebellion, and that Bonnie Prince Charlie had been on Raasay, the estate was not forfeited. Captain Malcolm had been taken to London but released without questioning. All three were pardoned. It appears that the authorities, satisfied that there would be no further trouble, were happy to release the leaders without taking any further action against them. Their losses were essentially financial. Unlike the people of Raasay, who had lost everything they possessed, the laird and his men were able to raise loans to re-establish themselves. Now that they were back home they set about regaining their position within the local region and within the wider society of Scotland and Great Britain.

In July 1747, Captain Malcolm of Eyre was released from custody in London and made his way home. It is said that he travelled back to Scotland in the same poste chaise as the famous Flora MacDonald, who had taken Bonnie Prince Charlie across the Minch to Skye. Captain Malcolm returned to Raasay, to the tack or farm of Eyre, in the south end of the island. There he was known as Fear Aire, or The Man of Eyre. His uncle, Murdo, held the tack, or farm of Brae in 1746. His house was close to Storab's Grave, mentioned earlier. Malcolm wrote his account of the events of 1745–46 and sent it to Bishop Robert Forbes in 1752. It was sent from 'Malcolm MacLeod of Brae in Raasay'. It is unclear whether Malcolm had both Eyre and Brae at that time, or whether he just happened to be at Brae when he wrote the account.

Like other lairds of the area, the MacLeods' outlook was changing. The pace of that change was to increase over the next fifty years. Signs of this could already be seen. The names of the MacLeods that have come down to us in various histories and documents are one of the most obvious signs. Previous lairds were referred to as MacGilleChaluim, and named as Calum, Alasdair and Iain. In their own accounts of events during the '45, their names were given as Malcolm and John MacLeod.

Notes

1. See Appendix 2.
2. J. G. MacKay, 'Social Life in Skye From Legend and Story', *TGSI*, vol. XXIX, pp. 270–2.
3. Master James Fraser (1634–1709), 'The Wardlaw MS', *SHS*, vol. XLVII, ed. W. MacKay (1905), pp. 498–9.
4. *The Book of Dunvegan*, ed. the late Rev. Canon MacLeod of MacLeod, printed for the 3rd Spalding Club, vol. 1 (1938), p. 65.
5. F. J. Shaw, *Northern and Western Islands, Their Economy and Society in the Seventeenth Century* (1980), p. 67.
6. Today, in general, five sheep are equivalent to one cow, and one horse is equivalent to two cows. However, because of the different ways that animals graze, it does not necessarily follow that someone with no cows could put the equivalent number of sheep on his land.
7. 'Muster Roll of Prince Charles Edward Stuart's Army 1745–46', ed. A. Livingstone, C. W. H. Aikman and B. S. Hart (1984, reprinted 1985), p. 184.
8. From a conversation with Dr Alasdair MacLean, Aird Bernisdale in 1998.

4

The History of Raasay, c.1750–c.1800

AFTER THE 1745 REBELLION

When the repercussions of the 1745 rebellion had passed, life in the north-west Highlands settled down again. Although his father was still alive, John MacLeod was now Laird of Raasay. Ownership of the estate had been passed from father to son before Malcolm 'went out' in 1745, to avoid the possibility of forfeiture. The tactic worked well in that respect. As might be expected, however, it caused other problems.

Matters were not helped by the fact that the estate was not financially sound at this time. An allowance for Malcolm had been agreed. In all probability this would have been a tack or farm granted to him for life.

On 10 May 1748, Malcolm MacLeod, with the consent of John, married his second wife, Seonaid or Janet MacLeod, the daughter of a tenant on the estate. Dr John MacInnes tells the story as he heard it from Seonaidh Dhòmhnaill Iain Bhàin, John MacLeod from Balmeanach, Raasay.[1]

> When Seonaid was a girl, probably in her late teens, she went to work in the tigh-mór [big house – Raasay House]. There she fell in love with a young man, one of Mac Gille Chaluim's servant lads. The lad, however, did not show any sign of interest in her. So she went to the cook to ask for advice and this woman said to her: 'That lad always comes in here for his meal at such and such an hour every evening. You stay here with me and just before he comes in – I'll let you know myself – go and stand behind the door there. As he comes in through the doorway, you jump out and steal a kiss from him. He'll notice you after that!' And so it happened. The cook saw the young man approaching, she told the girl, and the girl went and stood behind the door. But unknown to the cook Mac Gille Chaluim himself was there too and it was Mac Gille Chaluim who came in first. The girl jumped out from behind the door and kissed Mac Gille Chaluim. And that was how the affair began.

During their visit to Raasay in 1773, Dr Johnson and Boswell met Seonaid MacLeod, who was by then a widow. Boswell's description of her is rather disparaging. Her son, Charles, had taken the visitors to meet her. She lived in a small comfortable house at Ard na Bràthan, between Clachan and Oscaig. They were treated to cream and barley-bread. Boswell said of Seonaid, 'She was a stout fresh-looking woman, very plainly dressed, and could not speak a word of English.' He goes on to say

> It was not amiss to see the difference between her house keeping and that of Raasay's [John's]. Folly on one side, and probably interested cunning on the other, had produced the second marriage. She was called only Mrs MacLeod

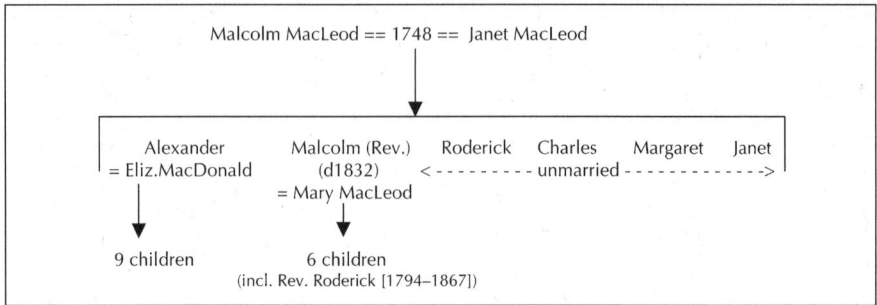

Figure 4/1. The second marriage of Malcolm MacLeod.

now. I know not if ever she was called Lady as her husband had previously given the estate to this gentleman [John].[2]

In Raasay tradition, Seonaid is known as Baintighearna Dhubh Oscaig. As *baintighearna* means 'the proprietor's lady', it must have been the MacLeods themselves, talking in English, who referred to her as Mrs MacLeod. The Dunvegan papers indicate that she was, in fact, a 'worthy woman, very much concerned for the welfare of her family and estate'.[3]

Some indication of the strained relations between Malcolm and John is found in the papers of the MacKenzies of Delvine, a family of lawyers who acted for both the MacLeods during the 1740s and 1750s.[4]

In 1747 John wrote to John MacKenzie in the hope that he could draw up an agreement (which no doubt his father would then be asked to sign) to ensure that neither John nor the estate would be bound by any debts his father might incur. John also wanted it made clear that Malcolm was not to meddle in estate affairs. In 1748 John MacLeod wrote again asking for a loan of £300, for a period of six months. The previous year he had made some money dealing in cattle, and wanted to do so again. He said, 'My affairs are in such order that without the help of friends it is impossible for me soon to recover them.' Relations between father and son did not improve, as shown by Malcolm's letter to the lawyer in 1751. In this he refers to 'that son of perdition my son'. John Mackenzie is asked to await instructions from Malcolm and to stop working with John. He finishes the letter, 'but let that wretch I mean Rona know nothing of the matter'. Clearly, Malcolm still regards himself as the real laird.

In 1754 John MacLeod asked his lawyer to recommend him as factor in Lewis, in the hope that this position would help his financial situation. There is no indication that he got the job. In 1759 Suisnish was mortgaged to John MacIver, tacksman of Delmore, Lewis, for 2000 merks – £1 333 6s. 8d. A sasine of 1761 confirms this transaction. The lands were redeemed fifteen years later.

John MacLeod estimated that his losses in 1746 amounted to £1 500 sterling. The most immediate concern was to get the laird's house habitable. He had been living with his wife's family, the MacQueens, at Totaroam, north of Portree parish on the east coast of Skye, on the Skye part of the MacLeod of Raasay estate. Before setting the house ablaze in 1746, the government troops had saved the oak windows. They were taken to Leith, where they were bought by a relative of the MacLeods and returned to Raasay. Some of the rebuilding work of this period shows signs of hasty workmanship. Not long after John moved back to Raasay, further building work on the mansion house began.

Malcolm MacLeod died in August 1761. The mortgage of Suisnish was concluded that year and may well have been used to finance further extension or refurbishment of the mansion house.

In July 1766, Sir James MacDonald of Sleat, 'The Scottish Marcellus', died in Rome. His sword was delivered to John MacLeod of Raasay in keeping with the tradition that on the death of either laird, the survivor always inherited the arms of the deceased man.[5]

A MacLeod Laird of Raasay is mentioned in Coinneach Odhar's prophecies, regarding the last of the MacKenzies of Seaforth. Coinneach Odhar was generally known as the Brahan Seer. The laird in question may have been John. Coinneach Odhar said

> I see into the far future and I read the doom of the race of my oppressor. The long-descended line of Seaforth will, ere many generations have passed, end in extinction and sorrow. I see a chief, the last of his house, both deaf and dumb. He will be the father of four fair sons, all of whom he will follow to the tomb. He will live care-worn and die mourning, knowing that the honours of his line are to be extinguished forever, and that no future chief of the MacKenzies shall bear rule at Brahan, or in Kintail. After lamenting over the last and most promising of his sons, he himself shall sink into the grave, and the remnant of his possessions shall be inherited by a white-coifed (white-hooded) lassie from the east, and she is to kill her sister. And as a sign by which it shall be known that these things are coming to pass, there shall be four great lairds in the days of the last deaf and dumb Seaforth – Gairloch, Chisholm, Grant and Raasay, of whom one shall be buck-toothed, another hare-lipped, another half-witted, and the fourth a stammerer. Chiefs distinguished by these marks shall be the neighbours of the last Seaforth: and when he looks around him and sees them, he may know that his sons are doomed to death, that his broad lands shall pass away to the stranger, and that his race shall come to an end.[6]

The last of the Seaforths was Francis Humberstone MacKenzie, who died 11 January 1815, aged fifty-nine. It is believed that Sir Hector MacKenzie of Gairloch was the buck-toothed laird. He was spoken of as An Tighearna Storach. *Tighearna* is a superior title of respect for a landlord or proprietor. *Storach* means having broken teeth or 'of crowded teeth'. Chisholm of Chisholm was the hare-lipped laird; Grant was the half-witted laird and MacLeod of Raasay the stammerer. The prophecy would appear to have been fulfilled in every detail.

In the autumn of 1773, Dr Samuel Johnson and James Boswell visited Raasay.[7] Their accounts of this visit give a record of life in Raasay as they found it. This is the earliest record that gives any detail about the lives of the people, albeit from the viewpoint of visitors living with, and being entertained by, the laird.

Captain Malcolm MacLeod of Eyre, or of Brae, Raasay, crossed to Skye in a strong, Norwegian-built boat with six oarsmen, to take the visitors to Raasay. The party consisted of Dr Samuel Johnson, James Boswell and Donald MacQueen, a Skye minister. They enjoyed the crossing, as the weather was calm and the oarsmen sang as they rowed across.

The laird, John MacLeod, and a group of gentlemen met them on the shore. The house, 'a neat modern fabrick', had a number of large trees about it, mostly plane or sycamore and ash. There were some rowan trees, loaded with berries, between the back of the house and the garden.

Boswell refers to the mansion house, commenting that a new house had been built before the 1745 rebellion. All but the walls had been destroyed by fire at that time. He says that stones from the previous building on the site had been used to build that house. On his tour, Johnson carried with him a copy of Martin Martin's book, which had been written about 1695.

In this instance, Boswell appears to have mis-read Martin, as he implies that the 'tower of three stories' stood at Clachan. However, Martin is quite clear when he says that the laird lives at Clachan, and that the village is 'adorned with a little tower and lesser houses'. Martin does mention a 'tower of three stories' but clearly states that it is 'called Castle Vreokle'. As stone from Brochel is most unlikely to have been used to build the new house at Clachan, it must be assumed that it was Martin's 'little tower' that was recycled in the building work before 1745.

The new house, that Boswell and Johnson were in, had eleven rooms, some having a number of beds, thus allowing extensive hospitality. The kitchen garden was well stocked with gooseberries, raspberries, currants, strawberries and apple trees. On the southern wall, fruit trees had been planted, but were neglected.

The guests arrived about six o'clock, and shortly after sat down to a meal of mutton chops and tarts, diet loaf, marmalade of oranges and currant jelly. They drank tea and coffee. There were some elegant books on a large table. During the evening they had 'excellent brandy', porter, claret, mountain and punch. The carpet was rolled back. Entertainment consisted of dancing, singing and fiddle music. Thirty-six people sat down for supper.

As well as John (the laird) and his wife (Jane MacQueen) there were three sons and ten daughters. A tutor was employed for the sons. Their mother educated the daughters. Johnson says, 'More gentleness of manners, or a more pleasing appearance of domestick society, is not found in the most polished countries.' Here in Raasay, in the house of John MacLeod he found 'civility, elegance and plenty'. The following morning, after enjoying goat's whey in bed, they breakfasted on chocolate, tea, bread and butter, marmalade and jelly, scones, a plate of butter and curd mixed, cakes of *graddaned* meal (meal burnt with straw, instead of being threshed and kiln dried), barley bannocks and cheese (which Boswell disliked intensely at breakfast time).

The visitors spent their time on Raasay being shown around the island. They went out shooting for blackcock, but found none. They did no better on their way to Dun Caan, when they saw moorfowl but could not get near them. Johnson declared that Raasay had no deer, hares or rabbits, but an abundance of wild fowl. Neither were there any foxes. It appears that there had been an unsuccessful attempt to raise roebucks in Raasay. Johnson tells us, 'The young ones it is extremely difficult to rear, and the old can very seldom be taken alive.'

In the morning, before setting out for Dun Caan, they had a dram and some bread. A boy named Stewart carried their provisions for them. When they reached the top they ate cold mutton, bread and cheese, drank brandy and punch, listened to some Gaelic songs and danced a reel. They saw Brochel Castle and the place where 100 men were reviewed before going off to fight for Bonnie Prince Charlie. All but about fourteen returned.

Johnson estimated the population at about 900. This would seem to be a very high estimate for the time. Around the mansion house were good grass fields and corn lands. There had been hardly any enclosing of fields, except for the kitchen garden. The laird had enclosed and planted firs on the south-east side of the island, and planned to enclose and plant more. The whole estate, including the area in Skye, gave £250–300 in rent. The laird lived 'in the greatest plenty' and although people from other areas were emigrating, 'not a man has left his estate'. The island had a corn mill, plenty limestone and a great quarry of freestone. Some of the lochs had trout in them, stocked by the laird.

Rona and Fladda were used only for grazing. The laird kept 400 head of cattle himself, and sold about 100 annually. It appears that cattle often perished by falling over cliffs. One hundred and sixty were wintered on Rona looked after by 'a solitary herdsman' (Johnson) who lives there 'with his family' (Boswell).

As Johnson and Boswell arrived at Raasay, they saw people harvesting corn. The women reaped with sickles, keeping time with their singing, and the men bound the sheaves. Boswell described the laird's barn in detail:

> The corners and a piece of wall at each door are built to the full highth of good stone and lime, to give it firmness. The rest of it has a wall of the same kind about the highth of an ordinary dike, and above that is work of wattles covered on the outside with heath. It is so open that the wind gets in and the rain is kept out. And it is well thatched with heath. In this barn he often dries his hay as well as his corn, which is a great advantage in so wet a climate.

Much of the land, we are told, was held in common, each man putting on it as many cattle as he wished. There could have been no pressure on the common grazing at the time. The system of soumming had been well known long before this time, and would have been used to control stock numbers if required. This also tends to confirm that Johnson's estimate of the population was too high.

There were some areas of natural woodland, none very old, as the people used them as required. They also used peat, or turf, as fuel. Cattle, sheep and goats were kept. Horses were used for ploughing and other work. The houses were on the shore, and most people had small boats. Plenty fish were caught in the seas around Raasay. A lot of potatoes were grown. The party called at a house, belonging to a MacLean, on the east side of the island. Boswell describes it.

> It was somewhat circular in its shape. At one end sheep and goats were lodged; at the other, the family. The man and his wife had a little bedstead. The place where the servants lay was marked out upon the ground with whinstones and

strewed with fern. The fire was towards the upper end of the house. The smoke went out at a hole in the roof, at some distance and not directly above it, as rain would hurt it. I found here sacks made of rushes very well plaited, so as to be strong and very compact. They really looked well and [made] very tolerable baskets. The art of creeling or working in wattles seems to be well practised among these islanders. I saw in this hut a little house-kiln for drying corn. It was about the size of a hogshead; was made of wattles, plastered with clay very firmly both on the outside and the inside. The convenience of it was that the man could dry a little at a time, as he could afford it, and instead of having one to attend in an outhouse, it could be watched by the family sitting by their fireside. The farmer here had no children, and he and his wife spoke only Erse. Adjoining to the house was another little circular room called a keep-house. The woman very hospitably went into it and brought us some very good milk. I went into the place. It was a kind of store-room for the few things that they had. She kept her milk in an earthen dish put within a wooden chest, which shut with a lid, so that it was very clean.

Having spent three days on Raasay, been shown around everything that they could possibly want to see, and been told a great deal of the history and traditions of the place, Johnson in his final paragraph is unstinting in his praise for the laird but dismissive of everything else.

Raasay has little that can detain a traveller, except the Laird and his family; but their power wants no auxiliaries. Such a seat of hospitality, amidst the winds and waters, fills the imagination with a delightful contrariety of images. Without is the rough ocean and the rocky land, the beating billows and the howling storm: within is plenty and elegance, beauty and gaiety, the song and the dance. In Raasay, if I could have found a Ulysses, I had fancied a Phaeacia.

It is interesting to note that two of the houseguests present along with Johnson and Boswell were Norman MacLeod, chief of the MacLeods of Dunvegan, and John MacLeod of Talisker. It was John MacLeod of Talisker who was, allegedly, so active in harassing the people of Raasay in 1746 and in the capture of Captain Malcolm MacLeod of Eyre. Yet here they were in 1773, enjoying each other's company, and MacLeod of Raasay's hospitality. Boswell's description of Captain Malcolm of Eyre is informative.

Malcolm was

now sixty-two years of age, hale and well proportioned – with a manly countenance, tanned by the weather, yet having a ruddiness in his cheeks, over a great part of which his beard extended. His eye was quick and lively, yet his look was not fierce, but he appeared at once firm and good humoured. He wore a pair of brogues; tartan hose which came up nearly to his knees and left them bare; a purple camblet kilt; a black waistcoat; a short green cloth coat bound with gold cord; a yellowish bushy wig; a large blue bonnet with a gold thread button. I never saw a figure that gave a more perfect representation of a Highland gentleman. I wished much to have a picture of him just as he was. I found him frank and polite, in the true sense of the word.[8]

Although the government had brought the Highlands under effective control, the method used had resulted in the laird now having a completely different outlook from that of the people living on Raasay. During the sixteenth century, the laird and the people had worked towards one goal, the good of the estate, and therefore one another. Now they had utterly different goals. That of the people had not changed. They worked the land, producing crops and livestock as before. Probably, they still paid their rent in livestock and produce. They would also have been essentially self-sufficient. There would have been a miller, weavers, carpenters, stone masons and blacksmiths, whose skills were passed down from father to son. It is most unlikely that any man could live by his trade alone. All would have had some ground as well, to plant potatoes and enough grazing for a cow. They all wanted to live in comfortable, clean houses and have enough food to feed their families.

The laird, on the other hand, was now enjoying a very comfortable and expensive lifestyle. He lived in a house, built and furnished according to the latest fashions. He and his family lived not only in comfort but also surrounded by elegance and style, comparing favourably with any gentleman's seat in any part of Great Britain. As well as a variety of good foods provided by the estate, food and drinks were imported from abroad. Extensive hospitality was provided for his friends and relatives as well as visitors. Boswell informs his readers that the whole of the Raasay estate did not provide more than £300 in rent. The trade in cattle was still strong at this time, so it must be assumed that John MacLeod derived a substantial part of his income from that. However, he had ten daughters, all of whom married. Given the social position of the MacLeods at that time, and the undoubtedly exalted circles in which they mixed, these weddings were probably most enjoyable, but expensive, affairs. In 1777, Flora MacLeod of Raasay married Colonel James Muir Campbell, who later became the Earl of Loudoun.

It is clear from the accounts that while the people of Raasay, including Seonaid MacLeod, the laird's stepmother, could speak only Gaelic, John and those around him were also fluent in English. They could converse easily with the visitors, imparting in the process a great deal of information about the history and present circumstances of the estate.

GENERAL CONDITIONS IN THE NORTH-WEST HIGHLANDS AFTER THE 1745 REBELLION

The Commission for Annexed Estates had been set up after the 1745 Rebellion, to run and administer those estates that had been forfeited because their lairds had supported the Stuart cause. By 1785 the Commission had become extremely concerned about the number of people who were emigrating to North America, mainly to North Carolina. At that time and for many decades later, those leaving the north-west of Scotland were tacksmen and gentlemen farmers, who could afford to finance the journey themselves and have enough capital to start again in America. When they went, they often took with them those of their own tenants and servants who wished to go. Landlords were losing people who could afford to pay their rent and emigration was therefore considered to be a practice that should be discouraged.

It was felt that action should be taken to stem the flow of people leaving and, with that in mind, the Commissioners wanted to encourage people to be less dependent on the land. They proposed the building of small villages, with each house having only a small plot of land. Thus tenants would have to find another trade, such as carpentry, shoemaking or fishing. By providing services, which other villagers would pay for, a man could support himself and his family. Periodically, merchants from the south could go round and buy up any surplus goods or produce. That was the theory; in practice things were very different.

Possibly as a result of the Commission's views, in 1786 the British Fisheries Society was formed as a joint stock company, with the object of extending the fisheries and improving the sea coasts of the kingdom. They acted as technical advisers to the government. As well as lobbying parliament, where they achieved a great deal, they proposed to set up fishing villages themselves.

By the time the 1745 rebellion was over, the government had realised that British sea power was not as it might have been and that the navy would have to be built up. It was decided that fishing – until then, carried out in open boats – could provide a training ground for seamen.

The Dutch had developed a system of fishing busses, which allowed their crews to stay at sea for long periods. These busses were large decked boats of twenty to eighty tons, and were used to transport everything, including small open boats, to the fishing grounds. Once there, they were used as a base or headquarters for the fishing operation. Smaller fast vessels, called jaegars, were used to run the catch from the busses back home, allowing the fishing effort to continue, but at the same time getting the fish to market.

An Act of Parliament was passed to encourage the building and operation of busses in Scotland by paying a subsidy, or bounty, to the operators. Initially this was paid at 3s. per ton, increased in 1757 to £2 10s. per ton. This had the desired effect, and in just six years the number of busses in south west Scotland had increased from 13 to 261, mainly in the Clyde area. To qualify for the bounty certain rules had to be adhered to.

1. Customs officers had to examine the boat to ensure that all the necessary equipment was aboard.
2. The boat had to appear at a set rendezvous on a given date. Fishing could not commence before that date.
3. The busses had to stay at sea for three months, without putting in to port.
4. Transferring fish between boats was not allowed.

These rules, although they may have been admirable for the training of seamen, gave no consideration to the requirements of the fishing industry. The date set for the British fisheries to start was later than that set for the Dutch, so by the time the British boats arrived at the fishing grounds, the Dutch were already fishing. It was possible for the busses to have a full catch after only a short period at sea, but they were not allowed to go in to port. Neither had they any way of getting their catch to market, as fish could not be transferred between boats.

The east coast of Scotland was well suited to fishing from busses. The lochs and bays of the north-west, on the other hand, were much better suited to fishing from small boats. However, local fishermen were not allowed to sell their catch to the busses, and the local market was limited as it was virtually impossible to obtain salt.

By 1785 the busses were allowed to catch cod and ling as well as herring. By then there were strict regulations for curing fish as well as for catching it. The royal burghs had acquired the exclusive rights to inshore fishing during the sixteenth century. They now organised themselves to withstand competition from foreigners coming into the rich fishing grounds of Scotland. Trading, both at home and abroad, was allowed by registered merchants only. At this time there was a lucrative trade exporting salt fish to Europe and the West Indies.

In 1786, John Knox undertook a tour, on behalf of the British Fisheries Society, throughout the Highlands and Islands of Scotland to find out how the fishing could be improved, to identify potentially suitable sites for the founding of villages and to raise funds for the society.[9] During his tour, he called at Raasay. The minister, Mr MacQueen, a son of the man who had accompanied Johnson and Boswell thirteen years before, accompanied the visitor from Applecross to Raasay. John Knox said,

> Here the natives have, with incredible labour, formed many little corn field and potato grounds. These heights decrease at the south end, where there are some farms, and a good looking country ... Mr Macleod the laird, was ill, and I believe in bed, when we arrived; but during our short stay, we experienced the hospitality and obliging manners of that family, so justly celebrated by Dr Johnson ... Till I arrived at this place, no person of the name of Macleod had subscribed, on any list, to the fund then raising by the British Society. Mr Macleod set the example, and in a short time the few gentlemen of that name contributed nearly 1000L [£1 000].
>
> The house of Raasay is pleasantly situated near the south-west end of the island, which is the most level part of it. It has an extensive and excellent garden and is surrounded with forest trees of considerable magnitude, another proof that trees will grow upon the edge of the sea, though it must be allowed that the channel here is narrow. Immediately behind the house of Raasay are the ruins of an ancient chapel, now used as the family burying place.
>
> This island contains 700 inhabitants (Dr Johnson says 900 inhabitants, but as my information was from Mr Macleod, who knew every particular of this island, I prefer his account), has plenty of limestone, freestone, and feeds great numbers of black cattle, but has no deer, hares or rabbits.
>
> The only appearance of a harbour in Raasay is at Clachan Bay, where Mr Macleod resides ... Mr Macleod is the sole proprietor of Raasay, and of Rona and Fladda at the north end of it, which are only proper for grazing ... On going into our boat I took a final leave of the worthy Laird of Raasay, who died soon after, and now lies among the remains of a long series of ancestors in the above mentioned chapel.

JAMES MACLEOD, LAIRD OF RAASAY FROM 1786

John MacLeod of Raasay died in 1786 and was succeeded as laird by his son, James. Like his predecessors, he was keen to embrace new ideas. The American War of Independence had finished in 1783. The Highland regiments were regarded as hardy and industrious and the soldiers worthy of help with agriculture and industry at home. The Board of Trustees for Manufacturers and Fisheries was in operation, and estates in the Highlands and Islands were open to new money and new ideas from the south. Prospects for the north-west Highlands were good. As many people of the time had realised, fish was a natural asset in the seas around the west coast and it seemed logical that this should be exploited.

James MacLeod of Raasay replied to a questionnaire from the British Fisheries Society in 1787. As well as giving his views on fishing, this gives an insight into the laird's view of the people on his estate. He says, 'the Lower Class of People in this part are so indolent, and so idly inclined, they will not be prevailed upon to begin any business – without immediate assistance ...' He advocated giving them 'a Sum of Money at the beginning to provide them with Boats and Nets, and besides give small Premiums to the best Fishers ...' The money suggested was £16 for a boat with cod and ling nets for four men, and £26 for a boat with cod, ling and herring nets for four or five men.

Rona was recommended as 'one of the most advantageous Places on this Coast for a fishing-situation'. The reasons given were that people from the mainland had discovered a number of fishing banks around it. It also had 'the best Harbours at every Creek both for large Vessels and small Boats'. At that time Rona was used for pasture and it 'rents about One hundred pounds a year'. He continued, 'I have been proposing to people it with a Colony of Fishers, but the people were so poor they could not be prevailed upon to begin the business, and indeed were not able to purchase a Boat & Nets, if they were made an Allowance for that purpose I would willingly give them my assistance.'

It is unclear what form the laird's assistance was to take, given that he did not seem inclined to grant his people financial assistance. Their reluctance to become involved in the fishing would appear to have been due entirely to lack of capital, as Raasay men were known to be good seamen and fishermen. The laird's comments about 'the Lower Class of People' being lazy is yet another example of how far removed he now was from the people of the estate.

In 1796 James MacLeod received a loan of £7 700. A loan of this magnitude was most likely required to finance the major building work on Raasay House that was undertaken about this time. A new building was constructed to the front of the old house and other renovation works were also carried out. This project may have given some local employment at the time, but that would have been unskilled, labouring work. The greater part of the cost would have gone to the skilled southern craftsmen who created the intricate finishings and to the city merchants who supplied the luxurious furnishings. The house was now fashionable, elegant and the perfect setting for the lavish entertainment hosted within it. Raasay people did not benefit in any way from this expenditure, which contributed in no small part to the financial problems of the MacLeods in later decades.

The Raasay laird was a member of upper class society of the country. In keeping with his position, James MacLeod had his own piper, John MacKay. Many lairds of the time supported piping in this way.

Some time during the second half of the eighteenth century, a Roderick MacKay came to Raasay from Sutherland. His reason for moving is not known. However, there would appear to have been MacKays living on Raasay prior to Roderick's arrival. They lived in the south end of the island, around Eyre. Faobairne MacCuidhein, the strong man of Raasay, has already been mentioned. Although it is not known when he lived, he was a MacKay from Eyre. Quite possibly Roderick MacKay was related to others already living there.

Shortly after moving to Raasay, Roderick died, leaving his two young children, John and Christina, orphaned. They were brought up in the house of Captain Malcolm, Fear Aire, the Man of Eyre. There, they helped around the house and John also worked as a herd-boy. Captain Malcolm was a good piper himself, and gave lessons to others. Unknown to him, John listened in, and later, while he was out on the hill with the cattle, practised what he had overheard. When Captain Malcolm found out, he realised that John had talent. After teaching the boy himself for some time, he sent him, in the early 1780s, to the MacCrimmons, pipers to the MacLeods of Dunvegan, for three six-month periods. Later, John was sent for tuition from Angus or his son, John Roy MacKay, the famous MacKay pipers of Gairloch. John MacKay became a piper of note, having won the Highland Society's first prize in 1792.

In 1794 a 'General view of the natural circumstances of the Isles, adjacent to the N.W. Coast of Scotland' was written by Robert Heron. He wrote:

> Black-cattle are the chief produce of the isle; and the annual exportation of quantities of these brings the money with which the rents are paid. Sheep, goats and small horses are also fed here in sufficient numbers. All the inhabitants have fishing-boats; and the fishes they take round the shores, form no small part of their provisions. Grey-oats, barley, and potatoes are raised here, in a similar proportion, as to quantity, and by the same practices of cultivation, as in the contiguous isles. Raasay has its abundance of lime-stone, as also of sandstone. Round the family-seat of the proprietor, are fields affording excellent grass and corn. His garden is plentifully stocked with pot-herbs, flowers, and fruit-bearing shrubs.

LIFE ON RAASAY AT THE END OF THE EIGHTEENTH CENTURY

During the last decade of the eighteenth century an account of each parish in Scotland was written, in many cases by the minister or schoolmaster. These were then collected and form the *Old Statistical Account* (*OSA*). This is an important source of information about the general population, as well as the lairds and tacksmen. The account of Portree parish was written about 1795 by Alexander Campbell, schoolmaster of Portree. The quotations given in the following section are from the *OSA*.

Many of the laird's tacksmen would have been relatives. They too held a prominent position in society, and mixed with others of similar status, both at home and elsewhere. After the '45, many tacksmen from the north-west, including some of the MacLeods of Raasay, joined the British Army as commissioned officers and took part in various campaigns of the time. The greater part of the income of both the laird and tacksmen was from the sale of black cattle, the small Highland breed, that were taken in large droves to the Lowland markets.

Land on Raasay, held and worked by the laird for himself, was around the Clachan/Oscaig area. The Home Farm continued the mixed arable and livestock production of past centuries. From it came food for home consumption. More refined produce came from the Raasay House garden. The Highland black cattle were also kept, giving James MacLeod a substantial part of his income. He was one of only two in the parish to try out the 'newly invented improved ploughs'. The new plough did a better job than the *cas-chrom*, or crooked spade, and required less labour. However, it was only suitable for use on large fields. The Home Farm on Raasay was therefore an ideal testing ground for it.

There is little information now available about the tacks held on Raasay at this time. Neither is it known precisely who held them. Mention of those at Eyre and Brae were found at the time of the 1745 rebellion. Genealogies of the MacLeods by Alexander MacKenzie in 1889 and Alick Morrison in 1974 refer to various branches of the MacLeods of Raasay. Many of these people appear to have settled on Skye, in the parishes of Portree and Snizort. There is also mention made of MacLeods of Glen in Raasay.

No detailed information exists. However, it seems likely that the south end and west side of the island, possibly from Eyre to about Manish, was either held by James MacLeod, the laird, or let by him as tacks. This assumption is borne out by information about population in the nineteenth century. Then the bulk of the population lived on the east side of the island, the west side being relatively sparsely populated. By now also, there were probably some people living on the islands of Rona and Fladda, as well as on Raasay, north of Arnish. This was the poorest land on the island and numbers there would have been very low.

Although the laird and tacksmen held the south and west of the island, others would also be in that area. The tacksmen, as well as the laird, would have had cottars working the land for them. These men would have held enough land to grow some potatoes and the grazing for a cow in return for their labour.

In the Clachan area, the main centre of the island near the mansion house, other tradesmen would be found. Each of them would have held some land, just as the cottars did. The mill, beside the Inverarish burn, bears the date 1720 and must therefore be one of the oldest buildings on the island. Probably the miller had his house nearby. Boatmen would have been based around Clachan. The blacksmith was an important man on the estate. The smithy was at the south end of Shore Street, Clachan.

The bulk of the population lived along the east coast from Fearns north. These townships would have been held under joint tenancies. A mixed arable and livestock system was worked on the run-rig principle. The mixed agriculture benefited both sectors. Animal manure and seaweed was used to fertilise the ground. Barley, corn and grass were the main crops. Some crops were grown to feed the animals over the winter. The bulk of the produce was for home consumption. After growing crops for three years or so, the land was manured and then left fallow for about the same time. The traditional *cas-chrom* was in general use. It was best for smaller plots of ground, and if the soil was wet, or the ground rough or steep. Cattle were raised and sold, to pay the rent and to buy in meal as required. Sheep, goats and hens were kept as well as some horses for farm work. By the end of the century, vast quantities of potatoes were grown. Along with fish, mainly herring, this was the staple diet of the population for at least half of the year.

The Raasay estate was more fortunate than many others in the area, in that estate income was not solely dependent on the land. The island had 'inexhaustible quarries of different sorts of fine free-stone'. This stone was so called because, due to its deep formation, it was unstratified. Therefore the mason was 'free' to saw it into blocks of whatever dimensions he wished, without fear of its splitting or weathering. It was in demand not only on Raasay but also elsewhere in the area, as it had been since the middle of the sixteenth century when Donald Monro commented on it. No mention has been found of Raasay men either as quarriers or stone masons, but it seems reasonable to assume that some local people would have been skilled in these jobs. Such employment was, however, probably sporadic.

Ard na Bràthan, the Headland of the Quern-stones, lies between Clachan and Oscaig, at the south end of the Oscaig parks. It was near this headland that Seonaid MacLeod, second wife of Malcolm of the '45, lived in 1773. Raasay was the sole supplier of millstones throughout the district and, as these stones were used extensively, some employment would have resulted.

James MacLeod and his father had planted trees on the island. The management of these woods would have yielded some employment. Perhaps the foresters also managed the natural woodlands of the island that were used by the people as required. Timber was sold to the neighbouring area, and would continue to be a source of revenue for the estate in the future.

The population of the north-west had been rising steadily for some time, a trend that would continue into the nineteenth century. About 1780, a count of 'examinable persons' was taken in Portree parish. Raasay had 318, accounting for about twenty-five per cent of those in the parish. Assuming the same percentage of the 'whole number of souls' in 1795, Raasay's population then would have been about 500. In the light of known population numbers and conditions in the nineteenth century, this seems more reasonable than Johnson's estimate of 900, twenty years before. It is, however, lower than John Knox's figure of 700 in 1786. Perhaps, by the end of the century, the true figure was somewhere about 600. In any case, although the population was undoubtedly rising, there does not appear to have been any pressure on the land, caused by over-population. In part, the population rise was due to inoculation against smallpox. By 1795 this 'now universally prevails', leading to far fewer deaths from that horrible disease. The run-rig system was well suited to accommodating more tenants, as the population increased. The township land could relatively easily allow new tenants to have a share. The use of cottars by the tacksmen and laird also contributed towards the increased population. A man could not get married until he was able to support his wife and family. First he had to have land on which to build his house, grow some crops and keep a cow. In return for their labour, cottars were given enough land to do so and this allowed earlier marriages than was previously the case.

Young people, particularly men, were going each year to the mainland (the 'low countries') to look for work. They left early in the year and came home about the end of October. Being particularly good seamen, Raasay men tended to go to the fishing rather than look for agricultural work. Many were employed at ling and cod fishing during the spring and summer and then engaged on board the herring busses until the end of the season, when they came home, more experienced, and with their earnings. One of the many changes that had taken place over the previous fifty years or so was that people were seeking employment outwith the area.

Two fairs were held each year at Portree, at the end of May and the end of July. These generally lasted from Wednesday to Saturday. Many people, from all over Skye, attended them. As well as drovers and people looking to hire servants, others went to meet with their friends and relatives from other districts. The innkeeper in Portree kept 'a large assortment of hardwares, grocery goods, and sundry other necessities'. There was a public house and post office at Sconser, from which two runners delivered the mail from Inverness to the rest of Skye. Mail for Raasay was collected by boat from Sconser. There were other 'petty merchants' in the parish, perhaps one on Raasay. Tradesmen, such as weavers (both men and women), tailors, carpenters, shoemakers (although most people made their own shoes), and blacksmiths lived in the parish, some certainly on Raasay.

Increasingly, over the last three decades of the eighteenth century, currency came into general circulation. Prices rose over this period too, causing Alexander Campbell in 1795 to blame inflation on the 'introduction of paper currency into the country' because 'circulation of money in greater plenty, helped to diminish its value'. There was certainly some truth in his statement. Previously, it was only the lairds and tacksmen who had any need for money. By the end of the century, however, the general population was moving towards a cash-driven economy. Once that move had begun, it gathered pace and, to an extent, took on a life of its own. Young people were working in other parts of the country for part of each year. There they saw how others lived, and their wages could buy goods both at home and away. Those people who went off each year for work would previously have been employed as servants by tacksmen and tenants at home. A labour shortage at home was now pushing up servants' wages here.

The people of Raasay had a £20 legacy that was the basis of a poor fund for them. In 1795 there were fifteen people on the list, and the interest from the legacy was distributed among them every year. There were others who were needy but were looked after by friends or relations. In any population of 600 people, there would inevitably have been some who, for whatever reason, were unable to support themselves. It was, however, a sign of the times that these people were now being supported by a poor fund, rather than by the laird.

At the end of his account in 1795, Alexander Campbell made an impassioned plea for a change in the Salt Laws. The tax on salt made it both difficult to get and very expensive. If small tenants were allowed some salt for their own use, he argued, they could provide themselves with a means of subsistence. Without salt, they had no means of preserving the fish they caught. As things stood, large quantities of meal had to be imported each year. He pointed out that it would be relatively easy to distribute salt to the tenants. If the authorities felt it necessary, they could sign an oath guaranteeing that the salt would be for personal use only. Even one barrel of salt per tenant would make a difference. The relatively small amount of salt involved would make an enormous difference, and could not be misused.

For decades, many people had argued the advantages of developing a fishing industry in the north-west of Scotland. One of the major obstacles to this was the difficulty and expense in obtaining salt. The Salt Laws imposed duty on salt and other chemicals. They were exceedingly complex, making distinction, for example, between salt from Ireland, England and Scotland as well as its eventual use. One Act of Parliament relating to the Salt Laws ran to seventy-three sections. Duty was imposed to protect home production as well as being a source of revenue for the government. The job of policing was given to Customs and Excise officers, much as whisky control is today.

Although many people were fighting hard for the abolition of the Salt Laws, for the good of the people and to benefit the fishing industry, others, notably the major landowners of the north-west, were doing everything in their power to keep the duty in place. The reason for this was the growing kelp industry. Because it was the major landowners who represented this region in government, the duty on salt was kept on for a considerable time.

Kelp is the burnt ash of seaweed. The ash is rich in soda and potash used in the manufacture of soap and glass and in the bleaching of linen. In 1811 it was discovered that iodine, used for medicinal and other purposes, could also be recovered from seaweed. The weed was gathered and left to dry until the following spring when it was burned, initially in the open, but soon in a simple kiln. This reduced contamination from sand and stones and also allowed the temperature to be better controlled. The kelp trade began in the eighteenth century and landowners saw the potential profits.

Thus, by the end of the eighteenth century, many conditions were being imposed on the people of the north-west that would, in the following decades, spell disaster for the area. The government had never considered fishing as an industry worthy of encouragement, for its own sake, on the west coast. Largely, this was because the area was represented by the major landowners. It was not recognised that west coast inshore fishing was different from that of the east coast. There was a whole tangle of regulations concerning the catching and trading of fish, not to mention the difficulty and expense of obtaining salt, that should have been abolished to give the industry in the north-west any chance of success. Those representing the area in government, who should have been pressing for these changes, were the very ones who opposed them. This was an early example of Acts of Parliament, created for entirely different reasons, adversely affecting the north-west of Scotland.

The men of Raasay preferred working at sea to agricultural work. They were good seamen, but instead of being allowed to take advantage of the rich seas around their own shores many went, each season, to the east coast fishing and the advantages of this natural asset were squandered.

The later decades of the eighteenth century were times of change for the people of the north-west. Conditions on Raasay were probably still comparatively stable, however, as there is no indication of any emigration from the estate, as there had been from some parts of Skye although few had left Portree parish.

By the end of the century the gulf between the laird and the people of Raasay had substantially widened. Although the MacLeods had financial problems as early as the 1740s, this had not diminished their appetite for the better things in life. Not only did they incur heavy expenditure on the alterations and refurbishment of Raasay House but also on entertainment and the lifestyle of upper class society of the time. Johnson and Boswell were surprised to discover that John MacLeod's rental income was only £250–300 per year, although it must also be said that further income came from the sale of cattle.

As well as financing his lifestyle, John MacLeod had ten daughters who all contracted good marriages. Commissions in the British army had to be financed also. The large loan James MacLeod took in 1796 is evidence enough that the financial troubles of the middle of the century had not been turned around. However, loans always needed security, and the security for the MacLeods' loans was the estate of Raasay.

Although they were now dealing to some extent within a cash economy, the objectives of the people had not altered substantially over the fifty-year period. Quite possibly, many still paid their rent in cattle or produce. They lived in reasonable comfort and were largely self-sufficient. Tacksmen stood somewhere between the laird and the tenants. In the old days of clan raids and feuds they had been part of the laird's retinue, supported entirely by the clan. During the seventeenth century they had been given tacks to support themselves. On Raasay, they spent a great deal of time in the laird's company and had, no doubt, come to enjoy that lifestyle. However, the income from their tacks was limited, and, unlike the laird who could use the estate as security, they would have been unable to raise large loans.

Notes

1. Dr J. MacInnes, 'Gleanings from Raasay Traditions, *TGSI*, vol. LVI, pp. 6–7.
2. R. Sharpe, *Raasay: Documents and Sources* (1978), p. 52.
3. Ibid., pp. 155–6.
4. A. Morrison, *The MacLeods: The Genealogy of a Clan*, Section 4 (1974), p. 43.
5. R. Sharpe, p. 44.
6. D. MacDonald, *Lewis, A History of the Island* (1983), p. 35.
7. R. Sharpe, pp. 42–59.
8. A. MacKenzie, *History of the MacLeods* (1889), pp. 377–8.
9. J. Knox, *The Highlands and Hebrides in 1786–87* (reprint, 1975), pp. 129–33.

5

The History of Raasay, c.1800–1846

THE EARLY NINETEENTH CENTURY

In 1805 James MacLeod married Flora Anne MacLean of Muck. Their children, born on Raasay, were Hannah Elizabeth in 1811, Loudoun Hastings in 1820 and Francis Hector George in December 1824, probably after his father's death. The birth of their oldest son, John, who inherited Raasay in 1824, is not found in the record of births for Portree parish. There is recorded, however, the birth of a child, Mary, in 1802 to James MacLeod Esq. of Raasay and Mary Reid. No further information has emerged about either mother or child.

By 1809, the perceived threat of a French invasion caused a flurry of activity in the north-west. The government, mindful no doubt of the 1745 rebellion that had originated in that country, were taking no chances. Sir James Grant, Lord Lieutenant of Inverness-shire, had suggested that five companies and a 200 stand of arms should be set up on Skye in case the enemy attempted a landing in the islands. In February 1809 two battalions, numbering over 500 men, were formed for home defence. James MacLeod of Raasay was lieutenant colonel of one battalion. He approached Lord MacDonald for permission to use one of his new buildings in Portree, as a store for the arms. About this time the Battery was built, near the landing place in front of Raasay House. One cannon is still on site at the Battery. Looking somewhat out of place, outside the perimeter wall, are two mermaids. Originally planned for the front of the mansion house, they now seem rather sad, and the worse for wear. It is unclear where the funding for either the militia or the Battery came from. However, as Lord MacDonald was unwilling to bear the full costs for his part of the set-up, it is likely that most of the money came from government, either local or national. The battalions were disbanded about 1815, after Wellington had defeated Napoleon at Waterloo, and all danger of invasion had passed.

The circumstances of the people of Raasay had deteriorated by the end of the second decade of the nineteenth century. Conditions for the people of Skye, by then, were possibly even worse.

The kelp trade, which had begun in the eighteenth century, had reached its height by about 1810. Although this trade continued into the 1830s, the price by then was fluctuating and eventually production became uneconomic. This trade grew up to supply the growing demand for industrial chemicals. An alternative was barrilla from Spain. This was an impure alkali, made from burning salt-rich marine plants. Manufacturers in the growing industrial cities of the south of Scotland and in England preferred barrilla because it was of better quality than kelp, but during the Napoleonic War with Spain it was unobtainable. At that time kelp production reached its peak. Even after the war ended, there was a tax of £12 per ton on barrilla. Chemicals, such as barrilla and salt, were subjected to a host of taxes and duties.

During the years from 1807 to 1809, it was estimated that the average cost of production of one ton of kelp was £2 7s. 6d. and the average price received was £16, giving a clear profit of £13 12s. 6d. per ton. At that time, the Highlands produced about 12 500 tons of kelp each year, giving the proprietors profits in excess of £170 000 per year. It was very much in the interests of these proprietors to fight any proposed reduction in the taxes of either barrilla or salt. This they did vigorously. As the number of manufacturers and industrialists grew, they put pressure on the government to reduce these taxes. The duty on salt was reduced in 1823 from 15s. 0d. to 2s. 0d. per bushel. The tax on barrilla was abolished in 1830, effectively ending the kelp trade.

Returns from agriculture in the area were, to a large extent, dependent on the weather. A bad storm in January 1801 was followed by late snow. In April that year the ground was white. There was very little meal and the fishing was poor. The next year also, bad weather damaged the crops.

About 1811, Lord MacDonald's estates on Skye abandoned the run-rig system in favour of each tenant having his own piece of ground, or croft. This idea had been proposed earlier by the Commission for Annexed Estates, who wanted tenants to find a trade rather than rely on the land. Earnings from kelp were considered good and, at this time, production was at its height. The kelp industry was labour-intensive and so crofting townships were formed near the shore. The estates and their factors allowed tenants to sub-divide their holdings. When a man had a piece of land on which to build his house and grow some crops, and a job – working at the kelp – he could support his wife and family. Therefore the population grew. Although sub-division of crofts encouraged the population to grow, the system was less flexible than run-rig, which had been based on township land rather than small crofts. The land consequently became poorer through over-use. Agricultural advisors of the previous century had argued for increasing the size of holdings, rather than reducing them.

Although it has been assumed by some that run-rig was abandoned on Raasay about this time, there is no evidence to support this. Unlike Skye, little, if any, kelp was produced on Raasay and so there was no reason to alter the system of land tenure.

Pressure on the land due to a growing population could perhaps have been relieved by emigration. There had been emigration from Skye, though not from Raasay, during the eighteenth century. In 1803 many people from both Trotternish and the south Skye parishes emigrated to Prince Edward Island, Canada, on the *Polly*. Although I. F. Grant maintains that the people of Raasay were 'strongly represented', no evidence is given in support of this statement. It may be suggested that if Raasay people did go abroad on the *Polly*, they had previously left Raasay to settle on Skye, probably in Trotternish. It would thus have been from Skye that they emigrated. That they did so is a possibility that cannot be discounted.

The *Polly* arrived at Orwell Bay, Prince Edward Island, in August 1803. By July of that year an Act of Parliament had been passed that increased the cost of the passage. Although it was apparently for the good of the people, so that they would not be tempted to leave in ships that were not suitable for such a passage, the increase in cost had the desired effect of stemming the flow of emigration. Yet again, the major landowners had acted out of self-interest. At that time they did not want people to leave, as the kelp industry required labourers. In spite of the increased cost of emigration, Donald Nicolson, who had emigrated from Stenscholl in 1803, came back to Skye in 1805 to get married. He also acted as an emigration agent for Lord Selkirk. This caused consternation on Skye as the buzz of emigration was again in the air. Two hundred and fifty people subscribed to go back to Prince Edward Island with Donald Nicolson.

In 1811 J. MacDonald published his 'General view of the agriculture of the Hebrides'.[1] His description of Raasay says

> ... the virtues of the people and of their landlord are universally talked of as eminently exemplary ... The appearance of both islands [Raasay and Rona] is by no means promising, being chiefly composed of rocky hills of no great elevation, and of moorish grounds and peat-mosses. There are, however, remains of woods in various parts of Raasay, but none in Ronay as in Dean Monro's time; and the beautiful and stately trees near the proprietor's mansion, at Clachan, evince clearly that timber of all sorts will thrive there by proper attention. His garden is well stored with fruit trees, and the new plantations behind it succeed to a wish, even at a very considerable elevation above the level of the sea.
>
> The great body of the island is free-stone. In the northern extremity, and in Ronay, vast quantities of breccia and of granite occur. The old castle, often remarked by sailors and travellers, Caisteal Bhreócoil, stands upon a solid mass of breccia of the firmest contexture, the stones of which are easier to be broken than separated. Not far from Raasay House are found large quantities of the finest porphyry, in pieces which look as if they had been artificially hewn or dressed; and which might be easily turned to good account as millstones, and materials for sepulchral and other monuments. They would also serve as ornaments to the corners and steeples of churches and the most exposed parts of public buildings. Lying contiguous to the sea, and in vast quantities of every size, it is surprising that such durable and beautiful stones have not become an article of export. It is this porphyry which Martin mentions in these words 'On the west side, particularly near the village Clachan, the shore abounds with smooth stones of different sizes, variegated all over'. Lime-stone also abounds in Raasay; and there is a calcareous petrifying spring, which has attracted much attention. Mr M'Leod the present proprietor has done much to improve the agriculture and livestock of his property. He cultivates green crops, sown grasses, and the best sorts of barley and oats upon his own farm, and encourages his tenants to follow his example. His stock of black cattle is one of the best in the northern division of the Hebrides, and is annually improving.
>
> The isles of Raasay and Ronay form a part of the vast parish of Portree in Sky. The population is about 1 000, of whom 200 individuals are occasionally engaged in the herring and other fisheries. The natives are good sailors; and every hamlet has a number of boats. The sound of these islands, or the strait which separates them from Skye, has of late years been one of the most

favourite herring resorts in the Hebrides. Upwards of 1500 boats, successfully employed, have been seen there at once; and 280 busses, of from forty to eighty tons each, have got complete cargoes of excellent herring in the space of six weeks. Small boats belonging to Raasay have been known to catch a *last* or twelve barrels in one night, which last was sold on the spot at twelve guineas. This was a most profitable occupation for five men, who subsisted in the interim upon a little oat-meal and potatoes.

He goes on to tell of the herring coming from the north, the 'countless sea-fowls' that accompany them and the whales which harass them. He goes on:

> The sea seems to boil; it teems with life and motion; and the happy natives of the adjacent shores, hail the welcome guests with every demonstration of joy. Every net strong enough to hold a fly, every boat that can swim, is prepared; man and boy become sailors – and those people who are so often branded with the epithets of *lazy* and *savagely improvident*, are all at once patterns of vigour and energy, of industry, ingenuity, and courage. How cruel is it at this season to put any obstruction in their way, and how unwise are the salt laws and regulations so often alluded to, which prevent those numerous islanders from availing themselves in their fullest extent of the blessings providentially offered upon their shores!
>
> The humane and intelligent proprietor of this island does all that lies in his power for the improvement of the people and the advancement of agriculture. He has planted a considerable quantity of trees; but many thousands of them have been destroyed by the roe-deer, with which Raasay abounds. He must, therefore, extirpate these animals before his plantations can be expected to thrive. Inclosures and draining are much wanted, though in some few places already commenced. Mr M'Leod himself has set a good example in both. A school is taught in the island, and attended by 46 scholars; but three or four additional ones ought to be established in the very extensive parish to which Raasay belongs. Upon the whole, the people are fully as happy and comfortable as any of their neighbours.

This account is very informative. MacDonald's account of the stone found on Raasay, gives not only locations for the various types, but also suggested uses to which it might be put. About this time the herring fishing appears to be very successful and his view of the industrious habits of the people do not agree with that given by the laird in 1787. Like so many others before him, he speaks out against the Salt Laws. In 1773, Johnson had said that the attempt to raise roe-deer had been unsuccessful. Since then it would appear that they had done very well, as they were now causing considerable damage to the trees that had been planted.

The poor years of 1801 and 1802 were repeated in 1815 and 1816. This was serious, but perhaps even more serious was the drop in the value of cattle. The Portree cattle market in August 1816 and the next one in 1817 saw poor prices paid. The people living on the extensive MacDonald estates on Skye were not in good circumstances, as the price for kelp was fluctuating.

The proposed solution was that people should turn their attention to manual labour and fishing, rather than rely on cattle and their land. In 1818, however, Lord MacDonald was still lobbying vigorously for support to oppose the repeal of the Salt Laws. This was a classic case of conflict of interests. The kelp trade required the protection of the Salt Laws – the fishing did not. Thus, at a time when there was a desperate need for an alternative to agriculture, and Lord MacDonald wanted the population on his estates to be less reliant on the land, he was not prepared to forego the profits of the kelp. The fishing, which could have been a substantial industry for the area, was grossly under-exploited, and the people of the area were subjected to grinding poverty then and more particularly in later decades. Lord MacDonald, it must be said, was not the only landowner who found himself in this position.

There were very few employment opportunities in the area. Road building schemes were funded by the government but organised by the estates. Apart from the kelp industry, they provided the only opportunity for employing large numbers of labourers. The estates therefore controlled both the land, and the only possibility of alternative employment.

By the 1820s, the downturn in the price of kelp saw that industry virtually eliminated in the islands. The fall in the price of cattle hit the population hard. There was now, on Skye as on much of the north-west mainland, a large number of people who had no secondary source of employment and who were therefore totally reliant on the land to support them. Destitution was rife.

Although affected by the conditions that were prevalent in Skye at this time, Raasay was in a somewhat different situation. Here the laird lived on the island and knew the people, although his opinion of them in 1787 did not seem to be the same as that of J. MacDonald, who wrote about Raasay in 1811. By the turn of the century, however, the financial difficulties of the MacLeods were almost certainly adversely affecting the people on the estate. It would appear that many of the tacksmen on Raasay had by then left the island, to go to Skye. Many seem to have settled in Trotternish, while others may have gone to Strath. However, the Raasay laird's problems were not related to the collapse of the kelp industry. Neither the laird nor the people had ever become dependent on income from that source. There is, therefore, unlikely to have been as large a population rise on Raasay, as there had been on Skye.

Information that has come 'back home' across the Atlantic indicates that in the early 1820s or possibly a year or so earlier, some tenants left Raasay and emigrated to Prince Edward Island, Canada. This appears to have been the first emigration from the island. These people financed the move themselves. This emigration will be discussed in more detail later. By then the price for Highland cattle at market was fluctuating. Butchers favoured larger, Lowland breeds that did not have to walk to market. This affected both laird and tenants.

By this time, various studies had been carried out into estate economies in general, and advisors believed that the best way forward for estates was sheep. The larger breeds of Lowland sheep were considered a good alternative to cattle. So began the age of the 'Great White Sheep'. James MacLeod set up a sheep farm at Glam. As well as the lands of Glam, the former tack of Brae was probably taken into this project. This would not have involved any great expenditure, apart from the cost of the stock. Only the land and shepherds were required. This was part of the area previously held either by the laird, or by tacksmen. There would have been relatively few people living on that land. Those who were would either have moved within Raasay, or emigrated.

POPULATION OF RAASAY IN THE FIRST QUARTER OF THE NINETEENTH CENTURY

John Nicolson had been minister of the parish of Portree since 1756. Although the only church in the parish was in Portree village, he came to Clachan in Raasay once a month to preach. In 1800 the Established Church of Scotland began keeping a register of births and marriages in the parish. These registers, known as the *Old Parish Records* (OPR), were kept only intermittently, so that by no means all births and marriages were recorded. However, it is the earliest detailed record of the general population of Raasay to give both names of the people and the township in which they lived.

For the period 1800 to about 1824, using the *OPR* as an indicator a possible population distribution has been calculated.[2] This had been done in percentage terms. The total population of Raasay and Rona at this time is not known for certain but in view of later evidence, may possibly be estimated at about 700. The results given below show the percentage, followed in brackets by an actual figure based on a total of 700.

14%	(98)	Rona, Fladda and Eilean Taigh
4%	(28)	North end of Raasay
5%	(35)	Arnish and Torran
5%	(35)	Castle
8%	(56)	Screapadal
11%	(77)	Hallaig
5%	(35)	Leac
19%	(133)	Fearns
11%	(77)	Eyre
13%	(91)	Suisnish to Oscaig/Holoman area
5%	(35)	Balachuirn to Manish
100%	(700)	Total

It must be stressed that the above figures can only be a guide. However, they do support the theory that the bulk of the population was on the east side from Hallaig to Eyre. The concentration around Clachan is to be expected as this was the main centre of the island. There were fewer people on the west side between Balachuirn and Manish, probably because this was the area that had been leased to the tacksmen. It can also be seen that the north end as well as Rona, Fladda and Eilean Taigh now had some people, although numbers there were low at this time.

One of the children of Malcolm MacLeod (Malcolm of the '45), by his second marriage to Janet MacLeod, was Alexander. In 1801 he and his family are found living in Castle, but by 1805 they had moved to Penifiler, outside Portree. It is not known why these tacksmen moved out of Raasay, but it is possible that as the MacLeods' financial trouble grew, they increased the rents on the tacks in an effort to gain more income.

There were, as one would expect, MacLeods throughout the island, and also on Rona. Castle and Hallaig show predominately MacLeods. Two of the MacLeods at Hallaig were named Torcall, probably descendants of Torcall Dubh from Lewis. Most MacSweens were in the Clachan area and on the west side of the island. Many of the MacKenzies were found in Fearns and Screapadal. MacLeans were in Eyre, Screapadal and Manish. MacKays were found in Eyre only. Most of the Cummings were on Fladda and the Arnish/Torran area. Other names found, but not seemingly concentrated in any area, were Gillies, MacLennan and Nicolson. It is, perhaps, more surprising to find the names MacInnes, MacKinnon, Matheson, Munro, Ross and Stewart. It is interesting that the name Stewart appears, as Johnson and Boswell mentioned that a boy named Stewart carried their provisions up to Dun Caan for them. There were a variety of names on Rona, although none predominated. They were MacLeod, MacLennan, MacKenzie, Gillies, MacSween, Nicolson and Stewart.

As may be expected in an island having so much connection with the sea, there were some dreadful tragedies, each of which would have affected the entire island as well as the immediate family. The earliest of these accidents, for which any detail is known, was that of a Rona boat in the 1820s.

Kenneth MacKenzie, from Lochalsh, was the tenant in Big Harbour, Rona. After a spell of dry weather, fresh water there ran short. Kenneth went with a neighbour and two servant girls from Rona to Portree to get supplies. Coming home after dark, they missed the entrance to the harbour, and all were drowned. Thereafter Kenneth's widow, Janet Nicolson, kept a light in her window to guide passing boats. About 1851, a Captain Otter made a nautical survey of the area for the Lighthouse Board. He reported that Janet MacKenzie had kept a light in her window, at her own expense, for ten years to help boats in the Sound of Raasay. The Lighthouse Board gave her £20 to help with the cost of oil for the light. The lighthouse boat stationed in Portree, until about 1986, to serve the Rona lighthouse, was called the *Janet MacKenzie* in her memory. Three sons of Kenneth and Janet MacKenzie were seamen. Two of them, Donald and William, owned the smack *Margaret*, of Stornoway, in the 1840s.

Writing in 1930,[3] William MacKenzie refers to Janet MacKenzie as 'Mrs MacRae, Bean Rona – meaning 'wife on or of Rona'. In calling her Mrs MacRae, he has confused her with her daughter, Catherine, who married Kenneth MacRae, also a Lochalsh man. Kenneth and Catherine MacRae lived in Big Harbour in 1841. By 1844 they had moved to Torran, and ten years later had moved to Camustinavaig, Braes. It is nonetheless Janet MacKenzie who is 'Bean Rona'. William MacKenzie continues, '[She] belongs to a Kilmuir family of good social standing. Her sister was the wife of Ronald MacDonald, Cnocowe, Kilmuir.' Janet's sister was Christine, and their parents were Donald Nicolson and Catherine MacDonald. Because, over the years, there has been more than one couple with these names, it has not yet been possible to identify this particular couple with any certainty. It would appear that Kenneth MacRae's wife had been called after her maternal grandmother.

THE MACKAY PIPERS OF RAASAY

In piping circles, the MacKays of Raasay hold a special place. Iain mac Ruairidh, John MacKay of Eyre, had become piper to James MacLeod, the Laird of Raasay. Living in Raasay House at that time were two nieces of James MacLeod, Eliza and Isabella Ross. The girls' parents had died when they were very young. Eliza was an accomplished musician with a good knowledge of musical theory. Based on John's playing, she transcribed a number of *piobaireachd* into pianoforte notation. She later married Sir Charles D'Oyly, who was in the service of the East India Company. On her return home from India, Eliza presented John MacKay with an elegant set of pipes. In her honour, John composed the *piobaireachd* 'Lady D'Oyly's Salute'.

John MacKay married Margaret MacLean from Eyre and they had a family of four sons and five daughters who survived infancy. As well as teaching his sons, John taught others. Both John and his pupils were very successful at Highland Society Competitions.

By 1823, James MacLeod of Raasay could no longer afford to keep his piper. John MacKay and his family left Raasay that year and walked to Crieff, their possessions carried by two ponies. John took up the position of piper to Lord Willoughby d'Eresby at Drummond Castle, where he remained until sometime before 1840 when he retired to Kyleakin to live with his daughter. John MacKay died about 1848 and is buried in an unmarked grave in the ruined chapel near Raasay House.

John's four sons and his other pupils all held positions as pipers. His oldest son, Donald, was piper to Clanranald in 1822 and, from 1834 until his death in 1850, was piper to the Duke of Sussex, Queen Victoria's uncle. John's third son, Angus, was piper to Davidson of Tulloch in 1829 and to Campbell of Islay in 1835.

Angus was the most famous of John's sons. As well as learning from his father, he also learned musical theory from Eliza, Lady D'Oyly. This knowledge he put to good use. It is known that Angus relied on his father's knowledge and teaching and continued to consult with him, even after John had retired. In 1843 Angus MacKay was appointed piper to Queen Victoria, a position that he held until 1854 when he began to suffer mental illness. He died in 1859. His contribution to Highland music is summarised by Neville T. MacKay[4] who says

> He published an impressive collection of sixty-one *piobaireachd* in staff notation, containing more material than its predecessor and providing pipers with a valuable reference for memorising the tunes as well as a guide to their interpretation. His manuscript record of 179 further tunes provided a basis for others to continue this work, notably Major General Thomason in his 'Ceol Mòr' and the Piobaireachd Society in its series of publications. He also made settings of 550 light melodies and contributed to the publication of two of the earliest collections of this music. He produced five outstanding marches in the newly developing 'competition' style, which are regularly played by present

day competitors. Finally, as the first royal piper, he took the Highland bagpipe to a new level of social acceptability, contributing to the revival of Highland culture and helping to secure the position of the bagpipe within that culture.

Christina MacKay, sister of John and therefore aunt of Angus, married Angus MacLeod, Raasay. They have many descendants, some of whom are still living on the island.

SCHOOLS ON RAASAY AND RONA IN THE FIRST HALF OF THE NINETEENTH CENTURY

The Scottish Society for the Propagation of Christian Knowledge, SSPCK, had established a school on Raasay by 1812. The teacher, James MacDonald, had forty-six pupils. This society, like the Gaelic Schools Society, GSS, provided schoolmasters, but not buildings, to teach the elements of reading and writing. The schoolmaster went to a township and stayed there until those attending had learnt the basics: then he was moved to another area where a greater need had been shown. Pupils, adults as well as children, were examined periodically by the minister of the parish. It is not known where on Raasay this first school was situated, but it was probably either in Clachan or in the Fearns area, where the bulk of the population lived at that time.

The GSS had proposed to set up a school on Rona in 1813, but Angus MacDonald, the schoolmaster, was sent to Raasay instead, where he had fifty-four scholars by November 1815. This school received a favourable report in 1817 from Rev. Coll MacDonald of Portree who heard pupils read in Gaelic from the Old and New Testament and Psalms. At that time there were about sixty-six pupils, one man, aged about forty, attending with his sons. Because the schoolmaster had by then been in place for four sessions, and had done so well in the south end of the island, it was proposed that he should be moved to the north end that winter. Probably all the teachers who moved about the island at that time would have taught in Gaelic. That was the language in common use, and everyone would speak it. However, those people who went away to work, like the men going to the east coast fishing, would have had at least some English.

From November 1817 until 1821, Angus MacDonald taught in Rona for the GSS. Here he had just fewer than forty pupils, ranging in age from five to over thirty, with about the same numbers of male and female. In February 1823 the SSPCK teacher in Rona was N. Gillies. It is not known how long he remained there. The GSS teacher in Rona in 1826 was Murdo MacMillan, until he was moved to Eyre in 1827. In Eyre he had thirty-one elementary pupils and twenty reading the Bible.

The SSPCK provided two teachers, Donald MacKinnon and John Cameron, for Raasay from 1825. In that year there were forty-nine pupils. There is no indication as to whether both men were in the same place, but probably not, as not all pupils would be able to attend at one centre. Possibly one man was in the Fearns area and the other in Clachan, or perhaps they moved about on the island as needs dictated. By 1827, both teachers were superannuated and received £12 per annum. Both remained on Raasay until the 1840s.

About 1839 a new teacher was employed on Raasay by the SSPCK. She was a Mrs MacDonald who taught 'spinning, sewing and other branches of female industry'. She was paid £5 per annum. She remained on Raasay until at least 1850.

By 1839 Alexander MacMillan, a Lochaber man, had moved to Arnish from Skye. He is found in the 1841 census living in Arnish, but the GSS records show that he was teaching thirty-six pupils in Torran. Later in 1841, he was moved to Fearns. By 1843 he was in Castle, where he remained until about 1846. By 1847 Alexander MacMillan was living in Balachuirn, although he was teaching in Holoman, where he had forty-six pupils. In 1850 he was moved to Fearns, where he remained until the last of the people left in 1854.

Angus MacDonald moved from Rona to Castle in 1821. In 1823 he moved to Arnish, where he stayed for two years. In Arnish he had twenty-six pupils.

From 1829, Duncan Gillies was the GSS teacher in Eyre, until he was moved to Castle in 1830. In Eyre he had seventy-seven pupils, including forty-five who could read the Bible in Gaelic. Twenty of his pupils were adults. He was a very popular teacher but drowned in July 1831 while crossing between Raasay and Skye. It is possibly his widow, Jean Gillies, and her family who were living at Clachan from 1841. The youngest daughter, named Nora, was born about 1829.

Donald MacDonald replaced Duncan Gillies at Castle in 1831. That year he had forty-nine pupils. He moved to Hallaig in 1832, where he stayed until 1837.

Duncan Morrison taught on Fladda for a year or so about 1846.

John MacDougall, who had been on Rona for the previous four years, was moved to Kyle Rona in 1837. He was there for little more than one year.

There was a school halfway between Fearns and Eyre, near the river. The ruin of the school building is up from the shore among the trees. The ruin of another school is found at Eyre, behind the four houses on the shore.

JOHN, THE LAST OF THE MACLEOD LAIRDS OF RAASAY

James MacLeod, Laird of Raasay, died in 1824. His eldest son, John, now took over the estate. Unlike his father, he did not live on Raasay. He was a lieutenant in the 78th Regiment of Foot, otherwise the 78th Highlanders.

By the late 1820s various people and institutions had a financial interest in the estate, as security for loans. Those included one of the MacKenzies of Seaforth,

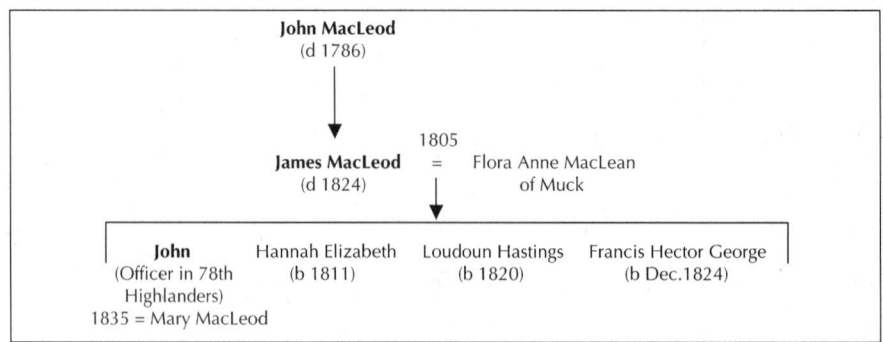

Figure 5/1. James MacLeod of Raasay.

a Moritz Hardman from the island of Grenada and Mathew Babington, a banker in Leicester. By 1828, John MacLeod's affairs were being managed by a trustee. John's mother, Flora, had an annuity as part of her marriage agreement in 1805.

Because John MacLeod did not live on Raasay, he relied on his factor to run the estate. In past times, when the laird lived on Raasay and knew his tenants personally, they could expect some leniency with rent payments if there had been a poor season, or if personal circumstances were difficult. A factor's loyalty, however, lay with the estate, and, aware of MacLeod's financial troubles, he had to maximise estate income. In the 1820s, just as conditions were becoming more difficult, tenants had to deal with the factor.

In 1835 John married Mary MacLeod, and their marriage contract gave her an interest in the estate. By 1837 Trustees for the creditors had an interest in the affairs of the estate. In May 1839, John's father-in-law appears to have given him a loan of £12 000. As with previous loans, it was secured by the estate.

FINANCIAL PROBLEMS OF THE MACLEODS AND THEIR EFFECT ON THE PEOPLE

It seems incredible that the Raasay estate was allowed to become so indebted to financiers and others. Unlike the major landowners of the area in the seventeenth century – MacLeod of Dunvegan, Lord MacDonald and the Earl of Seaforth – the Laird of Raasay was not obliged to send his children to be educated in the Lowlands, nor was he obliged to spend time in Edinburgh himself each year. He lived on Raasay, and did not have to rely on others to run his estate in his absence. It appears that during the period 1600 to 1745, general conditions on the Raasay estate were no worse, and were possibly even better, than in other parts of the region. In the time of Iain Garbh, Raasay was in a relatively good position. The people had a strong sense of identity and worth. Even by the time of the '45 Rebellion, this was the case. After the '45, however, it seems that the lairds took a quite deliberate decision to emulate 'High Society' of the south, effectively placing themselves apart from, and above, the people.

The massive expenditure on the mansion house required loans at each stage of new building and refurbishment. It is unlikely that the estate, even with very careful financial planning and management, could ever have financed this expenditure, and the opulent lifestyle enjoyed by the MacLeod lairds. In those days, lairds who could offer their lands as security had no problem in securing loans. Unfortunately, no one would have asked for a business plan or financial forecast. Had they done so, many ordinary people might have been saved a great deal of hardship and deprivation in later decades.

The loan to John MacLeod (laird from 1745), secured by mortgaging Suisnish in 1761, took fifteen years to repay. James (laird from 1786) secured a large loan in 1796. Poor seasons made it difficult for tenants to pay their rent in the early 1800s. The market for Highland cattle also suffered shortly afterwards. This hit the laird a double blow. His personal income from selling his own cattle had gone. The laird's income from rents on the estate was also hit because his tenants, who had previously relied on cattle to pay their rent and buy in extra meal and other necessities, suffered too from the fall in the price of cattle. At the very time when they might have expected some leniency in rent payments, the laird was in greatest need of money himself. The stone and timber, sold by the estate, were profitable by-lines, rather than a source of serious income for the estate. Certainly they were not enough to service the current debt.

Tacksmen had managed to follow the trend set by the laird for a time, but by the turn of the century had found it impossible to keep up. Probably even before the uncertainty in the price of cattle, which would also have affected them, they had little alternative but to move away from the island to an area where they could obtain a tack or lease on better terms than they could on Raasay. That, no doubt, explains why those who remained in the area are found on Skye.

By now it was clear that the land alone could not provide a living for the people. The fluctuations in the price of cattle, and poor seasons for weather and crops were the final blow. Some stock had to be kept, but the people knew that they were an unreliable source of income. The land they worked had to provide for their families as never before. Raasay men looked to the sea, and as well as fishing in home waters, they were employed on herring busses, and at the east coast fishing, thereby earning wages, although it meant being away from home for much of the year. Poor seasons at the fishing contributed to a general fall in the standard of living of most west coast families at this time.

The tables in Figures 5/2 and 5/3, taken from old estate records, were given to the Deer Forest Commission in 1893 by James Ross, factor for the estate. The total rental for Raasay and Rona in 1827 was therefore £695 8s. 7d. In 1773, Johnson and Boswell found that the rents for the whole estate, including the lands in Snizort, were £250–300. There has clearly been a very large increase in the fifty-four years between the two. Arrears in 1827 amounted to seventy-six percent of the annual amount, and by 1831 had risen to 142 per cent. This shows clearly that times were bad. There were greater arrears in the north end and Rona than in the rest of Raasay. In 1827 the arrears of the north end townships amounted to eighty-eight per cent of their rental, and by 1831 had risen to 157 per cent.

Not surprisingly therefore, there were further emigrations from Raasay in the

Figure 5/2. Rent and arrears 1827 and 1831 for townships that became part of the sheep farm in the 1850s.

Township	Rent in 1827			Arrears in 1827			Arrears in 1831		
	£	s.	d.	£	s.	d.	£	s.	d.
Manish	24	7	6	29	18	10	36	8	1
Castle	51	0	0	36	10	4	78	12	4
Screapadal	65	19	6	34	17	4	96	7	11
Hallaig	77	1	8	57	7	7	151	11	10
Leac	21	12	0	29	0	0	51	15	2
Fearns	126	5	6	80	3	11	154	13	4
Eyre	76	5	9	33	7	8	52	3	7
Suisnish	53	6	8	50	9	8	48	19	2
Total	**495**	**18**	**7**	**351**	**15**	**4**	**670**	**11**	**5**

Figure 5/3. Rent and arrears 1827 and 1831 for townships that did not become part of the sheep farm in the 1850s.

Township	Rent in 1827			Arrears in 1827			Arrears in 1831		
	£	s.	d.	£	s.	d.	£	s.	d.
Arnish	21	0	0	12	1	8	21	1	8
Torran	10	5	6	8	15	0	12	4	4
Fladda	22	15	6	18	3	2	40	13	6
Umachan	12	6	0	16	7	8	16	9	11
Eilean Taigh	6	1	6	—			—		
Kyle Rona	31	15	0	32	10	7	62	1	11
Doire na Guaille	17	17	6	20	18	6	32	6	5
Big Harbour	17	14	6	16	17	6	27	16	6
Dry Harbour	59	14	6	51	1	5	101	13	5
Total	**199**	**10**	**0**	**176**	**15**	**6**	**314**	**7**	**8**

1820s and 1830s. It is not clear whether these later emigrants went directly to Cape Breton, or went first to Prince Edward Island.

The story of one emigration from Raasay has come back from abroad.[5] There had been Cummings living on Raasay for quite some time, possibly having come with, or later joined, the MacLeans who are believed to have arrived on Raasay in the sixteenth or seventeenth century. At the beginning of the nineteenth century, the only Cummings found in Skye parishes were living either on the Skye part of the MacLeods' estate, or on Fladda and the Torran/Arnish area of Raasay. In 1833, two families of Cummings from Raasay arrived in Sydney, Cape Breton, and settled in the River Denys area. The first family, four brothers and two sisters, were cousins of the second family, five brothers and at least one sister. As with all information recorded many years after the events by people who were not themselves participants, there are discrepancies, mainly with dates. It is suggested that these Cummings had gone to Cape Breton directly from Raasay, although one of the sisters is said to have left Raasay with her husband, between 1818 and 1821, going first to Prince Edward Island. Hopefully more information will yet emerge.

Of the eleven Cummings from Raasay, found in Cape Breton in 1833, nine married. The surnames of their spouses were MacLean, MacKenzie (2), MacLeod (3), MacSween, Gillies and Nicolson. It is significant that all these surnames are found together on Raasay, suggesting perhaps that these families had all left Raasay, although they did not necessarily emigrate on the same ship, or at the same time.

The son of one of the Cummings men married a daughter of Donald MacLeod, son of Torcall. Donald (b c.1817) is said to have emigrated from Skye to Prince Edward Island, date unknown. The name Torcall MacLeod is found only among the descendants of the MacLeods of Lewis, and not among either the MacLeods of Dunvegan or the MacLeods of Raasay. As it is known that MacLeod descendants of Torcall Dubh of Lewis were living on Raasay, it is highly probable that Donald, son of Torcall, was originally from Raasay. It may well be, as discussed earlier, that the family had previously left Raasay and that they emigrated from

Skye. Indeed this tends to confirm that hypothesis. Also in the River Denys area of Cape Breton, in later years, are found other MacLeods who are believed to have come from Raasay.

An interesting emigration story has been handed down in a Gillies family in Raasay. Seonaidh Iain Dhòmhnaill, John Gillies, knew that a family of Gillieses, who lived in the Isle of Lewis in the 1920s, was related to his family in Raasay, although the exact relationship remains elusive. It is said that people from Raasay were emigrating. When their ship put in to Stornoway, presumably to take on more emigrants, at least one of the Raasay men jumped ship. Mr Bill Lawson, of the genealogical research centre 'Co Leis Thu' in Harris, says that the Gillies family in question turned up in Lewis 'from nowhere' in the early 1820s.

Thus we have two separate pieces of information, one from each side of the Atlantic, both indicating that people left Raasay in the 1820s and 1830s to emigrate. The information about the Gillieses suggests that not all of them wanted to go.

As with all emigrations at this time, people tended to leave in family groups, as the Cummings did. After they went, no Cummings were left on Raasay. There were, however, still Cummings on MacLeod lands in Snizort, probably related in some way to those who had left Raasay. Because so many family groups left together, little knowledge of many of them now remains on Raasay. Generally, information about the past is handed down within families, and when no relations remained on Raasay, information was lost. Perhaps it may yet come back 'home' and add to our knowledge of this time.

THE CHURCH

The minister of Portree parish, of which Raasay was a part, continued to come over to preach once a month. After John Nicolson's death in 1799, Alexander Campbell, who had been the teacher, became minister until 1811. Rev. Coll MacDonald was minister from then until 1854. As well as the parish minister, there were others who, working for various organisations, traversed the area preaching to the people.

During the 1830s, the factor for the Raasay estate was John MacLeod, a relative of the MacLeods of Raasay. John, Iain mac Dhòmhnaill mhic Alasdair, was tacksman of Balmore, Struan in Skye, and had previously been a factor for MacLeod of Dunvegan. John's brother, Alexander, was a missionary and catechist, working about 1833 in the parish of Portree. He toured the parish, going from one township to another, preaching to the people. Once in Hallaig he questioned a man who could give no satisfactory answers. 'Poor man', he said 'you have a heavy burden on you.' 'Well', said the man, 'I think you should keep quiet on that point. If I have a heavy burden, it was your brother that put it on me'. He was in arrears of rent at the time.

Alexander MacLeod died in 1836. Rev. Duncan MacCallum was on Raasay from 1836 until 1844, when he went to Duirinish. Although the heritors, or landowners of the parish were responsible by law for building and maintaining a church in every parish, the only church in Portree parish was in the village of Portree. Rev. MacCallum pressed for a church to be built on Raasay, and collected funds from members of the Established Church of Scotland for that purpose. The church on Raasay, now the Free Church, was built about 1836. It was not until 1843 that the Free Church of Scotland was formed.

ESTATE MANAGEMENT IN THE 1830S AND 1840S

John MacLeod, the factor, died in May 1834. Either before or after him, the factor was Donald MacRae, Auchtertyre. He too was related to MacLeod of Raasay, his wife being a cousin of John MacLeod. The last factor of Raasay under the MacLeods was Alexander Kenneth MacKinnon of Corry, from the parish of Strath, Skye. The MacLeods of Raasay were also related to the MacKinnons of Strath, and quite possibly to this man too.

MacKinnon of Corry became factor for Raasay either in 1834 or shortly after. By that time the MacLeods' creditors were becoming increasingly anxious. As factor, MacKinnon set about trying to maximise estate income. In the first instance, tenants in arrears were warned to pay up, or threatened with removal.

Now, again, the estate looked to sheep to solve the problem. This was a 'solution' for the estate only. It was never intended to be a solution for the people. The idea was that sheep, unlike cattle, were profitable. The traditional tacksmen had gone. If a tack was leased to one man to run as a sheep walk, the estate would not have the trouble of dealing with small tenants who were in arrears, and likely to remain so. However, a tacksman working sheep did not want people and their animals on the land. The people had to go!

The years 1836 and 1837 were poor seasons, when bad weather affected the crops, leaving both the people and their livestock seriously short of food. Peats could not be dried for fuel. In the later years of that decade, the fishing too failed. As far as is known, no estate papers relating to this period have survived. It is therefore most fortuitous that a great deal can be learned from estate papers of 1847 and 1851.[6] These documents show clearly that the desperate plight of the people of Raasay in the late 1840s and 1850s was due, in very large part, to the management of the estate in the late 1830s and 1840s.

It would have been fairly easy for the factor to clear an area of people to make way for the sheep. If they were in arrears of rent, and after successive poor seasons many would be, he could apply to the court for a writ of removal. Nice and simple, and with the law on his side too! Neither would there have been any particular problem with those who were able to pay their rent on time. Tenancies had been verbal and probably on a yearly basis. Cottars had no rights at all, and could be moved at will. Although this had always been the case, it had never before caused any difficulty. Tenants and cottars felt secure in the knowledge that the laird and the tacksmen would not do anything that was not in their best interests. As long as they paid their rent, to the best of their ability, they had no reason to suppose that anything would change.

Now, however, tenants and cottars alike were moved as the factor wished, to wherever the factor wished. About 1836 or shortly after, certain areas were cleared to make way for single tenants. The two tacks of Suisnish and Eyre were created. That of Suisnish included the small townships of Borrodale and Ramisdal in the Glen. Richard Sharpe[7] indicates that some writs of removal have survived. Some people were cleared off their land because they were in arrears of rent; others were cleared to allow the land to be leased as a tack to a single tenant.

Thus the south end was cleared. From Eyre, MacKays were moved to Rona and MacKinnons to Fearns. Other families received similar treatment. No doubt some emigrated or left Raasay for Skye or the mainland. Angus MacLeod became tacksman of Eyre, and John MacLeod held the tack of Suisnish. Both these men were from Skye, although they may have been related in some way to the MacLeods of Raasay. Only a few cottars and fishermen remained on these lands.

John MacLeod, who had the tack of Suisnish, was known as Iain mac Sheoc, John son of Jock. He had a shop as well as the farm. The rock below Suisnish House was known as 'Sgeir Dubh Iain mhic Sheoc'. He left Raasay in 1849 and went back to Skye. John is said to have emigrated to Australia.

The tack of Glam and Brae had been part of the MacLeods' sheep venture of the mid 1820s. It remained practically devoid of people, except for a couple of shepherds. It is unclear whether it was under the control of the estate, or was leased out.

Upper Hallaig was also cleared, probably during the 1830s. It is not known who took over this tack, but it is clear that there was some movement of people in the area. By 1847 there were six families living there, but only one of them had been there in 1841. The old parish records of births and marriages shows that descendants of Torcall Dubh of Lewis were living in Hallaig in the early 1800s. The information from Cape Breton indicates that some of them emigrated. All these pieces of evidence seem to fit together, and show that the MacLeods did clear these people from Hallaig. They left Raasay, going first to Prince Edward Island and later moving on to Cape Breton. Although some of these MacLeods went abroad, others remained on Raasay. By 1841 they are found on Fladda, later moving onto Raasay itself where descendants are still to be found.

By the time of the 1883 Napier Commission, and the 1893 Deer Forest Commission, the overriding impression on Raasay was that when MacKinnon of Corry became factor for the estate, things became steadily worse for the people. The evidence indicates that MacLeod and his factor cleared Eyre, Suisnish and Upper Hallaig. This is confirmed as shown above. There was no mention of Brae and Glam, but that was possibly because clearances there had been earlier, in the 1820s, and memory of them had faded, in light of the later clearances.

The population at this time was probably about 700, and growing. Because of poor seasons and the failure of the fishing, people were finding it difficult both to feed themselves and to pay their rent. MacKinnon, the factor, was pressing them for their rent, and had moved some to allow new tacksmen to come into the island. What happened next defies belief!

The estate (whether MacKinnon, the factor, or John MacLeod, the laird, or both) now began granting tenancies on Raasay to others from outwith the island. A few new tenancies in such circumstances might have been expected, given that they had cleared some local people out. However, from about the late 1830s, until the estate was sold in 1846, the population of Raasay rose by approximately fifty per cent. By 1847 fully one third of the people living on Raasay and Rona had come onto these islands during the previous decade.

People came from Skye, from the parishes of Portree, Stenscholl and Strath. They came from the mainland too, from Kintail, from Lochalsh and from Lochcarron and Applecross. Conditions were certainly as difficult in those areas as they were on Raasay. Land there too was being cleared to make sheep walks. That these people were actively encouraged to come to Raasay is shown by the case of a family of MacLeods from Stenscholl who, although they were cottars on Skye, were given a tenancy in Balmeanach.

By 1847, all the tenancies in Balmeanach, and half of those in Balachuirn, were held by incomers. Manish too had no local people. There were two shepherds in Glam. It is interesting that the only tenant at Doire Domhain was Iain Mòr MacSween, and that no new tenants went there. Some new tenants, although relatively few, even went to Eilean Taigh, Rona and Kyle Rona. Fladda, Torran and Arnish had only local people. Hallaig, too, was essentially local. Fearns, Leac and Screapadal, however, received a fair number of the incomers. Given the plight of the local population of Raasay at that time, the most obvious reason for this course of action by the estate would be to maximise the income of the Raasay estate in the short term, giving no consideration to the long-term consequences.

Although it has been assumed, by some, that the run-rig system was abandoned on Raasay shortly after that happened in Skye, in 1811, other evidence suggests that this was not the case. The townships of Arnish, Torran and Fladda were still working on the run-rig system as late as the 1950s. This system suited the land in the north end better than crofts, as arable land was in small patches here and there. Descriptions of the east side of Raasay also suggest that arable ground was in small patches. In 1786 John Knox, on his journey between Applecross and Raasay, commented on the 'many little corn fields and potato grounds'. Unlike Skye, where the kelp industry dictated practice, Raasay had no reason to change. Most, if not all, of the townships on Raasay were probably still operating on the run-rig system at this time. If that were so, the immediate effect of allowing extra tenants into them would have had less overall impact on tenants, than if individual crofts had to be divided and shared with the incomers.

Apart from the clearances of people at Eyre and Suisnish, others were also moved or cleared out. Anyone in arrears would have been pressured into paying up or getting out. In the circumstances, conditions could not improve. The island was now carrying a far larger population that it ever had previously. As the rental and arrears table shows, conditions had been deteriorating even before the influx of outsiders. There is every likelihood that there was more than one wave of emigration. It is not easy to interpret the evidence about this period given to the Napier Commission in 1883. There is a clear memory of people emigrating. Some said 'one boat-load of people' went. This is most likely to refer to people going abroad. There would, almost certainly, have been others going to Skye or the mainland. This internal emigration is seldom mentioned, but is equally important. From the point of view of those moved, it was upsetting and disruptive. It did not solve anything. It just moved the problem along with the people.

In the event, even those short sighted desperate measures were not enough to allow the MacLeods to keep their estates. Matters did not improve, and by the 1840s those people and institutions that had a financial interest in the Raasay estate took action to secure their interests. In 1840 the 'Fund for the Relief of the Widows and Children of the Burgh and Parochial Schoolmasters of Scotland', were securing a bond for £10 000. A David Sandeman appears in 1841 securing £7 000. In 1843 his creditors forced the sale of the estate, and John, the last MacLeod Lairds of Raasay, emigrated. From then until 1846 when the sale of Raasay and Rona was completed, it must be assumed that the estate was run for the benefit of the creditors. So ended nearly 400 years of traceable history of the MacLeods of Raasay.

It is interesting that another prophecy of Coinneach Odhar, the Brahan Seer, concerns the downfall of the MacLeods of Raasay. It is given here as found.

> During a recent visit to the Island of Raasay we received a peculiar prediction regarding the MacLeods from an old man there, over eighty years of age, who remembered seven proprietors of Raasay, and who sorely lamented the fulfilment of the prophecy, and the decline of the good old stock, entirely in consequence of their own folly and extravagance. Since then, we had the prediction repeated by a Kintail man in identical terms; and as it is hardly translatable, we shall give it in the original vernacular: *Dar a thig Mac-Dhomhnuill Duibh bàn; MacShimidh ceann-dearg; Sisealch claon ruadh; Mac-Coinnich mor bodhar; agus Mac-Gille-challum cama-chasach, iar-ogha Ian bhig à Ruiga, 'se sin a Mac-Gille-challum is miosa 'thainig na thig; cha bhi mi ann ri linn, 's cha'n fhearr leam air a bhith.*
>
> [When we shall have a fair-haired Lochiel; a red-haired Lovat; a squint-eyes, fair-haired Chisholm; a big deaf Mackenzie; and a bow-crooked-legged Mac-Gille-challum, who shall be the great-grandson of John Beg, or Little John, of Ruiga: that Mac-Gille-challum will be the worst that ever came or ever will come; I shall not be in existence in his day, and I have no desire that I should.]
>
> Ruiga is the name of a place in Skye. When the last Macleod of Raasay was born, an old sage in the district called upon his neighbour, and told him, with an expression of great sorrow, that Mac-Gille-challum of Raasay now had an heir, and his birth was a certain forerunner of the extinction of his house. Such an event as the birth of an heir had been hitherto, in this as in all other Highland families, universally considered an occasion for great rejoicing among the retainers. The other old man was amazed, and asked the sage what he meant by such unusual and disloyal remarks. 'Oh!' answered he, 'do you not know that this is the great-grandson of John Beg of Ruiga whom Coinneach Odhar predicted would be the worst of his race'. And so he undoubtedly proved himself to be, for he lost for ever the ancient inheritance of his house, and acted generally in such a manner as to fully justify the Seer's prediction; and what is still more remarkable, the Highland lairds, with the peculiar characteristics and malformations foretold by Kenneth, preceded or were contemporaries of the last Mac-Gille-challum of Raasay.[8]

It must be assumed that 'Ruiga in Skye' is Rigg. The last of the MacLeods of Raasay was John, son of James, son of John, son of Malcolm of the '45, said to be son of Alasdair who received the estate in 1692 when his cousins, Seonaid and Sileas, resigned in his favour.

One genealogy of the MacLeods states that Alasdair (who became laird in 1692) was the son of a John MacLeod of Rigg. However, in that case, John of Rigg's great-grandson was John, son of Malcolm of the '45. The last laird, John MacLeod, would have been a great-great-great-grandson of John of Rigg.

Another genealogy states that John (first of Rigg) was the son of Alasdair (who became laird in 1692) and was thus a brother of Malcolm of the '45. This does not fit either. If it is correct, descendants of the Rigg branch were not the Lairds of Raasay.

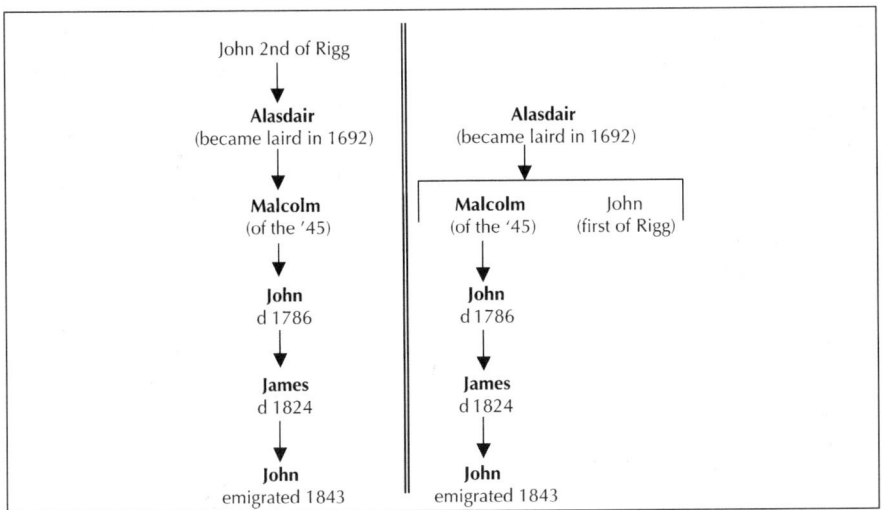

Figure 5/4. MacLeod lairds of Raasay 1692–1843.

Perhaps there is another explanation! There can be no doubt, however, that none of the lairds of Raasay after 1745 made any attempt to match their spending with their income. It was the people of Raasay who paid the price for that, and a heavy price it was.

Notes

1. R. Sharpe, *Documents and Sources* (1978) pp. 38–9.
2. There are inherent difficulties in using the OPR to extrapolate general information about population in this way. However, it is the only source for this period giving specific names and places.
3. W. MacKenzie, *Old Skye Tales, 1930* (edited and amalgamated by Dr A. MacLean, 1995), p. 45.
4. N. T. MacKay, 'Angus MacKay (1812–1859) and his Contribution to Highland Music', *TGSI*, vol. LV, p. 214.
5. Thanks to Mrs P. Cummings for providing the information that formed the basis of this research about these early emigrants. Such information adds greatly to our knowledge of this period.
6. Thanks to Mr M. Cumming, Inverness for allowing me to make use of these

documents. The are very important as they give details (not available elsewhere) for the period 1847–51.
7. R. Sharpe, *Raasay: A Study in Island History* (1977), p. 61.
8. A. MacKenzie, *The Prophecies of the Brahan Seer, 1877* (Foreword, Commentary and Conclusion by Elizabeth Sutherland, 1977), pp. 60–1.

6

The History of Raasay, 1846–1872

George Rainy: 1846–1863

John MacLeod emigrated in 1843, leaving the Raasay estate in the hand of trustees and creditors. By this time the estate had been set firmly on course for the misery and poverty that was to come over the following decade. The sale of Raasay and Rona finally went through in November 1846. The buyer was George Rainy, a West India merchant from London, who bought it for £27 600. Many Highland estates, about this time, were being sold to merchants and industrialists from the south, who were financially able to fund such ventures. Often such estates were looked upon as summer retreats, away from the cities. George Rainy took a keen interest in his newly acquired property.

Raasay House, the extensions and modernisation of which had already contributed largely to the financial downfall of the MacLeods, was redesigned again in 1848 by Charles Wilson, to comply with modern fashion. These classical additions were plain but expensive. Ladies and gentlemen had their own living areas and met in the common ground of the library, dining and withdrawing rooms. Servants' quarters were in any remaining available space. The alterations were completed in June 1851.

Rainy brought some key estate workers onto the island. The butler, Thomas Bunning, had worked in London and Paris before moving to Raasay with his family. It was he who kept a diary, giving an insight as to how events were viewed by the owner and his employees. The agricultural manager was Thomas Anderson. Although born in Roxburgh, he had come to Raasay from Gairloch. Duncan Campbell, the ground officer, was born in Oban. He had been the grieve for the MacLeods and was living on Raasay when he married in 1829. The new owner did not live on Raasay all the time, but in his absence, these key employees kept the estate running according to his instructions. Also newly arrived with their families was the ploughman, Thomas Matheson from Dornoch, and the gardener, John Rennie from Wigtonshire. Labourers and house servants were local men and women.

This was a definite break in tradition. Although people had come to live on Raasay from outwith the area in the past, they had all been from the Highland area. Their background was therefore similar to that of the people of Raasay. Now both the owner and those he took onto the island came from completely different backgrounds. Naturally, this would have given rise to some suspicion and apprehension among local people about what the future might hold. Thus there were now two groups of people on the island, the local people and those employed directly by the estate.

Unusually for a proprietor, George Rainy strongly supported the Free Church of Scotland, which had been formed in 1843. He had subscribed £1 000 to its funds. In 1847, Rev. Roderick MacLeod, Maighistir Ruairidh, Free Church minister of Snizort, told a parliamentary select committee that everyone on Raasay supported the Free Church. This was true of many areas in north Skye at that time. The church on Raasay had been built in 1836 for the Established Church of Scotland. Now, because everyone on Raasay belonged to the Free Church, Rainy took over the church on their behalf, and denied access to the other minister. On 26 November 1851, Rev. William Stewart MacDougall was inducted as minister of Raasay. Mr Bunning notes 'Church crowded, supposed 450 present'. Prior to Rev. MacDougall's arrival, Rev. Roderick MacLeod sometimes preached in Raasay. The minister and his wife lived at Raasay House for a few weeks until the manse was ready, in January 1852. It is not known whether the manse was being built, or refurbished, at this time. Rev. MacDougall preached, not only at the church at Clachan, but also at other places on the island, such as Torran and Castle and on Rona. In his diary, the butler makes a point of noting who preached the sermon each Sunday, and how many people attended the service. On some occasions, as in September 1851 when Rev. Fletcher, minister of Bracadale took the service, 'about six Boats from the opposite side' came to the service and the 'Church was full'. This must refer to people coming over to Raasay from Braes and Sconser. Rev. MacDougall stayed on Raasay until October 1855, when he left on the *Clansman* for Appin. Services were then taken occasionally by ministers from Skye, until in April 1857 Rev. James Kippen arrived on Raasay to take up the charge.

When George Rainy took over the estate, there were about 1 100 people living on Raasay and its satellite islands. Just over twenty-five per cent lived in the area north of Arnish, including Fladda, Eilean Taigh and Rona. Seven per cent lived on the south end farms of Eyre and Suisnish. Less than twenty-five per cent are found on the west side, between Clachan and Manish. Thirty-three per cent were in the area between Fearns and Hallaig, and the remaining ten per cent were at Screapadal and Castle.

The settlement pattern at this time appears to follow the pattern set by the MacLeods at the turn of the century. When talking in percentage terms, there is little difference between the two. However, it must be remembered that it was not until after the turn of the century that the north end of Raasay and the islands carried any significant numbers of people at all. At the turn of the century, the total population was in the region of 600–700 people. There had been a very large increase in population over a relatively short time. In part, this was due to the natural increase of population that had been taking place over the whole region for the previous fifty years. In the period between January 1848 and March 1851, seventy-six children were born on Raasay and Rona. However, the increase was, to a large extent, due to the short sighted measures taken by the MacLeods and their creditors in allowing, indeed encouraging, so many people from other areas to come into Raasay, over the previous five to ten years. By the end of the decade, almost twice as many people were trying to eke a living from the land, at a time when poor seasons and general changes in agricultural revenues and practice made conditions even more difficult.

The impression is given that George Rainy was a practical man, who tried to run his estate on sound economic principles. Since 1845, a combination of poor seasons and potato blight had caused problems for the whole area. The results of these natural disasters had been widely recognised.

Firstly, Rainy needed to know about the people on his estate. To this end he had his ground officer, Duncan Campbell, conduct a census of the people. This census did not include either estate workers, or those who held their land on lease. Perhaps the most astonishing fact to emerge was that one third of the tenants and cottars, living on Raasay at the end of 1847, were not local Raasay people. In cases where one or other parent was from Raasay, the family has been considered to be local. This large group of non-local people had come into Raasay within the previous ten years. As discussed in the previous chapter, they appear to have been encouraged to settle on Raasay by MacLeod or his factor, to increase rental income in the short term. The medium term effect, showing now after at most ten years, was to subject the whole population of tenants and cottars to severe poverty.

During the later years of the 1840s, bad weather again caused poor crops. By this time, far and away the most important crop was the potato. When potato blight hit the area, the population was left starving. The almost total lack of any alternative employment spelt misery for many. Government relief, through the Highland Destitution Relief Board, was given in return for labour, but this was only bare food rations, with no provision for clothing or any other necessities. In the years between 1847 and 1851 Rainy imported several shiploads of meal, selling it at barely cost price. In one five-month period, 1 200 bolls were sold. Thomas Bunning's diary shows that this continued into 1852. On Saturday 17 January 'Vessel arrived with Indian Meal' and on Friday 14 May 'The vessel *Mary Ann MacLeod* discharged meal for Raasay – 100 Bolls'. These conditions prevailed over the whole of the north-west Highlands at this time. No permanent solution was being sought and conditions for most of the people continued to deteriorate.

In 1847 the Central Board for the Relief of Destitution in the Highlands and Islands of Scotland spent £8 15s. on roadworks and £3 on a boat-quay on Rona. They spent a further £14 11s. 8d. on roadworks on Fladda and £21 10s. 9d. for fishing gear for Raasay fishermen. Over the next year or so there were further small stretches of road built at Kyle Rona and Balachuirn. In 1848 roadworks in the south east of the island cost £134 1s.

EVIDENCE TO THE M'NEILL COMMISSION OF 1851

In 1851 Sir John M'Neill headed a Royal Commission that had been asked to look into the problems of destitution of the late 1840s. As the son of a laird, it was to be expected that he would take his evidence from proprietors, and that his report would reflect their attitude. George Rainy of Raasay submitted his views to the commission. This and other records show how he viewed his estate and the people living on it.

When he bought the estate in 1846, the population was about 1,100 By 1851 it was less than a thousand. Some of the better-off families had left and some tenants of the larger farms had either come to the end of their leases or had gone bankrupt. There had been, over the previous four years, three births to each death. There were 104 small tenants, or crofters, and sixty-five cottars. Crofts were generally three and a half to six acres. Many families had nine to twelve people.

At this time it was generally believed that the failure of the potato crop, due to blight and bad weather, was the principal cause of the poverty in the west Highlands. However, Rainy believed that both the fall in the price of cattle and the alteration of the Corn Laws were of more significance, and he argues the case strongly. Until 1846 each crofter was in the habit of selling up to three cows every year at local fairs, for £7–8 each. With this money, he paid his rent and bought meal. By 1851, cattle were going to market in such poor condition that many could not be sold for £3. They were virtually valueless. Larger, heavier breeds from the south, and foreign imports, that were closer to the main British markets, were meeting the demand. This area was at a disadvantage, both because the breed was small and because of distance from the markets. Because of the change in the Corn Laws, there was now generally more permanent grazing and pasture at the expense of corn. Land in the Lowlands, around the centres of population, which had previously been used to grow corn, was now grazing land, on which cattle were raised.

About this time, it was being argued strongly by many that conditions would improve for the people if there were improvements in general agricultural practices. It was said that if draining, trenching and manuring were carried out in larger, enclosed fields, the land would be able to support the present population comfortably. Rainy was scathing about this idea. His evidence to M'Neill points out that these proposals had not been put forward 'by any parties who can appeal to the results of their own experience in these islands in confirmation of their speculative opinion'. By 1851 he had tried these methods and found them wanting. The cost of draining, trenching and enclosing was about £21 per acre. A relatively sheltered eight-acre field of the Home Farm had been drained and trenched, then left fallow for a year. The following year it produced a good crop of turnips, mainly used for the sheep. The next year oats and grass were sown, but by the end of November very little of the crop had been recovered, most having been destroyed by wind and rain. Thus he talked from experience. In this climate, trenching was a disaster as good soil, once turned over, was carried downhill by the rain, and often completely washed away. In 1850–51 meal could be bought for between 12s. 6d. and 14s. per boll on the east coast and he felt that it was a waste of capital and labour to try to produce it on the west coast. The ground was fit for pasture and green crops for winter fodder only. Rainy further pointed out that, even during the best of times in this area, grain had been imported and paid for by the sale of livestock.

The Highland Destitution Committee worked with proprietors to alleviate conditions. In February 1849 the committee agreed the amount of £366 13s. 4d. which they would spend on roads on Raasay if the proprietor provided the same and supported the people until the harvest in September. The committee that year reported a satisfactory inspection both of the condition of the population and the roadworks carried out. It seems that initially Rainy had been dubious about the workforce, as they had not appeared to make any effort to support themselves. However, although at first they had been reluctant, they soon worked willingly in gangs, earnings per day being from 1s. 6d. down to 3d. for little boys. The workmanlike habits and performance of the men employed had impressed the inspector. It was also noted that there had been fewer claims for charitable aid than in previous years, and that both people and proprietor appeared to appreciate and understand one another better. Rainy said that if another year of destitution should occur, he would be willing to continue the works and undertake the care of the people as he had done that year.

Unfortunately the period of destitution continued into the 1850s and because of that, by 1851, Rainy's opinion had to some extent changed. For the previous four years the population had received, and was now dependent on, charitable aid. He points out that prior to 1845, there had been some emigration, but that had stopped.

Rainy also said that in the past many people went to the mainland for work during the season, but now very few did. Those enterprising enough to go, tended to stay away. Changes in general agriculture at this time, probably meant that there were fewer jobs for people to go to on the mainland. Quite possibly that was the main reason for the people not taking up seasonal work away from home. Rainy felt that the people had, on the whole, lost all energy and spirit of enterprise, and were depressed physically and morally. This, he said, was not surprising. Because living was a continuous struggle, they could not afford to be concerned with the future. He does, however, make it clear that they were good people, peaceable, orderly and very patient in enduring their hardships and privations.

George Rainy had seen that despite aid from the Destitution Committee and the money that he had put in himself, things, far from improving, were actually getting worse. The people were, after more than four years, becoming less able to help themselves. In part this was financial, but it was also due to a sense of hopelessness.

He could not afford to continue spending money on relief as he had been doing. The money he spent was neither producing any improvement in circumstances for the people, nor was their any significant gain in agricultural improvement. No one wanted a croft with a rental above £6 per year. He found it impossible to let any holding larger than that. The land was only capable of supporting the people for three months each year. Although, because of that, he had strictly prohibited any sub-letting, he knew that it was still going on. Most people just wanted a small bit of land and a site for a house. He also stated that reckless, early marriages were another factor in the poverty of the people. He felt that men were getting married before they had the means to support themselves and a family.

It had been claimed by some people that the granting of longer leases was the way forward, because then the crofter would have some incentive to improve his land. However, Rainy found that this was not the case. The outlay for improving was known to be over £20 per acre, as well as the time involved. The crofter could not afford the expense, and had to crop annually to support his family.

Any improvements would have to be carried out at the proprietor's expense, but it would only be reasonable to do so if he could then charge a higher rent for the land. Because of the uncertain returns, and the difficulty in leasing larger areas, this was unrealistic. For those reasons, he granted tenancies on a yearly basis.

George Rainy spent a great deal of money on his estate, much of it for the direct benefit of the people. Later in the century Mr Wood was the owner of the estate. In 1883, the Napier Commission was told that Mr Wood spent over £3 000 per year in works to the inhabitants. Commenting on that figure, Rev. Angus Galbraith, minister on Raasay at that time, said 'I have no doubt as to the amount expended; I only wonder it is not greater, although it is small compared with the sum expended yearly in the time of Mr Rainy, senior.'

CLEARANCES FROM RAASAY IN THE LATE 1840S AND EARLY 1850S

Having taken over the estate about the time when conditions were becoming desperate, and seeing that they were deteriorating even further, Rainy did what he believed had to be done to alleviate, as far as he could, conditions for the people. He began with those who were not natives of Raasay. Many of those people now left the island, returning in the main whence they had come. This was done, most likely, by not renewing yearly tenancies. In the three years from about 1848 to 1851 nearly 120 people left the island. In 1851 a further ninety moved away, and the following year saw 120 more leave. Thus, approximately 330 people left Raasay for Skye and the mainland between 1848 and the early 1850s. Of those, at least forty had come to Raasay after the 1841 census had been taken in June, and left before the 1851 census. A further 110 appear in the 1851 census only. The remaining tenancy agreements were now, on the whole, with local Raasay people, although there were still many locals without tenancies.

It appears that many of these removals were by agreement. There may have been some incentives given. The method, for most, seems to have been 'the carrot' rather than 'the stick'. It is clear that the estate did assist in the removals, as shown by Thomas Bunning's diary. In May 1852 he notes that someone, perhaps Duncan Campbell, was 'ferrying the sheep belonging to the tenants of Manish and Screapadal'. The tenants of these townships moved to Skye, so presumably the sheep were taken over there for them. There are some, however, that are noted as 'Removed', or 'Ejected' and in a few instances 'Warned Out'. These people all left to go to Skye or the mainland. None of them emigrated from Raasay, although some may have emigrated later.

Having drastically reduced the population, Rainy now took such measures as he could to try to control things. It was generally seen by now that the sub-division of land, and consequent earlier marriages, had been one of the key factors in causing the general population rise in the Highlands. Tenants were now banned from allowing any more cottars on their land, probably with the threat of eviction if they ignored the ruling. He also insisted that any proposed marriages on the estate should not go ahead without his express permission. Marriages did take place on the estate at this time, with the owner's permission. There is no information, today, as to how many marriages were actually refused.

These measures, particularly the latter, were naturally resented. One man, John MacLeod from Arnish, did not have Mr Rainy's permission when, on 18 June 1850, he married Margaret MacLeod, also from Arnish. The estate retaliated. Men were sent to burn down their house. This left them without shelter, the most specific indication that Rainy's instructions were to be followed. Donald MacLeod, Kyle Rona, gave details of this to Lord Napier. He said

> Mr Rainy enacted a rule that no one should marry on the island. There was one man there who married in spite of him and because he did so he put him out of his father's house and that man went to a bothy, to a sheep cot. Mr Rainy then came and demolished the sheep cot upon him and extinguished his fire and neither friend nor anyone else dared to give him a night's shelter. He was not allowed entrance into any house. His name was John MacLeod from Arnish.

The 1851 census shows John and Margaret living with his father in Arnish. On 3 August 1852 they left Liverpool on the *Ontario*, arriving in Sydney, Australia on 15 December that year. With them were their son, Malcolm, and Margaret's sister, Hannah.

EMIGRATION FROM RAASAY TO AUSTRALIA – 1852 AND 1854

Largely as a result of Sir John M'Neill's report in 1851, the Skye Emigration Society, later absorbed by the Highlands and Islands Emigration Society (HIES), was set up to assist those who wanted to emigrate to Australia but could not afford to do so. Their aim was to try to help people to help themselves. The society was absolutely against any kind of compulsory emigration; neither did it actively encourage emigration. Having said that, it was certainly the case that many people sincerely believed that emigration was the only way to help both the people and the estates at this time. It must be assumed, therefore, that the benefits of emigration would have been stressed. The society raised money by public subscription. Aid from the society was in the form of a loan that had to be repaid within one year. The proprietor was also expected to give financial support to intending emigrants from his estate, both in the form of writing off any rent arrears and in meeting one third of the cost of emigration.

Many people from Raasay emigrated to Australia. There were two waves of emigration, in 1852 and 1854. Initially, some families approached George Rainy, with a request for assistance to emigrate. He made it clear that he would support anyone who wished to go. The notes from the butler's diary show that various people came to Raasay in connection with emigration, particularly in the period March to June 1852. Mr Harry MacDonald, factor for the estate, was involved with the necessary documentation. Doctor MacLeod was concerned with medical checks and inoculations.

As well as coming over to see emigrants, Dr MacLeod was also called to see people who needed his services. When in Raasay, the doctor stayed at Raasay House, the costs of his visits being met by the proprietor. In April 1851 he was over for a week, going each day to Fearns 'on a Black Pony'. In May 1852, Dr MacLeod was called and came over to 'visit sick people at Fearns'. This refers to an outbreak of typhoid that claimed the lives of some Fearns people at that time. Rachel Gillies, the wife of Iain Bàn MacLeod, died in May and their baby, aged just two months, died one month later.

Before they left the island, clothes and shoes were distributed to intending emigrants. Duncan Campbell, manager of the estate, arranged the sale of sheep belonging to emigrants and their removal from Raasay. Although the HIES did give assistance to some Raasay emigrants, many others went without assistance from them. Some of those were able to contribute a part of the costs themselves although others could not.

On Saturday 6 September 1851 Mr Kingston came to Raasay 'on Emigration business'. The following Monday he 'went to Fearns and Balmeanach'. Mr Bunning does not note any further visits with respect to emigration until the following year. On Friday 26 March 1852, 'Mr MacDougall at Raasay to meet the Fearns People and to take the statements of such as wish to Emigrate'. The following day 'A large packet of shoes for Emigrants arrived per Duntroon Steamer'. Mr MacDonald, the factor, and Dr MacLeod came over on Monday 5 April, 'to meet the intended Emigrants'. They left the following day. On Friday 9, Mr MacDonald was back 'to fill up the Papers for the Emigrants'. A week later he was back again with Dr MacLeod, who had come to 'vaccinate the intended Emigrants'. Monday 26 saw the factor 'distributing clothes among the Emigrants', and he was doing so again with Dr MacLeod on 3 and 4 May, the day before the first families left the island. On Wednesday 16 June, Duncan Campbell collected 'sixty-one sheep belonging to the Raasay Emigrants and other tenants leaving the Island' and sold them to a Mr Weir.

It is clear that Rainy did as much as he could to assist those who emigrated. He paid for the clothes and shoes distributed, and the cost of the passage to Liverpool where they left this country. Arrears of rent were written off. Some of this expenditure would have been recovered by the sale of stock belonging to these people, but given the low market price of cattle at the time, it is unlikely that much was recovered. There were many visits by the factor and the doctor to the island. These visits too would have been paid for by the proprietor. Essentially, therefore, he met all the costs that the people could not meet themselves. However, it must be said that by going, these emigrants were helping the estate, particularly if there were to be further years of poor harvests. It can be argued ad infinitum as to whether or not these emigrations were by choice or by force. Available evidence suggests that the people made the choice, and that Rainy took no part in it, except to make it clear that he would assist with finance where necessary. The people who received financial assistance from Rainy were almost exclusively Raasay people. Very few, if any, of those who had come onto Raasay in the decade before 1846 when he bought the estate were given financial assistance to emigrate. They were moved out, but they moved back to Skye and to the mainland. Therefore, it does not appear that Rainy, either himself or by instructions to others, forcibly removed anyone from Raasay or Rona with a view to making them emigrate. He, as much as the people, was a victim of economic circumstances, albeit one who was not, himself, going to starve.

In May 1852, seven families (thirty-four people) emigrated from Fearns and

Hallaig. They left Raasay on the *Islay* on 5 May for Glasgow. The butler notes 'Islay Steamer passed south at 11 p.m.'. Bell Gillies, who left on this boat with her husband and family, died in Glasgow Infirmary from typhoid. She must have been ill before leaving Raasay, as there was known to have been an outbreak of the disease in Fearns in May of that year. The family carried on to Australia. A further twelve families (sixty-six people) left Raasay on 23 June on the *Cygnet*. The diary states 'Twelve Families, in all seventy-nine souls, left Raasay per Sygnet Steamer for Glasgow as Emigrants to Australia. The Sygnet came into Raasay Bay at ½ past 2 p.m. and in fifteen minutes the Emigrants were all on Board.'[1] None of those Raasay people was assisted by the HIES. In July six families (eighteen people) left from Upper Fearns and Arnish, all but one receiving HIES assistance. On 6 July 1852, Thomas Bunning recorded that 'Three Families, consisting of eighteen Persons, left Raasay per Duntroon Steamer for Glasgow as Emigrants to Australia'.

They went from Glasgow to Liverpool and from there to Australia. The only records, in this country, of emigrants and the boats in which they sailed are those of the HIES. They recorded details of people whom they assisted to go. Some of the boats that took HIES assisted emigrants also carried others. Thus, it is not possible to say which boats many of the Raasay emigrants sailed on, but those leaving Liverpool about May and June 1852 were the *Borneuf* on 26 May 1852, arriving in Geelong, Victoria on 3 September. The *Medina* sailed on 25 June, arriving at Adelaide on 19 October. Those who left Raasay in July 1852 went on three different ships. The *Georgiana* sailed on 13 July, arriving at Geelong on 17 September. The *Ontario* sailed on 3 August, arriving at Sydney on 15 December. The *Ticonderoga* sailed on 4 August, arriving at Melbourne on 22 December.

In September 1852, Thomas Bunning's entry reads 'William Bunning left Raasay for Glasgow to join the Ship *Typhoon* for Australia'. He must surely have felt apprehensive as his eldest son, aged no more than eighteen at the time, left. In September just four years later, his wife died and was buried in the old cemetery.

There was no further emigration from Raasay to Australia until June 1854, when a further 129 people left, all with HIES assistance. Most of them were from the east side, Fearns, Hallaig and Leac, along with a few families from Balachuirn, Balmeanach and Holoman where they had gone to live after they had decided to emigrate and given up their tenancies. On 6 June 1854 the *Chevalier* put into Churchton Bay at 4 a.m., and took those emigrants on board. They all sailed from Liverpool together on the *Edward Johnstone* on 17 June, arriving at Portland, Victoria on 3 September.

James Ross, factor for the estate, gave evidence to the Deer Forest Commission in 1893. Ross was not factor in Rainy's time, but took his information from estate records and by questioning 'old residents on the island'. He stated that

> In 1851 four families in Fearns applied to Mr Rainy for assistance to emigrate to Australia. He promised to assist, not only these four families, but all who cared to go. On this offer becoming known, a good many people from the townships of Fearns and four cottars from Hallaig took advantage of it ...

The people had by this time sunk into such a state of poverty that only two families out of all those who wished to emigrate could raise sufficient money and the necessary outfit for the voyage. Mr Rainy took the cows belonging to the tenants of Fearns which they were unable to dispose of otherwise, as part payment for outfit and passage money, which he paid for all, except the two families already mentioned. He also paid full fares and expenses for them all to the port of embarkation, and full passage money to Australia for all those over 55 years of age. He likewise gave up all the arrears of rent due by those emigrating, which were very heavy.

Family connections being a good deal broken up by this emigration, most of those remaining in Fearns, as well as those in the townships of Leac and Hallaig left for Australia in 1853 [This was in fact 1854]. These last were granted free passages to Australia, and had outfits provided and all expenses paid by the emigration agent, acting on behalf of the Australian Government. In these cases Mr Rainy also gave up all claim to the arrears of rent due.

The 1850s

When George Rainy bought the estate in 1846, Suisnish and Eyre had been let to tacksmen. By 1849, they had both given up their tacks and returned to Skye. In 1850 the tacks of Suisnish, including the lands of Glen, Eyre and the farm of Glam and Brae, previously run by the estate, was granted to Royston MacKenzie who ran them as a sheep farm. He brought in his own workers and shepherds, and ran his own enterprise within the estate of Raasay. Both he and his wife, Hughina, were from Assynt. They lived at Suisnish House. She was very supportive of the Free Church in Raasay.

In Castle, Farquhar MacRae from Kintail, who had thirty cows and sixty sheep, was the tenant until he gave up the farm in 1851, when he left the island. The five cottars in Castle also left at this time. Three of them are noted as 'Ejected'. This tack was now taken over by Royston MacKenzie who had a shepherd living there.

MacKenzie also intended to take over Doire Domhain in 1851. However, Iain Mòr MacSuain, John MacSween, was the only tenant there at that time. It is interesting to note, from Figure 6/1, that Iain Mòr was the most substantial local tenant on the island at that time. He had ten cows, two heifers, four stirks and eighty sheep. By 1841 he was living on the west side of the island, an area dominated from the time of the MacLeods by themselves and their tacksmen. It is said that he had been moved there from Hallaig by the MacLeods. Most likely he had been in Upper Hallaig which appears to have been cleared in the 1830s. It seems likely, therefore, that Iain Mòr, descended from the MacSweens who had held Raasay when it belonged to the church at Snizort, was still enjoying some of the benefits of that time. Perhaps that is the reason he was given another tenancy when Upper Hallaig was cleared. After he died in 1851, his family was moved to Dry Harbour, and in 1852 Doire Domhain was added to MacKenzie's sheep farm.

In 1851 there were four tenants at Manish. Three of them 'gave up their lands

Figure 6/1. Stock held by tenants and cottars in 1851.

Township	Description		Cow	Heifer	Stirk	Sheep
Clachan	1 tenant, 1 miller, 1 herd	**Total**	7	1	—	14
Eyre & Suisnish	None					
Balachuirn	7 tenants, 1 grasskeeper	**Total**	22	5	6	84
Balmeanach	4 tenants	**Total**	15	1	8	26
Balachuirn & Balmeanach		**Total**	37	6	14	110
Brae & Glam	none					
Doire Domhain	1 tenant	**Total**	10	2	4	80
Manish	4 tenants	**Total**	16	10	7	80
Doire Domhain & Manish		**Total**	26	12	11	160
Arnish	5 tenants	Total	15	1	5	84
Torran	1 tenant	Total	8	2	1	60
Arnish & Torran		**Total**	23	3	6	144
Fladda	6 tenants	**Total**	19	3	4	62
Eilean Taigh	1 tenant	**Total**	4	—	1	12
Kyle Rona	9 tenants, 1 cottar	Total	20	11	6	123
Umachan	3 tenants	Total	12	2	3	60
Kyle Rona & Umachan		**Total**	32	13	9	183
Castle	1 tenant, 2 cottars	**Total**	30	10	6	60
North Screapadal	6 tenants, 1 cottar	Total	26	4	11	154
South Screapadal	1 tenant	Total	12	3	8	300
North & South Screapadal		**Total**	38	7	19	454
Upper Hallaig	1 tenant	Total	5	—	3	300
Lower Hallaig	9 tenants	Total	20	3	9	68
Upper & Lower Hallaig		**Total**	25	3	12	368
Leac	6 tenants, 1 cottar	**Total**	16	4	5	69
Lower Fearns	10 tenants, 1 teacher	Total	19	9	6	100
Upper Fearns	15 tenants, 1 cottar	Total	37	8	9	191
Upper & Lower Fearns		**Total**	56	17	15	291
Doire na Guaille	2 tenants	Total	10	3	5	26
Big Harbour	1 tenant	Total	8	4	4	40
Dry Harbour	12 tenants, 2 cottars	Total	39	8	9	119
Rona		**Total**	57	15	18	185

Figure 6/2. Summary of stock held by tenants and cottars in 1851.

Township		Cow	Heifer	Stirk	Sheep
Clachan		7	1	—	14
Eyre & Suisnish	None				
Balachuirn & Balmeanach		37	6	14	110
Brae & Glam	None				
Doire Domhain & Manish		26	12	11	160
Arnish & Torran		23	3	6	144
Fladda		19	3	4	62
Eilean Taigh		4	—	1	12
Kyle Rona & Umachan		32	13	9	183
Castle		30	10	6	60
North & South Screapadal		38	7	19	454
Upper & Lower Hallaig		25	3	12	368
Leac		16	4	5	69
Upper & Lower Fearns		56	17	15	291
Raasay	**Total**	**313**	**79**	**102**	**1927**
Rona	**Total**	**57**	**15**	**18**	**185**

Note: Eyre, Suisnish, Brae & Glam formed the sheep farm held by Royston MacKenzie. His stock is not included in the above tables.

by agreement' in November 1852 and moved back to Skye. The only local man there, Donald MacLeod, went back to Arnish to live with his father, Calum mac Iain 'ic Ailein.

By 1852, the west side of the island, from Eyre in the south to Manish in the north, was held by Royston MacKenzie. The only exceptions were the Home Farm and the townships of Balachuirn and Balmeanach which were held by Rainy. The Home Farm would have taken in the area from Clachan north to the boundary with Balachuirn. In that area lived estate employees, whether incomers or local people, and others as might be expected in the main centre of the island. The postman and the miller lived there, as well as some cottars, who probably made their living by fishing and occasional work for the estate. The tenants in Balmeanach had been taken onto Raasay by the MacLeods before they left. Now three of them returned to Skye, and the only local man there emigrated in 1854. This township was then used to house those people from the east side who had given up their land and were waiting to emigrate. Those families who were not locals in Balachuirn left the island.

Isabella Murchison held South Screapadal, running 300 sheep until the mid 1850s. The tenant in Upper Hallaig, Alexander MacRae, also had 300 sheep. He too gave up in the mid 1850s. The people from North Screapadal had returned to Skye by 1852. As these leases came up, Royston MacKenzie took them over.

Of thirty-seven households in Upper and Lower Fearns in 1851, only eleven stayed on Raasay. Only three of the nine families in Leac stayed on the island. In Hallaig, only four out of fifteen households remained. It appears that the

Munros on Raasay lived in Hallaig, but it is impossible to say now if they had always lived there, or if they had been moved from the south end in the 1830s, or indeed from 'the centre' in the previous decade.

Evidence by the people of Raasay and Rona in 1883 to the Napier Commission told of forced emigrations to Australia. Donald MacLeod of Kyle Rona, told of the people leaving in Rainy's time being sent away against their will. Alasdair Ruadh, Alexander MacLennan from Fladda, repeated the same story. He said, 'I was at the quay when the people were sent off and they were like lambs separated from their mothers. There was one old man there who said – should I go to Australia I may die on my arrival, I should prefer remaining in Raasay but I must go.'

The evidence given by the crofters to the Deer Forest Commission in 1893 gave a different view. It was more in agreement with that given by James Ross, the factor. Donald MacRae from Balachuirn, told that

> The clearances were made by Mr George Rainy, the proprietor, between 1851 and 1853, when a large number were sent to Australia, who expected that those who remained in the townships would be much better off. When those were got away, the remaining tenants in the thirteen townships were violently and forcibly cleared out of the country, their houses being pulled down about their heads, their fires put out, and some of the people taken to the steamers half dead. Thereafter these townships were made into a sheep farm.

This supported the evidence given by Tormod Dhòmhnaill, Norman Gillies from Oscaig. He said

> On the potato famine the proprietor, Mr George Rainy, started public works, and for some time gave the people work and a fair wage. When these works ceased, a number of the crofter tenants emigrated to Australia, at the expense of the proprietor. Before this the crofting townships were overcrowded, and a few left each township. Those who remained expected that the condition would thus be improved as all the towns were overcrowded before. But those who remained were afterwards evicted, every one of them by the proprietor about 1853, and the whole of the following townships made into one sheep farm.
>
> It is right to add that the two glens were cleared before Mr Rainy's time, and that if young Mr Rainy had lived he would have undone much of the evil caused by his father on the evil advice of the local factor whom he afterwards found out in his true character and dismissed.

When Alasdair Ruadh, Alexander MacLennan from Fladda, had given evidence to the Napier Commission ten years earlier, he confirmed that the factor was harsh. He says, 'At the time Rainy sent the people away Mr Harry MacDonald, father of Mr Alexander MacDonald Portree, was the factor, and if any one of us happened to be 10s. in arrears we would be served with a summons of removal and would have to pay 10s. for the summons.'

From the time of the 1841 census the MacLennans had been living on Fladda, Alasdair was born in the south of Raasay. Although he is clearly talking about the time of George Rainy, it is possible that the serving of summons of removal happened about 1870, when Rainy's son owned the estate. The factor, however, was still Harry MacDonald.

Iain Aonghais, John Gillies from Umachan told the Napier Commission that two families had been moved to Umachan from Hallaig because they would not go to Australia. This would appear to confirm that it was after the emigrations that the forced evictions took place.

Therefore, it seems that after the people had emigrated in 1854, or perhaps when all those who wished to emigrate had been identified, either Rainy or his factor set about clearing all those who were left from the east side townships. This seems to have been done forcibly, the people going either to Skye or to the north end of Raasay. The people of the north end remembered most clearly that part of the process which had affected them most directly. They had to make room within their townships for people forced to go there. They remembered the cruel, forced evictions.

By about 1854, Royston MacKenzie had all the ground from Eyre in the south end, to Manish and Castle in the north, on both east and west sides of the island, except the Home Farm, which was run by Rainy for himself, and Balachuirn and Balmeanach. Both these townships had had some tenants. There were also some tenants, although very few, in the townships within the Home Farm ground. Otherwise the island was entirely given over to sheep and a few shepherds. The population was now from Arnish northwards, and on the islands of Rona, Fladda and Eilean Taigh. In 1773, at the time of Johnson and Boswell's visit, the north end of Raasay and the islands had been used only to graze cattle. That area now held the bulk of the population.

The pattern for the settlement of the population had now been set, and it would remain thus for the next seventy years, until the people in desperation took matters into their own hands. The following figures are from the 1861 census. The south end had only Royston MacKenzie's family in Suisnish. Clachan had about eighteen per cent of the population. The townships of Oscaig, Holoman, Balachuirn and Balmeanach had the same. Castle, Fearns and Hallaig had only one family each, accounting for four per cent. Torran and Arnish had nine families, ten per cent. The north end, including Rona and Fladda, had fifty per cent of the total population of Raasay. That is made up of Rona, twenty-five per cent, Fladda eight per cent and Raasay north of Arnish seventeen per cent. The total population was now only 578, half the number that were on the island when Rainy bought it in 1846.

Although in percentage terms the number of people in the north end and the islands had increased, there was virtually no change in the number of people on Rona and Fladda. The increase is accounted for by the addition of the two lighthouse keepers and their families who now tended the lighthouse that had been built there about 1857. On the north end of Raasay, there had been an increase in numbers, from seventy-three to one hundred, owing to people being moved there and natural increase.

Since 1846, in spite of the disruption caused by people leaving the island for various destinations, those in the north end got on with their lives as they had done in the past. On the whole, they probably had little to do with the estate in the south end. Because of lack of roads, their nearest 'main centre' was Portree, just across the water. They had boats. Indeed boats and the sea were an important part of their lives. The land there could not, and never had been able to support the people for more than a part of the year. They made their living primarily from fishing. From the 1700s, when the men had gone to the herring busses, they had been fishermen and seamen. Now, some had their own boats. Many went to the east of Scotland for work at the herring fishing. That meant being away from home for a great part of the year. After the spring work was done, they left home, staying away for the season. Some seasons were poor and they made little money; others were more profitable.

Teachers from the SSPCK were still employed on the island. In the north end, there were schools at Dry Harbour, Rona and at Torran. John MacLeod from Assynt, moved to Dry Harbour at sometime between 1848 and 1851. Prior to that, he had been in Malacleit, North Uist. About 1855 John MacLeod moved to Torran, and James Urquhart, also from Assynt, came to Dry Harbour. He remained in there until his death in 1874.

Life in the south end was almost entirely centred round the mansion house and the estate. The people who were in this part of the island were, for the most part, employed directly by George Rainy working for the estate. Wages were 12s. per week. Houses were provided rent free and each man had as much potato land as he wished to plant. Coal was used here, as there is little peat in the south of the island. Coal came by boat, and was landed and carted by the proprietor's horses, free of charge. In April 1851 the *Bell Mary* arrived with coal. 'All people very busy working on Coals' one week later.

In January 1851 Malcolm MacQueen, the smith, was drowned at Portree. His wife, Marion MacInnes from Iona, and three young children left Raasay later that month. The family had moved to Raasay from Glasgow about 1842.

There was a regular boat service between Glasgow and Stornoway in the summer months. These steamers regularly called in to Clachan Bay on their way north and south, to pick up or drop off passengers and goods. The steamer lay at anchor in the bay and small boats ferried goods and passengers ashore. Thomas Bunning's diary notes various boats on this run. The service began between Glasgow and Stornoway in June 1846 with the *Mary Jane*, built by Sir James Matheson of Stornoway, and called after his wife. Two years later, the *Marquis of Stafford* joined the *Mary Jane*. The *Duntroon Castle* began the fortnightly Glasgow to Skye service in 1850. The *Islay* had been on a Glasgow to Islay service, but this was later extended to Skye and Lewis. The *Cygnet* is also mentioned. In 1853 the *Chevalier* was in service. She had been built for all-year sailings between Glasgow and Lewis, but was wrecked after only two years in service. The *Clansman* replaced her in 1855 and along with the *Dolphin* catered for Mull as well as Skye and Lewis. This regular service must have been very useful for George Rainy and others who had interests both in the area and in the south, making it possible for them to travel easily between the two.

Many visitors to Raasay, as well as George Rainy and his wife, used this service. The steamer appeared to deliver 'a Bread Basket' from Glasgow on her way past Raasay. Occasionally unforeseen circumstances could delay the boat. At the beginning of April 1851 she had to lie off the Black Rock at Portree, waiting for the weather to moderate. On Saturday 23 August that year she 'put into Sconser Bay at 8 p.m. with Lord MacDonald'. In May 1852 the *Duntroon* 'arrived at 12 o'clock today being two days after her time, by some accident to her Boilers'.

The estate also had their own boats. The yacht, the *Falcon*, was for pleasure, and business trips to Portree and elsewhere. There was also the 'Gig Boat', which seems to have been used more as a general work-boat. Both were kept busy taking people back and forth to Portree on estate business, as well as on pleasure trips for the owner and his guests. In April 1857, Duncan Matheson, from Plockton, came to Raasay to take charge of the yacht.

Produce from the Home Farm was used in Raasay House, and any surplus was sold in Portree. The butler records on 25 October 1851 that 'a cow killed, half for the House and half sold at Portree by Mr Anderson'. In December that year, John Rennie, the head gardener, 'went to Applecross for seeds with the new boat'. He returned the following day, but 'left the boat at Screapadal'. In August 1851 at least twenty-nine fine salmon were taken from Screapadal, six of which were sold in Portree. In 1852, however, the estate appears to have leased the salmon fishing rights. In May the bag net, with ropes and anchor was 'sold to the man that has taken the Raasay fishing'. A bull was killed in December 1859, and the meat was presumably sold. The butler's diary tells that 714 lbs was sold at 3*d*. per pound, realising £8 18*s*. 6*d*. The hide fetched 14*s*. 2*d*.

At the end of May 1852 although we are told that 'two ripe cherries pulled in Raasay Garden' we are not informed who ate them. There are various notes regarding crops. In 1851 by the end of October, they had 'Finished cutting the corn at Oscaig' and carted 'a few loads of Barley'. At the end of March 1852, they were 'Clearing stones of trenched field'. By mid May the 'Lower Field was sown with bare or Barley'. By the end of August they had 'Finished Cutting the Oats'. In October 1855 'Two Turnips taken from Church park weighing 15 lbs and 4 lbs, girth 34 inches, purple top'. Towards the end of April 1857, they 'Commenced sowing Barley on the West side of front Park'. In October they began to plough the 'Middle Park at Oscaig'.

In February 1852 a 'New Bell erected at the Square'. The 'Square' was the Steading in Clachan. The steading at Glam was also referred to as the 'Square', but it was not built until the time of the Woods' ownership of Raasay, after 1876. Two days later it was noted 'A new Rope for the Bell'. So it was then fully operational!

In February 1856, 'The Heather Barn was destroyed by fire, supposed to be by a spark from the Ploughman's Chimney'. The ploughman and other estate workers had living quarters on either side of the top entrance to the square at the steading. This barn was probably the same one as was described by Boswell in such detail in 1773. It was rebuilt on the same site, behind the steading.

It is surprising that no attempt to build a pier or any other kind of landing was made until 1854. Johnson had commented in 1773, how relatively simple it would have been to construct a landing area out of the rocks in front of Raasay

House. On Friday 26 May 1854 the 'First Stone of new Pier was laid'. This pier, although very close to Raasay House, would have been screened by one of the roundels. Two roundels, round areas planted with trees and surrounded by iron railings on either side and to the front of the mansion house, were planted specifically to hide any workmanlike activity that might have spoilt the view from the front of the house. It is not known whether they had been planted in the MacLeods' time, or later. On Friday 17 December 1858 'some of the pier was washed down by heavy seas'. Thomas Bunning did not note when the building of the pier was completed, but the weather must have been very rough to damage the pier. The pier, well constructed, still stands today and, although tidal, it is used by pleasure boats on a regular basis. It is generally referred to as the Wee Pier or the Old Pier.

Then, as now, the weather was commented on. In mid October 1851 the 'Parks were flooded by Rain'. There were gales in January 1852 when 'Man nor Horse not able to stand to work today'. During the winter months, quite often the 'Church thinly attended' because of bad weather. On Tuesday 27 February 1855 'after a severe frost of seven weeks duration great Thaw set in this evening'. The end of the year also saw severe frosts. On Tuesday 11 December there were 'People sliding on Loch'. In June 1859 the 'Farm people stop Turnip sowing owing to dry weather which lasted eight weeks'.

It is clear from the butler's diary that life in the house became much more interesting when George Rainy and his family were living on the Island. They had many family friends to stay, as well as those that came over on business. The yacht was used for pleasure trips, to see the surrounding area. One trip to the Storr resulted in the party being 'caught in a Thunder Storm on top of Stor'. On another occasion there was a trip to the 'Chuchullens'. Yet another was to the Quirang, when they left 'at 7 a.m. and returned at midnight'. They went to Scalpay and to Sconser 'to pick shells' returning at the more reasonable time of 6 p.m. On 31 May 1852 'Her Majesty's Tender anchored in the bay – Capt. Smith passed the evening in Raasay House'.

Those were the days of shooting and fishing trips. In 1852 a party of four men 'caught near 200 trout at Dun Caan loch'. The following day there was a trip to Rona to shoot seals. Rona, it seems, also had otters for shooting practice. Birds were not exempt either. A golden eagle was shot in October 1858.

On Friday 27 June 1856, there was an accident recorded by Thomas Bunning:

This morning about 10 o'clock, a large fishing boat, belonging to Fladda, Raasay, was struck by a squall and was sunk. All hands, six in number, perished. The names of the men were John and Donald Gillies, Fladda, two sons of Malcolm MacLeod, Fladda, a son of Donald Gillies, Torran and old Malcolm MacKenzie. The boat was going to Portree.

This is the first drowning relating to Raasay that was recorded officially in the register of deaths, which had begun only the previous year. That tells that the men were 'drowned in consequence of the upset of an open boat'. Malcolm MacKenzie, aged fifty, was the weaver from Torran. The family of Calum mac Thormoid, Malcolm MacLeod of Fladda, was particularly affected by this tragedy. Calum and his wife, Margaret, lost two sons, Angus – aged twenty-three, and Norman – aged eighteen. Both boys were unmarried. Their sister, Anna Bhàn, lost her husband, John – aged thirty-two. His brother, Donald, was twenty-eight. John and Donald were the sons of Ronald Gillies and Betsy Nicolson. John and Anne Gillies had been married only eighteen months. Calum Gillies, aged twenty-one, was the son of Donald Gillies, Torran, and a cousin of Anna Bhàn.

SCHOOLS AND THE CHURCH

During the 1840s the SSPCK had provided two teachers, Donald MacKinnon and John Cameron. As they do not appear on the 1851 census, it may be assumed that they had left before that. The SSPCK records do not mention Raasay after 1850. Mrs MacDonald, who taught all branches of 'female industry', in the 1840s cannot be identified in the 1851 census.

By 1851 Alexander MacMillan, the Gaelic teacher, had moved from Balachuirn to Lower Fearns. Presumably he had left there by 1854 when all the people from that area had left, most of them emigrating. In 1861 the census records that he was in Oscaig and had retired. He lived at the Craobhan Mòr, the Big Trees near the cattle grid at the north end of Oscaig. There he taught Latin and Greek for a time, and had at least one scholar who had come to Raasay from Braes to take advantage of his teaching. Alexander MacMillan died in 1871, by which time he was living with his son, John, in Clachan. Although the census of that year indicates that he was living at the 'Gardener's Cottage', he was not in the house known by that name today. He lived either in the house now known as the 'Old Post Office', or in another in that general vicinity.

In April 1851 Murdo MacDonald from Lewis, the Inspector of Gaelic Schools, stayed at Raasay House. He appears in the census for that year, and also in the butler's diary. The result of his inspection is not known. In July 1853 Rev. Roderick MacLeod, minister of Snizort, and Rev. MacDougall, minister of Raasay, inspected the schools. Rev. Kippen, minister of Raasay, and Mr MacPhail, inspected the Torran School in 1859.

In November 1858 the opening of the new school and schoolhouse at Clachan was celebrated with a tea party for the children after which they were addressed by Rev. Roderick MacLeod. The name of the teacher is not given.

Rev. James Kippen came to Raasay in 1857, replacing Rev. MacDougall who had left in 1855. Rev. Kippen remained on the island until 1866. Rev. Robert Rainy, nephew of the proprietor, was on Raasay during August 1859. He took the services while he was there. He later became principal of the Free Church College in Edinburgh. John MacLeod, schoolmaster at Torran, was ordained an elder on 4 April 1858.

The 1860s

From the 1860s information about people and conditions are available from more varied sources, and we no longer have to rely on the proprietor and estate records to find out about life on Raasay.

One such source is the census of 1861. As with all the censuses, Raasay was divided into three districts. The first of these was the south end, including Balachuirn and Hallaig. Arnish, Torran, Castle, Umachan and Fladda made up the second district. In the north end, Kyle Rona was included with the island of Rona in the third district.

Daniel MacMillan, the eighteen-year-old son of the former teacher, covered the south end. Fearns, Hallaig and Balmeanach had only one family in each village. In this area all the houses have some rooms with a window, most having two. The seven houses in Balachuirn each have three. Otherwise the most substantial houses, as expected, are Raasay House with thirty-one windows, the manse with nine, Royston MacKenzie in Suisnish House with ten, the Schoolhouse with four, Peter Nicolson in the shop with five, John Bethune the miller with six and John Rennie the gardener with eight.

Housing in the second district is very different. John MacLeod, the teacher at Torran, was the enumerator for that area. He notes that 'owing to the regulation of the Proprietor, the population is limited and widely scattered'. Both houses in Torran have windows. Three of the seven houses in Arnish have one window each. On Fladda, two houses have two windows, four have one, but five have none. In Umachan only two of the eight houses have a window.

In the north end conditions are even worse. James Urquhart, the teacher on Rona, was the enumerator for this district. He had had to cross the ferry twice, once to deliver and once to collect the schedules. The houses were 'scattered here and there' so it 'was not easy for me to keep the Schedules in a proper order'. However, in spite of that, 'no persons were missed'. None of the fourteen houses in Kyle Rona, Scorr or Doire Dubh had any windows. On Rona, the two lighthouse families had three and four windows respectively. The schoolhouse had three windows, and one of the two houses in Big Harbour had a window. Fifteen houses in Dry Harbour and five in Doire na Guaille were without windows.

The teacher in Clachan in 1861 was Abraham Park, aged twenty-four, from Rutherglen. His wife, Janet, is shown in the census as the 'schoolmistress'. It is not known when this family came to Raasay, but they had gone before February 1862. On Saturday 1, Mr Stewart, the new schoolmaster, arrived on the island, opening the school on Tuesday 4. He had gone by 1871 when the teacher was Alexander MacFarlane from Lochs, Lewis. In the north end, James Urquhart was at Dry Harbour, and John MacLeod at Torran.

In February 1860 there was an outbreak of smallpox at Umachan. Torcall MacLeod died on 7 February and was buried at Clachan. Within two weeks both his sister and his young daughter had also died. They were both buried on Rona. Torcall's wife and another child survived.

The south end of the island continued according to the pattern set during the previous decade. The estate had control over most aspects of life here. The proprietor was far and away the major employer. Royston MacKenzie employed a few shepherds. The teacher, the minister, the shopkeeper and possibly the miller are the only people with employment independent of the estate. Although Raasay had a visit from Mr Beal, the Post Office surveyor, along with the factor in March

1861, it is not until 1881 that a postmistress is recorded in the census. In December 1860, Thomas Bunning records that the servants were put on Board wages.

An accident occurred in Portree Bay, just after noon on 22 May 1861, when three estate workers from Raasay were drowned. John Rennie, aged thirty-six, was the head gardener on the estate. He was from Whithorn, Wigton-shire and had come to Raasay about the time that George Rainy took over the estate. In 1850 he married Catherine MacNeill from Tiree, who was also working on Raasay at the time. Alexander Finlayson, aged twenty-seven, was from Peinchorran, Braes. An agricultural labourer, he was living at Clachan with his wife and two young children. Murdo MacLeod, unmarried, was from Clachan. His parents were John and Jane MacLeod. His father, John, was a ferryman in 1841 when the MacLeods still owned the estate, but later census' show him as a labourer and fisherman, although the family remained in Clachan.

George Haygarth Rainy: 1863–1872

On 9 June 1863, George Rainy died in London. His son, George Haygarth Rainy, did not come of age until March 1866, when he was able to take control of the estate himself. Until then it must be assumed, affairs were conducted by the factor. Estate business continued. In June 1865, 1,417 feet of larch timber was sold to the master of the schooner *Flora MacDonald* at 9d. per foot for the total sum of £53 2s. 9d. The trade in timber from the estate, that had been mentioned in the time of the MacLeods, was still ongoing. Further alterations were made to Raasay House in 1865, when the billiard room on the upper floor of the west wing was created. In October the joists were laid, and in December the joiners began roofing the new addition. On Monday 19 March 1866, Thomas Bunning records that there was 'Great rejoicing at Raasay of the coming of age of G. H. Rainy. A great Bonfire on the top of Duncan, Rona and other places'.

Evidence given to the two Royal Commissions in 1883 and 1893 indicates that young Mr Rainy was highly thought of. Iain Uilleim, John MacLean from Oscaig, told the Deer Forest Commission that Mr Rainy had intended to restore the grazing lands to the Balachuirn tenants that had been taken away from them about 1854. In 1868 Royston MacKenzie's lease was being renewed. He offered £1 000 per annum if the tenants were removed from Balachuirn, but £900 if they were not. Rainy wrote to Harry MacDonald, the factor, to the effect that he could have the lease for £970 per annum without their removal. MacDonald was not to accept any less than £950. This was successful, and MacKenzie paid £970. At this time, Rainy was holding out against any more ground being given up to the sheep farm.

In 1866 the tenants of Dry Harbour felt able to approach Rainy directly with a joint letter, asking that they be allowed to use the 'black ware', a seaweed used for fertiliser. At the time it was being taken to Applecross. It is not known how this ended, but it is likely that the young owner allowed their request.

Rev. James Kippen left Raasay in 1867 and was replaced by Rev. Angus Galbraith. In his evidence to the Napier Commission in 1883, he said that Mr Rainy had done everything he could for the comfort of the people.

Under the Volunteer Act of 1863, the 7th Inverness-shire Rifle Volunteer Corps was created as part of the 8th Inverness-shire Highland Rifle Volunteers – the MacDonald Highlanders. Fifteen men from Raasay signed as Volunteers in November 1867. These men were all between sixteen and twenty-six years of age, from the south end of Raasay.

Emile Bunning was the butler's son.

William and Roderick Matheson were sons of Thomas, the ploughman.

John MacLeod was the son of Iain Bàn from Clachan.

Allan, Duncan and William MacInnes (although he appears to be three years younger than the age given) were sons of Duncan from Clachan.

John MacLean was Iain Uilleim from Oscaig.

John Matheson was the son of Duncan, Captain of the *Falcon*.

John MacKenzie was the son of James from Balachuirn.

Murdo Bethune's father, John, was the miller and joiner from Clachan.

Alexander Whiteford's father was Archibald, a drainer at Fearns.

Donald and Lachlan MacRae were sons of Donnchadh Beag from Balachuirn.

John Matheson was the son of Malcolm from Balachuirn.

These men took their first drill in March 1868. After inspection in Portree, Mr Rainy brought twenty-five muskets back to Raasay and they began target practice. In 1893 Iain Uilleim gave evidence to the Deer Forrest Commission. His statement said that he had attended a Volunteer Soiree in the time of the last Mr Rainy. He said

> Mr Rainy at that time had enrolled fifty rifle volunteers in Raasay. He said that evening, that if he was spared another year he would get the sheep farmer to renounce his lease, and that he would put some of the people back to the townships that his father had cleared. Unfortunately he died before the end of the year, and a sporting proprietor bought the estate, and the whole of those fourteen townships are now one sporting preserve. There is not one volunteer in Raasay today.

In Raasay today, young Mr Rainy is spoken of as having been a much better landlord than his father had been, as far as the people were concerned. This may be due, at least in part, to the evidence given to the two commissions. It appears, however, that he too was a businessman, and much of the estate management was left in the hands of his factor, Harry MacDonald, Portree. From 1866, when he took over the estate, anyone who had not paid their rent on time was 'warned'. If the rent money was still not forthcoming, they were 'charged to remove'. The factor kept records of those people. Two tenants in Holoman and two in Balachuirn received warnings, as did one in Fladda and one in Torran. Virtually all the Arnish tenants received warnings and four were 'charged'. In Umachan although only one was 'charged', more than half were 'warned'. Six people in the Kyle Rona area were 'warned'. On Rona, all three in Doire na Guaille were both 'warned' and 'charged'. Nine were 'warned' from Dry Harbour and three were 'charged'.

It must be assumed that anyone who could pay their rent on time, did so. Security of tenure depended on prompt payment. None of these people could afford to be turned out of their homes and off their land. It is clear from these figures that conditions steadily deteriorated towards the north end. There were comparatively few warnings in the south end. On Rona however, many people were being both 'warned and charged'.

It was mentioned above that Alasdair Ruadh from Fladda told the Napier Commission about the factor being harsh. He said that, 'if any one of us happened to be 10s. in arrears we would be served with a summons of removal and would have to pay 10s. for the summons'.

He is talking about the time that 'Rainy sent the people away' implying that he means George Rainy Senior. It may be asked, however, if his memory was of the period from 1866 to 1871, when George Rainy Junior, held the estate.

Although many people were 'warned' at this time, it appears that only two actually left Raasay. On the factor's list, only these two have no rent figures beside their names, only a note 'Mr Rainy'. Tormod an Tàilleir, Norman Nicolson, was the son of Donald, the tailor, from Dry Harbour. He was married and had a tenancy in Arnish. In 1870 or early in 1871 he moved with his wife and family to stay with his in-laws in Bernisdale. He remained there. The other man who moved away from the island at this time was Tormod Dhòmhnaill, Norman Gillies from Torran. He moved across the water to Portree, where his family was living in 1871. He himself was away at the fishing at the time of the 1871 census. By 1881, however, he had moved back across the Sound and was living in Eilean Taigh. He later moved to Oscaig.

A census was taken in 1871, as it had been ten years before. The area was again divided into three districts for the purpose. In the south end, John MacMillan, another son of the former teacher, was the enumerator. Royston MacKenzie had the sheep farm of 700 acres, eighty of which were arable. He employed six shepherds, five labourers and a boy. Fearns, Hallaig, Balmeanach and Castle had only one family living in each place. Rev. Angus Galbraith was the Free Church minister, and Alexander MacFarlane was the teacher at Clachan. A visitor in Clachan was Thomas MacDonald, sergeant drill instructor, who may have been involved with the Volunteers set up by young Mr Rainy.

John MacLeod, who was still the teacher in Torran, was again the enumerator for that area. None of the six houses in Arnish had any rooms with windows. In Torran only one was without windows, while four of the ten on Fladda were without. On Fladda, however, Neil MacLeod, age eighteen, was the 'elementary teacher'. This was the only census that notes a teacher in Fladda. None of the eight houses in Umachan had rooms with windows.

James Urquhart, the teacher in Dry Harbour, was the enumerator for Rona and the Kyle Rona area. In Kyle Rona, Alexander Nicolson, age eighteen, was noted as being the 'teacher's substitute'. He was lodging with Raghnall Beag,

Ronald MacLennan, and his family. Housing in this area had not improved over the ten-year period. The lighthouse, the lodge in Big Harbour with nine, and one in Doire Dubh with three, were the only buildings noted as having rooms with windows. Not even the schoolhouse was recorded as having any windows, although this may have been an omission.

In 1872 George Haygarth Rainy died. Raasay and Rona were sold. Particularly in view of the proposals that he had voiced to Iain Uilleim, Rainy's death at such a young age, was a blow to the island.

Note

1. Thomas Bunning's diary notes do not correspond in the detail with information given by Duncan Campbell in the estate papers. As the butler would not have been directly involved, it is assumed that Duncan Campbell's version is more accurate.

7

The History of Raasay, 1872–1900

George G. MacKay: 1872–1874

George G. MacKay paid £55 000 for the estate in 1872. He held it for only two years. His stewardship was entirely negative. The overriding memory of the man was that he raised the rents substantially. This was stated time and time again to both Royal Commissions. In 1883, Rev. Angus Galbraith said of this time:

> The purchaser was Mr G. G. MacKay, whose chief aim appears to have been to make pecuniary gain by the purchase. Accordingly he set immediately about increasing the rents. Rents were imposed on a number who paid none, and the rents which were before, and which were considered high enough, were in some cases nearly doubled. Taking an average of the whole, the rise was nearly fifty per cent. The people at the time remonstrated, and were almost driven to open resistance. Whether rightly or wrongly, I did my best, in the interest of peace, to influence the people to agree to Mr MacKay's terms, though I considered them very hard. The people were quite willing to take their lands at valuation; but the proprietor, perhaps thinking such a course might in some cases rather diminish than increase the rents, told them they must either agree to his terms, or leave the island. The poor people were unable, and probably unwilling to leave, and so they were compelled to submit. Since then the people believe – and I think justly – that they are far too highly rented; and it is not true, so far as I know, that in appearing before the Commission, they were influenced by any parties whatsoever, but by a sense of injustice which they think was done to them, in imposing a rent far beyond the value of their holdings. Looking at the extent and quality of their lands, the inconvenience resulting from their insular and outlandish position, the want of roads, and several other disadvantages, I have, after careful comparison with other places, come to the conclusion that their rents are among the highest, if not the highest, in the West Highlands.'

James Ross, factor for the estate in 1893, gave evidence from estate records and from questioning 'old residents on the island'. Information about this period would appear to have come mainly from estate records. He said

> During the two years Mr MacKay owned the property, a good many men were employed, chiefly in making walks and bridle paths on different parts of the property, but these were of little permanent benefit to the estate. Soon after entering into possession Mr MacKay took the township of Balachuirn, consisting of six crofts and pasture land, together about 500 acres, into his own hands.

Though deprived of their lands the tenants of this township continued to occupy their dwelling houses. Hitherto, or as far back as we have any record, the crofters' rent on Raasay estate remained practically unchanged, but during Mr MacKay's ownership they were raised all over, from seventeen to sixty-six per cent. In one township – Arnish – the increase was seventy-three per cent, the average increase over all the crofter townships on the estate being forty-three per cent. Soon after this, and before the increased rents came due, Mr MacKay sold the estate for £62,000 to Mr W. J. Armitage, who took possession at Martinmas 1874.

MacKay also created the township of Braig on Rona. Tenants were very reluctant to move there, as it was considered to be a poor area. Ailean Liath, Allan MacLeod from Dry Harbour, was eventually persuaded to move there, and did so with other members of his family. Twenty people, five households, are found there in 1881. Many of those MacLeods died young. By 1891, there were only two families left. The heads of both households were widowed.

The minister's judgement about MacKay would appear to have been soundly based. The man bought the estate, made some insubstantial paths on it, took the Balachuirn land into his own hands and substantially raised the rents over the whole island just before selling the estate. All these measures were designed to increase its value when sold. His plan worked. A £7,000 increase in price over two years was not bad going. But yet again, it was the people who paid the price.

Figure 7/1. Rents for north end townships, 1827–76.

Township	Rent in 1827			Rent in 1870			Rent in 1876		
	£	s.	d.	£	s.	d.	£	s.	d.
Arnish	21	0	0	19	18	0	35	0	0
Torran	10	5	6	10	5	8	15	0	0
Fladda	22	15	6	22	17	0	31	0	0
Umachan	12	6	0	12	6	0	15	0	0
Eilean Taigh	6	1	6	8	0	0	10	0	0
Kyle Rona	31	15	0	26	14	0	30	0	0
Doire na Guaille	17	17	6	17	17	6	25	0	0
Big Harbour	17	14	6	17	17	6	12	0	0
Dry Harbour	59	14	6	50	10	0	79	1	6
Balachuirn	—			27	1	0	33	1	0
Total	**199**	**10**	**0**	**213**	**6**	**8**	**285**	**2**	**6**

William James Armitage: 1874–1876

If MacKay's motives were reasonably transparent, the same cannot be said of his successor's. William James Armitage, of Southgate, London, spent only one summer on Raasay. Rev. Galbraith says of him

> Mr Armitage, a kind, gentlemanly man, was the purchaser. He only kept the place about eighteen months, and having spent but one summer in it, he did

little in the way of giving employment to the people, and left things pretty much as he found them. He spoke repeatedly to me of the injustice of having all the good land devoted to sheep, and all the worthless land given to the poor people. That is a grievance which still exists.

James Ross said,

> Mr Armitage provided no work for the people. He restored the land at Balachuirn to the crofters dispossessed by Mr MacKay at an increase of £1 per croft, on the original rent. He also let Isle Tigh, which had been vacant for a year, to a tenant at £10 rent per annum, being an increase of £2 on the rent paid by the former tenant. Mr Armitage then sold the property ...

Some insight into the man is found in a letter he wrote to Professor John S. Blackie at Edinburgh University in 1875. In this he refers to Raasay as 'our little kingdom'. His own lack of Gaelic makes it difficult 'in our intercourse with our subjects'. Nevertheless, when he sold the estate, he received £3 000 more than he had paid.

James Ross' statement to the Deer Forest Commission in 1893 states that Armitage let Eilean Taigh. By the time of the 1881 census, Tormod Dhòmhnaill, Norman Gillies, was living there with his family. He had been in Portree since the time of George Rainy Junior. The Valuation Roll, however, shows that Eilean Taigh had been held by the proprietor from the year 1873–74 up to, and including, the year 1877–78 after Mr Wood bought the estate.

Edward Herbert Wood from 1876

In 1876 Armitage sold the estate for £65 000 to Edward Herbert Wood, Sudbourne Hall, Suffolk. His family was originally from the Stoke on Trent area, and had made their money in the potteries there. This allowed Edward, who was then little over twenty-five years old, to buy his sporting estate.

Mr Wood and his family lived on Raasay for most of the year. Once again, Raasay House was subjected to extension and modernisation. This time it was divided into areas for the family, guests and servants. A service wing, almost as big as the house itself, was added to the rear on the east side of the building. This work was finished about 1877. In 1881 the census records that the house had forty-nine windows, an increase of sixteen since the previous census. Many servants were employed within it. Some, including the footman, were brought onto the island by the new owners. Others were local people.

Mr Wood spent a very great deal of money on the estate. First and foremost, he created a sporting estate. Royston MacKenzie, the sheep farmer, had died in December 1873. Mr Wood now took over the sheep farm and the stock of 3,200 sheep. The number of sheep was halved to allow deer to be brought in. In October 1876, the *Inverness Courier* reported

> Fallow Deer for Raasay – people who happened to be present at the Strome Ferry railway station on Saturday last were a good deal astonished at seeing

the unusual spectacle of several cases of deer arriving from the south by the afternoon train.

Sending coals from Strome to Newcastle would, in the estimation of Lochalsh men, be alone comparable to the arrival of deer from England in the far west of Ross-shire. But the matter soon was explained when it was stated that these were fallow deer imported by the new proprietor of the Island of Raasay. Unfortunately, a number of the strangers had died in transit.

Raasay is not much more than a good rifle shot's distance from Skye and yet the fertility of it is in striking contract to the sterile nature of the greater part of the neighbouring island.

A curious fact is that while sheep reared in Raasay will feed well and fatten when removed to turnips in the 'low country' sheep bred in Skye and other western islands will not improve, and are at their best just 'off the hill'.

Because the game could not be allowed to roam free around the mansion house or wander into the north end townships, deer fences were erected. At the north end, one ran from a point at the north edge of the woods at Brochel, up and over the hill to Loch an Uachdair, and from there to Loch Arnish on the west coast. This fence has now been replaced with an ordinary stockproof fence. In the south end of the island, another fence ran from just north of Oscaig, up the hill and over the Glen. From there it turned south, through the woods behind Inverarish and back to the sea just south of Suisnish House. This enclosed the Raasay House policies and the Home Farm. Remnants of this fence can still be seen. Where it crossed the roads, at Oscaig, Creachan and Glen, lodges were built. Estate workers lived in these lodges and were expected to keep an eye on the gates. The bulk of the island, therefore, was given over entirely to game.

There were now a large number of people employed as estate workers. Indeed there were very few people in the south end of Raasay who were not totally dependent on Mr Wood. Most lived fairly close to the mansion house. Alexander Stewart, the estate manager lived in the newly built Borrodale House – now Raasay Hotel. The sheep farm manager, William Brown, lived at Suisnish House, previously the residence of Royston MacKenzie. There were three shepherds, living at Hallaig, Glam and Castle. The head gamekeeper, James Hands, lived at Clachan and had three keepers working under him, one of whom lived at Glen Lodge.

The gardener, Thomas Coysh, lived in the Gardener's Cottage, behind the mansion house garden. He was unmarried and lived on his own in the house with six windowed rooms. He had two gardeners, an apprentice and a labourer working for him. Many people were brought into the island, as estate workers and house servants. The coachman was Alexander MacInnes, grandson of Donald MacSween who had been the postman in 1851 and was still the 'letter carrier' in 1881, then aged eighty-seven! John, son of Alexander MacMillan the teacher, became a forester rather than a gardener. He lived in the building now known as the 'Old Post Office' beside Borrodale House. His wife was the postmistress.

As well as bringing new estate workers onto the island, the new owner made other changes on Raasay for the benefit of himself and his family as well as their guests.

The area in the south end enclosed by the deer fence was, as far as possible, created to resemble a fashionable park. As well as forestry plantations, ornamental trees and rhododendrons were planted out. The whole area around Raasay House, Dun Borrodale, the Free Church and manse and around the Home Loch was littered with paths criss-crossing one another along the way. These paths still exist, and meandering along them is a very pleasant way of passing as much time as one can afford. The Home Farm continued as in the past. In the early years of the Woods' ownership, the clock tower was added to the Steading at Clachan.

In 1878 Edward Wood bought the *Amy*, a schooner. She was a clinker-built boat of 144 feet, nineteen feet breadth, with a round stern and two masts. Her name was changed to the *Rona*. The captain was Duncan Matheson, originally from Plockton, who had moved to Raasay in the time of George Rainy and been captain of his yacht, the *Falcon*. The 1881 census shows Duncan's family at home in Oscaig, but he was not with them. Although the reason for the visit is not known, Duncan and the *Rona* were in Port Bannatyne, Bute, at that time.

In spite of the heavy expenditure by the Woods during the early years of their ownership of the estate, economic conditions of the tenants and cottars in the north end of Raasay and on Rona were steadily deteriorating. The quality and size of their holdings made it necessary for them to have a secondary source of income – for most people that was fishing.

There were many fishing boats on Raasay and Rona. Most had a keel length of between thirteen and fifteen feet. They were open boats, with a lugsail and oars. A crew of two or three men worked nets for herring and lines for cod, ling or haddock. The lines were baited with herring for cod and ling (on long lines) and with mussels for haddock (on small lines). Winter fishing was mainly for herring. Cod and ling fishing was generally in the spring. Lobsters were caught in pots set not far off shore. If the weather was unsuitable for net or lines, it was often possible to try for lobsters. In practice the type of fishing carried out, whether nets, lines or pots, depended largely on the weather.

Although all the crofters and cottars depended to some extent on fishing to supplement the produce of the land, there were some who derived the main part of their income from fishing. They had larger boats. The *Janet*, owned by William MacLeod, Dry Harbour, was a half decked smack with a keel length of twenty-five feet. Ewen Nicolson, Doire na Guaille, had the *Hero*. She was an open boat of seventeen feet. Both these boats had a crew of four men. John Nicolson, a son of Alasdair Donn from Fladda, lived at Torran. He had the *Helen*, a decked boat of twenty-six feet. Five crewmen worked on this boat. Torcall MacLeod, Fladda, had a thirty-six foot decked boat called the *Swan*. She had six crewmen.

On 13 December 1880 three men were drowned at Duirineasgach, near the shore at Rona. They were fishing for lobsters at the time. Christopher MacRae, aged fifty, was unmarried. The MacRaes, originally from Lochalsh, had come to Balachuirn from South Uist in the early 1840s. About 1878 the family moved to Big Harbour. The same accident claimed the lives of two brothers, Murdo and Roderick MacLeod from Dry Harbour. Both unmarried, Murdo was twenty-six years old and Roderick two years younger. Their parents were Iain Mhurchaidh, John MacLeod, and Margaret MacLennan. John and Margaret had been living with her family in Lower Fearns, but moved to Dry Harbour in June 1853. John's family had also been in Fearns. They had moved to Bernisdale. The bodies of the MacLeod brothers were recovered within days, but that of Christopher MacRae was not found until about three weeks after the accident.

In the Sound of Raasay on 7 February 1885 another drowning occurred. John Nicolson, a son of Alasdair Donn from Fladda, was forty-eight years old. He was married to Anna Mhòr, a daughter of the teacher, John MacLeod, with whom they lived in Torran. Murchadh Dhòmhnaill, Murdo Gillies, was forty-three, married with two young children. He and his family lived with his parents in Torran. His brother, Calum, had been one of those drowned in 1856. The third man who was drowned in this accident was Angus Gillies, age twenty-eight. He was unmarried and lived with his parents, Iain Aonghais, John Gillies and Isabella MacLennan in Umachan.*

THE NAPIER COMMISSION – 1883

The 1880s saw the fishing industry in decline, and undergoing structural changes. There was also a slump in the wider British economy, resulting in fewer employment opportunities in the industrial areas of Scotland. It was not just the crofters and cottars on the Raasay estate who were suffering badly at this time. Similar poverty was being experienced in many parts of the Highlands.

In response to land agitation throughout the area, such as that in Braes, Skye, in 1882, the government was forced to act. A Royal Commission – now generally referred to as the Napier Commission, after its chairman, Lord Napier – was set up in 1883 to look into conditions of crofters and cottars in the Highlands. Four of the six members who made up the commission had, to a greater or lesser degree, an interest in history. Much of the rhetoric during the agitation had centred on the loss of crofting land over the previous one hundred years or so. The commission therefore encouraged crofters to give the history of their townships as they remembered it.

The commissioners travelled around the Highlands taking evidence. They sat at Torran, Raasay on Tuesday 22 May 1883, when twelve crofters gave their evidence and were questioned. John Munro, the missionary on Rona, and James Ross, factor for the estate, also gave their evidence that day. Rev. Angus Galbraith, the Free Church minister on Raasay, was away from home when the commissioners were on Raasay, and his evidence was given in the form of a written statement.

James Ross, now the factor for the estate, was an Inverness solicitor. He gave evidence both to the Napier Commission and the later Deer Forest Commission in 1893, on behalf of the proprietor. In each, he is at pains to present the owner as a benevolent man, who, at great cost to himself, did everything he possibly could for the good of the crofters living on the estate. He also presented the crofters as being in reasonably good circumstances. Some of the information he

---

* A poem in memory of these men will be found in Appendix 2.

gave was quite incorrect. Indeed, his evidence in 1893 corrects some of the errors of 1883.

A great deal of information about the running of the estate at this time is found within the Napier Commission's evidence. By considering the evidence given by the factor, who was at pains to present the owner in a good light, with that given by the minister, who presented the view of the crofters, a reasonably accurate view of conditions can be found. The minister's statement began, 'Personally, I had no wish to act as one of their representatives; but as they have chosen to elect me, and have since urged me to send in a written statement of their chief grievances, I cannot, consistently with my relation to them, refuse to comply with their wish.'

James Ross says, 'Since Mr Wood purchased the estate of Raasay, he has made it the home of himself and his family, making the condition of his population a matter of personal interest and care.'

In the six years since he had bought the estate, said James Ross, Mr Wood had spent nearly £32,500 as well as the total income of the estate over that time.

Figure 7/2. Expenditure by Mr and Mrs Wood, 1876–1882.

Year	Total
1876–77	11,909
1877–78	9,883
1878–79	8,127
1879–80	10,040
1880–81	10,414
1881–82	10,050
Total	£60,423

The figures given in Figure 7/2 do not include £14 800 spent by the Woods on the additions and alterations to Raasay House, the building of Borrodale House, and the work carried out on the farm buildings at the Steading.

Given the massive amount that was clearly being spent on the estate, and his acknowledged concern for the people living there, it is most unfortunate that Mr Wood does not appear to have had any great understanding of local conditions. Often, he appears to have incurred great expense, before finding out that his plans would not work in practice. That aside, his overriding ambition was to create a sporting estate over the main part of the island, and that could never sit easily alongside the local crofter population.

The plan that seems to have been least expensive, was Mr Wood's proposal to open a slate quarry on Fladda. Ross said, 'Mr Wood thought, at one time, with some degree of reason, that possibly a slate quarry might be opened there, and he took every means to ascertain the way it could be opened, first with a view of getting slates, and secondly, with a view of providing labour, but scientific people reported it would not work.'

In 1878 Mr Wood began the reclamation of a tract of 'waste land' at Glam, about four and a half miles north of Clachan. The old settlement of Glam was to the west and slightly north of the farm buildings erected at this time. This project was the brain-child of Mr Wood's brother-in-law. Its primary objective was to supplement the produce of the Home Farm, and thus save having to buy in supplies for Raasay House. It was a spectacular and expensive failure.

Although only seventy acres were actually reclaimed, it had been planned to reclaim two hundred. The land was 500–600 feet above sea level, and facing west. The soil was clay and peat. No farmhouse was required, but four labourers' houses and the farm steading, known as the Square, were built. These were of corrugated iron on concrete foundations. The steading blew down twice during building. The buildings, costing over £2 000, were finally completed by spring 1881.

Seventy acres were drained at a cost of £600. They were trenched and ploughed. Climate and exposure to the prevailing winds made this site unsuitable from the outset. It was found that grain crops, although heavy, did not ripen and had to be cut green and dried to be used as cattle fodder. Turnips grew well until mid August, but did not bulb well. Potatoes were a failure.

The project was totally abandoned after only three years, having cost £4 000. The factor's description of the project to the Deer Forest Commission in April 1893 made clear that the whole episode was a total failure. He blamed climatic conditions for the failure. He also maintained that a large portion of the expenditure had gone to the people of the island in wages. It is not know if that was the case.

THE OSCAIG TOWNSHIP

Six new slated houses were built at Oscaig. Iain Uilleim, John MacLean from Oscaig, gave evidence to the Napier Commission, and described the houses. They were built of stone, lime and slate, one storey high, without any stair or ladder to the loft. At each end of the house was a room and off it a closet, about eight feet square. Each room had a fireplace. There was no wash-house. The croft had a byre and a barn.

Water was piped from a spring, about half way between the two cattle grids on the Oscaig road, to a stand-pipe at the bottom of the township road. A tank was built around the spring. Lead pipe was used finishing in a 'swan neck', cut at an angle. The pipe ran continuously as there was no tap. People gathered around it with their pails and chatted while they waited for them to fill up. This system was still in operation in the 1920s, and was not known to have run dry. Sometime in the 1950s, probably after each house got its own water supply, it did tend to dry for a time in the summer. To solve the problem an additional supply was piped from the stream beside the southern cattle grid. Each house contributed towards the cost of the polythene pipe.

In his evidence to the Napier Commission, James Ross said,

> With regard to the Oscaig cottages, there was a man here who said he paid £14, which was quite true. The original intention of these was not with a view to crofters at all. When Mr Wood took possession of the estate, he was of the opinion it would be a good thing if he could induce such men as tailors and shoemakers to come, and encourage them to work, and these cottages

were originally built for those men as trade cottages; and they cost more than they would have done for other purposes. But then that would not suit, so he added small crofts to them.

Rev. Galbraith had this to say of them:

> The high rents I consider a real grievance. I take as an example the township of Oscaig, one formed by Mr Wood himself. The tenants here are crofters on a small scale, the most of the men being employed by himself. The whole arable land here is not quite six acres, and the rent charged is, I believe, £18. That is more than £3 per acre, and the quality of the land is not good. Each tenant is supposed to keep a cow, and if he occupies a whole house of two rooms and a closet (not too much for an ordinary family), he pays a rent of £13. That is £10 for his house, and £3 for the bit of land connected therewith. If he must be content with half a house, then his rent is £8 – being £5 for the one end of the house, and £3 for his land.
>
> This land I consider more than double its value. As to the houses, after careful comparison with such houses elsewhere, I consider the Oscaig houses are at present double rented. They are plainly built, and should not have been costly houses. But I know not, and care not to ask, how much they cost; but simply as a question of value between man and man, I think they would be fully rented at from £5 to £6 each house. The people in this township are very poor, and becoming poorer every year. They are getting into debt, and by this time they have learned by experience that they cannot with their earnings pay their present rents and support their families.

The six houses were built as tradesmen's houses, and were thus expected to command a higher rent. Ross claimed that they had cost £1 200 to build, but clearly the minister had his doubts about that figure. The idea of bringing in trades people harks back to the 'estate improvers' earlier in the century, who had advocated that people should be encouraged to be less dependent on the land. Instead they should make their living from a trade. Unfortunately, the execution of this plan, then as in the 1880s, depended entirely on the traders having a steady supply of customers with whom they might trade. Given the economic circumstances of the island, this was quite unrealistic, as Mr Wood soon found out. When the houses could not be let to trades people, small pieces of ground were added to each and they became 'crofts'. By the 1880s all but one of the tenants had found it was impossible to pay the rent for the full house, and five of the houses had two households in each. Mr Wood employed many of the tenants in these properties on the estate, and it would have been quite impossible for them to pay the high rents without this secondary source of income.

John MacLean could remember two tenants having the whole area plus a park of about nineteen acres, which Mr Wood himself now held, as well as common grazing. Each man had been able to have fifty or sixty sheep and a pair of horses, as well as a soumming of eight milk cows and some yeld cattle on the hill. The total rent was then £20. The total rent of Oscaig in 1883 was £60, chiefly because of the houses.

The croft, in front of the house, was about 1.25 acres. John was allowed to keep just one cow, but no sheep. There was scarcely enough feeding to keep the cow in winter and extra had to be bought in. That part of the croft nearest the house was fenced as a garden or potato ground. When asked if he grew good vegetables, carrots or peas, the reply was that he supposed it would be possible, but he couldn't really see the point of it. 'Well I don't know of any garden into which they have put either carrots or peas except one, and I dare say it is more for curiosity than for the good of it, because carrots and these vegetables do no good to a working man when he has no meat to go with them.' The question – 'Don't they make broth sometimes?' was met with 'They can do that with meat.'

He had regular work from Mr Wood, but complained about 'the smallness of the wages as much as the smallness of the land'. He depended on a week's wages of 13s. for his family with four children. He said that was 'barely enough to support me in meat and clothes and to pay the rent'. When asked if he let any part of his house or if he took in lodgers, he replied that he was not supposed to let it, but that sometimes he took in lodgers at 2s. per week, the usual charge.

These six new houses are known as South Oscaig. At North Oscaig a row of six houses, of two rooms each, was built. James Ross informed the Deer Forest Commission that they were granted rent free to widows, who each received four bolls of meal, two tons of coal and half a boll of potatoes each year, as well as a money allowance of 1s. per week.

This area was known as Camus Froineach, meaning fern or bracken. It became known locally as Manitoba. Iain Choinnich Chaluim, John Gillies, had emigrated to North America, presumably to Manitoba. He sent for his relations to join him. His father, Kenneth, and family had been living in Doire Dubh near Kyle Rona, but by 1881 were in Torran. The family sold up their stock and had come up to the south end of Raasay, before they learned that the ship on which they were to travel had been delayed for some reason. Mr Wood gave them accommodation at the new houses at Camus Froineach (North Oscaig) for a month or so until their ship was ready. Although some accounts maintain that the family remained on Raasay, they do not appear in the 1891 census, either at Manitoba or elsewhere on the island. It must therefore be assumed that they were eventually able to leave. By the time he left, Coinneach Chaluim would have been in his late sixties, or perhaps even older. Iain Raghnaill, John Gillies from Balachuirn, referred to the place as Manitoba, and the name stuck.

HOUSING ON RAASAY

Possibly Mr Wood's greatest achievement on Raasay was the improvement he made to housing conditions on the island. Not only did he renovate and put up new buildings in the south end, he also made it possible for the crofters in the north end and on Rona to substantially improve their housing. James Ross says:

> Thirteen crofters have been each allowed £10 to build better houses, £130; and there has been expended in wood for doors and windows, roofing and inside fittings, and ironmongery to a large number of crofters for the six years

for the same purpose, £137 18s. ... When Mr Wood first took possession of the estate of Raasay he felt disposed to erect houses for his tenants. Experience, however, showed that such a system would be both expensive and unsatisfactory. He consequently came to the resolution that it would be much more advisable to furnish the tenants with wood and slate, and make a certain allowance of money for building purposes, leaving it to themselves to do the work. This course was carried into effect with considerable success, and will no doubt eventually tend to the clearance of the present houses.

The results are found in the 1881 census, where very few houses are shown as having no rooms with windows, and most have at least two. As described by the factor, other improvements were also made to the houses at this time.

Houses, probably at Mill Place and Clachan, were improved. Six cottars' houses were rebuilt at a cost of £265, and four new ones were built at a cost of £165. It is noted in the 1881 census that a new house was being built beside the shop at Mill Place. Probably the others had been completed before then.

Although the factor claimed that three lodges were built for cottars at a cost of £450, it is likely that he was referring to the lodges at Oscaig, Creachan and Glen, which were built as gatekeepers' houses where the deer fence crossed the road. Estate workers lived in these lodges.

The factor also makes the point that Mr Wood had 'planted nine new tenants on a portion of the sheep farm'. While this might imply that Mr Wood was concerned about overcrowding of the population in the north end, in fact six of these 'new tenants' went into the houses at Oscaig, after it was discovered that tradespeople could not be found to take them on. Of ten households in Oscaig in the 1881 census, only two held a full house. Of those ten, only three had come from the north end of the island – one from Fladda, and two from Dry Harbour, Rona. The other seven households in Oscaig had either already been living in the south end of the island or had come onto the island in the recent past.

The other three new tenants on the sheep farm were at Brae and at Balmeanach. The one croft at Brae was occupied by Iain Eachainn, John MacLeod, who had moved from Umachan. It was his son, Eachann, who incurred the wrath of Catriona Uilleim – Kate MacLean, Oscaig, a great tradition bearer of her day – by allegedly making a haystack over Storab's grave. Dòmhnall Iain Bhàin, Donald MacLeod from Kyle Rona, and Murchadh Aonghais Mhòr, Murdo MacKenzie from Balachuirn, were at Balmeanach.

The factor, in his evidence in 1883, stressed the improvement that Mr Wood had undertaken on behalf of the crofters and cottars on the estate. He provided well-bred Highland bulls to improve the stock, and the benefit of this exercise was already being seen. He gave loans to buy stock.

Everyone had 'the privileges of free peat, fuel, and sea-weed', on which the factor attempts to put a monetary value, and notes that this is 'exceptional' in the Highlands. Although perhaps in theory, 'free' peat for fuel and seaweed for fertiliser were a 'privilege', the rights to such privileges were traditional.

Mr Wood had erected fences between pasture and the arable land. He believed that a proper system of crop rotation would be of great benefit, and he had presumably tried to encourage that. However, because of the smallness of the holdings, this was unrealistic. Financial pressures forced tenants to crop the land to its maximum each year. Even so it yielded only enough to maintain the family for a small part of the year.

A one-third rent abatement of the year's rent at Martinmas 1882 was granted by Mr Wood. In spring 1883 he had supplied sixty-three tons of seed potatoes and seed, 'so that all his tenants might have a thorough change of seed'. This was provided free of charge. His tenants would have appreciated both the rent reduction and new seed. One has to wonder, however, if perhaps they were granted in anticipation of a Commission of Enquiry into conditions being set up. Whether or not it was a deliberate exercise, it certainly had the effect of making all the delegates to the Napier Commission speak in glowing terms of Mr Wood.

Mr Wood had built 3.75 miles of road, six feet wide, between Torran and Kyle Rona, and church meeting houses at Torran and on Rona. A Bible, from the church in Rona, is held by the Skye Museum of Island Life in Kilmuir. Mr Jonathan MacDonald was given this Bible shortly after the museum opened, about thirty years ago.

The proprietor had also granted two-thirds of the cost of replacing fishing boats destroyed by high tides and gales in November 1881.

According to James Ross, when Mr Wood took over the estate in 1876 there were twenty-four estate workers. Because he had bought Raasay from Mr Armitage, who had spent only one summer on the island and took little to do with the running of it, this is not surprising. In 1883, ninety-four people were employed. He said that 'Labour at good wages and at convenient places has been offered to all his people who are disposed to accept it'. He claimed that during the six years that Mr Wood held the estate over £20,000 had been spent 'in work to the inhabitants of the island', and that over half of that had gone 'directly into the hands of the crofters' or members of their families.

This was clearly a very large sum of money, and had it been spent as stated, the factor's belief that 'The position of the people now, as compared with their state in 1876, is one of great improvement'. However, Mr Ross was at great pains to show the proprietor in a good light, and in emphasising the positive he tended to be rather economical with the truth.

The minister said

> I think it due to him [Mr Wood] also to add, that in cases of sickness, and to widows, orphans, and other helpless persons, Mr Wood has been very kind and very generous. But notwithstanding all this, the crofter population have real grievances, and I am not going to say who is to blame for this, although I cannot help having my own opinion on the subject.
> ... The sums said to have been expended on the place do not benefit the crofters to the extent that might be supposed ... The larger portion of the money must have passed into the hands of various tradesmen and strangers from without ... I have no doubt as to the amount expended; I only wonder it is not greater, although it is small compared with the sum expended yearly in the time of Mr Rainy, senior ... It is well known that large sums of money

are yearly expended on the raising of game, and the payment of gamekeepers, as well as on the importation of feeding stuffs for cattle – a thing not formerly required when rabbits were fewer. It is very difficult to understand how money spent on these objects could benefit the crofters.

Then it is further stated that the number of people permanently employed in the place is about ninety-four. I have taken some trouble to ascertain accurately who compose this permanent staff. I find that a goodly number are mansion-house servants, yachtsmen, gamekeepers, gardeners, shepherds, tradesmen of various kinds, salmon-fishers, farm-servants, etc. I find, further, that only about one-half of this permanent staff are natives, and fewer still – I would say not more than one-fourth – are in any way connected with the crofters. I do not say these things in the way of undervaluing the employment hitherto given by the proprietor, but simply to show that only a small portion of the sums expended really benefit the crofter population ...

As to those generally employed on day's pay about the farm, I do not think there is any improvement. In Mr Rainy's time the wages were, as a rule, 12s. per week. With this they had as much potato land as they wished to plant, got their coals landed and carted by the proprietor's horses free of charge, and had their houses rent free. Now they receive, as a rule, 13s. per week for six full days' work. Some have little or no potato land; they pay for the landing and carting of their coals, and pay *full rent* for their houses besides. In face of these facts, I regret I cannot say with the factor, in his statement, that 'the position of the people now, as compared with their state in 1876, is one of great improvement'.

Thus the circumstances of the crofter population were not nearly as good as the factor suggested. It appears, in fact, that estate employees had been far better off thirty years before when George Rainy owned the estate. Although Angus Galbraith had come to Raasay as the minister in the time of George H. Rainy, he clearly knew of conditions in the time of Mr Rainy senior.

Rev. Galbraith said:

The people are very poor, and worse off this year than I have seen them during my time ... As to the general health of the people, I regret to say that sickness is on the increase. Two young men who were last year at the fishing, died this summer of consumption – a disease which is on the increase, and which, I believe, in most cases is traceable to cold and poor feeding, when the men are from home at the East Coast and elsewhere. In order to save as much as possible, they live too cheaply for their comfort and health. I have no doubt that poverty has a good deal to do with most of the cases of sickness. A medical man of considerable experience, who spent a couple of years in the island lately, on being asked what the prevailing disease in the island was, replied – 'The prevailing disease is poverty, and the chief remedy is food.'

John Munro, the missionary on Rona, also spoke of the poverty on that island. He said:

Since I came to Rona, I never saw a place like it. They toil away all spring, men, women and children. Sometimes I am grieved to see the women and perhaps I should not speak about some things I took notice of here in public. It might be very unsatisfactory to some minds to see in the public print that a woman carrying seaware might be working at that today and in child-bed tomorrow ...

They have been reduced to poverty by the laws that made the people so long grind them down, and I think the government should help them out of their difficulties and they would work like other men. They are willing to work and if they got the chance I think they would do it. The people are good people, willing to pay everybody their own.

The evidence of these two men speaks for itself, and does not lie easily with the factor's view that everyone was much better off than in the past.

THE EVIDENCE FROM CROFTERS AND COTTARS TO THE NAPIER COMMISSION

Tenants in Balachuirn and the new tenants in Brae, Balmeanach and Oscaig were the only ones in the south end of the island, and therefore most affected by the sporting estate. They did not have an easy life.

Tormod Iain Ghairbh, Norman MacLean, was from Balachuirn. He said that 'every man's arable land is cut out for him'. This area, therefore, had crofts as distinct from run-rig. The land may have been divided into crofts about 1875, in William Armitage's time as proprietor.

Norman told the commission that rents varied according to the quality of the soil. The hill pasture was held in common, but much of it had been taken from the tenants. They had lost some in Rainy's time to Royston MacKenzie's sheep farm, and George MacKay had taken the remainder. Armitage had restored the arable and some hill grazing, but increased the rent.

In 1884 Norman paid £5 17s. rent plus rates. He had four cows but 'they do not get justice'. No one had sheep. Living a mile from the shore, the tenants were allowed to take as much seaweed as they wanted free of charge. Some of it had to be taken three or four miles by sea. Norman was unmarried. The family had moved to Balachuirn from Fearns in the mid 1850s.

He explained about housing on the island. Every man at first built his own house and it belonged to him. If he left his lot, his successor took over the house at a valuation. When Norman got his lot, the house on it was 'not fit for human habitation'. He wanted it valued as a 'broken house', as he would have to rebuild it. However, he received a letter from the factor saying that he was not allowed to rob his predecessor, and if he would not take the house at a valuation, he would find a man who would. Norman therefore had to pay £4 for the house, and then rebuild it at his own expense.

The real grievance for this area was the lack of land, particularly hill grazing, and the infestation of rabbits. Norman believed that they were not allowed to trap the rabbits. They were certainly not allowed to keep either a dog or a gun. The minister confirmed this, saying, 'I believe dogs are not allowed, except in a few instances; and if a cat should venture outside a door, a gamekeeper is watching with poison, traps, or gun to destroy it.'

Rev. Galbraith wrote at length about conditions regarding the game, in particular about the rabbits.

> In my opinion the greatest grievance in this island now is the loss by game. I do not profess to be able to state this fully, nor can it be understood by any who are not eye-witnesses. Mr Wood's representatives admitted, I believe, before the Commission, that 'he bought Raasay as a sporting estate more than anything else'. The manner in which the estate affairs are managed shows that this statement is strictly true. Game is the first and principal consideration, and everything else appears very secondary as compared with this. This being the case, however kindly Mr Wood is disposed to be – and he is kindly disposed – yet the crofters must suffer serious loss. The Rona people have no ground of complaint on this score, as there are no rabbits there, and winged game are comparatively few. But the Raasay crofters suffer very serious loss. I am aware that three parties received compensation at Martinmas last. Probably the rest did not apply, partly because they did not wish to be troublesome to their proprietor, and partly because they might fear that if the complaint became as general as the loss, they might expose themselves to serious consequences. They are tenants-at-will, and such a state of things is not fitted to cherish a spirit of independence. I believe the island of Raasay is at present fully stocked with rabbits, although all the sheep and cattle were at once cleared off. This is becoming more apparent every day. The large sheep farm in Mr Wood's own hands formerly carried over 3 000 sheep. Now the stock is about the half of that number, and the reduction is mainly through the want of grass. The losses during the past year have been so great, that now, I understand, it is proposed to send off the remainder of the sheep, rather than leave them here to starve. One thing is plain, the island cannot support a full stock of sheep and a full stock of rabbits. Meanwhile the rabbits have practically cleared the ground for themselves, or will speedily do so, unless they receive a very effectual check.
>
> I have been told by the keepers that so many as 14 000 rabbits have been killed in a season. The number that die of starvation and other causes is very great ... The crops and grazings of the tenants in the north end of the island are entirely unprotected from the ravages of these vermin, and the loss, as I can testify from observation is very great ... The people have been feeling it a sore grievance, that they should have to cultivate the most inferior land, and pay such high rent for it, while the best part of the island was under sheep. But instead of diminishing, it will only increase the grievance manifold, if, as is now supposed, the best land in the island is to be practically, if not wholly, converted into a rabbit warren ...

Clearly, even those few tenants in the south of the island were having a struggle to make ends meet. This was partly due to the fact that their holdings were small, and that they had very little grazing land, which severely limited the stock they could keep. Rabbits devastated their crops and their rents were high. They were therefore forced to take employment from the estate, at wages that were little more than George Rainy had been paying in the 1840s, nearly forty years before. But if things were bad in the south end of the island, they were even worse in the north.

❦

Alasdair Mòr, Alexander MacLeod, gave evidence from North Arnish. At that time he was seventy-five, and felt that the land he had would serve him for the rest of his life. However it was dear and spoiled by the game. The rabbits were thick on the arable ground. He made it clear that it was very difficult for a man to complain, even if his crops had been spoilt.

The second man to give evidence from Arnish was Charles MacLeod. He was a great-great grandson of the MacBeath from Applecross, who changed his name to MacLeod when MacGilleChaluim gave him land near Dun Caan. Charles told the Commission that the land was poor, and the crop yield did not justify the work put in. Rents were raised in MacKay's time, in the 1870s. The arable ground was in spots here and there, and could not be measured. The seed and potatoes sown each year would be sufficient for the family if the ground were good, and the crops were not being spoilt by game. The feeding boxes for the pheasants were at the end of the arable ground. Tenants were not allowed to kill, or trap, the rabbits. Conditions were worse now, because of this. They had two cows each, with their calves and, on average, six sheep. There were no horses.

❦

Murchadh Alasdair Dhuinn, Murdo Nicolson from Torran gave his evidence. He had moved to Torran from Fladda about 1874 because he had no land on Fladda. At Torran there were three tenants, paying £5 each. The soumming was two cows and a stirk, with four or five sheep. Again, MacKay had put their rent up. The rabbits and pheasants spoiled the crops.

The hearing where the men gave their evidence was being held at Torran. One of the commissioners had commented on it being a pleasant place, with its 'pretty little woods'. Murdo was quite clear that 'the pretty little woods are not as pretty as that'. They sheltered the game that then came out and spoiled their crops.

He had a small boat of fifteen feet, and fished for lobsters and herring. Spring work on the croft stopped the men fishing at that time of year. He went to the east coast fishing, and depended on that to supply his family, but some years were poor. Because he went away to the fishing, he did not work for Mr Wood. There was a good landing place at Torran for small boats. Fladda was a reasonably convenient place for bigger boats, had they been able to afford them. Larger boats would have allowed them to take advantage of good fishing in other areas, such as Gairloch, which they could not do with their small boats.

The point about the game, in particular the pheasants, doing damage was expanded on by Rev. Galbraith who said:

> Over 2 000 pheasants are reared annually, and these are to be found over all parts of the island. The factor is reported to have said that these are amply fed in the preserves, and consequently have no inducement to wander into the crofters' crops. The fact is, they wander wherever they can get food. He lives

in Inverness, and does not see the crofters, or their crops, but seldom. He generally sees the crofters at 'rent time'; but as for their crops, I question if he sees them at all. I live, however, in Raasay, and see for myself – hence the difference of our observations and experience.

<hr />

Two men from Fladda gave evidence. Iain Raghnaill, John Gillies, said that there were about fifty people on the island. Altogether they paid £30 rent, while before MacKay raised it, they had paid £22. He repeated the complaint of poor land and high rents. He had two cows, one stirk and one two-year-old along with five sheep, although he was allowed to keep six. No one had more than seven. There were no horses, because 'they would be drowned'. Everybody had been given a change of seed from Mr Wood's manager that year, and in a good year John might expect to have three returns of oats and potatoes. Seaweed, from the rocks about the shore, was used as fertiliser.

The fishing ground around was not good. Only eels and skate were about their shores because the ground was foul and too deep. He had not been at the east coast fishing for the previous three years, but prior to that had been there for eighteen seasons. On some nights, at the fishing, John had made £8 but on other nights nothing at all. He had stayed at home to work for Mr Wood. Others from Fladda worked for Mr Wood for a short time about May each year 'just to get sufficient money to take them away to the fishing'. Although they could all get steady work from the estate, they would expect to make three times as much by going away to the fishing. Everyone took any and all work that came their way.

John had steady work and wages of 13s. per week. Most of the work was at Mr Wood's own house, twelve miles away. Only some of the Balachuirn people got work at the Square at Glam. Therefore, he had to be away from home all week and out of his week's wages, he had to pay 2s. for lodgings and also his personal expenses. During that time 'the family would be starving at home'. Some of the women worked at the whelks, making 1s. 6d or 2s. 6d. per bushel but it could take two days to collect a bushel.

John also spoke about the channel between Fladda and Raasay, which was not more than thirty yards wide at high tide. The people of Fladda wanted a bridge, or to be re-housed somewhere else so that their children could go to school in safety. John had eight children. As things stood, if the men were away from home, the children were often starving while waiting for a suitable tide to get home. There were in fact many days when they could not go to school at all. The 1881 census shows twelve scholars on Fladda.

Alasdair Ruadh, Alexander MacLennan from Fladda, aged seventy-four, also spoke. However, probably because of his age he was questioned about past times, rather than the present. Some of his evidence has already been given, and can be found in a previous chapter.

Alasdair spoke of Mr Wood as being a 'good landlord'. Boats had been replaced after the storms. They had been given a rent reduction of one third, because of its being a poor year, and they had been given seed potatoes.

The man who spoke for the people of Umachan was Iain Aonghais, John Gillies, who had lived in Umachan for nearly forty years. He said that they had poor land and that there were too many people on it. There were two families on each lot (or croft), and two families who had no lot – a total of eight families.

In 1883 John paid £5 rent, but the rental for the whole township had been £12 6s. until MacKay had raised the rents in the mid 1870s. In the past there had been three families at Umachan. Then others had come from evicted townships. Two families had come from Hallaig to one croft, because they would not go to Australia. They went onto a croft, previously occupied by a man who had gone to Australia. Another man had come from Hallaig as a boy, and had married a girl from Umachan.

John told the commissioners that each man in Umachan had one cow, a young beast and seven or eight sheep with lambs. He himself had two cows and two stirks, but the others hadn't got as much as he had. He did not have the right to keep any more stock. If he had done, he would have had to pay extra for the grass for them. In good years he might have been able to make a boll or two of meal.

In 1851 there were indeed only three tenants in Umachan. They were John's father, Angus Gillies, who remained there. The others were two brothers, Donald and Alexander MacLennan. By 1861, Donald MacLennan and his family had moved to Kyle Rona. Alexander MacLennan had died before 1851, but his widow and family were still living in Umachan at that time. By 1861, Alexander's widow was living with her married son, Murchadh an t-Saighdeir, on Fladda. No reference has been found of any of them emigrating.

At the time of the commission, Iain Aonghais was in Umachan, probably with two married sons and their families. They were either living with him, or at least on his ground. That accounts for the two families without any ground. A further two families appear to have been moved from Hallaig. The man who married the local girl was from Eyre and does not show up in the Raasay census of 1851. He was quite possibly working in Portree at that time. He appears to have taken over his father-in-law's ground. Both the father-in law and the remaining two families appear to have come to Umachan from Kyle Rona.

Donald MacLeod, one of the older inhabitants at seventy-eight, represented Kyle Rona. He had lived there all his days and had been elected to speak for nine others. Poverty sent him to speak to the commissioners. He could remember when there were five families, twenty-nine people, in the township and they paid £15 rent. In 1883 there were ten families, eighty people, paying £30 rent. The division of holdings, to allow married sons to stay, had caused the increase in the number of families. Donald could not remember others coming in from other townships.

He could not remember the first removing in MacLeod's time, but thought that 'not many' were put out. He did not think that they had gone 'of their own accord ... People were not living in Rona at first, they were sent to Rona'. He could remember Rainy clearing fourteen townships about thirty years before. He said, 'the only occupants of that land today are rabbits, deer and sheep'. It was Donald who told the commissioners about Mr Rainy's rule about marriage.

One of the commissioners had read in an old book that there had once been a large place in the middle of the island that was free to anybody to take their cattle to in summer, the summer shieling. He asked if Donald had heard of that, and was told that it was true, but that it was not there now for the people.

The people lived on meal and fish, and very seldom got meat. Food was more plentiful in former times. The rabbits ate the grass and there was nothing left for the cows to produce milk. The calves were dying for want of milk, and there was very little milk for the children. They had no sheep. Wool from the sheep had, in the past, allowed them to make their own clothes, but now they had to buy cloth. Rabbits were free to go through the townships, and he had seen them there, so thick that they could not be counted. Donald 'had been sowing but had not been reaping'. He had not been to the mill for the past two years.

In 1841 there were five families, probably all tenants, in Kyle Rona, just as Donald had said. By 1851, however, there were nine tenants. Two of the 'new tenants' had moved from Torran during the time of the MacLeods, before Rainy took over the estate. Sometime after 1847, one tenant had moved from Arnish and another from Dry Harbour to Kyle Rona. Of those nine tenants, two had moved to Umachan by 1861.

⁂

The man chosen to represent the people of Dry Harbour was Ruairidh Nèill, Roderick MacKay. He told the commission that there were some people in the township who could remember when there were only seven families there. Now there were fifteen, and even if they were 'to get the place for nothing they would not make a living out of it'. He told the commissioners about the rent rises. The seven families had paid £50, now they paid £80, although the land was the same. One man's lot was divided to make room for another family from Fearns. In all, two families came to the township from areas that were cleared. Otherwise, the increase in numbers was caused by the natural increase of the place. The population of Rona had never been as high as it was then, and 'if Rona would carry sheep as well as the rest of Raasay it would have been cleared the same as the other townships of Raasay'. Most of the people wanted to leave Rona to go to any of the 'places that are lying waste' on Raasay. Ruairidh believed that the township of Dry Harbour could comfortably sustain only five families.

He paid £5 12s. 6d. plus road money and poor rates. They had all been granted a one third reduction of their rent that year. His soumming appeared to be two cows, a two-year-old and two sheep. He had kept three cows, but the land would not do justice to two. He had nine or ten sheep. He said, 'Though I have two cows that are named upon me, they don't belong to me. They belong to merchants in Portree and Glasgow. It is they who are keeping me in meal ... I am rearing a family on poverty.'

The arable ground was very soft. Ruairidh said that while they were making ditches on part of the arable land they had to have planks under their feet. 'If a man missed that plank another one will need to help him out of the bog'. The arable land was in spots here and there, far away from the township. He said, 'Our arable land is so far from us that should I leave at six o'clock in the morning I would not get home before eight or nine o'clock at night'.

They cut peat for fuel, but the peat would not last for much longer as there were too many families using it. The peat mosses used by the Dry Harbour tenants was 'far from our houses', and Ruairidh could see the time coming when it would be completely used up.

For the last twenty-eight years he had gone to the fishing at Peterhead and Fraserburgh on the east coast. He would have preferred to have enough land at home, so that he did not have to go away to the fishing. Everyone on Rona depended on the fishing for their subsistence. They all 'live by the sea'. They had small boats. Some were destroyed in the storm of 1881. Of the replacements, some were better than the old ones, but some were not. With these boats they fished around Rona. Most of the fish caught they cured, as they were not conveniently placed for market. There was a 'pretty good harbour at Rona', but a pier would have been an advantage.

There was a school on Rona. The children from the south end of the island had to walk two miles to it. They took pieces to school. They could not attend in bad weather, as there was no road. Since the 1872 Education Act had made schooling compulsory, they had not had a teacher who could speak Gaelic. That was a disadvantage.

They had a meeting house on Rona. Although the minister did not come regularly, there was a missionary staying on the island. Everyone on the island belonged to the Free Church.

Ruairidh said that some could remember only seven families living in Dry Harbour. Of those seven families, only four were Rona people. The other three appear to have moved to Rona shortly before the 1841 census. It seems likely that the MacLeods moved them from Raasay, when the south end tacks were being created in the late 1830s. By the early 1840s, therefore, the number of tenants living in Dry Harbour had already been increased from four to seven. Some other families who showed up in the 1841 census in Dry Harbour had come from outwith the area, and moved away again in the early 1850s. By 1883, the number had again increased from seven to fifteen. Little wonder then that the people there were living in poverty. Ruairidh said that he believed that five families could live in reasonable comfort in Dry Harbour. His estimate is shown to be well based, as only four lived there before the MacLeods began clearing people from Raasay.

☙☙☙

Giving evidence for the people of Doire na Guaille, Rona, was Seonaidh Mòr, John Nicolson, aged thirty-six. He began by describing conditions:

> We are working on land and sea, summer and winter and spring, every quarter of the year and after that we have only poverty. I cannot fully disclose the

poverty of Rona ... I can say with truth that my skiff is my cart and that the wives and the children are the horses and there is truth in that because it is the work of the horses which they perform. The creel is on their back continually and after being worked so hard at that they cannot make a living out of it.

He could remember the township being held by one man, then four. By 1883 there were eight families in the township. Two of those families had come from Kyle Rona, but the rest were the natural increase of the place.

John could not see that it was worth his while to build a house, considering the quality of the land. He lived in an 'old block house', because he wanted to be moved to the mainland of Raasay. None of the houses in the township were slated. Mr Wood had paid for the building of all but one of the houses in the township. The men had quarried stone for the new houses and had been paid for doing so. Mr Wood also provided wood for internal fittings for the houses, but had not increased the rents. He had not made any improvements, such as fencing or draining. The soil was peaty, and rock would have had to be blasted to drain the land effectively.

John had been going to sea, but considered that the fishing was a lottery. Some years, he knew of men who had hardly made enough money to get back home. He would prefer to get a good bit of land than go to the fishing. When asked if the Rona men could work big boats, such as were on the east coast, he said that they could, but felt that fishing and croft work were not easy partners, the 'one thing is only spoiling the other'.

Niall Ailein Lèith, Neil MacLeod, aged thirty-five, gave evidence about Braig, Rona. There were three families living there. MacKay had shifted them all from Dry Harbour to Braig, near the lighthouse, and charged £20 for the township.

The Valuation Roll shows this township as the 'Rona Lighthouse Farm'. Mr Wood had done nothing in the way of improvements. Their houses were built by the people themselves when they had moved. Neil worked as one of the hands on the 'lighthouse packet'.

About 1857 the lighthouse at Rona came into service. The Stevenson family, who had been responsible for many of the lighthouses around the coast, built it. It was manned by two permanent keepers, who lived there with their families.

When Neil moved to Braig he had taken four cows with him, but two had died. He also had one stirk and five ewes. He paid £10 rent. He would like to see the people get proper pieces of land in the townships that were then lying waste. He did not know of anyone who wanted to emigrate.

Just as Rev. Angus Galbraith had sent in a written statement giving details of the crofters' grievances in the south end of the island, so John Munro, the missionary on Rona, spoke for the people of that island. He attended the hearing and answered questions put by the commissioners.

John Munro was from Skye and had held some land there before going to

Glasgow, where he had had many different jobs. Six years ago, after thirty-two years in Glasgow, he had come to Rona. He told of the poverty of the people.

He was questioned about the school. There had not been a regular school in Rona, but a schoolmaster came now and again. Many of the adults could not read or write and few could speak English. They all very much wanted their children to be educated. No one ever spoke of the school rates as being a burden. Their only grievance, on that score, was the want of a road from the south end to the schoolhouse in Dry Harbour. There was only a track among the rocks and bogs. Ruairidh Nèill, Roderick MacKay from Dry Harbour, had made the point that since 1872 there had been no Gaelic-speaking teacher on the island. The young lady teaching at the time was there on a temporary basis. Not only did she have no Gaelic, but also she was from Aberdeenshire. Small wonder then that she and the children had a communication problem.

The herring had been very scarce the previous winter and they had few potatoes. The people, therefore, had to live mainly on meal and fish. They had very little milk. He agreed that if the people were able to have porridge and milk for breakfast and potatoes and herring for dinner they would consider themselves not badly off. But potatoes were scarce and there was very little milk.

Raasay and Rona people used to make all their own clothing and blankets. It was good and substantial. Most still made their own blankets. There was a weaver on Rona, but she did not keep very well, and could not work regularly. No one now made their own shoes.

He was questioned about possible emigration as a 'cure' for the overpopulation. Two of his own brothers had gone abroad. Nothing that they had said in any of their letters had encouraged him to emigrate himself. He had heard from others who had emigrated that the work had been very hard. The men of Rona were willing to work hard. If they were given government help to stock new holdings, they would be more willing, he believed, to work hard on Raasay than abroad.

Most people had voluntarily given up drink. However, people from Rona used to smuggle. They had shown the missionary some of their stills. The people were now very attentive to religious duties. There had been 'a great deal of nonsense' at ceilidhs, but now they seldom sang songs or heard the bagpipes.

EVIDENCE GIVEN BY THE HIGHLAND COMMITTEE OF THE
FREE CHURCH OF SCOTLAND

As well as taking evidence from the crofters and their representatives, the Napier Commission took evidence from other bodies, including the Highland Committee of the Free Church of Scotland. This was written by J. C. MacPhail and Robert Rainy, principal of the Free Church College in Edinburgh and nephew of George Rainy who had previously owned Raasay. This report makes clear that the authors were proud of their Church's role in minimising disorder in the Highlands at that time. Describing the role of Free Church ministers and laymen, the report stated that 'the influence of the ministers ... has not been used to embitter questions of this kind. On the contrary, the tendency has been to maintain peace and quietness'.

Later, many members of the church regretted its failure to back up the more radical land campaigners. In his written submission to the Napier Commission, Rev. Angus Galbraith of Raasay appears to question his own stance in 1874, when George MacKay substantially raised the rents on Raasay and Rona. The minister said that he had influenced the people to agree to MacKay's terms 'in the interest of peace'. This passage has already been quoted when discussing MacKay's time as landowner. Whatever his feelings about that time, it must be said that Rev. Galbraith wrote a very clear and detailed statement of the crofters' case to the Commission. Rev. Angus Galbraith left Raasay in 1890, when he went to Ferintosh in the Black Isle.

He finished his statement to the commission by highlighting the problems he saw on Raasay, and making recommendations. His remedies were

- That the people should be given more land, but it had to be good land, at its true value. It had to be protected from vermin, by which he meant primarily rabbits. They would thus be in a better position to support themselves when bad years occurred. Neither the people, nor the proprietors would lose under this arrangement.
- The power of the factors should be limited. Many grievances were largely due to them.
- Crofters should have better security for their holdings. Tenancy-at-will involved uncertainty. That not only prevented the improvement of their houses and lands, but also denied them any measure of independence. Every man who conducted himself properly and paid his way should be entitled to that.
- Competent valuators should settle all disputes as to the value of land.
- Valuators, not the proprietor or the factor, should estimate all damage to crops and grazing by game.

He stated the case clearly:

> It could scarcely be expected that any parties who prefer rabbits not only to sheep, but to people, could be impartial judges as to the amount of damage done. I am thoroughly satisfied that if the crofter population generally are to receive justice – and we ask no more for them – this must be secured to them by the law of the land. I trust the Report of the Commission will be followed up by practical legislation, and I do not know any places that more urgently require this than properties bought as sporting estates more than anything else.

Clearly the people of Raasay and Rona had been suffering from severe poverty for many years. This was due, not to natural forces – such as climate, and geographical position – but to a landholding system that allowed one young man who had inherited a great deal of money to buy this estate and manage it, first and foremost, for his own pleasure rather than for the good of the land or of the people living on it.

Lord Napier himself, had asked James Ross, 'Do you think 700 people a great population for 29,000 acres?', to which the reply was 'No, I don't say it is.' James Ross had said that the estate was 29,000 acres, although the actual figure was 18,000 acres. By exaggerating this total figure, he implied that the crofters in the north end had more land than they did.

During the general debate on the land problem at this time, many landowners had argued that the talk of 'pre-Clearance paradise in the Highlands' was false. It is clear that on Raasay, although 'paradise' in the true sense was an exaggeration, certainly compared to the 1880s it must have seemed so. Those Raasay and Rona men who gave evidence of past landholding in their townships were entirely accurate, and without exaggeration.

Their evidence seems to show that their memory of the MacLeod lairds had dimmed. Inevitably, the more recent memory of the people of Raasay was that large numbers of people had left in Rainy's time. They did not give evidence about the forced evictions or about the large increase in population during the time of the last MacLeod laird, perhaps because that had been forgotten. They did remember these people leaving in the late 1840s and early 1850s, when Rainy cleared the non-local population off the estate. They also remembered Raasay people emigrating and many appear to have assumed that these emigrations were forced. Those who had emigrated in the 1850s had done so in family groups, leaving very few relatives on the island. It was also remembered that the people remaining on the east side were forced to move to the north end.

The good land on Raasay, that could have been worked by and for the people, was lying waste, while they were crowded on small plots of poor land in the north end. All that was being asked was a reasonable amount of good land at a fair rent, to enable them to pay their way.

Everyone spoke of Mr Wood as a 'good landlord'. He had granted a general rent abatement the previous November and given out free seed that spring. Both of these things would have been of great benefit to the people, and were very much appreciated. Whether these 'acts of kindness' were done at that time knowing that the Napier Commission would be taking evidence in the near future is not known. Certainly James Ross stressed both as evidence of Mr Wood's consideration and generosity towards the crofters. It must also be remembered, however, that the crofters and cottars were not allowed to keep dogs (at Balachuirn) and were not allowed to kill rabbits (at Arnish) although 14,000 rabbits had been killed on the estate in a single year.

The people were industrious and well behaved, as spoken for by the minister and the missionary. It will be remembered that George Rainy also made this point to the M'Neill Commission in 1851.

AFTER THE NAPIER COMMISSION

Although Lord Napier recognised the complaints of tenants with regard to the size of their holdings, the commission members were not able to agree on a solution to the problem. Napier wanted to create economic security. The final report, based largely on his views, proposed

– The re-creation of a township system, responsible for common pasture.

- Limited security of tenure – tenants paying over £6 rent should get thirty-year leases, but those paying less should be helped by a scheme of voluntary emigration.
- Partnership between proprietor and tenant.

His long-term solution was to help people to form 'habits of industry and self-respect'. In stating this, he does not appear to appreciate the main problem of the people of Raasay and Rona, and probably other areas as well. It was the system of land holding that was keeping the people in a state of severe poverty, and grinding them down year after year. It has been said already that the people of Raasay and Rona would work well and willingly, if they were given the chance to do so to better themselves. The landholding system also denied them independence. Self-respect would follow if they had their independence and were able to pay their way.

A period of calm followed the publishing of the report. As it was debated, tenants waited for action. The government, realising that the proposals contained in the report addressed only part of the problem, was reluctant to commit itself to legislation. It was well aware that the scheme of voluntary emigration was unlikely to meet with approval. The government waited, hoping that proprietors and tenants could reach agreement among themselves.

THE CROFTER HOLDINGS (SCOTLAND) ACT OF 1886

Because the problems concerning land in the Highlands did not go away, as the government had hoped, it was forced to legislate and the Crofter Holdings (Scotland) Act of 1886 resulted. The main points of this Act were

- Tenants, paying less than £30 rent per year were granted security of tenure, subject to certain conditions.
- The Crofters' Commission was created to determine fair rents, adjudicate on arrears, and set levels of compensation for improvements when a crofter left his holding.
- A group of five crofters could apply for extra grazing land, but only if that land bordered on their holdings and was owned by the same landlord.

As far as Raasay and Rona were concerned, this Act defined a crofter – a tenant who paid less than £30 rent per year for his land – and gave him security of tenure for a fair rent. However, it did not begin to address the main problem – the availability of suitable land. The Act, therefore, created crofters but it did not give them adequate crofts.

THE LATE 1880S

In spring 1886 Edward Wood died of a spinal disease, aged only thirty-six. Mrs Wood continued to run the estate after her husband's death. Suisnish House was refurbished and servants' quarters added, for the family's use while Raasay House was let to shooting tenants.

Although Mrs Wood continued to spend large amounts of money on the estate over and above the income it generated, expenditure was not as great as in the early years of the Woods ownership. The number of servants and other estate workers was reduced. In July 1887 Mr Woods yacht, the *Rona*, was sold to a Mr James Weston Clayton of London. He kept it for eleven months before selling it to Count Pierre Pastre of Marseilles. Duncan Matheson, who had come to Raasay as captain of George Rainy's yacht, the *Falcon*, retired.

The Crofters' Commission began the huge task of dealing with applications from crofters to have 'fair rents' set. Owing to the large number of applications received, it was not until 1889 that they were able to deal with those who applied from Raasay and Rona. At that time there were eighty-four crofters and cottars on the estate, paying a total rental of £368 11s. 6d. Fifty men, who were between them paying a total rental of £248 7s. applied to the commission for fair rents to be set. Their new fair rents were fixed at a total of £153 4s. – a reduction of thirty-eight per cent. The applicants had arrears amounting to £677 16s. 10d. They were granted a reduction of arrears of sixty-six per cent, leaving only £229 14s. 7d. to be paid. Mrs Wood applied the same reduction of rent to all the crofters and cottars on the estate, and dealt similarly with the their arrears.

Figure 7/3 shows only the rentals of the tenants. Cottars' rents are not included. This probably accounts for the difference between the total of £287 1s. shown in the table and the figure of £368 11s. 6d. given by James Ross.

Figure 7/3. Rent of tenants in 1827, 1884 and 1889 and arrears in 1889 after the Crofters' Commission ruling.

Township	Rent in 1827			Rent in 1884			Rent in 1889			Arrears in 1889*		
	£	s.	d.	£	s.	d.	£	s.	d.	£	s.	d.
Arnish	21	0	0	31	0	0	19	10	0	33	0	0
Torran	10	5	6	12	0	0	6	0	0	8	0	0
Fladda	22	15	6	24	0	0	12	0	0	12	0	0
Umachan	12	6	0	13	0	0	7	19	6	6	0	0
Eilean Taigh	6	1	6	8	0	0	4	10	0	4	10	0
Kyle Rona	31	15	0	30	0	0	19	14	0	25	0	0
Doire na Guaille	17	17	6	20	0	0	12	0	0	17	0	0
Big Harbour	17	14	6	15	0	0	9	0	0	6	9	4
Dry Harbour	59	14	6	63	10	0	35	10	0	50	0	0
Balachuirn	—			33	1	0	22	16	0	—		†
Oscaig	—			37	10	0	29	10	0	—		†
Total	**199**	**10**	**0**	**287**	**1**	**0**	**178**	**9**	**6**	**161**	**19**	**4**

* James Ross said that 50 applicants applied to the commission for fair rent to be fixed. Those 50 had arrears of £677 16s. 10d. Of that amount £448 2s. 3d. was cancelled, leaving £229 14s. 7d. to be paid.

† No arrears are given for Oscaig and Balachuirn. That may account for the difference in the amounts of arrears shown above and determined by the Crofters' Commission.

That the crofters had good reason to complain of high rents was proven beyond all doubt. The figures in the table are worth further consideration. Rents for the townships of the north end of Raasay and Rona remained fairly static until

George G. MacKay raised them dramatically before selling the estate in 1874. Although Mr Wood had reduced the rentals of some townships prior to 1884, others had increased, so the overall figure remained much the same.

The earliest rental information is for 1827, shortly after John MacLeod, the last of the MacLeod lairds, inherited the estate. It is interesting to note that the fair rents set in 1889 were substantially lower than the rents charged by John MacLeod in 1827, over sixty years earlier. Certainly, farming rents generally were being reduced in the late 1880s, because of the difficulty in letting sheep farms, and because stock prices were variable. However, this must surely indicate that very high rents were being charged in the time of the MacLeods. No doubt that is why many Raasay people emigrated in the 1820s and 1830s.

The reduction in rent and arrears for all the tenants and cottars on the estate would have been very welcome. It may be noted, however, that the old rental income of £368 was a very small percentage (less than four per cent) of the average annual expenditure (£10 070) of the Woods on the estate in the six years since 1876.

The crofters on Raasay now had security of tenure and fair rents. However, they could get no increase in the amount of land that they held. James Ross had made it clear to the commission that Mr Wood would not consider increasing even the common grazing land for his tenants. Although he admitted that new crofts could be colonised to the advantage of the crofters, 'so far as Mr Wood is concerned ... it would not suit his views, because we know he bought Raasay more as a sporting estate than anything else'. Therefore, as far as the factor was concerned, the only 'cure' for the overpopulation on the north end of the island was emigration. The crofters' evidence to the commission, however, made it clear that very few, if any, of them would consider emigration. Therefore the Crofter Holdings (Scotland) Act of 1886 was of limited benefit to the crofters of Raasay. It did absolutely nothing for the cottars living on the estate.

In 1887 the east coast fishing gave little return. There was now a growing import market for chilled and frozen meat from New Zealand and both North and South America. This resulted in changes to the livestock market in Britain. The growing consumerism in the second half of the nineteenth century was also by now very evident in the Highlands.

In 1888 a Conservative government came into power. There was therefore a change of policy on the 'Highland problem'. The intention now was to deal with the problem of congestion without altering the land tenure system, and emigration was again proposed. In an attempt to end at least some of the people's dependence on the land, full time fishing was encouraged. This was done by large-scale investment in infrastructure. At this time roads and harbours were built. Steamboat subsidies were introduced. Of great benefit to the fishing industry later on, telegraphic extensions were also made.

In the few years up to 1891 there was some slight improvement. Winters were mild, livestock prices were higher and there had been some improvement in the fishing industry. However, early in 1891, bad weather again hit the west coast, and yet again there was destitution in the Skye and Wester Ross area. The previously mild winters had allowed a build up of livestock, which now could not be wintered. Seed and meal were used to feed that livestock, leaving a large part of the population starving. Authorities reacted much as they had done in the 1840s, and levels of wages paid for relief work were set so low that only the really needy would take the work. The Conservative government had done nothing to reform land tenure, and that was still the main objective of the crofters.

RAASAY AND RONA IN 1891

At the time of the 1891 census, Mrs Wood was in London. Four of her children were at home with their German governess and other servants. Altogether twelve people from Raasay House were in London, probably most being servants. The head gamekeeper was now John MacLean who had moved to Raasay, probably about 1890 from Kirkhill, Inverness. William Minty was the head gardener. A shepherd and a farm labourer were at Glam, a shepherd and gamekeeper at Castle, and only one shepherd and his family lived at Fearns.

There was no minister on Raasay, Rev. Galbraith having left the previous year. Alexander MacLennan from Lochalsh was the missionary at Dry Harbour, Rona, having moved there from Applecross about 1886.

The teacher in Clachan was still Alexander MacFarlane. He taught seventy-six pupils, some having to walk a distance to school. There were twenty scholars from Oscaig, North and South, five from Balachuirn, nine from Balmeanach and five from Glam. There were four from Creachan, but the loneliest walk must surely have been that of the one child from Fearns.

Neil MacLeod was the teacher in Torran. He was possibly the same man as had been the 'elementary teacher' in Fladda in 1871. Since then he had been in Dunnet, Caithness and Edinburgh, coming back to Raasay after 1886. In Torran he had forty-seven pupils, including six from Castle, ten from Fladda, two from Eilean Taigh, three from Umachan and eighteen from Kyle Rona.

At this time, Rona had two teachers, each described as 'elementary school teachers' on the enumeration book. Ewen MacKenzie from Gairloch was at Dry Harbour. His schoolhouse was having an addition built onto it. The two masons carrying out this work were in lodgings with Alasdair Dhòmhnaill 'ic Uilleim, Alexander MacLeod. Dòmhnall Alasdair Dheirg, Donald Nicolson, was employed labouring for them. The school had thirty-seven pupils, including nine from Braig. That township now had only two families living there; the heads of both households, although only in their thirties, were widowed.

Doire na Guaille had its own school. The teacher was John MacBeath, a grandson of John MacLeod who had been the teacher at Dry Harbour for a time, before moving to Torran in 1852. John had twenty-two pupils. He was boarding with Raghnall Beag, Ronald MacLennan, who, twenty years earlier, had the teacher at Kyle Rona staying with him.

The lighthouse on Rona employed two keepers, neither of them local men. They also employed Murchadh an Tàilleir, Murdo Nicolson, as one of the boatmen and Alasdair Dearg, Alexander Nicolson, as relief keeper. Although the work as boatman was all year round, the wage paid was low – just 5s. per week in 1893.

John Munro, the missionary on Rona who had given evidence to the Napier

Commission in 1883, died the following year. His widow was now living in Doire na Guaille with her two married sons.

There was little employment opportunity on Raasay and Rona, apart from working for the estate. The four teachers and the lighthouse employees have already been mentioned. John MacMillan, son of the former teacher, was the postmaster. His daughter was employed as assistant postmistress. Norman MacLeod, living in Mill Place, is the only 'letter carrier' identified in the census. Peter Nicolson and his daughter worked in the shop. There were three dressmakers, four domestic servants and a joiner, Fionnlagh Alasdair Ruaidh, Finlay MacLennan from Fladda, who were probably not estate workers.

Thirty-nine people worked for the estate in the south end of the island, as well as those from Raasay House who were in London. Three more were at the 'salmon fishing', also owned by the Woods. Another dozen labourers or servants were, most likely, also estate workers.

About fifty-five men were described as crofters and a further forty were employed in some capacity at the fishing.

There was another significant employer, although not on Raasay itself. The Conservative government's investment in infrastructure created jobs building the new railways. A total of fourteen men, nine from the south end, three from the north end and two from Rona, were working as labourers on the schemes.

THE DEER FOREST COMMISSION – 1893

In August 1892, Gladstone's Liberal government was elected on the promise that they would legislate on behalf of cottars and others who had been excluded from the 1886 Act. Although they promised that more land would be brought under crofting tenure, the means of doing so were vague.

In December that year, the Deer Forest Commission was set up, not to advise on policy, but to identify land that could be put under crofting tenure. Their report was published in April 1895. This commission sat in Portree on Tuesday, 18 April 1893 and took evidence from eleven men from the Raasay estate. All but three of these men were examined in Gaelic through an interpreter.

Two men from Doire na Guaille gave evidence to the commission. The first was Raghnall an Scòtaich, Ronald Nicolson. He told the commission that there was no land available for the formation of new holdings on Rona. He did not know how much land he had, because it was scattered amongst rocks and stones. He had cows and seven sheep. He worked at fishing, labouring and 'every sort of work that comes in my way'. The previous year he was labouring on Raasay, at 13s. to 15s. per week, and lived by labouring, rather than either fishing or the croft.

At that time there were eight holdings in Doire na Guaille, but 'it is only enough for two'. All the Rona tenants complain about the smallness of their holding, and most were anxious to leave. Some had lived on Raasay in former times. There was land available in Brochel, North and South Manish, Hallaig, Leac, Fearns, Haer, Eyre, Suisnish and North and South Screapadal. Ronald had been told that crofters occupied all these townships in the past, until removal and change took place about forty years ago. That land was now held by the landlord, and was under sheep and game – rabbits and deer.

Ronald would have liked fifteen acres of arable land along with grazing up to the extent of the old township marches. He did not know what the rent would be on that size of croft. He would require financial assistance to put up a house and steading and buy stock for a new holding, but had no idea where that assistance might come from. His friends were as poor as he was.

The township that is named Haer by Ronald is not mentioned by others in their evidence, nor does it appear in estate rentals. It may be the small township of Tòrr, the ruins of which can be seen beside the stream that flows out of Loch a' Chadha-chàrnaich (a stony or rocky pass). This loch lies in the deep gully to the east of Dun Caan.

The second man from Doire na Guaille who gave evidence was Raghnall Beag, Ronald MacLennan. Born about 1830 on Rona, Ronald had lived in Umachan, then in Kyle Rona, before he moved to Doire na Guaille in the 1870s.

In 1893 he had half a croft and four cows. He would have liked to be able to have five or six cows, about fifty sheep and a horse. Because 'we are so accustomed to broken land' he had no idea how much land would be required for that stock.

Ronald had been the boatman on the lighthouse boat, earning only 5s. per week for the work, since about 1889. Perhaps he had taken over the job from Niall Ailein Lèith, Neil MacLeod from Braig, who had been one of the lighthouse boatmen in 1883 when he gave evidence to the Napier Commission. Neil died in 1889 aged just forty-three, leaving a widow and a young family.

Ronald MacLennan had 'seen seven landlords in Raasay', and told the Commission about previous times. He said

> I have seen the time when the mill in Raasay had more to do than it could manage. In one day I have seen no less than 300 evicted and leaving the island, and I have seen them going to the churchyard in their grief at being separated from their homes, and taking handfuls of the soil and grass that covered the graves of their kindred, as mementoes. It was myself and two other boys who ferried across for MacKenzie, the new tenant, the first lot of sheep that were to occupy the land which was thus cleared; and from that beginning the eviction process was carried on till the whole place was cleared.

He was asked, 'Were they all cleared at one time?' and replied, 'it was year after year. The two townships were cleared in Mac-Gille-Challum's time.' His evidence continued:

> Mr Rainy was the owner when the big clearance was made. They were left to settle on the top of each other, and shifted to the Isle of Skye, and cleared anywhere. Some of them reside in the parish of Portree at the present day; I know one man in Portree whose father was a tenant in Keistle, and had 80 cows and 50 sheep. His house was demolished over his head, and he was obliged to go into a little hovel there until he could dispose of his stock.

When asked, 'The island was then put under sheep?' he replied, 'Yes, it was cleared for MacKenzie, the tacksman.'

Most likely 'Keistle' was Castle, and 'eighty cows' was a misprint for eight. Even allowing for that, a man with eight cows and fifty sheep would have been in much better circumstances than the great majority of the people on Raasay. Although Ronald refers to clearances during the MacLeods' time, he does not emphasise that, remembering more clearly the large number of people leaving after George Rainy took over the estate in 1846. There appears to be no memory of the MacLeods' attempt at sheep-farming in the 1820s, but perhaps that had ended before the MacLeods left in the early 1840s. Farquhar MacRae, who held Castle before it was let to Royston MacKenzie, had had forty-six cows (including heifers and stirks) and sixty sheep in 1851. By that time he was the only tenant in the township. He gave up his lands in 1851 and, probably about the same time, the remaining five cottars were 'ejected' and went to Skye – only one of them being a local Raasay man.

The commission in 1893 did not take evidence about the crofters' circumstances, but life for Ronald had not been easy. In 1856 he had married Catherine MacLean from Eilean Taigh. Shortly after, he went away to the fishing. When the men left Raasay for work they did not know what boat they would be able to get a berth on, or even what port they would be working out of. It was, therefore, not possible for the family to contact him when his wife died in September 1856, and he was not aware of the sad news until he came home at the end of the season. In 1862, Ronald married Anne, a daughter of Donald Nicolson, An Tàillear from Dry Harbour. Incidentally, Catharine MacLean's sister, Isabella, known as Beileag Eilean an Taigh, was said to be the first person who was buried in the New Cemetery. She died in Oscaig in 1885.

✦

From Dry Harbour, Alasdair mac Iain Mhòir, Alexander MacSwan spoke for the crofters. He was the youngest son of Iain Mòr MacSween, who had been a substantial farmer in Doire Domhain until his death in 1851. The family then moved out of Doire Domhain to Rona, when Alasdair would have been about twenty.

He was a crofter, having succeeded his brother, John, who had died in 1892. He agreed with the evidence given by Raghnall an Scòtaich about the land available on Rona and Raasay.

He told the commission that he was in debt, because they had run to poverty in Rona. He said, 'There are no crofts at all in Rona; only bits here and there scattered among the rocks'. He lived by anything that came to hand, such as fishing. Why did he go to Rona from Raasay? – 'My father was put out of Raasay'. Was he in arrears of rent at the time? – 'No, we had a good stock too'. What was the reason given? – 'The township was evicted when MacKenzie, Suisnish, took it for a sheep farm.'

Alasdair would have liked a farm in either Manish or Castle, with enough ground for six or seven cows, eighty to one hundred sheep and a horse. If he could have a croft of ten acres arable, he knew 'how to cultivate, and make the best possible use of it ... I know how to manage stock and horses, and to use the scythe.' There were no horses in Rona 'but we had them in Raasay'. He could not afford to put up a house or buy stock.

Raghnall an Eilein, Ronald Gillies, spoke for the people of Fladda. He had been just ten months old when his father was drowned with five other men in 1856, and had lived on Fladda all his life. He was one of those who spoke to the commissioners in English.

The general size of a croft on Raasay was about three acres, with about ten sheep. 'The holdings will scarcely feed that stock, but they are kept alive in a sort of way.' He was in arrears of rent, but only for the present year. Ronald was a fisherman, with a share in a small fishing-skiff. However, 'I am sick-tired of the fishing: I would rather have a croft that would keep me entirely employed.' The fishing had not been good for some years past. He would have liked to have a croft that would keep seven or eight cows, eighty to one hundred sheep and a horse.

He told the commission that all the deer had been imported and added 'I believe they are endeavouring to improve the breed of rabbits'. The Fladda people had little complaint of damage by rabbits or pheasants.

About this point, the chairman read an extract of the report by J. MacDonald (quoted in an earlier chapter) which told that in 1811 the island of Raasay abounded with roe-deer. Ronald was then asked, 'Is it of the roe-deer that you complain?' In common with the other crofters, Ronald had not, in fact, been complaining about the deer at all. This line of questioning seems to have taken him rather by surprise. He replied, 'I never quarrel with the deer.' The next question, 'What kind of deer are they?' elicited the response, 'Big beasts', which brought the subject of deer to a close.

The next man to speak was Alasdair Chaluim Bhig, Alexander Gillies from Doire Dubh, although the Report of the Commission notes that he was from Kyle Rona. Like the other crofters, he would have liked to have had enough ground to keep seven or eight cows, fifty or sixty sheep and possibly a horse. However, he does say, 'I am not a practical farmer'. Two years previously he had been working on the 'Black Isle Railway' and because of that was not shown on the 1891 census. In 1892 he had been on contract work for the estate 'building a house for a crofter'. Alasdair gave his evidence in English.

Iain Dhòmhnaill, John Gillies, spoke about Torran. His rent was then £3, having been reduced from £6. He was very anxious to leave Torran and move to the south end, and could, 'with pleasure', have shown the commissioners ground suitable for crofts. He would only have been able to put his present stock on a new holding and wait until it multiplied. He had 'practical knowledge of the management of stock'. He would have preferred to get a good croft away from the sea.

Although it would be very difficult to move without financial assistance, he was so keen to move that he would have considered doing so even without assistance. He had 'no idea' where any assistance might come from. If he were to receive, say £100, of assistance and good stock, 'I would be anxious enough until it was all repaid'.

He complained of the poverty of the holdings and how they were infested with game – rabbits and pheasants, but not deer, 'the deer never trouble us'.

⁂

Although Alasdair Iain Aonghais, Alexander Gillies, was from Umachan, he is noted in the report as being from Kyle Rona. He was a cottar, who had a one third part of his father's croft. His father, at that time, had 'two small beasts', and he had 'two cows of a sort'. He made his living from fishing.

⁂

Iain Eachainn, John MacLeod, had been in Kyle Rona, and was then twenty years a cottar in Umachan, before he got the holding in Brae from Mr Wood. He referred to the townships previously mentioned as being suitable for occupation by crofters, 'I have seen them myself, occupied by crofters'.

Although there was land contiguous to his present holding, from which it could be enlarged, he would have preferred to move to another township, if he could manage the expense. Game was a constant problem in Brae, and he makes it clear that he would not have gone there, had he known how difficult life would be. When he went to Brae, the holding was empty, and 'I have now got the livestock and buildings. I believe if I got land in any of these townships I would do quite as well there.' He was prepared to go, even without financial assistance, but would have liked to have sheep on the new holding. If he could put a few on it, they would not be long in multiplying. He would like to go to Castle or Screapadal, because 'These are the best townships that have been cleared to my knowledge'.

Iain Eachainn was living with his parents in Kyle Rona in 1841. However, his view of Castle or Screapadal being the best land possibly comes from the fact that his father had been born in Screapadal, and was probably cleared from there by the MacLeods, after Iain was born about 1835.

⁂

Donald MacRae, Balachuirn and Murdo MacKenzie, Balmeanach had been elected to represent these two townships. Although Donald's parents were both born in Strath, they had moved to Raasay about 1831. From at least 1841 the family lived at Leac until they were moved to Balachuirn in 1854, when Donald was about eight years old. Donald MacRae gave a statement:

> The crofting townships in Raasay are, and unless relieved will remain, in a condition of chronic poverty; the reasons being (1) because the land occupied by the crofting tenants is the poorest land in the islands; (2) because the crofting townships are overcrowded with crofters and with cottars; (3) because these townships have not the hill pasture necessary for a fair living; (4) because the best townships in the island have been cleared, and now form a huge sporting

preserve; (5) because deer, rabbits, pheasants, and black game do incalculable damage to us. The townships that were cleared of the people, and that are now under sport, are thirteen in number. They are far the best land in the island, though now going back to a state of nature, having been forty years waste. Over ninety families lived in them at one time. They would make thirty-four new holdings at the least, and keep that number of families very comfortable, at a just rent, and game would be much more plentiful than at present.

Donald's statement has already been quoted, regarding the clearances by George Rainy. He said also that George MacKay introduced deer about twenty years before. Mr Wood had introduced more deer and rabbits and pheasants.

Rabbits are being imported every year since, though the island is swarming with them. If the people were put back to these thirteen townships, and this is what the people want, it would relieve the congestion of population in the existing crofting townships. Those migrating to the old depopulated townships would do well, and so would the existing townships when relieved of the over population. By such a scheme it would be found that there is plenty of land in Raasay for the people of Raasay.

Murdo MacKenzie's parents had been moved from Upper Fearns to Balachuirn in 1854. They had remained there, but he moved to Balmeanach when he married about 1878. Murdo gave his evidence in English.

In 1893, he had five cows, a heifer, a two-year-old and four stirks. The Crofters' Commission had told him to get rid of his sheep, so now he had only one black-faced sheep. There were no horses on the island, except those owned by Mrs Wood.

Mr Stewart, the estate overseer, explained the 'privilege of hill grazing attached to the crofts' of Murdo and Donald MacRae. They were allowed to put their cows on the hill of Mrs Wood's farm for six months in the year, but were not actually limited to the six months if they kept within ordinary bounds. Murdo used to feed his cattle well, and make some meal in Portree. The Raasay grinding mill had been turned into a saw-mill. He explained that 'One year when the game was clear of me, I fed my cattle and had £12 worth of corn'. He had been experiencing so much damage by game that in February that year he had written to Mrs Wood. The letter said,

Madam – I beg respectfully to submit to you that, since the death of Mr Wood, my crops of every kind have been destroyed by pheasants and black game and deer. At rent time in each of those years I was bringing my case to the notice of the factor. He always promised to look into it, but did nothing hitherto. The crop of 1891 was so much injured that I was obliged to buy feeding-stuffs for my beasts to the value of £8, besides being short of two bolls of oatmeal. The last crop of 1892 was practically altogether destroyed. I have not a handful of oats left for sowings, and already I have been obliged to buy to the value of £4, not to speak of what I must yet buy for my beasts before the end of May. For want of fodder I was compelled to have my beasts out on the hill

1. Mr Cameron, the factor
2. Peter MacLennan, Glam – Pàdraig Ruadh
3. Annie Gillies, Fladda – Anna Raghnaill
4. Katie Gillies, Torran – Ceit Iain Dhòmhnaill
5. Jane MacLeod, Fladda – Sìneag Iain Chaluim
6. Jessie Nicolson, Torran – Seasag Mhurchaidh Alasdair
7. Cathie MacLennan, Torran – Catrìona Thormoid an t-Saighdeir
8. Cathie MacKenzie, Fladda
9. Mary MacLeod, Arnish – Màiri Chaluim Dhòmhnaill
10. Malcolm MacRae, Clachan – Calum Dhonnchaidh

Back row from the left

11. John Allan MacLeod, Arnish – Seonaidh Ailean
12. Donald MacLeod, Arnish – Dòmhnall Bàn (Dòmhnall Chaluim Alasdair)
13. Alexander Gillies, Doire Dubh – Alasdair Chaluim Bhig
14. Alexander Nicolson, Torran – Alasdair Fada
15. John MacLeod, North Arnish - Iain Chaluim Alasdair Mhòir
16. Malcolm MacLeod, North Arnish – Calum Alasdair Mhòir
17. Johnnie MacLeod, North Arnish – Seonaidh Theàrlaich
18. Malcolm Graham, Kyle Rona – Calum Iain Graham
19. ?

20. Lexy MacLennan, Glam – Lexie Phàdraig Ruaidh
21. Mary Nicolson, Torran – Màiri Mhurchaidh Alasdair
22. John MacLeod, South Arnish – Seonaidh Alasdair Mhòir
23. Jane Gillies, Umachan – Sìneag Alasdair Iain Aonghais
24. Betsy Mary MacLeod, Fladda – Beitidh Màiri Iain Chaluim
25. Morag MacLeod, Fladda
26. John MacLennan, Fladda – Iain Fhionnlaigh
27. Kate MacLeod, North Arnish – Ceit Alasdair Mhòir
28. Alexander MacLennan, Fladda – Alasdair Fhionnlaigh

Second row from the left

29. John MacLeod, South Arnish – Iain Chaluim Dhòmhnaill
30. (behind) Iain Cumming, Doire Dubh
31. John Gillies, Umachan – Iain Alasdair Iain Aonghais
32. Roderick Cumming, Doire Dubh
33. Charles Gillies, Doire Dubh
34. Angus MacLeod, North Arnish – Aonghas Sheonaidh Alasdair
35. Donald John MacLeod, South Arnish
36. John Graham, the Schoolmaster

37. Bella Cumming, Doire Dubh
38. Mary Ann MacLeod, Kyle Rona – Màiri Anna 'n Achaidh
39. Johanna MacLeod, Oscaig – Johanna Mhurchaidh Iain Bhàin
40. Anne Gillies, Doire Dubh – Anna Alasdair Chaluim Bhig
41. Johnnie Cumming, Doire Dubh
42. Donald John MacLeod, South Arnish

Third row from the left

Behind
43. Donald Gillies, Fladda – Dòmhnall Raghnaill
44. Murdo Gillies, Fladda – Murchadh Raghnaill
45. Angus Gillies, Umachan – Aonghas Shandaidh
46. John Gillies, Umachan – Iain Shandaidh

47. Janet Gillies, Umachan – Seònaid Shandaidh
48. Julia Gillies, Fladda – Sìle Raghnaill
49. Margaret MacLeod, North Arnish – Mairearad Sheonaidh Alasdair
50. Alexander MacLeod, North Arnish – Alasdair Sheonaidh Alasdair
51. Alexander MacKenzie, Kyle Rona – Ailì Sheonaidh Alasdair Bhig
52. ?
53. Cathie MacKenzie, Kyle Rona – Catrìona Thorcaill
54. Angus MacLennan, Fladda – Aonghas Thormoid an t-Saighdeir
55. Johan MacLeod, Fladda – Seonag Ailein
56. Peggy Gillies, Umachan – Peigi Alasdair Iain Aonghais
57. Julia MacLeod, South Arnish
58. Cathie Gillies, Umachan – Catrìona Mhòr Alasdair Iain Aonghais
59. Lexy MacLennan, Fladda – Lexie Thormoid an t-Saighdeir
60. Murdo MacKenzie, Kyle Rona – Murchadh Thorcaill
61. Charles MacLeod, South Arnish – Teàrlach Chaluim Dhòmhnaill

Fourth row from the left

62. Peggy MacLennan, Fladda – Peigi Fhionnlaigh
63. Peggy Nicolson, Fladda – Peigi Iain Bhig
64. (behind) Peggy MacLeod, South Arnish – Peigi Chaluim Dhòmhnaill
65. Cathie Gillies, Umachan – Catrìona Bheag Alasdair Iain Aonghais
66. Rachel MacLeod, South Arnish – Raghnaid Chaluim Dhòmhnaill
67. Lexy Gillies, Fladda – Lexie Raghnaill
68. Ann Gillies, Umachan – Anna Shandaidh
69. Mary MacLeod, South Arnish
70. Rachel MacLeod, North Arnish – Raghnaid Sheonaidh Alasdair
71. Maggie Livingstone, Fladda
72. Cathie MacLeod, Fladda – Catrìona Mhòr Ailein
73. Murdo MacLennan, Fladda – Murchadh Thormoid an t-Saighdeir
74. Malcolm Gillies, Fladda – Calum Raghnaill
75. Murdo MacLennan, Fladda – Murchadh Fhionnlaigh
76. ? (one little girl has been missed out)

RAASAY

Torran School, taken c. 1905. The names were collected by Mary Gillies, Màiri Iain Iain Raghnaill. (Isobel MacLean)

RAASAY

Norman Gillies, Tormod Dhòmhnaill, Eilean Taigh & Oscaig. The original (c. 1875?) is on silk. (Norrie Gillies)

The Steading at Clachan, showing the front of the building, taken from the road down to Clachan. (Isobel MacLean)

Group at Balachuirn: John Gillies, Iain Raghnaill, with his daughter-in-law, Jessie (nee Nicolson), and grandchildren, John, Murdina, Bessie, Neil and James. Torcall MacLeod is third from the left. (Mary Gillies)

The Steading at Clachan from the south. The bell tower was taken down in the 1940s, as it was dangerous. On a clear day the bell could be heard in Braes. It was taken away by DAFS, as part of the war effort. (Isobel MacLean)

RAASAY

Raasay Public School, Senior Division, 1912. *Back*: Miss Tallach, Katie Tallach, Jessie MacLeod (Brae), Mary MacRae, James Nicolson (Orchard). *Middle*: Mima Nicolson, Malcolm MacLean (Clachan), Maggie Ferguson, Chrissie MacLean, Murdo Tallach, Katie MacLeod. *Front*: Willie Ferguson, Mary Ann Gillies, Murdo MacLean (Clachan). (Mary Gillies)

The Avenue (Mill Park), Raasay, looking towards Henderson's Bridge. (Isobel MacLean)

RAASAY

Raasay Public School 1928/29. *Back*: Jimmie MacLeod, John Nicolson, John Gillies, Murdo MacLeod, John Nicolson. *Middle*: Calum MacRae, John MacLeod, Neil MacLeod. *Front*: Miss Tallach, Lena MacVicar, May Duncan, Rita Nicolson, Chrissie Nicolson, Bella Gillies. (Iain Hamish MacLeod)

Raasay School c. 1950: *Back*: Miss Tallach, Mary Ann MacLeod, Allan MacLeod, Calum MacDonald. *Middle*: Ina MacLennan, Janet MacLeod, Judith Langford, Sheila MacLeod, Mary Gillies. *Front*: Janet MacLean, Mary Ann MacDonald, Gina Ferguson, Rosemary Langford, Sandy MacLeod. (Mary Gillies)

RAASAY

Alexander MacFarlane, born in Lochs, Lewis, taught in Braes (Skye) before moving to Clachan (Raasay) before 1871. He was also an elder and Kirk Session Clerk of the Free Church. With Rev. Donald MacFarlane (Raasay) and Rev. Donald MacDonald (Shieldaig), he was a founding member of the Free Presbyterian Church in 1893. He retired about 1909/1910. (Isobel MacLean)

Some of the family of Peter Nicolson, who had the shop in Mill Place, c. 1898 – (from back left) Dolly (ran the shop), John (JB), Jean (married Mr Finlayson), Margaret (seated centre), Annabella (milliner) and Johnnie Finlayson. (Isobel MacLean)

Free Presbyterian Church and manse at Holoman, built 1899. The roof from the church was used for the new manse at Inverarish in the early 1950s. (Norrie Gillies)

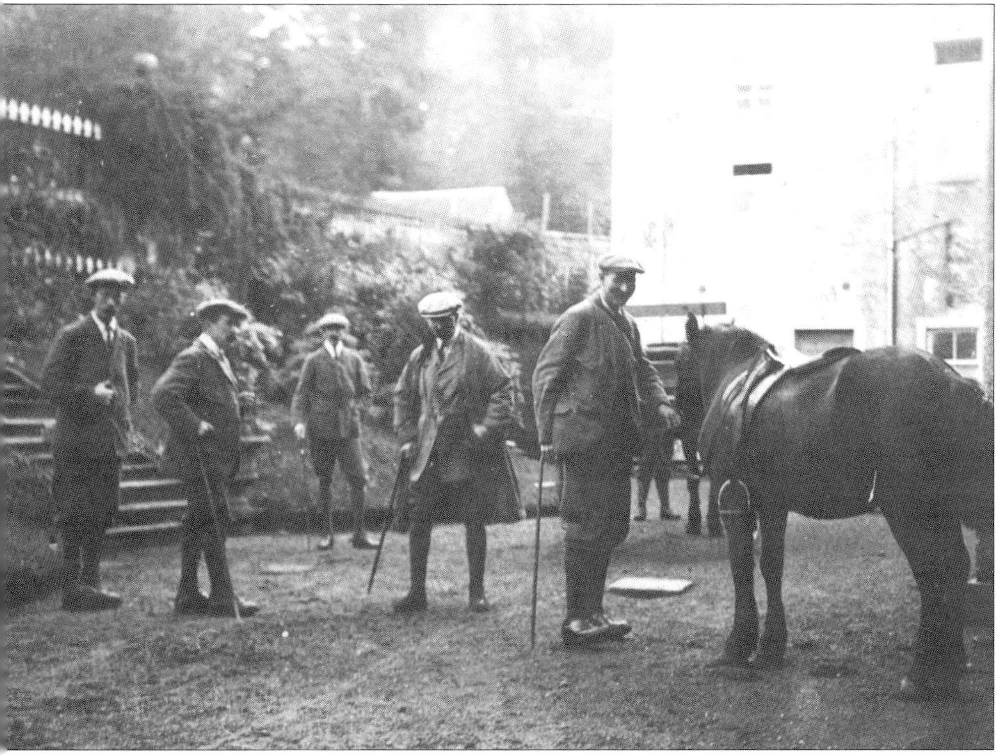

The back of Raasay House. Far left is John MacLeod, Balmeanach, Seonaidh Dhòmhnaill Iain Bhàin. Jonathan MacDonald, from Braes, is standing beside the horse. He was head keeper on Raasay before the First World War. (Norrie Gillies)

RAASAY

Taken at Glam c. 1912 and shows the corrugated iron buildings. Peter MacLennan, Pàdraig Ruadh, originally from Lochbroom, came to Raasay from Letterewe as a shepherd in 1877. He moved to Glam from Balmeanach when the new houses were ready in spring 1881. With him are his wife, Margaret (nee Ross); his daughters, Anne (back left) and Lexy (middle right); his daughter-in-law, Mary (middle left) and his grandchildren, Bett, Angus and Johan. (Norrie Gillies)

Taken c. 1905, showing Suisnish House, Mill Place and the Free Church Manse. The Free Church is barely visible in the trees. (Isobel MacLean)

The Raasay Football Team that played Portree School c. 1935/1936. *Back*: Donald John Gillies, Neil MacKay, Murdo J MacLeod, Calum Nicolson, Johnnie Gillies, Murdo MacLeod, Angie MacLeod. *Front*: Norrie Gillies, Donald Gillies, Alasdair MacLeod, Donnie MacKinnon, Norman MacLeod. (Norrie Gillies)

The Old Post Office, Clachan, in the time of the MacMillans. There were no windows on the end of the building. Taken 1910–1920. (Isobel MacLean)

Building Raasay Pier c. 1913. (Isobel MacLean)

Inside the power house at the Pier, Suisnish. (Norrie Gillies)

RAASAY

Left. John MacLennan, Johnnie Gillies and Murdo Nicolson dismantling the kilns above the pier.
(Norrie Gillies)

Below. Viaduct over the burn near Inverarish Dam. There were no metal sides on this viaduct, as there were on the one crossing the road to Fearns.
(Norrie Gillies)

RAASAY

This page and opposite, bottom. Advertising card for Raasay Hotel. From 1937 to 1960 Raasay House was run as Raasay Hotel by Mrs Davidson. (Andrew Gillies)

RAASAY HOTEL

ISLAND OF RAASAY
SKYE
SCOTLAND

THE HOTEL has a southern exposure and is ideally situated amidst magnificent scenery, facing the Blue Cuillins across the Sound of Raasay. It was the Seventeenth century home of the Chiefs of the Macleods of Raasay, and was visited by Dr Johnson and Boswell in 1773.

HOT AND COLD WATER IN BEDROOMS
FULLY LICENSED ● LOCH AND SEA FISHING

The Island is of Botanical, Biological and Geological interest.

HOW TO GET TO RAASAY

By Road or trains direct from London, Edinburgh or Glasgow to Mallaig or Kyle of Lochalsh. Thence by the MacBrayne steamer, which sails daily except on Sundays, or, from Portree, Isle of Skye, by the Macbrayne steamer.

LOCAL MOTORBOAT FERRY SERVICES TO AND FROM
PORTREE AND SCONSOR, ISLE OF SKYE.

Telephone RAASAY 2

Culross, C.A. 7427-2m-60

The Gardener's Cottage, behind Raasay House gardens. Taken 1900–1910. (Isobel MacLean)

Tariff

Inclusive Terms :

	£	s.	d.
WEEKLY TERMS	12	12	0
These Terms include Bedroom, Breakfast, Lunch, Tea and Dinner.			
BED AND BREAKFAST	1	1	6
BREAKFAST		5	0
LUNCH		6	6 *
TEA	2s. 6d. to	3	0
DINNER		8	0 *
MORNING TEA			10

* Tea, Coffee or Milk extra.

Special Rates for Children on application.

Postal Address : ISLE OF RAASAY
Kyle of Lochalsh . Ross-shire – Scotland.

RAASAY

This page and opposite. Taking the sheep away to the sales on the *Loch Arkaig*. The men are Calum MacKay, Neil MacKay, James Gillies, Torcall MacLeod and Charlie Gillies. Neil MacKay is taking a sheep down to the lower deck on the boat. (Peter Gillies)

RAASAY

Allan MacKenzie, Ailean Mhurchaidh Mhòir, was a gamekeeper in Raasay in 1891. (Isobel MacLean)

Chirstie Chaluim, a daughter of Calum Matheson, spinning. They lived at Holoman. The photo was taken on 3 February 1902 to enter a photographic competition. (Isobel MacLean)

The Old Churchyard at Clachan, showing St Moluag's Chapel with the nineteenth century memorial chapel to the right. (Isobel MacLean)

to keep them alive instead of having them housed as they ought to be during winter. Let it not be that my stock is excessive; for I have actually less stock now than when the Crofters' Commission fixed it. I have been paying the rent regularly up to last term, that is as long as I could.

When I had occasion to complain at the second last rent time, to our late proprietor Mr Wood, he allowed me £8 compensation when I had only one-third of the land under tillage that I had last year. Then the last rent time before his death that I submitted my case, he allowed me £5 compensation. As already stated, I suffered serious loss all those years since Mr Wood's death, and no attention has been paid to my complaints beyond promises. But the last two years have been simply ruinous. Mr Ross did, indeed, offer me, on the last occasion, £3 10s. compensation, but I could not accept of that as part payment of compensation. I am now obliged to submit these facts for your consideration, and I humbly trust you will order such inquiry into the above statements without delay as will be satisfactory to you, and that you will see to it that such compensation is allowed me as will be fairly proportionable to the loss that I have sustained.

     I am
     Madam,
     Your Obedient Servant,
     M. MacKenzie.

The result of this plea is not known.

Appearing on behalf of the Oscaig township was Tormod Dhòmhnaill, Norman Gillies. He and Iain Uilleim, John MacLean, had prepared a statement on behalf of the township. Their evidence concerned the past rather than the present, and has already been discussed.

James Ross, a solicitor in Inverness, was the factor for Raasay and gave his evidence the following year, due to a misunderstanding about the time of the hearing in Portree. He read his statement and was then questioned about it and the running of the estate.

Here he appeared to give more accurate information than he had done in 1883, to the Napier Commission. At that time he claimed that the estate was 29 000 acres, but in 1893 he gave the more accurate figure of 18 000. Much of the information he gave has been given previously. A great deal of detail about the expenditure is related, emphasising always how much this benefited the crofters and cottars.

Details of the Glam Farm were given, and he was questioned at length about the high expenditure on this project. £3 942 was spent on reclaiming just seventy acres, which after three years were abandoned and by 1893 were reverting to a state of nature.

The total expenditure, through the estate accounts, during the seventeen years that the Woods owned Raasay was £133 736. Gross income for the same period was just £50 182. Thus £83 554 (an average of £4 915 per year) was spent from sources outside the estate. These figures do not include £14 803 for the alterations to Raasay House, the building of Borrodale (the manager's house) or work to the Home Farm buildings. He included tables showing rent and arrears at various dates from 1827 to 1893, and was questioned about these.

About the time he bought the estate, Mr Wood took over the sheep farm along with 3 200 sheep. 'For personal reasons the late Mr Wood transferred part of the sheep stock to his English estate, thus reducing considerably the stock on Raasay.' The stock had since been increased and was then 1 800 sheep and fifty cattle. The sheep got good prices at market. He gave many reasons – including climate, stock prices, foreign competition and distance from the markets – for Raasay being unsuited to arable farming. He spoke from experience of the last sixteen years. 'Our manager is the son of an Aberdeenshire farmer, and no money has been spared to make that place a success; and yet we find that he cannot work it to satisfaction, and certainly not to profit.' It was suggested that some west coast men had managed to make a living by agriculture, and that Raasay had a beautiful garden where fruit was grown, but his replies were evasive.

When questioned, the factor was vague about the now derelict townships being occupied in previous times, and argued that they could not now be occupied profitably. He said, 'The arable land is limited in extent, and I hardly think a crofter would care to do it'. Later he said, 'I consider that any man of energy who is capable of going down there and erecting a house and getting a croft into cultivation would go somewhere else and get a better place. I don't think a plucky man would think of settling there.'

When asked about the possibility of building a harbour and setting up a fishing village somewhere on Raasay he said, 'I do not know whether you could make a harbour on the south with any possibility of success. There is not a single place on the south or east that is suitable; it is one severe coast line, thoroughly exposed all the way.' After persistent questioning, Ross did agree that small crofts for fishermen, if they could be got, would be an advantage in relieving the distress in the north end. Further questioning elicited vague responses:

Q: I think your statement comes to this, that you would be very glad to give the people holdings, provided the present arrangements would not be touched?

A: Raasay is a somewhat peculiar place, and ...

Q: You have no theoretical objection to enlarging the holdings of the crofters provided the present distribution of the land were maintained, – do I fairly state your position?

A: I am just thinking it over for one moment.

Q: You stated to Mr Gordon that you would have no objection to these people getting larger holdings provided the present arrangement of the land in Raasay were left as it is?

A: I should have no objection to that, if the land were left as it is.

Q: Do I correctly describe your position when I say that?

A: That so long as the present arrangement of land is not interfered with I have no possible objection to what you propose.

Ross later claimed that the large amount of expenditure on the estate was because the proprietor wanted 'to deal liberally with the people'. The commissioners did not see that it was fair 'to hold the climate and the people responsible' for the expenditure. They felt that if the money had been spent 'in a way suitable to the circumstances of the island' there may have been 'an adequate return, remunerative to both parties'.

The question of the rabbit population was also addressed. The factor had admitted that there were a large number of rabbits.

Q: In fact, the island is in an insanitary condition from the dead rabbits that are to be seen all over it?

A: I have not seen that.

Q: We saw the carcasses ourselves when we went over the place. Do you still think it is putting the land to the best use, to allow the rabbits to run all over the island?

A: No, it is a mistake to do that, but you must bear in mind that we have a large amount of the rental from a shooting tenant at this moment, – it is let on a three years' shooting lease.

It is clear from the evidence given by both the factor and the crofters to the Deer Forest Commission that the problems of the crofters and cottars on Raasay were very much the same as they had been ten years previously, when the Napier Commission sat. The Crofter Holdings (Scotland) Act of 1886 had granted them the right to a fair rent and security of their holdings, but had not begun to address the main problem – the lack of sufficient, suitable land. James Ross, the factor, made it clear that even in 1893, Mrs Wood would not be willing to alter, in any way, the land holding on the estate for the benefit of the people.

The Deer Forest Commission report was published in April 1895. Again there was a great deal of debate about the whole question of land holding in the Highlands, with many of the old arguments repeated along the usual lines.

The commission had concentrated on 'historic land use', and encouraged elderly crofters to name townships that had been cleared. This was necessary, as their remit was to identify land capable of being put under crofting tenure. Landowners argued that much of this was based on fallible memories, and that standards of living had changed, so that crofters of the 1890s would not tolerate conditions of the 1830s. They argued that if farms and deer forests were destroyed, this would be bad for Highland prosperity. Deer forests provided much needed employment and investment in areas that had little else. Many of the arguments used at this time are being repeated in the land debates of today, over 100 years later.

The commissioners identified 1.78 million acres, as suitable for crofters, either as extensions to grazings or as new holdings. Because they could not reach agreement among themselves, they were unable to put forward any solutions, or to recommend an ideal size of holding. Nothing was done, and the Liberal government fell in the summer of 1895. A Conservative government was elected, and land policy changed again.

THE FREE CHURCH OF SCOTLAND AND THE FREE PRESBYTERIAN CHURCH OF SCOTLAND

Rev. Angus Galbraith had left Raasay in 1890. It was not until early May 1893 that Rev. Donald MacFarlane was inducted as Free Church minister of Raasay. Later that month, he attended the Free Church Assembly in Edinburgh. There he read out the protest by which he severed his connection with the Free Church. On 28 July 1893, at a meeting held on Raasay with Rev. Donald MacDonald, minister of Shieldaig, Applecross, and Alexander MacFarlane, the schoolmaster at Clachan, Raasay, the Free Church Presbytery of Scotland was formed. Alexander MacFarlane, as well as being the schoolmaster, was also an elder and Kirk Session Clerk.

By the end of August 1893, Rev. MacFarlane was no longer Free Church minister of Raasay. The congregation of Raasay was now divided, most following Rev. MacFarlane. At a meeting in Inverness on 3 July 1894, the name of the new church was changed to the Free Presbyterian Church of Scotland. Both these ministers lost their churches and manses. The Shieldaig minister, by then an old man, had already lost his church and manse in 1843 when he had joined the Free Church. Rev. Donald MacFarlane remained as minister of the Free Presbyterian Church on Raasay until 1903.

THE CONGESTED DISTRICTS (SCOTLAND) ACT 1897

This Act created a board to administer a fund of government money to benefit certain 'congested' parishes. The legislation was based on land purchase. As well as freeing proprietors from the burden of crofting tenants, the government hoped that the creation of smaller estates would produce a new middle class of Conservative proprietors.

The aim was to provide land for crofters and cottars, helping them to settle in other less congested areas, and also to develop better agricultural practices. The board had responsibility for developing fishing and other industries and for extending the road and communications network in the congested areas. Because the government, naturally, wanted the Board to work with proprietors, there were yet again no compulsory purchase powers.

Because the board had to wait for land to become available, they began by trying to improve agricultural practices. Better seed was provided as well as encouragement to grow vegetables. They had some success in improving livestock by the provision of bulls, rams and stallions. However, the crofters' lack of good land and capital resulted in problems with the wintering of these animals and many of them died. Everything possible was done to encourage club-stock farming. The Crofters' Commission, continuing from the 1886 Act, had by now resolved the bulk of the 'fair rent' applications and had turned its attention to the administration of the Crofters' Common Grazing Regulations Act of 1892. The commission had the power to draw up rules for the effective management of common grazings in co-operation with the crofters involved.

On Raasay, the 1897 Act was of very limited effect. Mr Wood, had provided bulls to improve the stock, and new seed to improve the crops and potatoes. The crofters of both Rona and the north end of Raasay were still in desperate need of more land, and that was not forthcoming from Mrs Wood.

Over the Highlands in general the Congested Districts Board had only limited success in its objectives. Most people, such as those in Sconser, Skye, showed a distinct reluctance to move to another area, even to gain better holdings. The main problem with the 1897 Act was that land ownership was too expensive for most crofters. They simply could not afford to purchase. There were some successes, however, such as on the Glendale estate on Skye, bought by the board in 1903. There, 131 crofters had become owner-occupiers when the scheme was completed in 1907.

By the end of the century, therefore, the crofters and cottars on Raasay and Rona were no nearer achieving better land than they had been when the Napier commission was set up to address the problem in the early 1880s. Although various governments had been obliged to consider the problem and legislation had been passed, the main objective remained elusive. They now had security of tenure and 'fair rents'.

Employment by the estate had reduced markedly after Mr Wood's death in 1886. Mrs Wood had kept the estate and let the shootings and Raasay House to tenants. The result was that many people from Raasay and Rona had to leave the island to find employment.

8

The History of Raasay, 1900–c.1950

By the end of the nineteenth century, Mrs Wood was trying to sell the Raasay estate.

An Act of Parliament in 1910 relating to the value of property gave rise to the Ordnance Survey Name Books which were compiled, for the whole of Scotland, between 1910 and 1914. These are interesting as they give some details of the condition of buildings as well as noting other items of interest.

On Rona, the only slated buildings at that time were the lighthouse buildings and the shooting lodge at Big Harbour. The lodge had been built about 1866 for George Haygarth Rainy. He and his guests used it as a base for their shooting expeditions to the island. After the Woods bought the estate the MacRaes, who had been in Balachuirn, moved into the lodge as caretakers. They remained there after Mrs Wood sold the estate. The houses at Doire na Guaille, Braig and Dry Harbour were all thatched and in a 'poor state of repair'.

There is no description of the houses on either Fladda or Eilean Taigh. Fladda had a few acres of cultivated ground at the south end. The rest of the island was covered with heather.

As in Rona, all the houses at the north end of Raasay were thatched. At Kyle Rona several small croft houses with byres attached were, similarly, in a 'poor state of repair'. Some ground was cultivated. At Kyle Rona, opposite the Sound, there was a small schoolhouse. Although thatched it was 'in reasonable repair'. It was noted that this schoolhouse was provided entirely by a Society of Ladies in Edinburgh. The teacher, Mr A. Nicolson, taught only 'the first rudiments of education'. Average attendance was twenty-three.

Umachan had several houses, all 'in a bad state of repair'. The houses in Torran were not in good repair either.

At Balachuirn, several thatched houses were 'in a bad state of repair', as was the shepherd's house at Balmeanach. A few dwellings were noted on the north east coast of Holoman Bay and to the east of Holoman Island. There was only one shepherd's house at Brochel and one at Hallaig.

In the south end of Raasay, the school at Clachan was a one-storey building with schoolhouse attached, belonging to the Portree School Board. It was slated and nearly new. Only 'the first rules of education' were taught. Average attendance that year (probably 1910 or 1911) was thirteen. The previous year it had been nineteen. The Sub-Post Office received and despatched mails three times per week. The one-storey thatched house was 'in very good order'. There were a few cottages at Clachan. All were one-storey, slated and 'in thorough repair'.

Raasay House, described as a 'large beautiful mansion house', was three storeys high, slated and 'kept in excellent condition'. There were a number of cottages at Inverarish, all slated and in 'fair repair'. These would have been at Mill Place. Mr Barron, who at that time was the estate manager, lived at Borrodale House. Suisnish House was the residence of the farm manager.

The Free Church, it was said, was the only place of public worship on the island. It had seating for a congregation of 200. The manse, with a garden attached, was 'very commodious' and had a pleasant situation.

Clearly, although housing was reasonably good in the south end of Raasay, where most people were employed by the estate, those crofters and cottars in the north end and on Rona had seen no improvement in their situation.

THE CHURCH (1893–1929)

The Free Presbyterian Church of Scotland had been formed in 1893. A new church and manse were built at Holoman on land granted by Mrs Wood. The site was chosen to be convenient for the populations of both the north and the south ends of the island. Richard Sharpe indicated that these new buildings were erected about 1908.[1] However, the Ordnance Survey Name Books were not compiled before 1910 and although mention was made of a few dwellings at Holoman, it was stated that the Free Church was the only place of worship on the island. It appears that, for whatever reason, the Free Presbyterian Church and manse were omitted from the Ordnance Survey Name Books. The Church and manse had been built by 1899. The manse appears for the first time in the Valuation Roll of 1902/1903.

After Rev. Donald MacFarlane left the island in 1903, the Free Presbyterian Church was served by a succession of missionaries until 1934 when Rev. Murdo Morrison moved to Raasay from Assynt.

From 1895 Rev. John MacDonald, an Applecross man, was the Free Church minister on Raasay. In May 1908 he moved to Rosskeen in Easter Ross. Rev. Hector Kennedy became Free Church minister of Raasay in 1912 and remained on the island until his death in 1930. He was born in Sleat, Skye and came to Raasay from Kilmallie, just north of Fort William.

THE SMALL LANDHOLDERS (SCOTLAND) ACT 1911

In 1906 a Liberal government came into power and the Highland land policy changed again. Once more tenancy was favoured over ownership. Problems of overstocking and lack of fencing were partially addressed by The Common Grazings Act of 1908 which superseded the 1892 Act.

The Small Landholders (Scotland) Act was passed in 1911. This abolished the Congested Districts Board. The 1897 Act under which it had been created was based on a policy of land purchase. That policy had proved unsuccessful. The Crofters' Commission, whose job in revising rents was now complete, was also abolished. These two bodies were replaced by the Board of Agriculture for Scotland (BoAS) and the Scottish Land Court (SLC). It may be noted here that the present day Crofters' Commission was set up in 1955.

Under the 1911 Act

– holdings could be enlarged and new holdings created on private land

- if the landowner did not agree, the BoAS and the SLC could introduce an element of compulsion
- the landowner could be compensated by the SLC
- farms of less than 150 acres, home farms and those under lease at Whitsun 1906 were exempt from the creation of new holdings.

The crofters and cottars now had high expectations of an improvement in their conditions. There was a huge demand for land over the whole of the Highlands, the north west in particular. On Raasay and Rona, it appeared that they might now be able to have the land that was so desperately needed.

William Baird & Co. Ltd, Ironmasters of Coatbridge: 1911–1923

In May 1911 Mrs Wood sold the estate to William Baird & Co. Ltd, Ironmasters of Coatbridge. Bairds bought the island to exploit the deposits of iron-ore found there. A great deal of construction work was required for this project. It created the prospect of long term employment, not only in the actual mining, but also in all the associated work necessary before the ore could be shipped off the island.

Suisnish House now became the residence of David Munro, the Mining Engineer. Dr Burns moved into Borrodale House, giving the island a resident doctor for the first time. Churchton House was built for Baird's cashier, William Rankin. Because they were interested only in that part of the estate that involved the extraction of the ore, the remainder of Mrs Wood's sporting estate, including Raasay House, the Home Farm, the Sheep Farm and the sporting rights, were let to a tenant. He was a Mr Rawnsley, from Lincolnshire, who lived with his wife and son in Raasay House.

In 1913 Robert McAlpine & Sons began building the pier at Suisnish. It had initially been proposed to build it just south of Suisnish House, but anticipated problems associated with pollution from the works resulted in its being built further south. It was constructed of reinforced concrete and had, in addition, underwater walls, infilled with sand and gravel, for added stability. The pier had to be strongly built because as well as its exposed position, the superstructure was high and it had to support the weight of the machinery and ore. To prevent possible damage from heavy boats coming alongside, the hammerhead was not connected to the main gangway of the pier. The loading shute was fixed. Boats were moored to two large buoys that kept them about six feet out from the pier. They were then winched back and forth between the buoys, enabling even loading of their holds.

The railway from the mines to the pier involved the building of two high viaducts over the Inverarish Burn and the road to Fearns. They were constructed of iron girders with wooden decking. The one running over the road had sheet-metal sides to prevent accidents. Offices and power generating sheds were built near the pier, as were five huge kilns for burning (or calcinating) the ore. During the operation of the kilns, the sea between Raasay and Skye turned a rusty red colour and the land behind them was covered in fine ash.

During 1912–13 the two lower blocks of Inverarish Terrace were built with stone taken from Suisnish Point. The upper blocks were later built of brick. The terraced houses were erected to accommodate mine workers. Each house had two large rooms and a small scullery with a sink and cold water tap. The living room had a range for heating and cooking. Two houses shared an outside toilet. Between the two rows of houses was a drying green. Each washhouse, shared by eight houses, was built into a block that also had a coal shed for each house. Inverarish Cottages were built for the foremen. Shortly after the terrace houses were built, a recreation hall, with billiard table, was built beside them.

Miss Tallach, the teacher at Clachan, had over forty new pupils in 1912, compared with a previous pupil intake in the order of six per year. As well as the children of people who had come into the island, there were also the children of some local people who had moved from the north end for work.

There were two mineshafts opened, although the second never justified the money spent on it. A Bucyrus Steam Dragline that had been shipped to Raasay from the USA worked an open cast mine quite close to the main shaft beside the Fearns road.

In 1914, just when all ancillary works had been completed and the mining operation was ready to start in earnest, war was declared. Thirty-six local men were called up and, during the four years that the war lasted, many of them were killed.

A severe labour shortage led to the site lying idle. The German submarine campaign in 1916 made it increasingly difficult to obtain ore supplies from abroad, and the possibility of using German prisoners of war to work the mines was considered. By May 1916 it had been agreed that Bairds would manage the works on behalf of the Ministry of Munitions. Thus Bairds did not directly employ the prisoners.

Tall barbed wire fences were erected around the upper blocks of Inverarish Terrace, with guardhouses at opposite corners. The other two corners had lights, supplied by the powerhouse near the pier. Of the other houses in the terrace, No. 48 was the medical room, Nos 15 and 16 were for non-commissioned officers and Nos 46 and 47 were the guards' accommodation. Officers' quarters were in Churchton House. At most there were about 260 prisoners on Raasay. About sixty British people, including fourteen mining experts and approximately twenty local men, were employed.

However, Bairds did not have an easy relationship with the Ministry of Munitions. About July 1917, when Bairds wanted to increase production to 3 000 tons per week they were told that they must not do so. Yet, by February 1918, the ministry was complaining about trading losses and pointing out that production of 3 000 tons per week had not been achieved. Bairds felt that the ministry was entirely to blame for these problems, not least because they had failed to provide regular shipping to take the ore off the island. Storage space for ore on the island was in short supply, and any delay in shipping was liable to result in a shut down of the plant.

The British men and the prisoners worked well together. Responsibility for the welfare and guarding of the prisoners rested with the ministry. Very few prisoners escaped and those who did were all re-captured on Raasay, and then sent to a camp in the south of England. Prisoners' rations were short, but the British workers often managed to slip them some food. Two prisoners died on Raasay, one as a result of a roof-fall in the mine in December 1916, and the other in the camp the following May. Another of the prisoners, a stone mason to trade, carved a gravestone for them from a large boulder found near the pier. This stone now stands outside the cemetery. Sadly in January 1919, after hostilities had ceased, twelve prisoners died during a 'Spanish flu' epidemic shortly before they were due to leave the island at Easter that year. In 1967, all the prisoners' bodies were removed to the Cannock Chase war cemetery in Staffordshire.

In February 1917 local workers on Raasay were becoming increasingly dissatisfied with their conditions. Early in March Mr Morrison, Solicitor-General for Scotland, attended a meeting on the island. Although no satisfactory solution emerged local people were able to air their views. The main complaints were that wages were low, houses were not being repaired and no land was provided with the houses. Although, presumably, Bairds could see no need to provide land with the houses, apart from the small patches of garden behind them, local people had been used to working crofts and wanted to continue growing their own potatoes and keeping a few animals to supplement their income.

Things did not improve, and early in December the men went on strike. Later that month, a branch of the National Union of Scottish Mineworkers was set up on Raasay. Although questions were raised in parliament about the use of German prisoners as strike-breakers, it appears that no prisoners were doing work that they had not already done before the strike. By mid-January 1918, the dispute had ended and it is believed that the local men were given a substantial wage increase.

The price of ore, which had been 6s. in 1916, had dropped to 4d. per ton by November 1920. The operation was put onto a care and maintenance basis, employing only a few men to keep the machinery in working order and to paint the metalwork. The opportunities that the mining operations had promised, less than a decade before, had now gone.

THE LAND SETTLEMENT (SCOTLAND) ACT 1919

The high expectations of the 1911 Small Landholders Act did not materialise. By 1915 it was realised that the structure of the Act was flawed. It was being exploited by landowners who were able to use delaying tactics and take advantage of loopholes, particularly with regard to compensation payments. The result was frustrated applicants and unhappy landowners. Even the Liberals who had created the Act were not happy.

However, the land settlement programme was suspended after war was declared in 1914 because many of those involved, both applicants and adminstrators, were away. Also, the prices of materials and livestock had risen. This increased financial pressures at a time when available money was being directed to the war effort.

In 1919 the Land Settlement (Scotland) Act was passed. It was less complex than previous legislation. The BoAS could buy land and then either act as landlord or sell to owner-occupiers. Compensation rules were altered. The Act was presented as an attempt to fulfil a pledge to recruits that they would get land on their return home. Initially this may have deterred civilians from applying.

By now, however, people were becoming desperate and the period 1919–22 saw seven land raids on Skye and many more threatened. Land raids were a major problem for the government. Giving in to them would result in more raiding. If they did not give in, the original problem would be exacerbated. Landlords preferred to sell rather than have to create and administer small-holdings.

The BoAS used the raids, or the threat of raids, to get money from the treasury to enable them to buy estates. They recognised that raids were not a challenge to authority but a symptom of frustration, even desperation. Although the government was gaining political mileage by giving preferential treatment to war veterans, the land problem in the north-west was not a post-war problem.

Although the BoAS knew of the problems on Raasay and Rona before the war, they could do nothing to help under the terms of the 1911 Act. Bairds owned the whole estate but were interested only in the ore. They did not want crofting tenants.

The BoAS had been under sustained and increasing pressure to provide viable holdings for the crofters of Rona. After the 1919 Act, they began negotiations with Bairds for a scheme on Raasay.

The Scottish Land Court inspected the holdings on Rona and, having given full consideration to all the facts, issued their verdict in December 1920. This was a damning indictment of conditions on the island. The report said –

> Edinburgh, 17 December 1920 – The Land Court, having inspected the holdings and resumed consideration of the applications and the evidence adduced, ... have determined that the fair rent to be paid by each applicant respectively for his holding is as follows:

	Old Rent	Fair Rent
Hugh Nicolson	£4.10.0	£3.0.0
Donald Nicolson	£4.10.0	£3.0.0
Alexander Nicolson, Jr	£2.5.0	£2.0.0
Alexander Nicolson (Post)	£2.5.0	£1.10.0
Mal. and John MacKay	£4.0.0	£3.0.0
Donald MacLeod	£4.10.0	£3.0.0
Dun and Donald MacLeod	£4.10.0	£3.0.0
John MacSween	£4.10.0	£3.0.0
Norman Nicolson	£4.10.0	£3.0.0

Note: The general conditions under which these tenants live are miserable in the extreme. The land on the island, both pasture and arable, is of the poorest quality, and housing accommodation and sanitary arrangements are of the most primitive description. The arable land is scattered here and there over the island, and it is only small detached strips and patches which can be cultivated. The difficulty of transport to the island must be a great inconvenience and must give rise to hardship and distress during the winter or during rough weather.

It is difficult to know how anyone can carry on under such conditions, and still more so to understand how a living can be obtained, even with the help of the fishing. The whole of the applicants, except one, seem anxious to improve their position by procuring better holdings, and their claims in this respect are deserving of prompt consideration. If the scheme prepared for the settlement of new holders on the island of Raasay is put into force, it is only fair to say that the claims of the Rona tenants should be brought to the notice of the Board of Agriculture for Scotland.

The Court have great difficulty in fixing fair rents for holdings such as are occupied by the applicants, and which are situated on an island entirely unsuited for a settlement of smallholders. In the opinion of the Court, the island is suitable for nothing else than as grazing for a very limited number of sheep.

(Signed) Norman Reid.

The Rona men had made repeated application to the BoAS and to Bairds, the landowners, to be moved from Rona to new holdings on Raasay. Although the BoAS was in negotiation with Bairds, it did not appear that any satisfactory solution was being achieved. Time was going on and soon crops should be planted.

On 25 February 1921 they notified the board that they could no longer exist under their present circumstances and that they proposed to raid and cultivate the fertile land in Raasay to support their wives and families. They would do so on 15 March. They received the standard reply. Such action would 'prejudice their claims' and 'impede the Board'. Their applications would be 'kept in view in the event of a scheme of land settlement in Raasay'.

The men of Rona were not put off by this reply. There followed a period of five weeks of bad weather when Rona was entirely cut off and, it was reported, the people were 'reduced to living on a few potatoes'. When the weather moderated, the men took possession of the townships of Fearns and Eyre, carrying out a resettlement scheme of their own. A temporary house was erected, in which they all lived while they got on with the work of cultivating the land and building their houses.

About 1909 a new Highland Land League (HLL) had been formed. While the Crofter Movement of the 1880s had been strongly represented at the grass roots, this new League was largely made up of urban activists. Linked with the Independent Labour Party, they pressed for the nationalisation of land in the Highlands. Many members of the HLL were descendants of people who had been forced to leave the Highlands and seek work elsewhere. Information about the ongoing situation 'at home' was widely reported in the press. The SLC findings of December 1920 were reported in the *Greenock Telegraph*. On 29 March 1921 the *Dundee Advertiser* gave details of the land raid on Raasay.

Fund raising by the HLL in support of those in the Highlands, who were trying to improve their lot whether by raiding or other means, was ongoing. The Greenock branch of the HLL held weekly ceilidhs to raise funds. William

MacKenzie, the branch secretary who was originally from Strath, presided at one such ceilidh at the end of April. There, special mention was made of the Rona men's raid. The audience was told that a telegram had been received that day informing them that interdicts had been served on the Raasay raiders. This was reported in the *Greenock Telegraph* of 2 May 1921.

The Honorary Secretary of the HLL, Mr J. B. Malcolm, visited Raasay and met with the raiders in July. On 30 July his account was reported in the newspaper *Forward*, which strongly supported the HLL. By then, several new houses, built on the sites of the old ones, were ready for occupation. The first temporary house was now being used as a store. When it was suggested to one man that he might be imprisoned he replied, 'I have never been out of prison all the time I've been living in Rona. I go not back to Rona, although I stay here with my boat-sail for a tent.' Some of the crops had been badly damaged by rabbits, but the potatoes had done well.

When the people had been cleared from that area in the 1850s, stone from their houses had been used to build a park and sheep fank. The men had re-used these stones to build their houses. The factor challenged their right to do so, but was told that they were merely 'returning the stones to whence they came'. Wood for the roofing was taken from the birch wood nearby. The factor had objected to their use of 'estate timber'. The *Forward* article continued:

> It is interesting to note, especially as the case was not reported in the Press, that the tenant, an English military officer named Rawnsley, was haled before the Sheriff Court at Portree early this year by the local shoemaker on a question of payment of a pair of shoes, and the latter, conducting his own case, obtained a decree for payment and expenses. This is the gentleman who, along with the Baird Company, about whom so much was heard during the war in connection with the iron mines, is now suing the raiders for establishing their right to live. Possibly, however, he may find that even the landlord 'law' is not sufficient to drive the 'raiders' from their settlement, and as for the men themselves, and even more among their local sympathisers, the most frequently expressed sentiment is one of contempt for the aforesaid 'law' and its workings. The people have been so often gulled with specious Government promises (the Raasay affair of last year being a case in point), that they have no longer any faith in them. As a matter of fact, the opinion is often expressed that it would be better should no immediate settlement result, the expectation being that next year the men will each be working a small farm instead of the usual backgarden allotted by the BoAS and dignified with the name of a holding.

This article was severely critical of the lack of action by the BoAS and the size of the holdings granted by them. It was true that holdings were often smaller than the board would have liked, mainly because applicants were unwilling to move from their own area.

Because of the Raasay raid, the BoAS had to suspend negotiations for the resettlement scheme on Raasay. An explanation is given by Ewen A Cameron:

> The usual process of serving and breaching of interdicts led to the raiders'

incarceration in late 1921. The Secretary for Scotland, Robert Munro, responded to this situation with uncharacteristic firmness, declaring that henceforth, raiding would operate as a bar to land settlement. The BoAS, however, took a different view to that of the Scottish Office. It was much more sympathetic to the plight of the raiders; ... There was no doubt that the conditions on Rona were dreadful. The problem was that only one of the raiders possessed the ex-service qualification, so they could not be given priority treatment, if the letter of the law was followed.

While the Scottish Office was declaring against land raids, the Board was approaching the Treasury with a proposition to purchase Raasay: the only possible method of preventing the raiders from reoccupying the land was to 'project a scheme at once'. The Treasury was horrified at the potential expense of purchasing Raasay and settling penniless cottars on new holdings, but it was eventually persuaded to allow the Board to go to £20 000 in an effort to purchase. The island was secured in March 1922 for £18 000. Tentative BoAS predictions indicated that a further £14–15 000 would be required to take over the sheep-stock and to equip the new holdings.[2]

Thus the BoAS had to look at the wider context. In 1920 Raasay had not been considered a priority for a resettlement scheme. No politically defensive argument could be found to make Raasay a priority. There was a general shortage of money for the many schemes they had to consider.

The BoAS files covering the period of the land raid were not made public until 1981. At that time the *West Highland Free Press* carried an article about the Raasay raids by Brian Wilson. It appears that eight men had carried out a raid on the Home Farm on 20 March 1921. On 2 April, a police report said that the Rona men had been to the south end of the island to measure out plots, but the factor (Baird's mining engineer, David Munro) believed that this was a bluff.

However, the raid on the south end did take place. An interdict was served, but ignored. On 12 July, the men failed to appear at court in Portree. Although, on 15 August, the chief constable 'expected that the defenders will come quietly', he had underestimated the determination of the Rona men. Police officers were sent to Raasay. One week later the Sheriff Principal was informed that the men would not listen to reason and had finally dispersed in different directions.

There followed a request for permission to use the fishery cruiser *Mina* to take fifteen to twenty policemen over to Raasay to arrest the men. If they were arrested at night and taken to appear at court in Portree early the following morning, it would then be possible for the *Mina* to take them to Kyle to catch the Inverness train. This speedy action, it was hoped, would have them in prison in Inverness quickly and avoid possible trouble from sympathisers. The Fishery Board was appalled about this suggestion as it would badly damage their relations with crofter/fishermen. The secretary of state agreed, and refused permission to use the *Mina*.

In the event, a late night raid without the *Mina* was arranged and five of the Rona men were sentenced to six weeks in prison. A national campaign developed to support them. While they were still in prison, it was suggested that should they agree to give up their new holdings on Raasay, the government would undertake to seek to provide new ones legally. This was impossible. On 17 November, the men wrote from prison to say that they could not agree to this proposal as their families were already in Raasay, as were their cattle, peats and potatoes. They would not have their families made homeless. The precise terms of the eventual settlement are unclear, but by 25 April 1922 the affair was resolved to the men's satisfaction.

THE BOARD OF AGRICULTURE FOR SCOTLAND FROM 1923
In February 1923, with the consent of the Board of Agriculture for Scotland, William Baird & Co. Ltd sold the bulk of the estate of Raasay and Rona to the Trustees of the Scottish Rural Workers Approved Society for £16 150. The BoAS took over the estate immediately, under a 'Contract of Ground Annual' for a period of thirty years, paying £1 231 18s. 6d. per year. This 'Contract of Ground Annual' was discharged by the Minister of National Insurance in favour of the Secretary of State for Scotland in May 1953. Bairds retained the mineral rights and all areas necessary for the mining of the ore so that, should the price of ore recover, they could restart mining operations.

Within two years the BoAS had created thirty-three new holdings at Fearns, Eyre, East and West Suisnish, Inverarish, Brochel, Glam and Oscaig. At Oscaig, one of the Home Farm parks was divided into six new holdings, and at Mill Park, Inverarish, seven holdings were created. In addition nine existing holdings were enlarged.

As well as providing money for roads and fencing, the BoAS made available loans for the building of houses. These loans were repaid over a long period and had low rates of interest. The Board encouraged their tenants to have a share in a sheep stock club and advanced loans to buy the stock. North Raasay Sheep Stock Club was created at this time, and still operates today. Although perhaps some tenants were initially dubious about this venture, in 1933 each share was worth nearly eight times its original value and a dividend of £8 15s. was paid to each member. A further dividend payment was expected the following year.

The management committee of the South Raasay Common Grazing was responsible for the maintenance and repair of roads and footpaths in their area. Tenants of East Suisnish and Eyre paid any costs relating to the roads and paths to the east of the main railway line, while the tenants of West Suisnish and Inverarish paid the costs of those on the other side of the line. The present road from Inverarish to Eyre was cut by the railway going along the pier. Until the workings were dismantled in the early 1940s, the 'road' went onto the shore and under the pier.

In 1923, for the third time within fifty years, Raasay's new owner had bought the estate for one specific reason. In 1876 it had become the sporting estate of Mr Wood. Bairds had bought it in 1911 solely for the purpose of mining iron ore. Now the BoAS had taken over the island, to resettle crofters and cottars.

The 1919 Act which created the BoAS did so to enable it to carry out resettlement schemes and act as landlord where necessary. In this respect, in Raasay, they were very successful. However, to do so they became responsible for the whole of the island, except that part retained by Bairds. As well as the land, now under tenancies, the Board owned the mansion house and policies, the shooting and fishing rights, woodlands on the estate and much of the housing stock available on the island at that time. They also owned Rona, including the lodge at Big Harbour.

Probably because it had never been envisaged that the board would be responsible for such varied subjects, there appears to have followed a period of uncertainty about how to proceed. In February 1925, just two years after they took over the estate, sale particulars of these subjects were prepared to be ready for issue when the necessary authority to sell came through. This authority was not received.

It is unclear why the expected authority to sell was not given at this time. Possibly there was some complication because the BoAS did not own the estate outright. It is also possible that the head office in Edinburgh had not grasped the significance of their ownership of the remainder of the Raasay estate. In this, Raasay was unique. Although in many other instances the BoAS had bought estates, nowhere else did the economic survival of the whole community depend solely on them.

From about the beginning of the nineteenth century, the plight of the crofters and cottars, living in the north end of the island had gradually deteriorated. However those people living in the south end of the island, had depended on 'the estate' for employment. Clachan, around the mansion house, was the economic centre of the island. In the days of the Woods many people were employed. Employment created by Bairds, although not based around Clachan, was in the south end of the island. Now, under the BoAS, estate employment was virtually non existent. However, it must be remembered that Bairds still hoped to restart the mining operations in the future. Had that happened, a large number of jobs would have been created.

Some matters had to be addressed. The houses in Clachan, Mill Place and others that were not occupied by crofter tenants were let on annual tenancies to those people living in them at the time. The gardener was kept on to tend the mansion house gardens. A caretaker and a vermin control officer were also employed.

Over the following decade, various people expressed an interest in buying the estate, or a part of it. There were numerous enquiries about the island of Rona. Some enquirers wanted an isolated island for sporting pursuits. Others wanted it for grazing. The board, however, felt that it could not proceed with either sale or lease while there were still tenants on the island. Despite all efforts to persuade them to move to the south end of Raasay, the MacRaes remained at Big Harbour. It is far from clear what would have been done had the MacRaes moved. At one time it was suggested that the Raasay crofters might want the island for grazing in the future. Another suggestion was that the shooting rights would be a useful addition for letting along with Raasay House.

In 1919 an officer from the Forestry Commission valued the growing timber on the island at £5 547 10s. Damage caused by a gale had reduced this figure by March 1921. Sometime, probably in the late 1920s, timber merchants bought a large area of this wood. They cleared the trees from about the Avenue (behind Mill Park) right over to Temptation Hill and down Creagan Beaga (towards

Oscaig). That created some employment, but it was hard labouring work. Horses dragged the logs to the road. They were then loaded onto a big wagon and taken to the foreshore at Clachan. Huge stacks were made right along the shore, from the present day cattle grid across to the landing place in front of the boat shed. When the puffers came in to take it away, rafts were formed and floated out to them.

In 1928 the Home Farm was leased. Until 1935 Raasay House was let annually but on average, receipts of £310 were less than expenditure on the gardener's wages and general maintenance of £390. In 1937 Raasay House, fully furnished, along with Borrodale House and the sporting rights of the island were leased for a twenty-year period to Mrs C. Davidson, to be developed as a sporting and tourist hotel. An inventory of the furniture in 1929 valued it at £1 514. It was believed that by the end of Mrs Davidson's lease its value could be written off. Tourism then was very different from the 'bed and breakfast' regime of today. Families and others often returned to the same place for their annual two-week holiday. Local people, although probably not very many, were employed in the hotel. As was usual for such establishments, the hotel had a licence. The bar was a focal point for locals and an additional source of income for the hotel.

SCHOOLS

The 1872 Education Act stated that children should not have to walk more than three miles to school. As in the past, there were two main schools on Raasay – at Clachan and at Torran. Because of the three-mile-rule side-schools with uncertificated teachers, were set up at various times, operating under the supervision of one of the main schools. Miss Tallach was the teacher at Clachan from about 1910, while James MacKinnon was the teacher at Torran in the early 1920s.

A side school at Glam, under the supervision of the Clachan School, was opened in January 1921. Miss Annie MacRae was the teacher. The school functioned from a room in the home of the Glam pupils. The Education Authority paid an allowance for the provision of the room and fuel for heating it. An outbreak of whooping cough and influenza closed this school for five weeks from early February 1921. However, when Miss Tallach examined the children in April, she found that they were in no way behind those at Clachan. This school closed in July 1922 when the family moved away.

In September 1922 the parents from Balachuirn were concerned about their children having to walk to and from Clachan, a distance of over three miles, in the winter. The Director of Education agreed to re-open the Glam Side School, for the eleven children from Balachuirn, Holman and Glam, again with Miss Annie MacRae teaching. The tenant at Glam then was Mr MacPherson. Although Mr Munro, Baird's Mining Engineer and factor, became involved in negotiations, Mrs MacPherson was unwilling to place a room at the disposal of the Education Authority unless her daughter, who had just left school, was employed to teach the children. Because there was no bridge over the Storab Burn, the Balachuirn children would still have to walk over three miles to Glam. Thus the Glam Side School did not re-open.

Although there were some difficulties regarding distance to the Clachan School, these were minor compared to those affecting the north end school at Torran. In 1921 the teacher was James MacKinnon. Catherine MacLeod was the sewing teacher. As with all schools at that time, it could be closed on the instruction of the Medical Officer of Health. In February 1922 Torran School was closed for three weeks and in February 1929 it was closed for four weeks, because of outbreaks of influenza. The building was disinfected before re-opening.

In July 1925 concern was raised about the attendance at Torran. It was, at that time, one of the lowest in the county. The main reason for this was the distance pupils had to walk to school. Although the legal period of schooling was nine years, from age five to fourteen, poor attendance at Torran reduced the average schooling of pupils to only five years. The average age on admission was over seven. Four pupils had been over eight on their first enrolment. Two pupils were from Eilean Taigh and five from Castle. It had been suggested, two years earlier, that other provision should be made for the Kyle Rona pupils, as they were often absent. The attendance of pupils from Torran and Arnish was also deemed unsatisfactory, possibly because they were often needed for work at home. The Torran schoolmaster was also responsible for the side-schools on Rona.

About 1919 Miss Mary Ann MacInnes was appointed as teacher in Doire na Guaille. A year's supply of peats was arranged at a cost of £2. James Graham, one of the pupils, was paid £2 for cleaning the school for the year. In December 1920, Miss MacInnes wrote to the Director of Education asking if she could have a few days off at New Year and make up the lost time on Saturdays. If she were to leave the island, she would be dependent on the weather for the date of her return. It is not clear, if it was generally the case in the county that days missed could be made up on Saturdays, or if the unique position of Rona caused this. Communication difficulties were one of the many problems of living on Rona. Sometimes the island was cut off for weeks by bad weather, and mail was held up.

By 1921 the only children attending the school were the Graham family. A nephew of the family had come from Glasgow, from a house where the children had whooping cough. Inevitably, the Graham children caught it. Two of them were off school ill, but had returned to school before the other two became ill. In March, Miss MacInnes wrote the Director. Only two of the children were at school. The other two were likely to be off for some time, and were 'spoiling the register'. She was very disheartened, as there were so few pupils. She now thought that she might not stay for much longer. Eventually the medical officer closed the school on heath grounds for three weeks until the 18 May.

The children were taught, arithmetic (including money sums), English (essay and letter writing), geography, history, and Gaelic dictation. This school closed on 7 July 1926, when the Graham family moved from Rona to the north end of Raasay.

There was also a side school in Dry Harbour. In 1921 the teacher was Miss Catharine MacKinnon. Because of bad weather, the school did not close at New Year, but had the two week holiday later in the year. When the Doire na Guaille school was closed in April 1921 because of whooping cough, the Dry Harbour school was closed for holidays. When in May that year Miss MacKinnon was off ill for a time, Miss MacInnes from Doire na Guaille taught alternate weeks in both schools. This school was closed on 31 July 1930.

THE CHURCH (1929–1934)

Until his death in 1930, Rev. Hector Kennedy was the Free Church minister on Raasay. In 1932 Rev. Archibald MacDonald became minister but in 1934 he moved to Knock in Sleat, Skye after which the Free Church had no resident minister. The flitting to Sleat was by boat, from Raasay to Armadale. Because the minister's cow also had to move, a young lad, Norrie Gillies, went with the minister to walk the cow from Armadale to Knock. He returned home the following day.

The Free Presbyterian Church and manse had been built at Holoman, by 1899. This site, a compromise between the north and south ends of the island, was unsatisfactory, particularly after the BoAS took over the estate and most of the people had moved back to the south end. Consequently, in 1929 a new church was built just above the school, half way between Inverarish and Clachan. The roof from the church at Holoman was taken off and used for the new manse in the early 1950s.

WILLIAM BAIRD & COMPANY (1923–1943)

Bairds, it will be remembered, had an ongoing interest in the island. They had sold neither the mineral rights nor those areas necessary for the production of ore, in the hope that this might again become a viable proposition. In the early 1930s, most of the houses in the Terrace were vacant. In 1931/32 the valuation roll shows that only fifteen of the sixty-four houses were occupied. Even by 1941/42 only thirty houses were occupied. Only people who would work for Bairds, should the occasion arise, were given tenancies.

The plant had been put onto a care and maintenance basis after the First World War. Three to five men were employed to maintain the plant and paint the iron-work. This employment continued until about 1943 when the bulk of the machinery was dismantled and sold for scrap. Bairds then sold off all the houses in the terrace.

This 'pull out' by Bairds had not been expected by the Department of Agriculture and Fisheries (DAFS – which succeeded the BoAS in the late 1920s), and certainly not by those in the local office. A report on conditions on Raasay, written in 1943, makes this clear. When the BoAS had bought the estate, it had been assumed that 'considerable mining operations would form part of the economy of the island for a long time'. Matters had now changed and serious consideration, it was said, should be given to the future. Demolition of the machinery was in the hands of the scrap merchants. Quarries, pits and bore-holes, resulting from their previous operations, were a danger to both people and animals. The houses were now being sold off. Although substantial, they were not up to standard and the cost of improving them might be a drain on the public purse in the future. Many of the people moving into these houses were applying to DAFS for land, but all the land nearby was already occupied by shareholders. It is not known whether the head office in Edinburgh addressed these concerns.

Thus all hope of major employment opportunities resulting from the re-opening of the mines was gone.

Notes

1. R. Sharpe, *Raasay: Documents and Sources* (1978), p. 207.
2. E. A. Cameron, *Land for the People*, pp. 182–3.

9

Epilogue

Although it is too soon to attempt a comprehensive history of the last fifty years there are some aspects of those decades that may be considered.

About 1949, DAFS granted land on Raasay to the Forestry Commission. This gave some much-needed employment on the island. At most about fourteen men were employed. They were busy for a number of years fencing, clearing and planting. At that time all planting was done by hand. Although in the early years the work was labour intensive, as time went on fewer men were required and the numbers employed dwindled.

In the early 1950s, two township roads, to Balachuirn and East Suisnish were constructed by DAFS. Until the 1950s, a contractor maintained Raasay roads. Thereafter the Roads Department of the County Council took over this work, employing some men themselves. This source of employment reached its peak in the 1970s, when the then regional council employed six men. By the 1980s, however, local authority budgets were being cut and anyone who retired or left was not replaced. The ferry service by then made it possible for road maintenance to be carried out by squads from Skye. Now, no one on Raasay is employed by this department.

After his death, Peter Nicolson's family continued to run the shop at Mill Place. It was taken over by the Scottish Co-operative Wholesale Society (the Co-op) in the late 1940s but continued to operate from Mill Place. It was not until the 1950s that they acquired houses in the Terrace and moved their premises. In February 1973, the shop was taken over by Finlay MacLennan, formerly the Co-op manager, who ran it until he retired in July 1999.

In May 1956 Raasay was officially 'switched on'. The North of Scotland Hydro Electric Board had opened Storr Lochs power station in 1952, and thereafter worked to bring power to the whole of the Skye area. Laying the submarine cable from Braes to Raasay was part of that exercise. By the beginning of April 1956 the power lines on Raasay were in place, and all the townships that have electricity today were connected.

The 'switching on' ceremony was held at Braes and the speeches transmitted to Borrodale House in Raasay. The official party then crossed to the island. The occasion was celebrated at Raasay Hotel (Raasay House) and Borrodale, where a cookery demonstration was held. The coming of electricity to Raasay, as for the Highlands in general, was one of the great advances of the twentieth century.

Until 1959 the *Loch Nevis* was the boat that served Raasay. Six days per week, she left Portree and sailed to Mallaig, returning to Portree in the evening. In 1959, because of a reduction in passenger numbers, David MacBrayne Ltd rescheduled their sailings. From then, the *Loch Arkaig* served both Raasay and the Small Isles. Based at Portree, she called on Raasay in the mornings on

Mondays and Wednesdays and in the evenings on Tuesdays and Thursdays. On Fridays and Saturdays, she called at Raasay in the mornings and the evenings.

Mrs Davidson had run Raasay House as a sporting hotel since 1937. In 1960 she gave up the hotel and moved to Tokavaig in Sleat where she ran a boarding house. This, it must be assumed, was her decision and not that of DAFS. The hotel closed.

Thus, the department was once again faced with the problem of what to do with that part of the Raasay estate that was not required for its crofting tenants. By then it was known that, although Bairds still owned some land and the mineral rights on Raasay, there was no possibility of their restarting mining operations. It is not known how the solution to this problem was reached, or who took the final decision. It must be assumed that the decision to sell rested with officials at head office in Edinburgh. Who ran the advertising for the sale of these properties, and how widely they were advertised are two more unanswered questions.

In 1961 the DAFS sold nearly 10.5 acres including Raasay House, Borrodale House, the Gardener's Cottage, the Kennels and the Battery and Boathouse to Dr John Green of Cooden, Sussex. Dr Green had recently sold the island of Scalpay, just south of Raasay. In 1964 he acquired Suisnish House, by a private sale. Title to all of these holdings on Raasay was transferred to the Bank of Scotland in November 1967. It might be assumed that they were security for a loan.

The previous month, DAFS had sold Dr Green some small pieces of ground about the Old Pier, reserving the right to use the Pier. In November 1967, on the same date as the Bank of Scotland acquired title to all but 0.182 acres of Green's property on Raasay, DAFS sold him Glen Lodge and the field opposite. They also sold him Orchard Cottage, Loch a' Mhuilinn and other ground totalling ninety-eight acres, reserving only the right of way to the Old Pier at Clachan. By December 1969 title to all of these new holdings on Raasay, except Loch a' Mhuilinn, was transferred to Downbourne Finance Co. Ltd, again, it might be assumed, to secure a loan.

The land sold to Dr Green in November 1967 included the Home Farm. The BoAS (and later DAFS) had leased the farm, to various tenants, during the time they owned it. Presumably, it was not sold by DAFS until it became vacant.

In February 1968 William Baird & Co. Ltd sold Dr Green all their remaining interests in Raasay, including the mineral rights. Some areas, reserved by them in 1923, had already been sold off, most notably the houses of Inverarish Terrace and the Cottages.

Dr Green employed Norman Ellercamp to manage the farm. It was run as a dairy farm and equipped with modern milking and bottling machinery and a herd of pedigree Guernsey cows that produced the most delicious 'gold top' milk ever tasted. Some of this milk was exported to Kyle.

It is not known what Dr Green's plans for his Raasay property were. In 1972, the second issue of the *West Highland Free Press* quoted Mr Ellercamp as saying that Dr Green had spent thousands and thousands of pounds in trying to make Raasay House into 'the kind of hotel he wanted, but then just as quickly everything stopped.' The same article stated that Green had admitted (to whom we were not told) that his purchase of Raasay was purely as an investment.

Clearly, he had never intended to live on the island. It may perhaps be assumed that DAFS had not spent a great deal on the maintenance of Raasay House while it was leased to Mrs Davidson. She had been running it as a hotel for twenty-three years. If Dr Green had planned to create a high-class establishment, a substantial investment would have been required to bring it up to standard. Was this what he had in mind when he spent 'thousands and thousands of pounds' on the building?

Meanwhile, about 1968 it had been accepted that the *Loch Arkaig* was not providing an adequate service for Raasay, and it was agreed that the island should have its own dedicated service. This took some considerable time to put into practice. The new roll-on roll-off car ferry was to run from Sconser to the Old Pier at Clachan, requiring two new slipways to be built – at Sconser and at Clachan. Firstly, however, ground had to be acquired from Dr Green for the Clachan site. In March 1972, he refused to sell the necessary ground.

As reported in the *West Highland Free Press* of 13 April 1972, the Highlands and Islands Development Board (HIDB) had been trying to acquire Dr Green's entire holding on Raasay. At a recent meeting between Dr Green and the HIDB, he had apparently agreed to sell his properties to them. Negotiations were still in progress.

In early June a compulsory purchase order for the land required for the ferry terminal took effect. In the same month, Inverness-shire planning committee considered three applications from Dr Green for developments on Raasay. They were for

- a thirty bedroom extension to Borrodale House
- a seventy bedroom hotel and filling station at Suisnish House
- an extension to Raasay House with service station and shops

All three were thrown out by the planning committee and Dr Green was informed that his £530 000 plans were premature because of the lack of vehicular ferry access. Most likely, the three applications were submitted in the hope that one would be acceptable to the committee.

By mid August 1972 Dr Green had lodged an objection to the compulsory purchase order for the ground at Clachan. He did not object to the £10 compensation offered for the ground but claimed that the proposed ferry facilities would adversely affect the beauty and character of the island while the existing means of access were adequate. The project was then delayed while a public inquiry was held.

This was duly held and a compulsory purchase order obtained for the site. Only then was it found that the Clachan site would be too costly to develop. This caused further delays. Eventually, on 18 March 1975, because the slip at Sconser had not been completed, a temporary ferry service between Raasay and Portree began. A temporary slip was built beside the pier at Suisnish. Construction of the main slipway, to the south of the pier, and work on the pier itself was carried out after the service was introduced.

The *Eigg* now served Raasay six days per week, with two sailings per day to Portree. Although this service was not ideal, it was a vast improvement on the *Loch Arkaig*'s timetable. Because the slipway at Portree was narrow and tidal, vehicles could only be carried on some sailings. On Friday (Good Friday) 22 April 1976 the *Canna* began the Raasay–Sconser run, sailing three times per day, each journey taking only fifteen minutes.

As well as providing a very much improved ferry service this created three new jobs on the island. This was important, as the population had now fallen to about 130 people, many of them elderly. For the first time, people living on Raasay could take jobs on Skye. Perhaps of even greater importance, it allowed Raasay children to attend Portree High School without having to live in a school hostel. Before then, if the weather was reasonable in the summertime, pupils could get home on a Friday evening by small boat from Braes. In wintertime, however, they had only one day a week at home. Arriving at Raasay on the *Loch Arkaig* on Saturday morning, they had to go back to Portree on the boat in the late afternoon.

Meantime, negotiations between Dr Green and the HIDB had been ongoing. It was reported in July 1975 that, although no deal had been reached over the other properties, he was possibly about to sell Borrodale House. Over the intervening years his applications for planning permission for various schemes had been submitted.

In January 1977, the *West Highland Free Press* reported that Brian Wilson and Derek Cooper had interviewed Dr John Green at his home in Sussex. An article based on this interview is given here with the kind permission of Brian Wilson.

> In this second article based on an extensive interview with Dr John Green at his home in Cooden, Sussex, BRIAN WILSON relates the answers that he and Derek Cooper received from the man who has been held responsible for the strangulation of Raasay. A transcript of the entire interview, which was taped with Dr Green's permission, has been supplied to the Highlands and Islands Development Board.
>
> Our interview with Dr Green was certainly long and painstaking. I wouldn't claim that a great deal of new information emerged but, for the first time, the threads of Dr Green's story can be pulled together. I hope that the HIDB and others involved will respond to these articles so that, at last, some light can be shed on this astonishing story.
>
> I agree with Derek Cooper's remarks about the initial blame lying with the people who sold him the property – the Department of Agriculture and Fisheries. And Dr Green's account of how the initial sale was conducted does nothing to erode the grounds for criticism.
>
> Dr Green: 'When we purchased this property in '61 it was in a shocking state. So far as I know we were the only offerers. At that time we had just sold Scalpay – I personally was rather sorry but my wife found it too isolated. I went to see the Department and said: "Well, frankly, we don't know what sort of price you are expecting to get and we don't know what other offers you may have received, but we are interested."

'I have connections with Raasay – one of my grandmother's ancestors was a MacLeod of Raasay. I told them I'd leave an open offer. They told my solicitors the sort of figure they were expecting to get and we said: "Very well, if that's the price your're asking, we'll pay it." I think it was about £6,500.'

Cooper: 'But the furniture was worth more than that!'

Green: 'Well, I don't know about that.'

Cooper: 'But you must have known it was – wasn't there an inventory?'

Green: 'We merely said – you fix a price and we'll pay what you ask. It wasn't such a snip. You see, '61 values were very different. We sold the whole of Scalpay – house, furniture, everything – for just in excess of £20 000. It had cost us £5 000 to put in electricity.

'Having bought Raasay House we had a survey and decided that we must undertake major structural repairs. We had a lot of contractors – much of the roof was gone and there was a lot of dry rot around. The billiard room, for instance, was completely gone. Between 1963 when the work started and 1967 we spent somewhere in the region of £80 000.'

Later Dr Green produced his account books in respect of Raasay. Sure enough, the figures in the expenditure column added up to £84 409 9s. 7d, but we noticed that this figure included wages, insurance and farm expenses as well as building costs. Questioned on this, Dr Green suggested that he had spent £30 000 on Raasay House.

He claimed that, by 1967, 'the house was structurally pretty sound'. Then, 'I thought it might be sensible to apply to the HIDB for a grant to finish the internal work because we'd put a lot of money into the external work and the farm. We sent in an application in 1967. We had a certain amount of correspondence and then they asked if they could meet me to discuss the whole thing.

'So I met them in London. Prophet Smith was there and Fasken and so on and, to my great surprise, they said: "Well, what we are really interested in is acquiring the estate. We feel that it is the sort of project that the Board could use what ideas they have for developing an island estate."

'"Well," I said, "we haven't any intention or interest in selling but at the same time ... if that's what you want we'd be prepared to sell. But naturally in view of the money that's been put into the thing, although we wouldn't necessarily want to make a profit, we wouldn't want to make a great loss, especially selling to a public body."

'They asked my wife and I if we wouldn't do anything further; to mark time because they might wish to develop the interior in a different way to what we might do. And they would let us know their decision as quickly as possible ... We met again and they said they would like to go ahead, but they couldn't give a precise date because they had to get permission from the Secretary of State to proceed with the purchase.

'Well, we stopped work and time went on but I was always assured that they wished to go ahead. And so we dragged on until 1972 and then that storm blew up about the ferry and, of course, the wrong impression was put over that we were against a ferry. We opposed the ferry because they wanted to ruin the environs of Raasay House by sticking a ferry terminal in front of it – they were going to build lavatory blocks! We considered that the whole aspect of Raasay House would be ruined by such a development right in front of it – we had to oppose it. But in opposing it we offered them gratis an alternative site in front of Suisnish House.

'Then this storm blew up. The Nationwide programme was shown at that time, and perhaps the people were encouraged to go from afar and see Raasay House. From that time the vandalism started.'

At that stage the Board re-emerged with an offer. But, says Dr Green, it was a fraction of what they originally offered. We asked if he could put figures to these statements, but he replied: "I can't really – I've always been told that I mustn't say."

'Then they revised their offer – upwards. In 1974 we agreed a figure. They were to take over all the property at an agreed price apart from one or two things like the mineral rights. Then at the last moment they broke the bargain. They didn't go ahead. The reason was they ought to have the minerals.

'First they wanted the sporting rights which they hadn't mentioned before. Then when we'd agreed on that for a small extra sum they wanted the mineral rights – for the price they'd offered for just the properties. We said we couldn't do that because, after all, we had to buy them – what we would do was to include the minerals at about half the price we paid for them.' (Dr Green declined to state the price he paid to Messrs Baird, the previous owners of the mineral rights).

'I said to the Board – look, we can't go on like this; you've got to stand by the agreement. But then they came back and offered even less. Then they suddenly turned round and said that all they wanted to buy was Borrodale House. So that left us high and dry. We said: "If you're just wanting to buy this one house after all this waste of time and the legal expenses we'll agree to sell."

'The district valuer again came in and we agreed a price and then suddenly they turned round again when we were about to conclude and said they didn't want any of the properties at all. So they reneged every time and on every agreement.'

Dr Green claims that Raasay House will reopen as a hotel. 'I've now had estimates for the second restoration of Raasay House. The last estimate was somewhere in the region of £50 000 for the external work – it looks much worse than it is. I should imagine to do everything, to restore and bring it up to standard, you could do the lot for £150 000.'

We suggested that £500 000 might be nearer the mark and asked him when he had last seen Raasay House. 'I know all about the place – I had aerial photos taken three weeks ago ... The architects, MacKenzie in Dingwall, will be submitting the detailed planning application sometime in early March.'

Asked if he would be going to the HIDB for financial support, Dr Green said: 'Well, I don't know. None of my work is contingent on getting a grant from the HIDB.' He insisted that he has the money to do it.

The name of the Highlands and Islands Development Board kept cropping up: 'When one has been so badly let down by a public body I think at least they should have the courtesy to admit it. I mean, this new chairman goes there and says the farm ought to be supplying milk and it's a dreadful thing to see Raasay House standing there like that.

'Then he goes to a bit of my land and says: "This is where we want to put our new hotel." I mean all this nonsense when he knows – if he cares to look at the files he must be aware – that all these things he's saying are absolute rubbish. I've written to him about it.'

Dr Green is not at all pleased about the HIDB plans for its own hotel – 'a crackpot idea,' he says. 'The idea of putting some modern building within a few yards of Raasay House would be an act of sacrilege ... This is an old Georgian property which has very historic associations and interest ... We naturally would never agree to the Board putting a hotel in our grounds.'

Later he returns to the same theme. He had written to the Secretary of State saying that if the HIDB had that kind of money to put into Raasay then it should surely be put into Raasay House. 'After all, that is the focal point of the island.'

Cooper: 'Or was ... It hasn't been the focal point of anything since you bought it, has it?'

Green: 'Well, I don't know that it was much the focal point before.'

Cooper: 'So how do you mean it's the focal point of the island?'

Green: 'The house – the associations of the house.'

Cooper: 'But you can't have a ruin as the focal point of anything – except perhaps a car park and a toilet.'

Dr Green pointed out that the discontinuation of the licence at Raasay House was not of his doing. 'When I applied for a licence one set of islanders opposed it and the other set said that if they'd known it was being opposed they would have gone and supported it. The Wee Free minister was dead against liquor being served on Raasay again, and so the result was that the whole matter was left in abeyance.'

Cooper: 'You seem to be saying that, between them, the Board and the islanders have cooked their own goose?'

Green: 'I think they have.'

I have always thought the most puzzling aspect of Dr Green's behaviour to be the fact that he left the valuable contents of Raasay House to rot or to be pilfered. Our efforts to draw forth a rational explanation were notably unsuccessful. 'It is a great pity,' he said. 'But then one would hope that people would respect property.' The books of value had gone to the National Library in Edinburgh. 'I'm an antiquarian book collector myself and what's lying around is of no great value.'

Certainly, Dr Green seems to be in no way disposed towards dropping his long range interest in Raasay. The Board, he says, 'will never get planning permission' for their proposed hotel. What about the planning permission granted to ferryman Alistair Nicholson to extend his guesthouse to hotel size?

Well, Dr Green's not very pleased about that either. He pointed to the refusal of his own similar application for 'secondary site' development on the island and believes that the same planning criteria should be applied to Mr Nicholson's application.

Will he object: 'Being in possession of the minerals we do have some say. If we wanted we could create a lot of trouble. If any new house is built on any part of the island or if there is any extension they must really get the agreement of the mineral owner. If Nicholson wanted to drain onto the Suisnish land for his septic tanks, we probably would object. It all depends.'

As the interview drew to a close Dr Green returned to his favourite theme. 'The chief culprits are the Board. They should stand by the offer they originally made and although that offer has gone down in value because of inflation we were prepared to stand by it from our side if they were prepared to go ahead.'

Mrs Green re-entered to offer us sherry and to hurry her husband on the way to an appointment. We suggested that life might have been simpler if they had invested their money in a stamp collection, which they could at least look at. Somewhat wearily, she agreed.

From *West Highland Free Press*, Friday, 4 February 1977
'The View from Cooden'

The response by the Highlands and Island Development Board to our exclusive interview with Dr John Green, of Raasay fame, came this week in the form of the following statement:

'We have read with interest the articles based on an interview with Dr John Green which the *West Highland Free Press* has carried over the past two weeks. Readers will have been interested to learn of Dr Green's views about Raasay's problems and how they might be resolved.

'We do not agree with Dr Green on the reasons for the unfortunate condition of Raasay house and other parts of his estate. As landlord he is solely responsible for the care and maintenance of his own properties.

'The Board have tried to negotiate the purchase of the whole or parts of Dr Green's estate based on a district valuer's price. Our last offer for the whole of Dr Green's estate (13 November 1974) including the sporting rights and mineral rights was £80 400. Our attempts to buy Dr Green's properties were unsuccessful and we are no longer in discussion with him.

'The Board's advisors have informed us that Raasay House is now in such disrepair that it would be impossible for the Board to convert the building into an hotel at reasonable cost.

'Our main purpose now is to press ahead with efforts to help improve income and employment on the island. To that end we will give sympathetic consideration to any project on Raasay which will create opportunities for such change.

'The Board sees no purpose at present in reopening negotiations with Dr Green.

From *West Highland Free Press*, Friday, 11 February 1977
Board Reply to Green'

Epilogue

Since the start of the ferry service, other things had been happening on Raasay.

About 1975, the Highland Council began a scheme to provide mains water for most of the villages and townships. Water was piped from Loch na Meillich near Dun Caan. The works were completed in 1977 and mains water was then available to the townships of Balachuirn, Oscaig, Clachan, Inverarish, and East Suisnish. This had also provided some local employment.

In 1976, Calum MacLeod completed ten years' work constructing a road between Arnish and Brochel. After Calum's single-handed effort in building this road the Regional Council carried out some improvements and tarred it. This work, costing £45 000, gave vehicular access as far as Arnish for the first time.

Perhaps surprisingly, given all that had gone before, Skye and Lochalsh Licensing Board granted Dr Green a 'licence to sell strong drink' for the four-star hotel he planned to build around Raasay House in June 1978. At that time the proposal appears to have been for a sixty-bedroom hotel, costing about £1 million. He is quoted as saying 'Raasay House Hotel will be properly run and will give work for every employable person on Raasay.'

Dr John Green's career in Raasay came to an end in 1979, when the HIDB finally bought him out. As Brian Wilson said at the time, 'The irony of Dr Green's position was that he did more harm than anyone else to the reputation of absentee landlords, even though he hardly owned any land.' This is certainly true. Of the 18 000 acres that form the Raasay estate, Dr Green owned, at most, less than 200.

Dr Green's refusal to sell the ground for the ferry terminal had received widespread publicity in the press. Now both islanders and the general public looked to the HIDB for solutions to revitalise the island. They had an even bigger headache than DAFS had had in 1960. All the properties, which had then been in reasonable repair, were now derelict.

They began with the obvious and boarded up all their buildings. Surveys were carried out on Raasay House and the other properties. Raasay House underwent some repairs and was then leased to the Scottish Adventure Schools Trust late in 1980. Clearly the island needed a hotel. Because the cost of renovating Raasay House would be prohibitive, Borrodale House was extended and became the fifteen-bedroom Isle of Raasay Hotel. It opened in July 1981.

The leaseholder gave up the Home Farm, which had been worked throughout Dr Green's ownership, because the HIDB wanted vacant possession. Various improvements were carried out on the farm before it was again leased out. It was eventually sold to local people in 1995.

Raasay Outdoor Centre took over from the Adventure Schools Trust in 1983. By May 1985 the building was wind and watertight and structurally sound. Community groups use the west wing.

By 1981 the population, which had been as low as 130 in 1976, had risen to 145. That year, six years after it started, the Raasay ferry was carrying fifty cars per day during the summer season. Demand grew steadily. The original six-car ferry was replaced by one capable of carrying twelve cars. Between April and mid-October that ferry now sails nine times each day between Raasay and

Sconser, six days per week. For June, July and August, there is an additional sailing each day, and a late sailing on Saturdays. Now six people have full-time jobs on the ferry.

The fish farm in Loch Arnish employs six or seven people. Raasay Outdoor Centre has grown from strength to strength and, as well as six jobs all year round, it employs an additional twenty to twenty-five people from April to September.

When Richard Sharpe wrote his book on Raasay in 1977, his final paragraph was less than encouraging. He said

> Raasay remains a microcosm of the Highlands and Islands in the twentieth century. Crofting is declining. Transport difficulties threaten to cut the island off. The native population moves away and outsiders buy up houses for summer homes. It cannot yet be seen whether solutions will be found for these problems, and so it is too soon to write the history of the twentieth century. But as more documents become available at the Department of Agriculture and Fisheries, it may be possible later to see why its policy towards the island changed.

The prognosis for Raasay today is far more encouraging. The arrival of the car ferry in 1975 would appear to have heralded the beginning of better times. Population is rising. Young local people are setting up home on the island. Raasay children are attending the primary school. They are then able to attend school in Portree yet still take part in home and island life during term time. There is employment on Raasay itself, and those who wish to are now able to take jobs on Skye. The population is continuing to rise. There are now about 180 people resident on the island.

However, many questions remain unanswered.

Did BoAS and DAFS's policy towards Raasay change? They took over the Raasay estate in 1922 to set up and administer crofter holdings. The legislation that created this department never envisaged that it would become 'responsible' for a whole community. At that time, the local office believed that the part of the estate not required for crofter tenants would be sold off. This did not happen. While Bairds still retained an interest in the estate, it was believed that they would restart mining operations. When Bairds sold up about 1943, it is clear that the local DAFS office understood that their position had significantly altered. Did DAFS head office in Edinburgh understand this?

Perhaps the most obvious error made by DAFS was in the valuation of the contents of Raasay House. In 1929 a value of £1 514 was put on the contents. It was believed that this could be written off, presumably through depreciation, after Mrs Davidson's twenty-year lease had ended. Who carried out this valuation? Were they qualified to do so? One would suspect not.

Do government rules and regulations allow common sense to prevail, should a department find themselves faced with the unexpected? Common sense would suggest (albeit with hindsight) that an antiques expert should have been involved with the valuation of contents, and that the opinion of some expert on stately homes should have been sought before any decision was taken about Raasay

House. But realistically, how should DAFS have gone about this? Could the same thing happen again?

There also appears to be a number of unanswered questions surrounding the HIDB's part in the affair. If Dr Green's version is accepted, the HIDB, having stated their intention to buy his properties and having asked him to stop all work on Raasay House, then proceeded to change their minds constantly as the years went by. Why did this happen? Having been involved in negotiations with him for years, they then submitted their own planning application for a hotel on the island, on his land and close to Raasay House. That would appear to have been unnecessarily confrontational. Did they look for a site elsewhere?

Did Dr Green offer a site for a ferry terminal in front of Suisnish House as he claimed? If so, was that alternative examined? Why was it not realised that the Clachan site was too expensive for a ferry terminal before years and a lot of public time and money had been wasted with a compulsory purchase order and public inquiry?

The Dr Green/Dr No episode received a great deal of publicity in the national press at the time. Did that publicity help the island?

Nowadays, thankfully, the publicity that Raasay receives tells of the diverse activities, both economic and recreational, taking place on the island. The many benefits that the island has to offer tourists are widely advertised – the freedom to enjoy the natural beauty and wildlife and to see the evidence of part occupation, such as St Moluag's Chapel, Brochel Castle, townships previously occupied and, more recently, the iron-ore works. It tells of the many activities enjoyed by the present population.

The ferry link with Skye brought with it a diverse variety of benefits to the island. Long may it continue to do so!

Part II

Genealogy

10

Genealogy of the MacLeods of Raasay

Written Histories of the MacLeods

There are various written histories of the MacLeods of Raasay. The earliest, Alexander MacKenzie's *History of the MacLeods* published in 1889, has a chapter dealing with the MacLeods of Raasay. In his *History of Skye*, published in 1930, Alexander Nicolson included a chapter on the 'History of Raasay'. A second edition of this book was published in 1994, having been substantially revised by Dr Alasdair MacLean, Aird Bernisdale, a nephew of Alexander Nicolson. Richard Sharpe's *Raasay: A Study in Island History* was published in 1978 with a second volume giving *Documents and Sources – People and Places*. This study is extremely useful, as many references are quoted, both in the original Latin and with an English translation.

Dr I. F. Grant's *History of the Clan MacLeod* was published in 1959, with a reprint in 1981. This work is about the whole clan and references to the Lewis and Raasay branches are scattered throughout. Rev. Dr Donald MacKinnon, who had already amassed a considerable knowledge of the clan, was asked to write a companion volume dealing with the genealogy of the MacLeods. Thus *The MacLeods – The Genealogy of a Clan* was published in five sections. Alick Morrison continued this work after the death of Rev. MacKinnon. He wrote Sections 4 and 5, dealing with the MacLeods of Lewis and their various branches. He notes in his introduction to Section 4 that most of the work by Rev. MacKinnon had been lost and that he had to undertake research again into the history and genealogies of these families. This section was published in 1974.

All these publications gathered information from earlier works about other clans with whom the MacLeods had dealings and from public records and private sources available at the time. It is significant that all histories and genealogies of the MacLeods of Raasay have essentially followed that written by Alexander MacKenzie in 1889.

A great deal of new research has been done on the history of the Highlands and Islands over the last thirty years or so, and is indeed still ongoing. Rev. William Matheson and W. D. H. Sellar have both written about the MacLeods in the 'Transactions of the Gaelic Society of Inverness'. In particular, William Matheson undertook a great deal of research into the MacLeods of Lewis and his work substantially altered previous works on that subject.

There is thus a lot of information about the MacLeods of Raasay. Each source in itself appears to make sense but when they are read together, there are discrepancies and contradictions that have not so far been resolved. There is a lot more yet to be discovered about the MacLeods of Lewis and their various branches. Also so far unresolved is the relationship between the Raasay MacLeods and the MacLeods of Gairloch, another branch of the clan, which is believed to have been the cause of much grief in the second half of the sixteenth and the beginning of the seventeenth century.

Origins of the Clan MacLeod

The ancestor from whom the clan took its name was Leod (from the Norse Loitr or Ljot) who lived during the thirteenth century. Until the more recent research was undertaken, it was thought that Leod was the son of Olaf the Black, King of Man, and his wife Christina, daughter of Farquhar, Earl of Ross. Leod was said to have been fostered by Paul Balkason, vicecomes or sheriff of Skye. He was believed to have received the lands of Uist and Harris as well as some land on Skye from his father, the lands of Lewis from his grandfather (Earl of Ross) and Glenelg from his foster-father. By his marriage to the daughter of a Norse noble, called MacRaild, Leod gained Duirinish, Bracadale, Minginish, Lyndale and much of Trotternish on Skye.

W. D. H. Sellar[1] has shown Leod to be a descendant of Harold the Black. Leod's great, great, great grandmother was Ealga Follalainn, Helga of the Beautiful Hair, a sister of Godred Crovan, Rí Innsegall or King of the Isles who died about 1095. The chart of 'Kings of Man and The Isles/MacLeods/Lords of the Isles' shows this relationship.

There are two branches of the Clan MacLeod, the Siol Thormoid (offspring of Tormod or Norman) of Harris and Dunvegan and the Siol Thorcaill (offspring of Torcall) of Lewis. It was thought that Tormod and Torcall were brothers, and that they received their lands from their father, Leod. William Matheson[2] showed how that idea was incorrect. Tormod's son, Murdo, married the daughter of a Nicolson chief, who lived on Lewis. Their son, Torcall, named after his mother's people, inherited the Nicolson lands of Lewis, Assynt, Coigeach and Waternish, from his maternal grandfather. Thus, Torcall, the first of the MacLeods of Lewis, was a grandson of Tormod. Both branches of the MacLeod clan were important. W. D. H. Sellar explains:

> The Siol Thormaid and the Siol Thorcuil functioned effectively as separate clans, each under its own chief, neither holding their principal lands of the other, with separate coats of arms and separate places of burial; they even, on occasion, took separate sides in island conflicts. It is a sign of the aspirations and importance of both these MacLeod branches that their arms, together with those of the Lords of the Isles, appear in the Armorial de Berry a leading European mid-fifteenth century armorial, being the only Hebridean arms given; the MacLeods of Harris bear a castle in their arms (presumably for Dunvegan), and the MacLeods of Lewis a mountain on fire.

Mr Sellar has since indicated that the above quotations should be amended to read, 'being the only Hebridean arms given, save for the Lord of the Isles himself ...'

The MacLeods of Lewis – Siol Torcall

William Matheson substantially revised the genealogy of the MacLeods of Lewis. Details are found in the chart – The MacLeods of Lewis. This book is only concerned with the MacLeods of Lewis insofar as they impact on the MacLeods of Raasay. Therefore the previously accepted genealogy of the Lewis MacLeods will not be given here.

The MacLeods of Raasay – the MacGilleChaluim

The MacLeods of Raasay were known as the MacGilleChaluim. That they were a branch of, and descended from, the MacLeods of Lewis there can be no doubt. Tradition says so, and this tradition is otherwise confirmed.

In 1518 the Laird of Raasay accompanied MacLeod of Lewis on a raid to Ardnamurchan against a branch of the MacDonalds. Hugh MacDonald in his 'History of the MacDonalds'[3] records this event. Although his account was written about 1628, sometime after the event, MacLeod of Lewis is recorded as the chief of the Laird of Raasay. It says, 'Raasay had a consultation with his chief, the Laird of Lewis.' In 1549 Dean Monro states that, 'MacGilleCalum should obey MacLeod of Lewis'.[4]

Clearly, therefore, the MacLeods of Raasay were a branch, or sept, of the MacLeods of Lewis. However, the belief that the MacLeods of Raasay were descended from Calum mac Ruairidh, chief of Lewis early in the sixteenth century, cannot be accepted so easily. Alexander MacKenzie, writing in 1889, states that

> Malcolm Garbh MacGillechallum, second son of Malcolm MacLeod of Lewis, succeeded to Raasay early in the sixteenth century. The earliest glimpse which we get of the MacLeods of Raasay as an independent sept is when, in 1518–19, along with the MacLeods of Lewis, they accompanied Sir Donald Gallda of Lochalsh in an invasion of Ardnamurchan ...[5]

Descent of the MacLeods of Raasay from Previous Histories and Genealogies

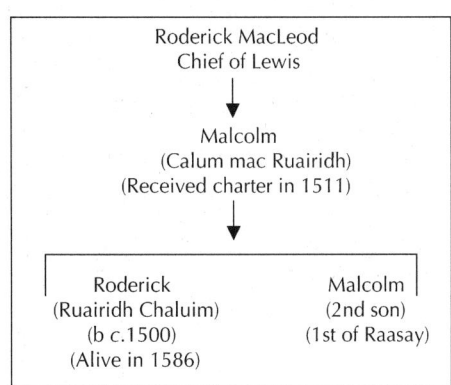

Figure R1. Descent of the MacLeods of Raasay as given by Alexander MacKenzie.

There are several reasons for questioning this.

Calum Garbh's older brother, Ruairidh Chaluim, is believed to have been born about 1500. Thus his younger brother could have been at most eighteen years old in 1518. It is most unlikely, therefore, that he was the laird who accompanied the MacLeods of Lewis to Ardnamurchan. If the Raasay laird were Calum Garbh, as described, the Laird of Lewis would have been his father, although Hugh MacDonald's account does not say so.

Because dates relating to this period in history are often vague, the possibility must be considered that Ruairidh Chaluim was born sometime earlier than 1500. During the second half of the sixteenth century there was a long-running dispute over the succession of the MacLeods of Lewis. Ruairidh Chaluim disowned his eldest son, Torcall Conanach. Torcall Conanach, backed by the MacKenzies of Kintail, fought his father for many years, resulting ultimately in the downfall of the MacLeods of Lewis. Although it is not known when Ruairidh Chaluim died, it is known that in 1586, as part of the disputed succession, Torcall Conanach made him a prisoner in Stornoway Castle. If Ruairidh Chaluim were born about 1500, by 1586 he would have been an old man. It is, therefore, unlikely though not impossible, that he was born earlier than 1500. If the 1500 date were to be revised, it is more likely that it should be later, rather than earlier.

It appears, therefore, that a younger brother of Ruairidh Chaluim would not have been old enough to be the laird of Raasay in 1518.

Ownership of the Raasay estate

Ownership of the Raasay estate must also be considered. Alexander MacKenzie, and all subsequent writers, believed that Raasay was granted by MacLeod of Lewis to his second son. There is good reason to question this belief, as no evidence has been found to suggest that the MacLeods of Lewis ever owned or held Raasay.

In 1511 Calum mac Ruairidh, chief of Lewis, was granted a charter by James IV for his lands. This charter names his lands as the lands of Lewis, Waternish, Assynt and Coigeach. Furthermore, all these lands were, at this time, conjoined into 'one free barony and Lordship of Lewis' with Stornoway Castle as the principal seat. Raasay is not mentioned.

In 1572, because of the disputed succession of the lands of Lewis, another Crown charter was granted. On this occasion the Lewis chief was Ruairidh Chaluim, son of Calum who had been granted the charter of 1511. Again the lands of Lewis are named as Lewis, Waternish, Assynt and Coigeach. Again there is no mention made of Raasay. Had Raasay belonged to the MacLeods of Lewis, it seems reasonable to suppose that it would have been included in both of these charters.

A Crown charter of 1596 to Calum Òg MacLeod of Raasay states that prior to the Act of Annexation of 1587 the lands of Raasay and part of Snizort had been Church lands, held by the MacLeods from the Bishop of the Isles. There seems no reason to question this.

It thus appears that the Raasay estate did not belong to the MacLeods of

Lewis, but to the Church. It could not, therefore, have been granted by Calum mac Ruairidh of Lewis to his second son, or indeed to anyone else.

Names of the Lairds of Raasay

Arguably of less importance, but nonetheless significant, are the names of the Lairds of Raasay. The chart of the MacLeods of Raasay shows that their names were Calum (Malcolm), Alasdair (Alexander) and John. The chart of the MacLeods of Lewis shows that their names were Torcall and Ruairidh (Roderick), although the names Calum (Malcolm), Norman and John also occur.

If, as claimed by Alexander MacKenzie, the MacLeods of Raasay were directly descended from Calum mac Ruairidh of Lewis about 1500, one might expect greater similarity in the naming pattern, particularly in the early period.

Thus, in all probability, the MacLeods of Lewis did not hold or own Raasay and the first of the MacLeods of Raasay, as described by Alexander MacKenzie, was too young to have been the laird in 1518. The question of the descent of the MacLeods of Raasay must therefore be addressed.

Who were the MacLeods of Raasay?

The early Lairds of Raasay, as given by Alexander MacKenzie and Alick Morrison are the same. Neither of these histories gives any substantial detail about the first two chiefs, Calum Garbh and Alasdair. They both indicate that Calum (Garbh), the third laird, was a child (aged nine – Alexander MacKenzie) in 1568, and escaped the massacre at Isay as he was being fostered away from home at the time. All (number not known) of Calum's brothers are believed to have been killed at Isay, along with a number of other relatives.

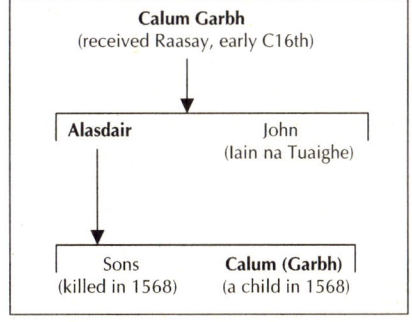

Figure R2. Lairds of Raasay as given by MacKenzie and Morrison.

Calum (Garbh), said to be the third laird and believed to have been born about 1560 (i.e. aged nine about 1568), is of interest. The disputed succession in Lewis and the Crown charter of 1572 resulting from it has already been mentioned. This charter names the Raasay laird as heir to Torcall Conanach in the lands of Lewis, if Torcall had no legitimate sons.

The Raasay laird is named as 'Calum son of Calum Garbh MacLeod of Raasay'. Thus by 1572, Calum Garbh MacLeod of Raasay had died and his son, Calum, was laird. It may be assumed that Calum, the laird in 1572, was known as Calum Òg (Young Calum) to distinguish him from his father. It must be assumed that he was, at the very least, aged twenty-one in 1572. He was thus born by 1550 at the latest. His father, Calum Garbh, could not, therefore, have been born about 1560. It may be estimated that Calum Garbh was born by about 1520.

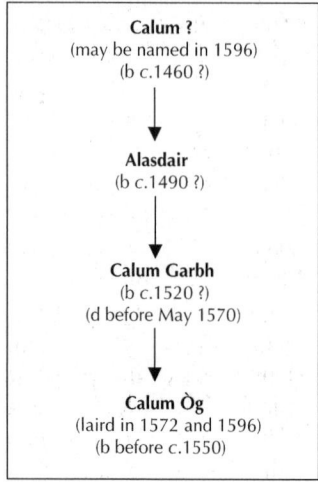

Figure R3. MacLeod lairds of Raasay from charters of 1572 and 1596.

In 1596 a Crown charter was granted to Calum MacLeod of Raasay. This was Calum Òg, the same man as was mentioned in the charter of 1572. Here he is named as Calum MacGilliChallum, son of Calum, son of Alasdair MacGilliChallum of Raasay. Calum Garbh's father was, therefore, Alasdair. It is possible, although not certain, that Alasdair's father was named Calum.

Thus the names of the successive Lairds of Raasay found in the Crown charters are the same as those given by Alexander MacKenzie, although the dates given by him cannot be reconciled with the charters. In the absence of dates it is usual, in genealogical terms, to assume thirty years per generation. Thus Calum Òg was born by 1550 at the latest. Calum Garbh was born about 1520, Alasdair about 1490, and his father (possibly named Calum) about 1460.

The charter of 1596 is granted to Calum Òg for the lands of Raasay and Snizort, eleven merklands in total, and states that Calum Garbh 'his father, grandfather and predecessors since time immemorial' had held these lands as 'feeholders and tenants of the Bishop of the Isles'. Clearly, this cannot be reconciled with Alexander MacKenzie's view that the lands had been granted by MacLeod of Lewis to his son, Calum Garbh, early in the sixteenth century.

Who were these MacLeods who had held Raasay 'since time immemorial' and certainly since the laird, possibly named Calum, born about 1460? Some things are known about them.

They were known as the MacGilleChaluim. They were believed to be related to the MacLeods of Gairloch, who were also known as the MacGilleChaluim. Alick Morrison refers to Sir Robert Gordon's 'Genealogical History of the Earldom of Sutherland' and says 'Sir Robert normally a very trustworthy historian, ... believed that the MacLeods of Gairloch and the MacLeods of Raasay were one and the same family'. The names of the MacLeods of Gairloch are of interest.

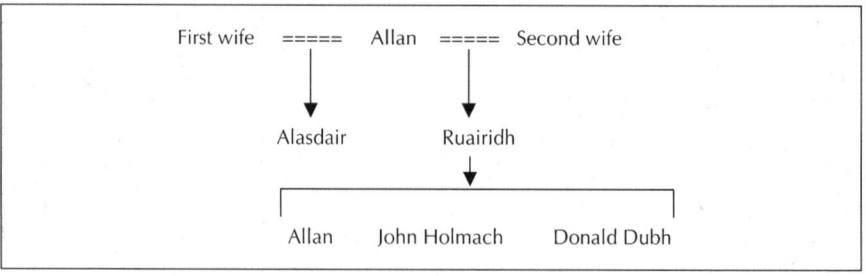

Figure R4. MacLeods of Gairloch as given by MacKenzie and Morrison.

Genealogy of the MacLeods of Raasay

Although admittedly very few generations of the MacLeods of Gairloch are given, it is significant that the names Allan and Alasdair occur. The name Alasdair occurs also in the MacLeods of Raasay, but not in the MacLeods of Lewis. The name Allan is not generally thought of as a MacLeod name. It does not occur in the names of the chiefs of either the Siol Thorcaill or the Siol Thormoid.

There is in Raasay a family of MacLeods, who are descended from Ailean Liath, Allan MacLeod of Dry Harbour, Rona, who was born about 1800. One descendant was John Malcolm MacLeod, the Shoemaker. Somhairle MacLean[6] tells that the Shoemaker 'said they came from Gairloch or Cóigeach. They were buried in the old vault of the Mac Gille Chaluim in the churchyard of Clachan in Raasay.' It is more likely that the family came from Gairloch, rather than Coigeach which was MacLeod of Lewis land. The names Allan and Alasdair appear frequently among the descendants of Ailean Liath. Somhairle also says that Beileag an Achaidh, Bella MacLeod, a noted tradition bearer of her day, said 'the family came from Lewis'. It is not impossible that both these statements are true, as the MacGilleChaluim of Gairloch were themselves descended from the MacLeods of Lewis.

On the shore on the east side of Raasay, between Brochel and Kyle Rona, is a place called Laimhrig Clann mhic Ailean, the Landing Place of the Race or Offspring of Allan. As its name describes, it is a natural jetty or landing place. This would have been ideally placed for MacLeods of Gairloch going back and forth to Raasay.

Therefore, in all probability, the MacGilleChaluim or MacLeods of Raasay were descended from the MacGilleChaluim or MacLeods of Gairloch. If this hypothesis is correct, they would seem to have diverged towards the end of the fifteenth century.[7]

When it was believed that the MacLeods of Raasay were descended from Calum mac Ruairidh of Lewis the name MacGilleChaluim, or descendants of Calum, made perfect sense. However, as they do not appear to be so descended, where did the name come from? Clearly there was a Calum at the 'top of the tree'. The most likely one, indeed the only other known Calum in the MacLeod of Lewis tree, was a brother of Ruairidh, the second chief of Lewis.

This man was known as Calum Beag nam Buadhan, Little Calum of the Accomplishments or Triumphs. He lived on Lewis. His sister, Sidheag, had married Angus MacKay of Strathnaver, Sutherlandshire. After she was widowed, her brother-in-law became tutor to her sons. It appears that he treated her badly, and her brothers in Lewis were not at all pleased about that. Calum Beag and some Lewis men set off for Sutherland to sort things out. Their mission was not successful however, and on their way home they 'laid waste' Strathnaver and Breachart, in Sutherland. When the MacKays heard of this,

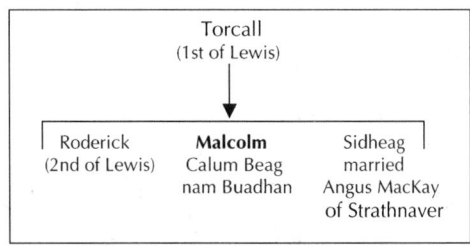

Figure R5. Calum, brother of Ruairidh MacLeod, second Chief of Lewis.

they sent word to the Earl of Sutherland. His men overtook the Lewis men, and there followed a skirmish at Tuiteam Tarbhach, between Ross and Sutherland. Calum was killed, and it is said that only one Lewisman escaped and got home to tell what had happened. This took place about 1406.

There are MacLeods in Lewis known by the patronymic MacGilleChaluim. It seems likely, therefore, that both they and the MacGilleChaluim of Gairloch, and consequently Raasay, were descended from this man. If that were the case, it would not be necessary for the first of either the MacGilleChaluim of Gairloch or of Raasay to have a father named Calum. The patronymic may be older than that.

The MacLeod of Raasay genealogies and histories by Alexander MacKenzie and Alick Morrison make no mention of the marriage of a MacGilleChaluim of Raasay and Marion Campbell of Craignish. It is, however, noted by Alexander Nicolson. The story of their meeting and subsequent marriage is told in a history of the Campbells.[8] Craignish Castle, near Craignish Point, is south of Oban, roughly level with the north end of Jura. Ardkinglass House is at the head of Loch Fyne. Campbells held both these areas.

Marion Campbell of Craignish had been living with the Laird of Ardkinglass as his concubine and had by him at least three sons. After some years he told her that he would marry her if she could 'procure a competent tocher [dowry]'. According to the customs of the time, a friend went, on her behalf, to her relatives to inform them of her position. The answer she got was 'that well favoured whores needed no tochers'. When Ardkinglass realised that her mission had not been successful, he said 'since you have no tocher, I'll marry you for God's sake and out of charity'. She was most offended and left him.

> ... and coming to visit some of her relations who lived upon the West Coast near Craignish, she accidentally met with Gillicallum MacLeod of Raasay, second son to the Laird of MacLeod who with his birlinn happened to be then in these parts, with whom upon very short acquaintance she strikes up a marriage, and went along with him to Raasay. The late famous John Garve MacGillichallum of Raasay was her great grandson or fourth from her. Her burial place is to be seen in Raasay to this day. The MacLeods of Raasay, and these descendants of the house of Ardkinglass kept a close and constant friendship with us, as being all descended from the same man John Gorm.

Thus, we are told, the Campbells of Craignish, the Campbells of Ardkinglass and the MacLeods of Raasay kept in close contact because of their relationship through Marion and her father, John Gorm.

The author of the manuscript believed that Marion had 'gone away with the Laird of Ardkinglass' about 1490, at which time her father was dead and 'she under the management of her brother Archibald'.

There seems no reason to doubt that a marriage between Marion Campbell and one of the MacLeods of Raasay took place, although it is difficult to reconcile the details as given. The Campbells of Craignish also figure in an account of how the MacLeods of Raasay acquired the money to build Brochel Castle. That two stories named them adds weight to both. Although this account names

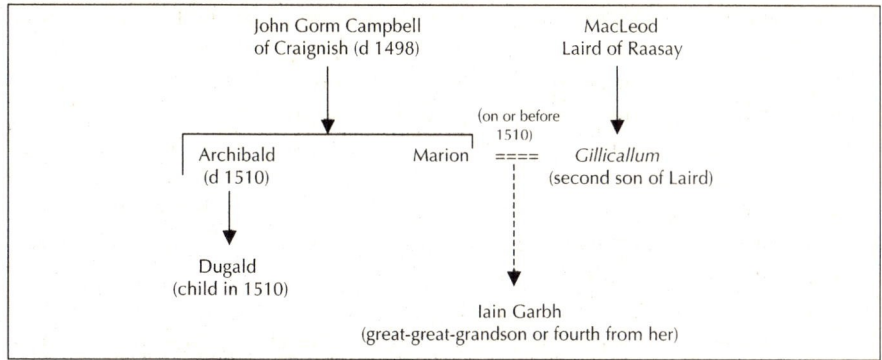

Figure R6. Marriage of Marion Campbell and MacLeod of Raasay.

Marion's husband only as 'Gillicallum MacLeod' it says that Iain Garbh, who was the Laird of Raasay in the mid seventeenth century, was directly descended from her.

The date of 1490 given as the time Marion ran away with the Laird of Ardkinglass may be too early, as her father John Gorm Campbell was still alive then. Marion's brother, Archibald, succeeded his father in 1498. Archibald is known to have died, a young man, in 1510 when his son Dugald was still a child. Marion's marriage with 'Gillicallum MacLeod' may therefore have taken place in 1510 or shortly before.

It is not known which of the MacLeods of Raasay Marion married. As Iain Garbh was said to be directly descended from Marion it would appear that, although her husband was the 'second son of the laird of Raasay', either he himself, or at least his descendants, became laird. The name, 'Gillicallum MacLeod' implies that he was one of those named Calum. It is not impossible that she married Calum (?) the father of Alasdair. It may have been Calum Garbh. Perhaps 'Gillicallum' here is used to mean 'the MacLeods of Raasay', in which case it could have been Alasdair who was Marion's husband. Counting back the generations from Iain Garbh does not clarify this matter, as the genealogy of the MacLeods of Raasay is no clearer in the seventeenth century than it is in the sixteenth.

Alexander Nicolson, in his *History of Skye*, believed that Marion's husband was John MacLeod, known as Iain na Tuaighe. Iain na Tuaighe makes fairly frequent appearances in the histories and genealogies of Raasay, Gairloch and Lewis. However, he does not appear to have been one of the Lairds of Raasay and for that reason it is unlikely that he was the husband. It is true to say, however, that so little is known about these early times that none of these people should be entirely ruled out as Marion's husband.

The Early MacLeod Lairds of Raasay

About 1460 the Laird of Raasay was visited by Hugh MacDonald of Sleat. The name of the laird at that time is not known, although he was probably a MacLeod.

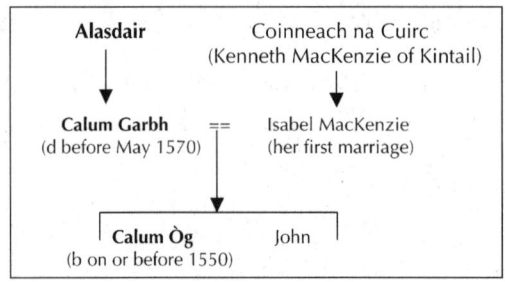

Figure R7. Lairds of Raasay/MacKenzies of Kintail.

It has been shown that Calum Òg, son of Calum Garbh, was the Laird of Raasay in 1572. He is named in a Crown charter of that year. Further information is found in a history of the MacKenzies of Kintail.[9] This tells that Coinneach na Cuirc, Kenneth MacKenzie of Kintail, had 'a bastard daughter that married first the Laird of Raasay and thereafter she was married to James MacKintosh of Stroine.' The MacKintosh Muniments, a book of legal documents of the MacKintosh family, shows that Isabel MacKenzie was married to James MacKintosh by May 1570, and was still married to him in June 1584.

Therefore Calum Garbh was married to Isabel MacKenzie. He had died sometime before May 1570, by which time his widow had remarried. The history of the MacKenzies gives some further information. It says that

> Gillichallum Garve married Isabel MacKenzie natural daughter to Kenneth MacKenzie of Kintail (agnamed Coinneach na Cuirk – Kenneth of the whittle). She was mother to Gillichallum Og that was killed in the ship by Gairloch men and to John MacGillichallum that was killed at St Bride's Logie at Conon.

Thus the laird of Raasay named in the Crown charter of 1572 was known as Calum Òg, and he was the son of Calum Garbh and Isabel MacKenzie of Kintail.

It is not beyond the bounds of possibility that Calum Garbh was married twice. Indeed, it is known that Isabel MacKenzie was still alive in 1584, at least twelve years after his death, so she may have been much younger than he was. However, the history of the MacKenzies states that Calum Òg was her son. If Iain Garbh was a direct descendant of Calum Òg, his father could not have been the man that Marion Campbell of Craignish married.

Iain na Tuaighe – John of the Axe

The name of Iain na Tuaighe has already cropped up, and it is time to consider this man in more detail. He makes fairly frequent appearances in the various histories of the MacLeods of Raasay, as well as those of Lewis and Gairloch. Very little was known of the lives of the early lairds of both Raasay and Gairloch. It is therefore remarkable that Iain na Tuaighe appears so frequently. Who was this man who was given such a 'bad press' by Alexander MacKenzie?

An epithet, or nickname, such as 'na Tuaighe', may not always have been given to the man. Those who knew how he acquired it would use it, while others might not. No indication is given as to how he acquired it. It may be assumed that he used his axe during battle, committing great slaughter, but it is equally possible that it was used for some other purpose that was memorable. Perhaps it was the axe itself that was unusual – well made or with a carved or decorative handle that was out of the ordinary.

The genealogies of the Raasay lairds, as given by Alexander MacKenzie and Alick Morrison, say that Iain na Tuaighe was the son of Calum Garbh, first of the MacLeods of Raasay. Thus he was a brother of Alasdair, and an uncle of Calum Garbh, the third laird. As such, Alasdair and Iain na Tuaighe would probably have been born about the early 1530s.

Given that, it is most surprising to find that, in the various histories, Iain na Tuaighe is said to have had no fewer than four wives, three of whom were born in the 1490s or even earlier, at least forty years before him. The descent of the MacLeods of Raasay from Calum MacLeod of Lewis has already been considered and found to be questionable. This is another reason for questioning that descent. Iain na Tuaighe's alleged wives were –

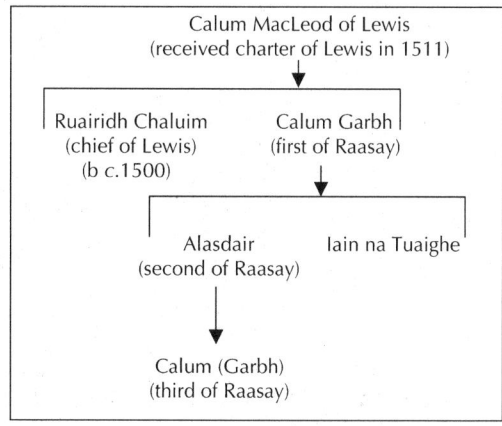

Figure R8. Previously accepted ancestry of Iain na Tuaighe.

- Marion Campbell of Craignish
- Janet MacKenzie, the first wife of Ruairidh Chaluim of Lewis
- A daughter of Allan mac Ruairidh of Gairloch (said to be a sister of Ruairidh Nimhneach)
- A daughter of Ruairidh Nimhneach

It has already been seen that Marion Campbell of Craignish married 'Gillicallum MacLeod of Raasay, second son to the Laird of MacLeod'. This marriage is noted only by Alexander Nicolson, and he may have assumed that Marion's husband was Iain na Tuaighe because he was the only 'second son' named in any of the genealogies. As far as is known, Iain na Tuaighe was not one of the Raasay lairds, so this 'marriage' may therefore have been a case of mistaken identity.

Another possibility was that Iain na Tuaighe married Janet MacKenzie of Kintail. Janet was a daughter of Coinneach a Bhlàir (Kenneth of the Battle, MacKenzie chief of Kintail) who died in 1491. She was therefore a sister of John of Killin, who was born about 1476 and later became chief of Kintail. Janet's first husband was MacKay of Reay (near Dounreay in Caithness). Her second husband was Ruairidh Chaluim of Lewis.

Janet MacKenzie was Ruairidh Chaluim's first wife. They had a son who was known as Torcall Conanach because his mother's people brought him up in Strathconon. Torcall was probably born in the early 1530s. Ruairidh claimed

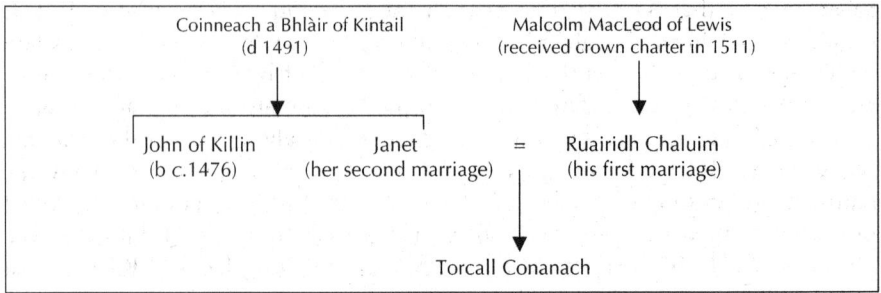

Figure R9. Janet MacKenzie, first wife of Ruairidh Chaluim MacLeod of Lewis.

that Torcall was not his son, but the son of Hugh (sometimes referred to as Hucheon) Morrison, the Brieve of Lewis. Ruairidh, therefore, divorced Janet and disinherited Torcall. Torcall's claim to the lands and chieftainship of Lewis, backed by the MacKenzies of Kintail, led eventually to the downfall of the MacLeods of Lewis at the end of the sixteenth century.

Ruairidh Chaluim married his second wife, Barbara Stewart, in 1541. Therefore he must have divorced Janet sometime before that. The first Earl of Cromarty [10] suggests that Janet was significantly older than Ruairidh Chaluim and, from what is known of both, that would appear to be correct. He says that, 'She had come to a greater age than suited well his youth, whereupon did shortly follow a dislike ... and putting away his wife, alleging a falsehood ...'

There are different accounts of what happened after Ruairidh and Janet separated. Alexander MacKenzie says of Iain na Tuaighe, 'It was he who carried off, and afterwards married, Janet Mackenzie ... This wicked act of John Na Tuaighe resulted in the ultimate ruin of the family of Lewis and was the cause of the massacre at Island Isay, ...' [11]

He later refers to 'the children' of Iain na Tuaighe and Janet MacKenzie. The massacre at Isay will be discussed later. His reason for blaming Iain na Tuaighe for the downfall of the MacLeods of Lewis is far from clear.

Alick Morrison says, 'John carried off Janet, ... and afterwards married her. By Janet Mackenzie John had several sons and a daughter.' Thus far, it seems clear enough. If it is accepted that Iain na Tuaighe was born about the 1490s rather than the 1530s, he and Janet MacKenzie would be of the same generation.

A history of the MacKenzies [12] appears to shed some doubt on this. Talking of Janet MacKenzie, it says, 'She was mother to Torcuil Cononach and John na Tuaighe. MacGilleCalum of Raasay's brother ravished her from his chief, MacLeod of Lewis. She bore him a daughter that was married to Alasdair Roy MacEachan that lived in Auchterneid.' At a later point in this same history, it says, 'MacKenzie's daughter [Janet] was taken away from him [Ruairidh Chaluim] by his own kinsman John MacGilleCalum the laird of Raasay who was named John na Tuaighe. He kept her five years in Coigeach and had a daughter with her that was married with Alasdair Roy MacEachan.'

Although the first quotation makes a clear distinction between Iain na Tuaighe (said here to be the son of Janet) and MacGilleChaluim of Raasay's brother, Mr

Sellar believes that the first quotation has at some time been mistranscribed. It should read, 'Iain na Tuaighe MacGilleCalum of Raasay's brother ...' Thus Iain na Tuaighe is described as the brother of the Laird of Raasay. This would now agree with all the other references to Iain na Tuaighe and Janet MacKenzie.

Although the second quotation names Iain na Tuaighe as the Laird of Raasay, this seems unlikely. The crown charter of 1596 does not name him as one of the lairds. Quite possibly both Iain na Tuaighe and his brother Alasdair were killed in the massacre at Isay (discussed later). If that were so, he could not have been one of the lairds. Whether or not Iain na Tuaighe was ever Laird of Raasay must remain an open question.

The second quotation, given above, indicates that Iain na Tuaighe kept Janet MacKenzie 'five years in Coigeach'. Why any of the Raasay MacLeods would keep someone in Coigeach is difficult to explain, as that was MacLeod of Lewis land.

Alexander MacKenzie in his *History of the MacKenzies* causes further confusion when he says 'Roderick of Lewis married first Janet ... the unfortunate woman, while attempting to escape his cruel treatment going in a birlinn from Lewis to Coigeach was pursued and run down by Roderick's followers. All on board perished.'[13]

Although there may be some doubt over the details, it appears that Janet MacKenzie, who had been married to Ruairidh Chaluim of Lewis, had a daughter by Iain na Tuaighe. That daughter later married Alasdair Roy MacKenzie. Because the history of the MacKenzies does not mention them, it is perhaps unlikely that Iain na Tuaighe and Janet had other children.

A different MacKenzie history,[14] talking of Alasdair Roy MacKenzie, says 'This Alasdair was married with a daughter of John na Tuaighe MacGilleCalum. She was mother to Hector MacAlasdair vic Eachan, who lived in Kinnellan, and was nicknamed The Bishop. He was married with The laird of Raasay his Daughter ...'

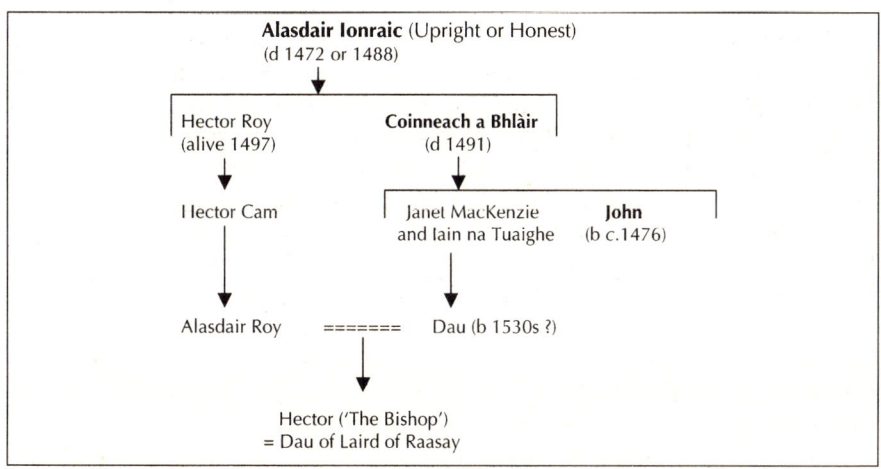

Figure R10. Janet MacKenzie and her relationship with the MacKenzie chiefs.

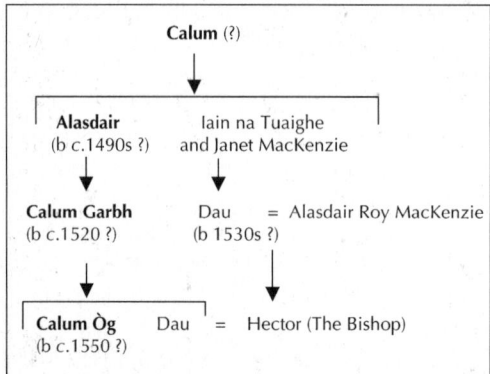

Figure R11. Relationship of the 'Bishop's' wife with the Raasay lairds.

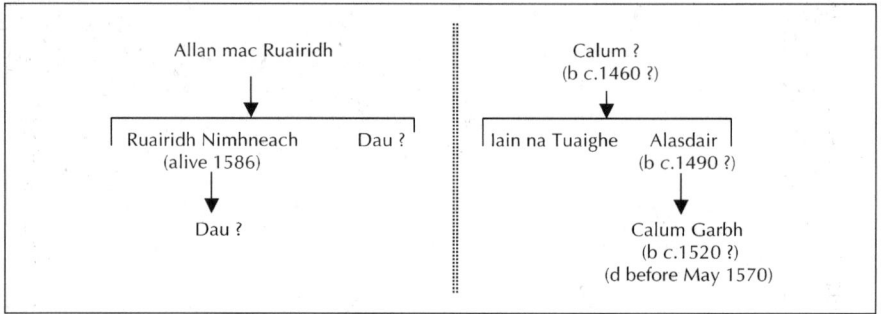

Figure R12. Ruairidh Nimhneach and Iain na Tuaighe.

Alexander MacKenzie makes no mention of this marriage but Alick Morrison states that the wife of the 'Bishop' was a daughter of Calum Garbh. It is known that Calum Garbh died before May 1570.

It is as well to consider together, the alleged marriages of Iain na Tuaighe to a sister and a daughter of Ruairidh mac Allan (called Ruairidh Nimhneach by Alexander MacKenzie). First, a recap on the people concerned.

Figure R12 above shows what is known about both Ruairidh Nimhneach and Iain na Tuaighe.

Alexander MacKenzie states clearly that Iain na Tuaighe's second wife was Ruairidh Nimhneach's sister. However, Alick Morrison's account appears confused. In his section on the MacLeods of Gairloch, his chart shows Iain na Tuaighe married to Ruairidh Nimhneach's sister, but the written part says that she was Ruairidh's daughter. In his section on the MacLeods of Raasay, he states that it was a sister of Ruairidh who married Iain na Tuaighe.

Although both Alexander MacKenzie and Alick Morrison refer to a sister and/or daughter of Ruairidh Nimhneach the older MacKenzie history makes no mention of either. It seems unlikely, therefore, that Iain na Tuaighe was married to either.

Most likely Iain na Tuaighe was a brother of Alasdair, Laird of Raasay. They were probably born in the 1490s. That at least three of the marriages attributed to Iain na Tuaighe were to ladies born about the 1490s or earlier tends to confirm this. It is unlikely that he married Marion Campbell of Craignish or a relative of Ruairidh mac Allan of Gairloch, although neither can be ruled out. He appears to have married Janet MacKenzie.

Although Alexander MacKenzie states that Iain na Tuaighe was, it would seem, personally responsible for both the downfall of the MacLeods of Lewis and the massacre at Isay, he gives no substantial evidence for either claim. The downfall of the MacLeods of Lewis was triggered by Ruairidh Chaluim's disowning of his son, Torcall Conanach, who fought for his rights with the backing of the MacKenzies of Kintail. The alleged massacre at Isay raises many questions, which will now be addressed.

Massacre at Isay

The island of Isay (pronounced 'easay') lies to the west of Waternish, Skye, near the mouth of Loch Dunvegan. In 1841 there were thirteen families, ninety people, living on Isay, but by 1861 they had all left. Waternish and Isay belonged to the MacLeods of Lewis, as shown in the Crown charters of 1511 and 1572. The dispute over the paternity of Torcall Conanach led to the downfall of the MacLeods of Lewis. At the beginning of the seventeenth century all the lands of Lewis, including Waternish, were taken over by the MacKenzies of Kintail. It suited both parties that Waternish, lying on their doorstep, was bought by the MacLeods of Dunvegan.

The massacre on Isay is said, by Alexander MacKenzie and Alick Morrison, to have taken place about 1568. Their accounts are essentially the same. Alexander MacKenzie [15] explains that Ruairidh Nimhneach, the son of Allan MacLeod of Gairloch by his second wife, was the perpetrator. He wished to open up the succession of Raasay for his sister's son (by Iain na Tuaighe) and the succession of Gairloch for his own son, by assassinating all those who stood in his way. He killed, 'all the direct male representatives of Alexander MacLeod of Raasay and the children of Iain na Tuaighe by his first wife, Janet MacKenzie, as well as the lawful heirs of the Gairloch Macleods – his own brother's children'. They were all killed 'except a boy, then only nine years of age, who was being fostered from home.'

The boy who escaped the massacre was Calum Garbh – the third of the MacLeods of Raasay, as numbered by Alexander MacKenzie and Alick Morrison. It happened as follows:[16]

> [Ruairidh Nimhneach] invited all the members of both families to a great feast at the Island of Isay, professing to each of them that he had matters of importance to communicate to him. They were thus led into the trap prepared for them. Roderick feasted his visitors sumptuously at a great banquet. In the middle of the festivities he communicated to them his desire to have each man's advice separately, at the same time stating that he would afterwards make known to them the business for which he called them together, and which concerned each of them closely. He then retired into a separate apartment, and called them in one by one, when they were each, as they entered, stabbed with dirks through the body by a set of murderous villains whom he had engaged and posted inside the room for that purpose.

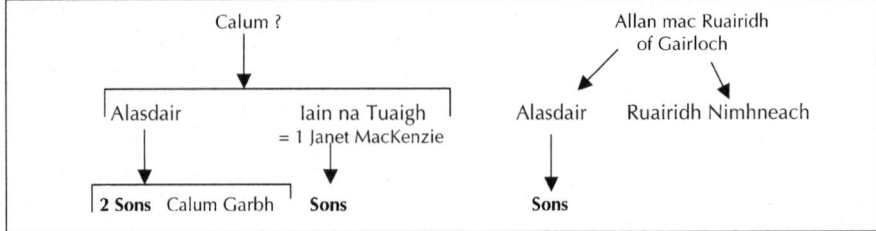

Figure R13. Those allegedly killed at Isay 1568 (marked in bold) as given by Alexander MacKenzie and Alick Morrison.

One must ask why should Ruairidh Nimhneach, who was from Gairloch, invite the hierarchy of the Gairloch and Raasay MacLeods to Waternish, owned by the MacLeods of Lewis. To commit a massacre, such as is described, he would have needed complete control over events. That would surely have been easier in an area owned by the Gairloch family, and closer to home. Would the Raasay and Gairloch families not have been rather suspicious of an invitation from Ruairidh Nimhneach to Isay?

Another problem with this account is the date – 1568. It has already been shown that Calum Garbh had died before May 1570, by which time his widow, Isabel MacKenzie, was married to James MacKintosh of Stroine. Alexander MacKenzie's account says that Calum Garbh was a child of nine in 1568. The date, therefore, cannot be correct.

Alexander MacKenzie says that Iain na Tuaighe and Janet MacKenzie had children, other than the daughter who married Alasdair Roy MacKenzie, who were killed at Isay. These children were not mentioned in the history of the MacKenzies. The impression given in this account is that children were killed. However, by 1568, all those allegedly killed must surely have been grown men, some in their twenties and others, possibly, in their forties.

The relevant points about this account of the massacre at Isay in 1568 are

- the perpetrator was Ruairidh MacLeod of Gairloch
- he killed members of the Gairloch and Raasay family, including his two nephews
- the impression created is that they were children at the time
- one child escaped as he was away from home
- the purpose of the massacre was to acquire the lands of Gairloch and Raasay for his own relatives.

A history of the MacKenzies [17] does tell of a massacre at Isay. This account is worth examining in detail. It begins by saying that Iain na Tuaighe had taken Janet MacKenzie, the wife of Ruairidh Chaluim of Lewis, away with him to Coigeach. It continues:

> afterwards Rorie MacLeod killed this John na Tuaighe with almost the whole family of Siol vic Gillichallum of the family of Raasay and Gairloch most treacherously being his spealest [closest ?] kinsmen; he did invite them all to

meet him in the Isle of Isay where he (as he alleged) had some business of consequence to consult with them. After their coming he feasted them with wine and such other things as he had prepared for their destruction; after he had ended the feast he caused call for each one of them singly and every one that entered the house [room] was apprehended and sticked [stabbed] so that there was none left alive of that whole family but a child of nine years of age that was a fostering. When the news of the murder of his father, uncle, brothers and whole race of Siol vic Gillichallum was divulged abroad a gentleman of the country of Raasay took him and carried him secretly to the Laird of Calder who kept him during his minority.

This description of the place (Isay), the feast and the killing is identical to that given by Alexander MacKenzie, and so it would appear that he is talking about the same event. However, in this account the perpetrator was Ruairidh MacLeod of Lewis, Ruairidh Chaluim – not Ruairidh Nimhneach of Gairloch – and this makes more sense, as the MacLeods of Lewis owned Isay.

The account then continues:

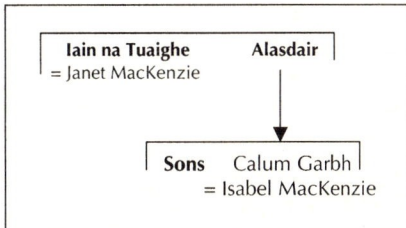

Figure R14. Members of the Raasay family killed at Isay as given by the MacKenzie History.

There was also a young man of the family of Gairloch left alive who was MacLeod's own sister son. He was with the rest of his brothers that were older than himself gotten with MacKenzie's daughter; MacLeod brought him aside from the rest, he being walking with his uncle he heard the cry of one of his brothers so he said to his uncle 'yon is the cry of my brother'. His uncle desired him to hold his peace that yon cry was to make him laird of Gairloch; that yon was the son of MacKenzie's daughter, that he was the son of MacLeod's daughter.

The young man for fear of his life was silent but afterwards he did what he could to revenge his brother's and kinsfolk's death on the murderers, and indeed this was the first step that Hector Roy MacKenzie got in the position of Gairloch to revenge his nephews they being his sister's bairnes [children] that were murdered in the Isle of Isay ...

Although it is clearly Ruairidh Chaluim who is described as the perpetrator of the murders, the nephew of the Gairloch family as described must be a son of Allan mac Ruairidh of Gairloch.

Allan's first marriage to a daughter of Alasdair Ionraic, chief of the MacKenzies of Kintail, is confirmed by histories of the MacKenzies. Allan and his first wife are said to have had three sons. Alexander MacKenzie names one of the sons, Alasdair, but the older MacKenzie history names none. Allan's second wife was a MacLeod of Lewis. Alexander MacKenzie states that she was a daughter of Ruairidh, fourth chief of Lewis.

According to the MacKenzie history, one young man of the Gairloch MacLeods

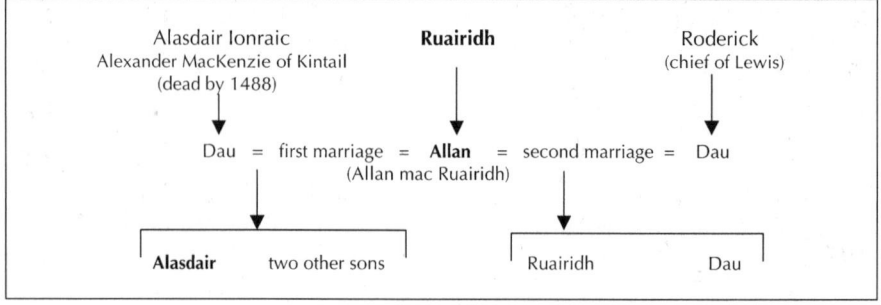

Figure R15. MacLeods of Gairloch.

was left alive. He is said to have been the nephew of the perpetrator, Ruairidh Chaluim. His older, half-brothers were killed to allow him to become Laird of Gairloch. Their uncle (mother's brother), Hector Roy MacKenzie, later avenged their deaths. The young man himself later did what he could to avenge the deaths of his brothers and other relatives.

The account continues:

> This young man of the family of Gairloch that was left alive after the murder possessed himself with Raasay thinking none to be alive of the family of Raasay qlk qn [which when?] Donald M'Neil the gentleman that carried away the heir of Raasay to Caddel [Calder] saw that the heir of Gairloch took possession in Raasay he went to Raasay and carried the heir of Raasay Gillichallum Garbh privately [secretly] to Raasay where he had him till the said Donald M'Neil got time of the special keeper that the heir of Gairloch left in the castle of Raasay who promised to Donald (when he informed him that he had the righteous heir of Raasay) to leave an entry open in the castle, that Donald M'Neil and his master might enter to possess the castle; but Donald M'Neil did not bring his master but went himself and when he murdered all the keepers he sent for his master Gillichallum Garve and cryed him Laird of Raasay. This Gillichallum Garbh married Isabel MacKenzie natural daughter to Kenneth MacKenzie of Kintail (agnamed Coinneach na Cuirc). She was mother to Gillichallum Og that was killed in the ship by the Gairloch men and to John M'Gillichallum that was killed in Laggan Bride.

Although somewhat confusing, it is clear that the child of the Raasay family who escaped this massacre was Calum Garbh, who later married Isabel MacKenzie of Kintail. He was nine and escaped, whilst his father, his uncle and his brothers were killed. It has already been suggested that Calum Garbh was born about 1520. If this massacre was committed by Ruairidh Chaluim after his first wife, Janet MacKenzie, left him it would suggest a date about the early 1530s. This appears to fit reasonably well with all the known facts.

The relevant points about this description of the massacre are:

- it was on Isay
- the perpetrator was Ruairidh MacLeod (Ruairidh Chaluim) of Lewis

- he killed most of the family of MacLeods of Gairloch and Raasay
- a young child of the Raasay family escaped as he was being fostered away from home
- his father, uncle and brothers were murdered
- a young man of the Gairloch family was not killed although his half-brothers were
- the purpose of the massacre was to allow his nephew, of the Gairloch family, to acquire the lands of Gairloch and Raasay
- Hector Roy MacKenzie took revenge over the murder of his nephews.

This account is remarkably similar to another related by Alexander MacKenzie and said to have taken place in Gairloch. Then, he said, Allan MacLeod of Gairloch and two of his sons by his first wife were killed. One son escaped as he was away from home. Hector Roy MacKenzie, the murdered boys' uncle, got a commission of fire and sword against the murderers, and a charter for the lands of Gairloch about 1494. This implies that Allan and his sons were murdered shortly before that date. The murderers on this occasion were said to be two of Allan's brothers who lived on Lewis. The beneficiary, on this occasion, was to be the son of Allan by his second wife – a MacLeod from Lewis. Thus the two massacres have many points in common. Only the names of those killed, the date and the place are different.

It is unlikely, even in these harsh times, that there were two such atrocities committed against the same family (that of the MacLeods of Gairloch and Raasay) barely forty years apart. Furthermore, the sons of Allan MacLeod of Gairloch could not have been murdered twice. The earlier account given in the history of the MacKenzies is probably therefore more accurate.

That still leaves the question of who committed this massacre on Isay. Could it have been Ruairidh Chaluim? He became chief of the MacLeods of Lewis about 1532. He had divorced Janet MacKenzie before 1541, when he married his second wife. The earlier account of the massacre is set after Janet left Ruairidh Chaluim – whether she went away with one of the MacGilleChaluim of Raasay, or was drowned while escaping from Ruairidh Chaluim is irrelevant. The massacre at Isay may, therefore, have taken place in the early 1530s. It is believed that Ruairidh Chaluim took over the estate and became chief of the MacLeods of Lewis in the early 1530s, so datewise it is not impossible. It is perhaps unlikely, though not impossible, that Ruairidh Chaluim's sister was married to Allan MacLeod of Gairloch, as she would have been of a younger generation than he was.

There are other significant details within this account. The 'family of Raasay and Gairoloch' implies that Raasay and Gairloch were one and the same family. The child of the Gairloch family left alive, although not named, must surely have been the man Alexander MacKenzie calls Ruairidh Nimhneach. Calum Garbh is named as the child who escaped. If he was nine years old at the time, this may be further confirmation that he was born in the 1520s.

One young man of the Gairloch family, the perpetrator's nephew, survived –

'Macleod's own sister son'. Thus his mother was a MacLeod from Lewis. He was with his older brothers, whose mother was a MacKenzie. This describes the family of Allan MacLeod of Gairloch. He was first married to a daughter of Alasdair Ionraic of Kintail, and then to a daughter of a MacLeod of Lewis. The young man of the Gairloch family must therefore have been Ruairidh Nimhneach. Far from being the perpetrator of the massacre (as stated by Alexander MacKenzie), he is said to have 'done what he could to revenge his brothers and kinsfolk's death on the murderers'. Ruairidh Chaluim's motive for this massacre, apart from benefiting his nephew, would appear to have been revenge against the MacKenzies of Kintail – perhaps because of the alleged adultery of his wife, Janet MacKenzie.

Alexander MacKenzie and Alick Morrison both say that Allan's second wife was the daughter of Roderick MacLeod who became the chief of Lewis in 1464. As such she was Ruairidh Chaluim's aunt, not his sister. Because Ruairidh Chaluim was alive in 1586, his date of birth (given as about 1500) has already been questioned. It is quite possible, however, that he had older sisters, although none have been mentioned. Neither is there any independent record of Allan's birth, or indeed of his death. It is not impossible that his first wife was the daughter of Alasdair Ionraic, and his second a sister of Ruairidh Chaluim of Lewis.

Interestingly, although the name of Calum Garbh's wife is given here as Isabel MacKenzie, Alexander MacKenzie does not name her. He says only that Calum Garbh was married. Their two sons, Calum Òg and John (who was killed at 'Laggan Bride'), are named, but Alexander MacKenzie names only Calum Òg and Alexander (of whom there is no mention here). Indeed, Alexander MacKenzie does mention John (who was killed at 'Laggan Bride'), but says that he was a son of Iain na Tuaighe.

It seems, therefore, that Alexander MacKenzie has described the massacre at Isay, which probably took place in the 1530s, as two separate events – one at Gairloch about 1494 and the other at Isay about 1568. If indeed only one massacre took place, during the 1530s, it may be unwise to assume that Allan MacLeod of Gairloch had died by 1494.

If Ruairidh Nimhneach was a 'young man of the family of Gairloch' in the 1530s, he may reasonably have been born in the period 1510–1520. This is more likely that the earlier 1494 date, as he is found to be alive in 1586.

The MacLeod Lairds of Raasay in the Sixteenth Century

Although there are many conflicting accounts of events during the first half of the sixteenth century, it seems likely that many of the MacLeods were massacred by one of the MacLeods of Lewis at Isay in the early 1530s. Alasdair and his brother, Iain na Tuaighe, were killed as were all of Calum Garbh's brothers. Calum was taken to the Laird of Calder, who kept him safely until he came of age, at which time he was taken back to Raasay and proclaimed laird, probably in the late 1540s. Calder is Cawdor and at that time the Laird of Cawdor was a Campbell.

Genealogy of the MacLeods of Raasay

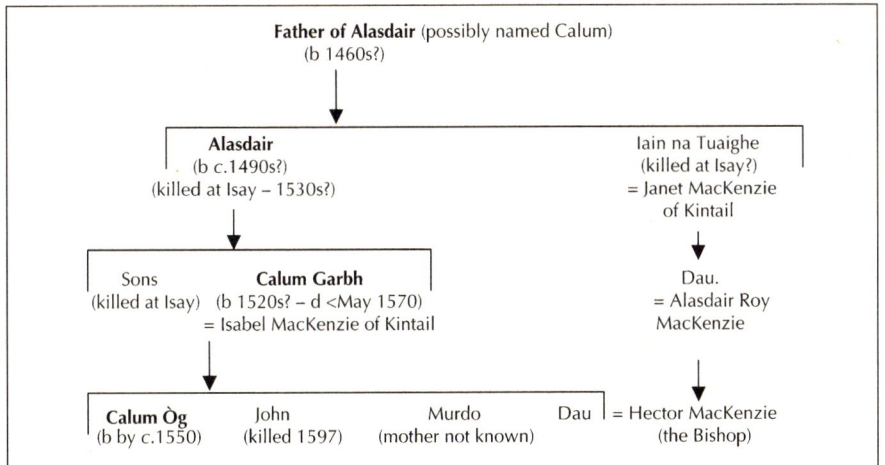

Figure R16. The MacLeods of Raasay.

Although there are an alarming number of question marks on the above chart it is also true that some facts are now known.

Calum Garbh is known to have died before May 1570, as his widow, Isabel MacKenzie had, by that time, married her second husband, James MacKintosh of Stroine. In a Crown charter to the MacLeods of Lewis in 1572, Calum Òg, son of Calum Garbh, is named as heir to the estate of Lewis if Torcall Conanach had no legitimate sons. It is interesting to note that in this charter Torcall Conanach places Calum Òg of Raasay and his heirs immediately after the heirs male of his own body, and before his own other nearest and legitimate heirs male (this would include his half-brothers).[18] In 1596 a Crown charter was issued to Calum Òg for the lands of Raasay, comprising eight merklands of Raasay and Rona and three merklands in Snizort, Skye. These lands had come to the king's hands following the Act of Annexation in 1587 which transferred ownership of all lands, previously held by the Church, to the Crown. Because this was the first crown charter for Raasay, the laird and his predecessors were named in it. He was Calum Òg, son of Calum, son of Alasdair. Alasdair's father may be named as Calum, although this is unclear in the charter. The charter further states that Calum Garbh's grandfather and 'predecessors since time immemorial' had held this estate as tenants of the Bishop of the Isles.

John, a brother of Calum Òg, was killed at Conon Market in 1597. This is recorded in MacKenzie histories, which also tell that a daughter of the Laird of Raasay married Hector MacKenzie (known as the Bishop) who was a son of Alasdair Roy MacKenzie of Applecross. Although the Laird of Raasay is not named he may have been Calum Garbh.

At a meeting of the privy council in 1610, Murdo, a brother of the Laird of Raasay, was denounced as a rebel for a second time. Murdo must, therefore, have been a brother of Calum Òg. He had been declared a rebel and put to the horn on 18 January 1609, but had still not been apprehended for his crimes in February 1610.

Although the reason for doing so is uncertain, in 1608 Calum Òg resigned superiority of the lands of Raasay to Andrew, Bishop of the Isles, knowing that the bishop would then transfer superiority to Lord Kenneth MacKenzie of Kintail. A Crown charter of June 1610 to Kenneth MacKenzie confirms this transaction.

Shortly after this, in 1611 it is said, a boat from Gairloch put into Clachan Bay, Raasay, and a sea fight took place between the men on board this boat and the Raasay men. During the fight, according to the history of the MacKenzies, 'Gillichallum Og, Laird of Raasay' was killed along with many of his men. All but three of the men who arrived on the ship were also killed, including Murdo MacKenzie, son of the Laird of Gairloch, and Alexander Bayne, eldest son of the Laird of Tulloch. Also involved in this fight was Murdo, the brother of Calum Òg. It is not known who Murdo's mother was, but it appears she was not Isabel MacKenzie.

There has been considerable debate in previous histories of the MacLeods over which member of the Raasay family was killed in this fight. Some maintain that it was Calum Garbh who was killed, while others believe that it was Calum Òg. Because Calum Garbh had already died before 1570, it could not have been him. Calum Òg was laird in 1572. Thus by 1611 he would have been at least sixty years of age.

An account of the incident given in the history of the MacKenzies[19] says that the man killed was 'Gillichallum Og, Laird of Raasay', and that 'he was made against his will by Gillichallum Mòr mac Donald mhic Neil to go to the ship to take MacKenzie prisoner'. This account was written about 1667, and by reason of that early date may hold more weight than later histories. Because Calum Òg's mother was Isabel MacKenzie, it may perhaps be assumed to be accurate. However, one might ask whether an experienced chief would do anything 'against his will' as described in this account. Could it have been a son of Calum Òg who was killed? Could 'GilliChallum Og' mean 'Young MacLeod of Raasay', referring to the heir apparent? The eldest son of a laird was often referred to in that manner. It seems most likely, however, that Calum Òg was killed in the sea fight at Clachan.

An account given by Sir Robert Gordon[20] states clearly that in August 1611 the Laird of Raasay was killed. He tells that on the first visit to the ship, Murdo MacKenzie kept out of sight. When the MacLeods came back to the ship to get the wine, MacKenzie showed himself. When the Laird of Raasay tried to take him prisoner, there was a fight on board the ship. Many were killed, before the Gairloch ship sailed away. The three who made their escape are said to have died soon after. There is no mention of drinking aboard the ship. Neither is there any mention of the Laird of Raasay consulting with anyone. In this account he was the man who took the decisions.

Although there were clearly other MacLeods, some of whom were no doubt closely related to the laird, on Raasay at this time, few names have come down to us.

There is some confusion, and by now this should come as no great surprise, over who succeeded Calum Òg as Laird of Raasay. Both Alexander MacKenzie and Alick Morrison describe two lairds named Alexander. One is said to have been served heir in 1617 and the other in 1643.

The first Alexander is believed to have married a daughter of MacLeod of Drynoch, Skye. After her husband's death, she married Thomas Graham of Drynie and later, Alexander MacKenzie of Hilton. Although it is also said that Alexander of Raasay received a letter from the king in 1611, Richard Sharpe was unable to trace this document. The second Alexander, it is said, married Sibella, eldest daughter of Roderick MacKenzie of Applecross.

It would appear that these writers have confused the two Alexanders. Indeed it may be asked whether they created one. Histories of the MacKenzies [21] record that Sibella (or Isabel), daughter of Roderick MacKenzie of Applecross, married firstly, Alexander MacLeod of Raasay, secondly Thomas Graham of Drynie, and thirdly Alexander MacKenzie of Hilton. In 1650 there was a sasine in her favour as widow of Alexander MacLeod of Raasay and future spouse of Thomas Graham of Drynie.

Both writers of the Raasay genealogy express surprise that Alexander was not served heir to the estate until 1617. No evidence is provided to confirm the proposition that Alexander was a minor until then. Given that Calum Òg was born about 1550, it seems most unlikely that his eldest son would not have come of age until 1617. It could be suggested, however, that the reason no heir was served until 1617 was that Calum Òg was alive until then. Perhaps the date given for the sea fight at Clachan is too early. However, Mr Sellar has indicated that he does not think that the gap between 1611 and the service of heirs in 1617 is significant: there were sometimes long gaps between death and a following 'service of heir'.

Thus, in all probability, Calum Òg died in 1611. He was succeeded by Alasdair who, it must be assumed was his son. Alasdair married Sibella, or Isabel, MacKenzie. It is most unlikely that Alasdair was Calum Òg's brother, as has been claimed, because it is not until 1650 that Sibella appears on record as the future spouse of Thomas Graham, the second of her three husbands.

Alasdair had therefore died before 1650. That appears to be confirmed by the fact that Iain Garbh is believed to have been served heir to his father in 1648. Iain Garbh's sister, Margaret, married Calum Nicolson of Scorrybreac, probably about the middle of the seventeenth century. His father was Donald, chief of the Nicolsons at that time. A song in celebration of this marriage mentions Iain Mòr and Iain Òg – Big John and Young John. Iain Mòr is, of course, Iain Garbh and this suggests that he had a younger brother, also named John, as well as two brothers, Calum and Alasdair.

It may be remembered here that the history of the Campbells of Craignish said that Iain Garbh was directly descended from Marion Campbell. He was said to be her 'great-grandson or fourth from her'. His great-grandfather, if this interpretation is correct, was Calum Garbh. This does not appear to fit datewise as Marion's marriage was believed to have been around 1510. Calum Garbh, on the other hand, was most likely born in the 1520s. It may be asked if 'fourth from her' would be a great-great-grandson. If that were the case, it would be Calum Garbh's father, Alasdair, who married Marion Campbell.

Iain Garbh married Janet MacLeod, a daughter of Sir Ruairidh Mòr, Chief of Dunvegan. Before Easter 1671, Iain Garbh and sixteen of his men went to Lewis to attend the christening of a child of the Earl of Seaforth. On their way home, all were drowned in the Minch. One of those who perished with him was his brother, Calum.

Based on the Wardlaw Manuscript, the date of this tragedy is taken to be 1671. However, in 1680 the Laird of Raasay is named as 'John MacLeod of Raasay', in a tack of teinds from Andrew, Bishop of the Isles to John MacLeod, Iain Breac, of Dunvegan. At this time, John MacLeod of Raasay owed money to MacLeod of Dunvegan, who appears to have taken steps to recover it. It is believed that Iain Garbh's youngest brother, Alasdair, succeeded him. If that had happened in 1671, it is strange that in 1680 the Laird of Raasay is named as John.

Although it has been said that Iain Garbh died at the early age of twenty-one, this cannot have been the case. If he was served heir in 1648 he must have been at least twenty-one then, putting his date of birth about 1627 or earlier.

The MacLeod Lairds of Raasay in the Seventeenth Century

Because Iain Garbh was succeeded by his youngest brother, Alasdair, it may be assumed that neither he nor his other brothers had any sons. Alasdair died in 1688, or shortly before. This gave rise to a retour, in which his daughters were served 'joint heirs of line, conquest and provision'.22 Alasdair's daughters were named Sileas and Seonaid, usually 'translated' as Giles (or Julia) and Janet.

The retour of 1688 names Alasdair as the ladies' father. Their father is said to be the son and heir of the late Alasdair MacLeod, their grandfather. He, in turn, was the son and heir of Calum MacLeod, their great-grandfather.

Although Alexander MacKenzie believed that the retour went on to name the ladies' great-great-grandfather, it does not appear to do so. He also believed that Sileas and Seonaid were sisters of Iain Garbh. That belief is perhaps based on the supposition that there were two lairds named Alexander following Calum Òg. That, as already considered, was unlikely. Furthermore, if the ladies were

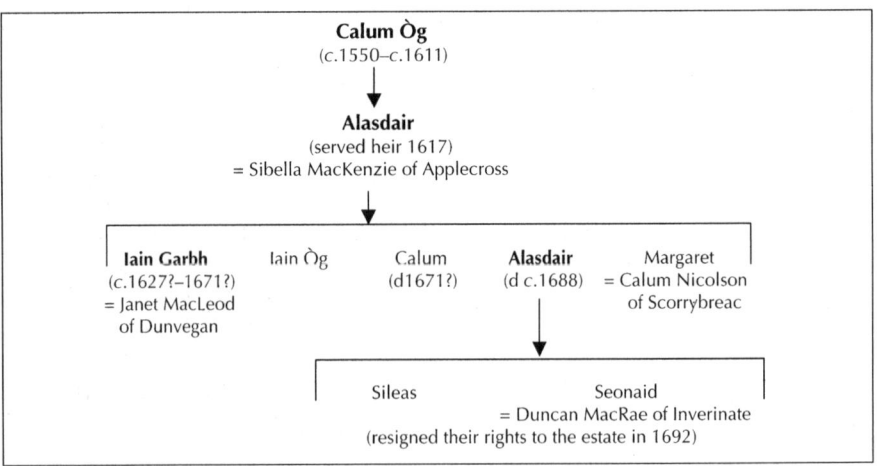

Figure R17. The MacLeods of Raasay in the seventeenth century.

sisters of Iain Garbh, would they not have been served heirs to their two brothers, Alasdair and Iain Garbh, rather than to their father? If they were Iain Garbh's sisters, it may also be asked why his sister, Margaret – who married Calum Nicolson – was omitted.

Sileas was unmarried. Seonaid was married to Donnchadh nam Piòs (Duncan of the Silver Goblet), Duncan MacRae of Inverinate. He was born about 1640 and died sometime between 1693 and 1704. He is the man who made the collection of Gaelic poetry now known as 'The Fernaig Manuscript'. This manuscript has over 4000 lines of verse, written phonetically, and from authors who lived at different times. In Gaelic literature it is of immense value, firstly because many of the poems are not found elsewhere and secondly because it is written phonetically. Some of the verses were Duncan's own composition. Others were written by people known to be related to him.

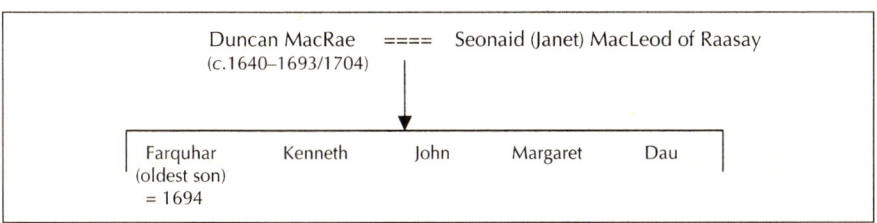

Figure R18. MacRaes of Inverinate.

In 1692 Sileas and Seonaid resigned their rights to the estate of Raasay to their cousin, Alasdair.

It is by no means clear who this relative was. Both Alexander MacKenzie and Alick Morrison believe that Alasdair was a minor until 1692 when he inherited the estate. It appears more likely, however, that there was a protracted legal dispute over the inheritance at this time, as Richard Sharpe makes reference to various sasines regarding this. Different ancestries have been suggested for Alasdair.

Alexander MacKenzie says that he was the son of John, son of Alasdair who was served heir in 1617. He believed that the MacLeods of Rigg were descended from Alasdair (who inherited Raasay in 1692). Alick Morrison, on the other hand, believes that Alasdair was the son of John, son of John of Rigg, who was the son of Alasdair (served heir in 1617).

Both MacKenzie and Morrison believed that Alasdair, who was served heir in 1617, was a brother of Calum Òg. It has been shown that he was much more likely to have been his son. It is suspected that Seonaid and Sileas were nieces, rather than sisters of Iain Garbh. It will be noted that, unlike Morrison, MacKenzie makes no mention of Iain Garbh's brother, Alasdair, who is believed to have succeeded him. If he was unaware of this Alasdair, it may explain his assumption that Seonaid and Sileas were sisters of Iain Garbh, because their father and grandfather were both named as Alasdair.

If both the charts in Figure R19 were to be amended by removing Alasdair (served heir in 1643), it would be noted that Iain Garbh and John become brothers,

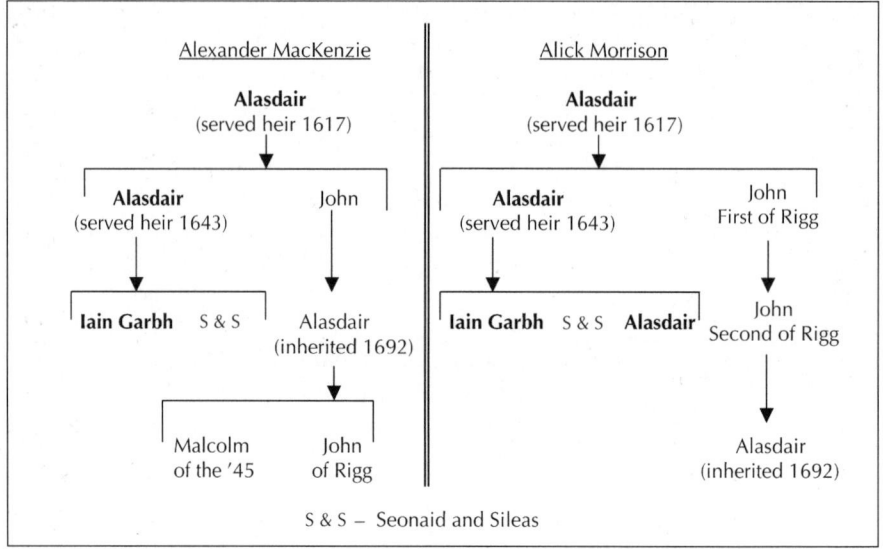

Figure R19. Alasdair – as given by MacKenzie and Morrison (previous lairds in bold).

sons of Alasdair (served heir in 1617). Could the song celebrating the marriage of Iain Garbh's sister, Margaret, to Calum Nicolson confirm this? In it, there is mention of Iain Mòr and Iain Òg. If that were so, however, one might ask why did Sileas and Seonaid inherit the estate in the first place?

Alick Morrison believed that Alasdair was a minor until 1692, and because of that his uncle Murdo, a brother of John second of Rigg, became his tutor. Because he was tutor, Murdo held land in Glen, Raasay. Morrison gives details about Murdo. He was born about 1620 and had many descendants.

Figure R20 below shows some substantial age gaps between the generations. In genealogical terms, when an estimate is required, it is usual to allow thirty years per generation. There will, of course, be times when this will not hold true.

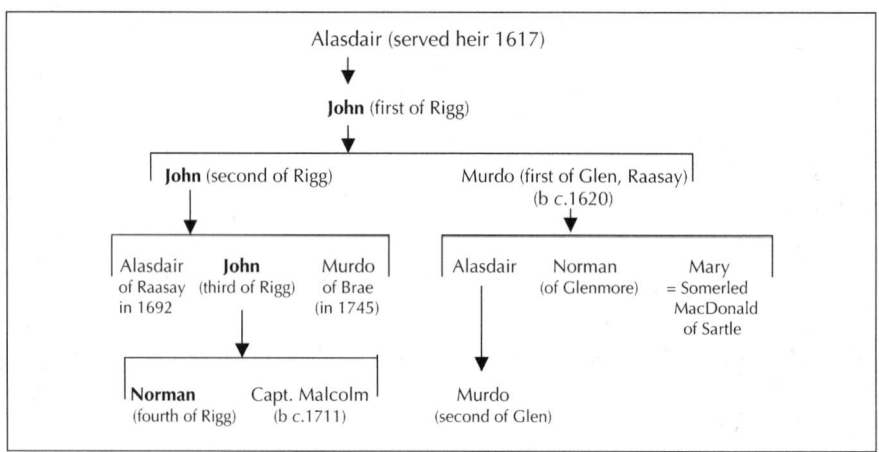

Figure R20. MacLeods of Rigg: as given by Alick Morrison.

There are clearly far more questions than answers about this period. Perhaps later research will help to clarify matters.

Although we do not know who Alasdair was, it appears that he did inherit the Raasay estate in 1692. It is also clear that he was not a minor, as in 1692 Alasdair MacLeod of Raasay granted lands in liferent to his wife, Florence, giving her an income for life. This too poses a query, as both MacKenzie and Morrison state that Alasdair married Catherine MacLeod of Bernera, Harris. Morrison believes that Alasdair and Catherine had an only son Malcolm who, as Laird of Raasay, became known for his support of Bonnie Prince Charlie during the 1745 rebellion. MacKenzie, on the other hand, believed that Alasdair and Catherine had two sons – Malcolm and John. Malcolm, the Laird of Raasay, took part in the 1745 rebellion. John, it is said, was the father of Captain Malcolm who joined his uncle, the laird, in the '45.

There appears to be agreement that Malcolm who was Laird of Raasay in 1745 was the son of Alasdair, who had become laird in 1692 after his relatives, Seonaid and Sileas, had resigned their rights in his favour.

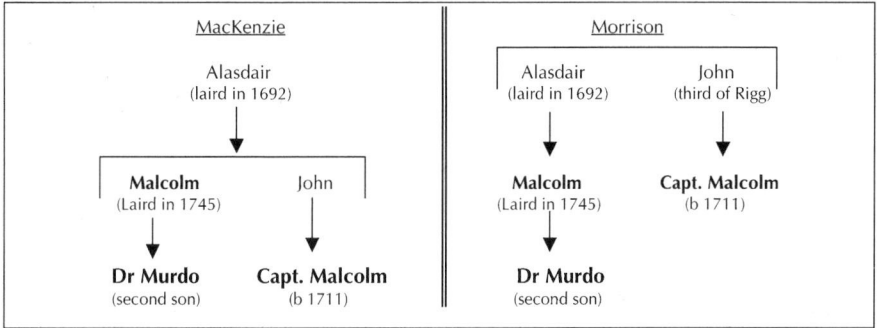

Figure R21. MacLeods of Raasay who took part in the 1745 rebellion.

Malcolm – Laird of Raasay (date not known – 1745)

At Tarradale in Ross-shire, in December 1713, Malcolm MacLeod of Raasay married Mary, daughter of Alexander MacKenzie of Applecross. It may therefore be assumed that he was born by 1692 at the latest. Their children were John, Murdo, Norman and Janet.

Before 'going out' in 1745, Malcolm signed the Raasay estate over to his eldest son, John, to avoid any possibility of forfeiture. Norman was an officer in the service of the States General. He was in Raasay in 1773 when Johnson and Boswell visited the island. Janet was married to John MacKinnon of MacKinnon who, like her father, was a strong supporter of the Stuart cause.

Malcolm's second son, Murdo, was a medical doctor. He settled in Eyre, Snizort, in the Skye part of the estate. In naming Murdo's eldest son as Captain Malcolm, who was 'out' during the '45, MacKenzie illustrates the confusion surrounding the relationships between the MacLeods of Raasay at this period. Clearly Captain Malcolm, who it is known was born about 1711, could not

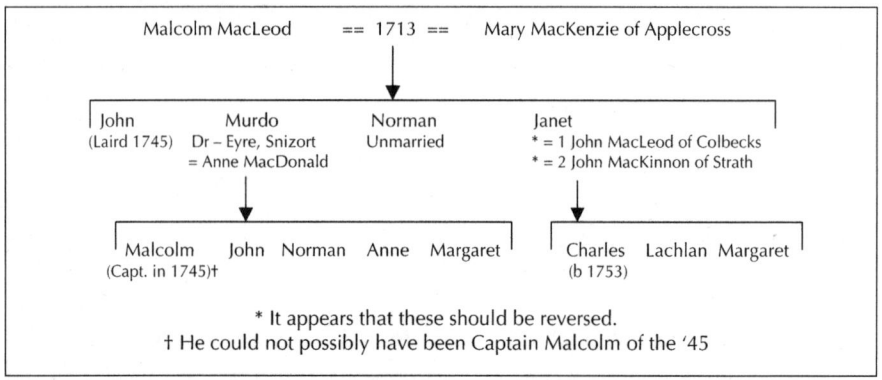

Figure R22. The first marriage of Malcolm MacLeod: from Alexander MacKenzie.

possibly have been a son of Dr Murdo of Eyre. Indeed, MacKenzie himself has already given a different version of who Captain Malcolm was.

Alick Morrison gives some more information about these people. Dr Murdo of Eyre is believed to have had four children – Anne is not mentioned. His eldest son, Malcolm, died unmarried in the West Indies. Norman, son of Malcolm and Mary, was in the service of the States General in Holland.

Janet is said to have married Iain Dubh, John MacKinnon of MacKinnon, as her first husband, with family as given by MacKenzie. Iain Dubh died about 1755 and Janet's eldest brother, John, was appointed by the Court of Session as 'Tutor Dative' to young Charles and Lachlan MacKinnon. In 1757, John MacLeod took a 'Tutelar Inventory' of the estate. The lands of Strath, belonging to the MacKinnons, had been taken over by John MacKinnon of Mishnish. John MacLeod now began proceedings to restore the estate to his nephew, Charles. However, a private sale of the main estate of Strath had been made, in 1751, to the agent of Sir James Macdonald and this could not be set aside. Only the estates of Mishnish and Strathaird were restored to Charles. He did not keep them for long. Mishnish was sold, and then Strathaird. Although his tenants offered to make it possible for the MacKinnons of Corry to buy Strathaird, Charles opposed it, saying that if it went out of his own family, no-one else of the name MacKinnon should ever possess it.[23]

Janet MacLeod's second husband was John MacLeod of Colbecks, Jamaica. John MacLeod of Colbecks registered arms in 1762. He gave his genealogy as

> John MacLeod of Colbecks, son of Donald of Lewis, son of John, son of Torcall, son of John, 'only brother germane' of Roderick, last Baron of Lewis.

Roderick, last Baron of Lewis, was Ruairidh Chaluim. Because of this believed relationship with Ruairidh Chaluim, the MacLeods of Colbecks claim to be male heirs of the MacLeods of Lewis and representatives of that branch.

Malcolm MacLeod, Laird of Raasay, married his second wife on 10 May 1748. She was Janet MacLeod, who became known as 'Baintighearna Dhubh Oscaig'. The marriage contract was found in the Muniment Room in Dunvegan Castle.

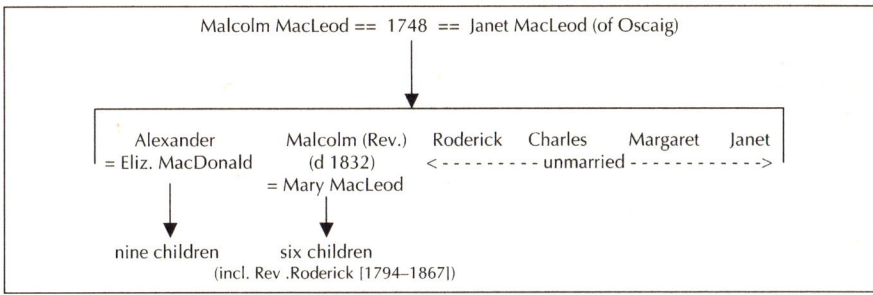

Figure R23. The second marriage of Malcolm MacLeod.

The above chart is based on Alexander MacKenzie's genealogy. Alick Morrison states that Malcolm and Janet had eight children. The two not included in the above chart are Marjory and Elizabeth, but he says 'nothing is known' about either of them. Morrison says also that Rev. Malcolm MacLeod had eleven children.

It may be noted here that Alexander MacLeod and his wife, Elizabeth MacDonald were living at Castle, Raasay in 1801. The birth, on 7 May 1801, of their daughter, Chirsty, is recorded in the Old Parish Records. Alexander is designated 'Captain'. By 1805 the family had moved to Penifiler where their children, Alexander Donald and John Murdo, were born on 17 June 1805 and 5 December 1812 respectively.

John – Laird of Raasay (1745–1786)

John, eldest son of Malcolm MacLeod by his first wife, was born about 1714. He took over the estate of Raasay in 1745. John married Jane, daughter of Angus MacQueen of Totaroam, between Rigg and Storr Lochs on the east coast of Skye. They had thirteen children. John and his family entertained Johnson and Boswell when they visited Raasay in 1773. Information about the family is based on Alick Morrison's genealogy. The children of John and Jane were:

- James, who succeeded his father as Laird of Raasay
- John, who died young
- Malcolm, who was a captain in the Indian Army and died unmarried
- Flora, who married Colonel James Muir Campbell, afterwards 5th Earl of Loudoun.
- Margaret, who married Martin Martin of Bealach, Trotternish
- Janet, who married Archibald MacRae of Ardintoul
- Catherine, who married John, second son of Dr Murdo MacLeod of Eyre, Snizort
- Isabella Rose, who married Major Thomas Ross of the Royal Artillery
- Julia, who married Olaus MacLeod, who had the tack of Bharcasaig, near Orbost, Skye

- Jean, who married Colonel John MacLeod, 2nd of Colbecks, Jamaica
- Anne, who married Donald MacKenzie, son of Thomas of Applecross
- Mary, who married Rev. Donald Campbell, D. D. of Kilninver in Argyll-shire
- Christina, who married Alexander MacSween, an Indian judge

There were many descendants from these marriages, only some of whom will be noted here.

Flora MacLeod and the 5th Earl of Loudoun married in Edinburgh on 30 April 1777 and had an only daughter, Flora Muir (1780–1840), who became the Countess of Loudoun on the death of her father. Flora MacLeod of Raasay died at Hope Park, near Edinburgh, on 2 September 1780. In 1804 her daughter married Francis, Earl of Moira, who became the 1st Marquis of Hastings in 1816. He was Governor General of India from 1813 to 1823.

Janet MacLeod married Archibald MacRae on 9 September 1783. Archibald was for many years chamberlain of the Seaforth estates. Their eldest son, Colonel Sir John MacRae, joined the staff of Lord Moira and was his Military Secretary when he became Governor General of India. Janet, daughter of Archibald and Janet MacRae, was born in 1791. In 1817 she married Donald MacRae of Auchtertyre (1775–1843). He was, for a time, a planter at Demerara, and afterwards tacksman of Auchtertyre. Donald MacRae was one of the factors of the Raasay estate in the time of John, the last of the MacLeods to hold Raasay.

Isabella Rose MacLeod married Major Thomas Ross. He fell ill abroad in 1799 and was invalided home, but died on the way. His widow and young daughter, Elizabeth Jane (or Eliza) set off to come back to Britain. Isabella gave birth to her second daughter, Isabella Rose, but died at her birth and was buried at sea. James MacLeod, Laird of Raasay, learned of his sister's death when he met the ship. He took his two young nieces to Raasay, where they stayed until they were old enough to be educated in Edinburgh. There they lived with their aunt, Catherine, widow of John MacLeod of Eyre, Snizort.

Eliza and Isabella left for India with their cousin, Flora, Marchioness of Hastings. There, Eliza met and married Sir Charles D'Oyly, an artist who was

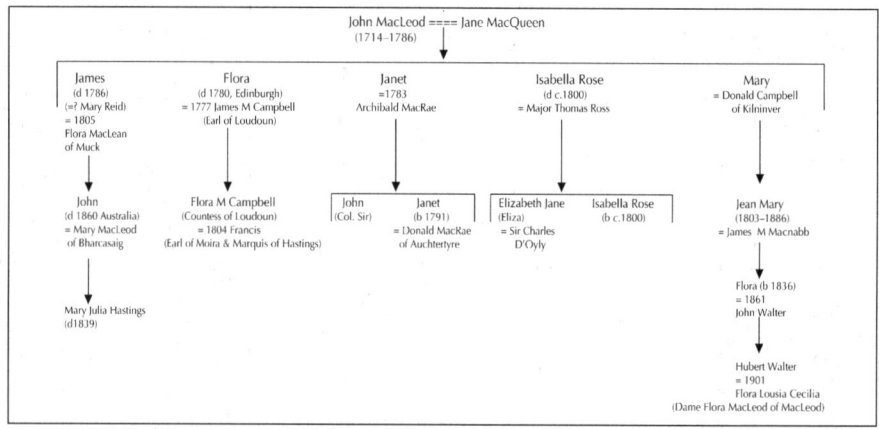

Figure R24. Some of the descendants of John MacLeod and Jane MacQueen.

employed by the East India Company. Eliza was an accomplished musician. While at Raasay, she transcribed a number of piobaireachd into pianoforte notation, as she heard them played by John MacKay, piper to her Uncle James (the laird). While she was in India, she had an elegant set of pipes made for John MacKay, which she presented to him on her return home. In her honour, John composed the famous *piobaireachd* 'Lady D'Oyly's Salute'. It is believed that Angus MacKay, son of John, and later piper to Queen Victoria, learned much of his musical theory from Eliza. Eliza died on 1 July 1875.

Mary MacLeod married Rev. Donald Campbell of Kilninver. They had three children, the youngest of whom was Jean Mary Campbell (1803–1886). In 1820 she married James Munro Macnabb (1790–1860). James and Jean Macnabb had ten children, including Flora, who was born in 1836. As his second wife, she married John Walter of Bearwood in 1861. He was the principal proprietor of *The Times*.

Hubert Walter (b1870) was one of their six children. In 1901 he married Flora Louisa Cecilia, Dame Flora MacLeod of MacLeod. Hubert was thus a great-great-grandson of John MacLeod, Laird of Raasay, and his wife Jane MacQueen of Totaroam.

James – Laird of Raasay (1786–1824)

John MacLeod, the laird who took over the estate of Raasay in 1745 and entertained Johnson and Boswell in 1773, died in 1786. His eldest son, James, now became laird. Although Alexander MacKenzie does not give a date, Alick Morrison believes that James MacLeod married Flora MacLean of Muck in 1805. Alexander MacKenzie notes five children of this marriage, although only four are mentioned by Alick Morrison.

The *OPR* show that a daughter, Mary, was born on 9 March 1802, to James MacLeod Esq of Raasay and Mary Reid. Neither the marriage nor the child is mentioned in the genealogies and nothing more is known of either mother or daughter. The *OPR* records the births of four children of James MacLeod Esq of Raasay and Flora Anne MacLean. They were Hannah Elizabeth on 6 March 1811; James on 22 January 1813; Loudoun Hastings on 13 December 1820 and Francis Hector George on 24 December 1824.

Neither the marriage of James and Flora Anne MacLeod nor the birth of their eldest son, John, is recorded in the *OPR*. Perhaps John was not born on Raasay, or he may have been born during the period 1806–1811 when there is a gap in the Portree parish records. All four sons were married with families.

John – Laird of Raasay (1824–1843)

It is not said in the genealogies when James MacLeod died, or when John MacLeod became Laird of Raasay. Other sources indicate that his father died in 1824. If the date of the marriage is correct at 1805, and his father died in 1824, John would have been a minor, and not able to succeed to the estate until he was twenty-one. Whenever he became laird, he did not live on Raasay, as he was an officer in the 78th Highlanders. He married Mary, daughter of Sir Donald MacLeod of Bharcasaig, near Orbost, Skye. Sir Donald was a distinguished officer in the Indian Army.

The only daughter of John and Mary MacLeod, Mary Julia Hastings MacLeod, died in 1839, aged three. There is a chapel in her memory in the old churchyard at Clachan. In 1843 John and Mary emigrated to Australia, where he died. His headstone bears the inscription:

> Erected in memory of John Macleod Esq., of Raasay and Chief of the Clan Torquile who died June 6th 1860 aged 53.

It would appear, therefore, that John was born in 1807, and did not come of age until 1828, some four years after his father's death. No indication is given as to who ran the estate during his years as a minor.

In 1846 John MacLeod's creditors sold the estate. Raasay and Rona were bought by George Rainy.

After 1843

Although the MacLeods no longer owned the Raasay estate, the genealogy of this branch, or sept, is continued by Alick Morrison. The 'head of the sept' after John's death was his nephew, James, who died unmarried. James was succeeded by his cousin, Loudoun Hector MacLeod. He, in turn, was succeeded by his eldest son, Torquil Bright MacLeod, who was succeeded by his son, Torquil Roderick.

Perhaps it is easier to follow in chart form.

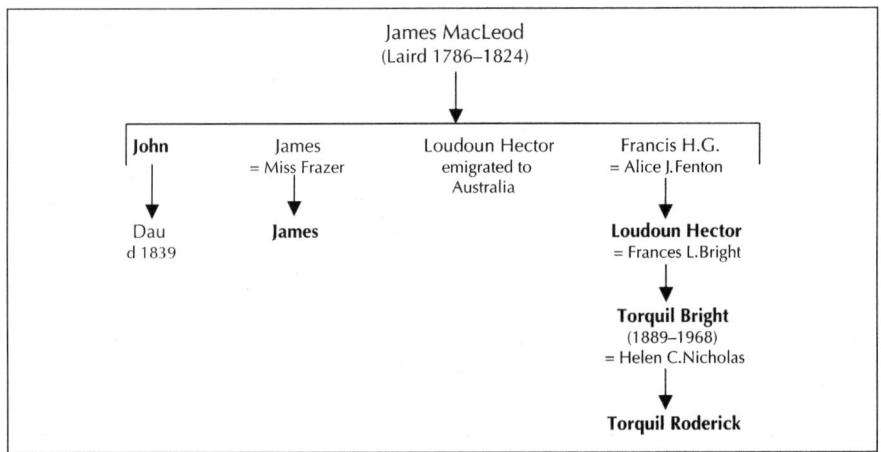

Figure R25. The MacLeods after 1843.

It has been noted that by the early 1800s, the only close relatives of the laird known to have been living on Raasay were Captain Alexander MacLeod and his wife, Elizabeth MacDonald. In 1801 they were living at Castle, Raasay, but shortly after had moved to Penifiler, near Portree. The genealogies as given by Alexander MacKenzie and Alick Morrison are shown in chart form. These suggest that there were many relatives of the MacLeods of Raasay living in Trotternish. Possibly they left Raasay at the end of the eighteenth or early in the nineteenth century if the financial problems of the lairds made life difficult on Raasay.

In any case, it certainly appears that many of these MacLeods lived on Skye by the nineteenth century. There are undoubtedly descendants living on Skye today. Further research into these families may well produce more information resulting in better understanding of the history of both the MacLeods and the area. Information, as given by Alexander MacKenzie and Alick Morrison, is shown as charts.

Notes

1. W. D. H. Sellar, 'The Ancestry of the MacLeods Reconsidered', *TGSI*, vol. LX, pp. 235–58, where all references to W.D.H. may be found..
2. W. Matheson, 'The MacLeods of Lewis', *TGSI*, vol. LI, pp. 320–37, where all references to W. Matheson may be found.
3. H. MacDonald, 'History of the MacDonalds', *SHS*, Highland Papers, vol. I, ed. J. R. N. MacPhail (1914), p. 56.
4. D. Monro, 'Description of the Western Isles of Scotland, 1549', Monro's *Western Isles of Scotland*, ed. R. W. Munro (1961), p. 70.
5. A. MacKenzie, *The History of the MacLeods* (1889), p. 344.
6. Dr S. MacLean, 'Some Raasay Traditions', *TGSI*, vol. XLIX, pp. 379, 392.
7. Thanks to Mr W. D. H. Sellar for this comment.
8. 'The Manuscript History of Craignish', *SHS*, 3rd series, vol. IV, 'Miscellany of the Scottish History Society', pp. 231–2.
9. J. MacKenzie, 'Genealogie of Surname of M'Kenzie', written *c.* 1667, *SHS*, Highland Papers, vol. 2, ed. J. R. N. MacPhail (1916), pp. 33, 52.
10. W. Fraser, *The Earls of Cromartie*, vol. 2 (1876), p. 512.
11. A. MacKenzie, *History of the MacLeods* (1889), p. 346.
12. J. MacKenzie, 'Genealogie of Surname of M'Kenzie', written *c.* 1667, *SHS*, Highland Papers, vol. 2, ed. J. R. N. MacPhail (1916), pp. 25, 50.
13. A. MacKenzie, *History of the MacKenzies* (1894; reprinted 1998), p. 174.
14. 'The MacKenzies', *SHS*, Genealogical Collections, vol. 1, ed. J. T. Clark (1900), p. 71.
15. A. MacKenzie, *History of the MacLeods* (1889), p. 348.
16. Ibid.
17. J. MacKenzie, 'Genealogie of Surname of M'Kenzie', written *c.* 1667, *SHS*, Highland Papers, vol. 2, ed. J. R. N. MacPhail (1916), pp. 50–1.
18. Thanks to Mr W. D. H. Sellar for this comment.
19. J. MacKenzie, 'Genealogie of Surname of M'Kenzie', written *c.* 1667, *SHS*, Highland Papers, vol. 2, ed. J. R. N. MacPhail (1916), pp. 52–4.
20. Sir Robert Gordon of Gordonstoun, Baronet, *A Genealogical History of the Earldom of Sutherland* (1813), pp. 276–8.
21. 'The MacKenzies', *SHS*, Genealogical Collections, vol. I, ed. J. T. Clark (1900), p. 99; A. MacKenzie, *History of the MacKenzies* (1894), p. 598; D. Warrand, *Some MacKenzie Pedigrees* (1965), p. 122.
22. See Document Sources.
23. A. M. Downie and A. D. MacKinnon, *Genealogical Account of the Family of MacKinnon* (1883), p. 4.

11

Genealogy of the MacLeods of Gairloch

Alexander Mackenzie,[1] writing in 1889, gave some details of the MacLeods of Gairloch at the beginning of his chapter on the MacLeods of Raasay. He wrote, 'It is thought that the same branch of the Clan, descended from the House of Lewis, inherited both Gairloch and Raasay long before Malcolm Garbh MacGillechallum received the latter as his patrimony from his father, Malcolm Macleod of Lewis, early in the sixteenth century.' There is some doubt concerning the descent of the MacLeods of Raasay from Malcolm MacLeod of Lewis. This has been considered.

Alick Morrison, writing in 1974,[2] discounted Alexander MacKenzie's version, claiming that the MacLeods of Gairloch were about 200 years older than the MacLeods of Raasay. He described this branch as being descended from a Malcolm MacLeod, chief of Lewis about the middle of the fourteenth century. However, that chief named Malcolm does not appear in William Matheson's revised genealogy of the MacLeods of Lewis.[3] There are also other doubts regarding Morrison's account of the early history of the Gairloch MacLeods.

Early Generations of the MacLeods of Gairloch

The first two chiefs are described as follows:

> In 1430 it is recorded that King James I of Scotland granted to 'Nele Nelesoun' for his homage and service in the capture of his deceased brother, Thomas Nelesoun a rebel, the lands of Gerloch and others in the Earldoms of Ross and Sutherland ...

The name Thomas is not found as a MacLeod name in any history of the clan. There is an account,[4] however, which may serve to shed some light on this story.

> Thomas Macneill, son of Neill Mackay, who was engaged in the battle of Tuttum Turwigh, possessed the lands of Creigh, Spaniziedaill, and Palrossie, in Sutherland. Having conceived

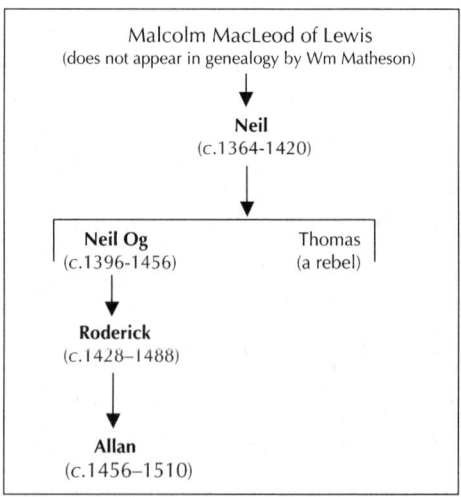

Figure G1. MacLeods of Gairloch as given by Alick Morrison.

some displeasure at Mowat, the laird of Freshwick, the latter, with his party, in order to avoid his vengeance, took refuge in the chapel of St Duffus, near the town of Tain, as a sanctuary. Thither they were followed by Thomas, who not only slew Mowat and his people, but also burnt the chapel to the ground. This outrage upon religion and humanity exasperated the king, who immediately ordered a proclamation to be issued, denouncing Thomas Macneill as a rebel, and promising his lands and possessions as a reward to any one that would kill or apprehend him. Angus Murray ... held a secret conference with Morgan and Neill Macneill, the brothers of Thomas, at which he offered, provided they would assist him in apprehending their brother ... to aid them in getting peaceable possession of such lands in Strathnaver as they claimed.

The lands of Strathnaver belonged, at the time, to Angus Dubh MacKay. Neil and Morgan duly apprehended their brother, Thomas, and delivered him to Murray, who presented him to the king. Thomas mac Neil was executed at Inverness about 1430. Neil and Morgan are described as 'cousins-germane' of Angus Dubh MacKay.

It would thus appear that the first two Lairds of Gairloch, as given by Alick Morrison, were MacKays and not MacLeods.

There may, however, be a link between these MacKays and the MacLeods of Lewis. When considering the origin of the MacGilleChaluim patronymic, mention was made of Calum Beag nam Buadhan, Little Calum of the Accomplishments, or Triumphs, and his visit to Strathnaver in 1406 on behalf of his sister. The relationship between the MacLeods of Lewis and these MacKays is shown in the following chart.[5]

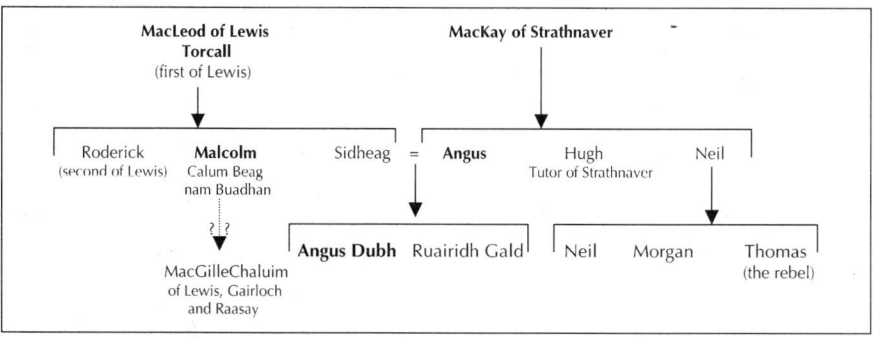

Figure G2. MacLeods of Lewis and MacKays of Strathnaver.

Calum Beag nam Buadhan lived on Lewis, and about 1406 he had set out with some men to visit his sister, Sidheag, in Strathnaver. She was then a widow and was allegedly being ill-treated by her brother-in-law, Hugh (sometimes referred to as 'Houcheon Dow' [Black Hugh]), who was then tutor to her young sons. The visit by Calum Beag from Lewis did not rectify the matter, and he and his men 'laid waste Strathnaver' on their way home. This resulted in the skirmish at Tuiteam Tarbhach when the MacKays, along with some of the Earl of Sutherland's men, caught up with the Lewis men. Calum Beag was killed, as were all but one of the Lewis men. It appears that Thomas MacKay was one of those who took part in the skirmish at Tuiteam Tarbhach.

Although this incident does introduce some relationship and dealings between the MacLeods and the MacKays, it does not readily explain how Alick Morrison considered the MacKay brothers to be MacLeods. Although surnames were not then in common use, clans and their historians were well aware of who people were and how they were related to one another.

Later Generations of the MacLeods of Gairloch

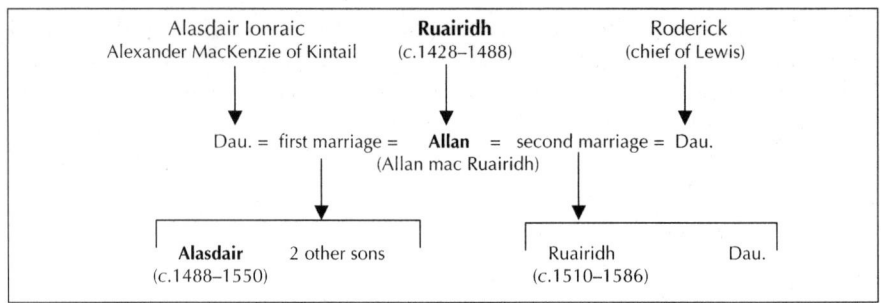

Figure G3. MacLeods of Gairloch as given by Alick Morrison.

The next of the MacLeods of Gairloch, named by Alick Morrison, is Ruairidh. He is known only by the patronymic of his son 'Allan mac Ruairidh'. Otherwise, 'tradition is silent about him'.

Allan mac Ruairidh is the first of the MacLeods of Gairloch for whom any substantive information exists. Allan married, as his first wife, a daughter of Alasdair Ionraic (Honest or Upright), Alexander MacKenzie, chief of the MacKenzies of Kintail. This marriage is confirmed by a MacKenzie history,[6] which says 'Alasdair Ionraic had one daughter who was married to Allan MacLeod younger of Gairloch. This Alasdair Ionraic died very aged at Kinnellan in the year 1472' (a footnote says that the date may be 1488). By his first wife, Allan had three sons.

Allan's second wife was a daughter of Ruairidh MacLeod, chief of Lewis. By her he had a son, Ruairidh. The following events are given by Alexander MacKenzie and followed by Alick Morrison. The following quotation is from Alexander MacKenzie. Talking of Allan, he says:

> Two of his brothers are said, according to tradition, to have resided with their relatives in the Lewis; and to have resolved that no Mackenzie blood should flow in the veins of the future Chiefs of the Gairloch family. Allan mac Ruairidh ... [lived] with his second wife, his two sons by his first wife, and a daughter. His brothers determined to murder Allan and his three boys by Mackenzie of Kintail's daughter, so that the estate should revert to themselves and their relations. For this purpose they sailed across the Minch to Gairloch ... They found him [Allan] ... and without any warning, there and then 'made him short by the head'.

They then went to Allan's house

> where Allan's wife, with two of her three step-children resided, they, in the most cold-blooded manner, informed her of her husband's fate, tore the two boys – the third being fortunately absent – from her knees, ... carried them along to a small glen ... and stabbed them to the heart with their daggers, and carried their blood-stained shirts with them.

The shirts were taken

> ... to the boys' grandfather, Alexander Mackenzie of Kintail, at Brahan Castle. Hector Roy, [the murdered boys' uncle], immediately started, carrying the blood-stained shirts along with him as evidence of the atrocious deed, to report the murder to the King at Edinburgh. His Majesty, on hearing of the crime, at once granted Hector a commission of fire and sword against the murderers of his nephews, and gave him a grant of the lands of Gairloch in his own favour, by charter, dated 1494, from the Crown. The assassins were soon afterwards slain.

The relevant points about this incident are that:

– the murderers were MacLeods from Lewis

– Allan MacLeod and his sons by his first wife, a MacKenzie, were killed

– one son escaped, as he was away from home at the time

– Hector Roy MacKenzie, uncle of the murdered boys, took revenge for their deaths, and consequently acquired the lands of the MacLeods of Gairloch

– no-one with MacKenzie blood should be laird of Gairloch, although it is unclear from this account who would become the laird.

The history of the MacKenzies names Allan as 'Allan MacLeod younger of Gairloch', implying that he was not the first of that branch of the MacLeods.[7] It does not use the patronymic, 'Allan mac Ruairidh', given by MacKenzie and Morrison. They say that 'tradition is silent' about Allan's father, but that two of his brothers lived on Lewis, suggesting, perhaps, that his father did also.

Although no date is given for the killing of Allan and his sons, there is an implication that it took place shortly before Hector Roy received the grant of

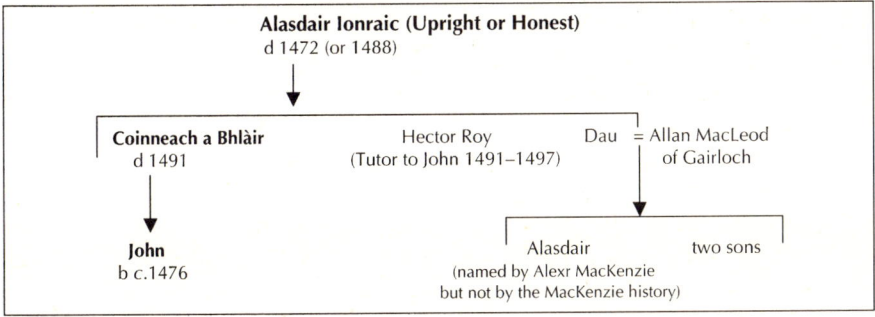

Figure G4. MacKenzies of Kintail.

Gairloch in 1494. Why, one might wonder, did the assassins stay in Gairloch awaiting retribution, rather than return to Lewis?

The blood-stained shirts were taken to Alasdair Ionraic (Upright or Honest), but he had died by 1488 at the latest. His son, Coinneach a Bhlàir, died in 1491. At that time Hector Roy became tutor to his nephew, John, who was then a minor. Thus, by 1494, Hector Roy himself was acting chief of the clan.

Alexander MacKenzie gives an account of another massacre, said to have taken place on the island of Isay, off Waternish, in 1568. According to his account, most of the MacLeods of Raasay and Gairloch were killed, including grandsons of Allan of Gairloch and children of the Raasay family. We are told that one child, of the Raasay family, escaped since he was being fostered away from home. His brothers were killed.

A history of the MacKenzies,[8] written about 1667, gives a different account of a massacre at Isay. Here no date is given. Again, we are told that one child, Calum Garbh, escaped through being fostered away from home. He later became Laird of Raasay. His father, uncle and brothers were killed, as were members of the family of the Gairloch MacLeods. They were not named as such, but the account clearly describes the sons of Allan MacLeod of Gairloch by his first wife, a MacKenzie. It is said that the perpetrator of this massacre was a Ruairidh MacLeod from Lewis, and that its purpose was to enable his nephew, the son of his sister and Allan MacLeod of Gairloch, to succeed to the estates of Gairloch.

This affair was recorded in the history of the MacKenzies because their relatives were affected by the event. Grandsons of Alasdair Ionraic were killed, and Calum Garbh of Raasay later married a MacKenzie. Known information about Calum Garbh suggests that the massacre at Isay took place, at the very latest, in the early 1530s.

It cannot be a coincidence that there are so many similarities within these three accounts. Indeed, Alexander MacKenzie's description of the massacre at Isay has been taken, almost word for word, from the MacKenzie history. Clearly, the sons of Allan MacLeod of Gairloch and his MacKenzie wife could not have been murdered twice. Because of its earlier date, it seems reasonable to accept the version given in the MacKenzie history.

Why Alexander MacKenzie should have translated an account of the massacre at Isay, that took place in the early 1530s, into two massacres – one at Gairloch about 1494, and one at Isay about 1568 – is a mystery. Because of the doubt raised over the authenticity of the massacre at Gairloch, it would be unsafe to make any assumptions based on it.

Although much has been said, little is known of the MacLeods of Gairloch. Allan, possibly described as 'younger of Gairloch' by the MacKenzie history, first married a daughter of Alasdair Ionraic, chief of Kintail. By her he had sons who were most likely murdered at Isay in the early 1530s. By his second wife, a MacLeod of Lewis, he had another son. He was a 'young man' when his older brothers were killed. It is not stated that Allan himself was killed at Isay; perhaps because he was already dead. Confirmation of Allan's patromymic, 'Allan mac Ruairidh', has not been found. There is also some doubt as to whether he had brothers living on Lewis. They were supposedly the murderers of his children. However, the MacKenzie history states that the murderer was the brother of his second wife and perhaps that is more readily acceptable.

Unfortunately, the history of the north west Highlands for the period between about 1450 and 1650 is relatively obscure and tends to raise more questions than it answers. Nowhere is this phenomenon more evident than in the relationship between the MacLeods of Lewis, the MacLeods of Gairloch – and therefore the MacLeods of Raasay – and the MacKenzies of Kintail.

Some information about the people and events of this time is found in manuscripts written in the early seventeenth century and histories of later date. However, much of it, such as the accounts of the MacLeods of Gairloch, appears contradictory. At least part of the reason for this is that certain events have been attributed with dates which are possibly incorrect.

One such event is the killing of Allan MacLeod and his two sons. According to Alexander MacKenzie, Allan was killed about 1494. His children must therefore have been born by 1495. MacKenzie says that Ruairidh Nimhneach was a son of Allan by his second wife. Indeed, he maintains that he was responsible for the massacre at Isay. His assertion that Ruairidh Nimhneach was not only alive in 1586, but also 'molesting fishermen' at that date, must be questioned. The man would have been over ninety! Although essentially following MacKenzie's account of events, Alick Morrison maintains that Ruairidh Nimhneach was born about 1510. This would have been impossible had his father been killed in 1494.

Some further information about people and events of this time may be helpful. Both Alexander MacKenzie and Alick Morrison say that Allan MacLeod's second wife was a daughter of Ruairidh MacLeod, Chief of Lewis. Some further information about the MacLeods of Lewis is found in the history of the Mac-Donalds.[9]

This was a very unsettled period in Highland history. In 1476 John, fourth Lord of the Isles, surrendered his lands to the king. Many of his closest relatives were against this, none more so than his own son, Angus Òg. The struggle between Angus Òg and his father created a virtual state of civil war in the area, with some clans supporting John and others supporting his son.

One of Angus Òg's supporters was Ranald, son of Allan MacDonald of Moidart. Ranald was married to a daughter of Ruairidh Dubh MacLeod, tutor to the heir of Lewis. It appears that Ruairidh Dubh, the tutor, had decided to dispossess the rightful heir and take over the lands of Lewis for himself. However, Angus Òg displaced Ruairidh Dubh and put the rightful heir in possession. Ruairidh, fourth chief of Lewis, was served heir to his father in 1464.

There were, it appears, repercussions from Angus Òg's intervention in the affairs of the MacLeods of Lewis. Ranald MacDonald's wife, a daughter of the tutor, was not at all pleased about Angus Òg's part in the affair. With John MacKenzie of Kintail, she hatched a plot to kill him. An Irish harper carried out their plan about 1488. There seems to have been a fairly lengthy time span between Ruairidh Dubh being displaced in 1464 and the killing of Angus Òg in 1488.

It is known that Angus Òg was dead by 1490. Ruairidh, fourth Chief of Lewis,

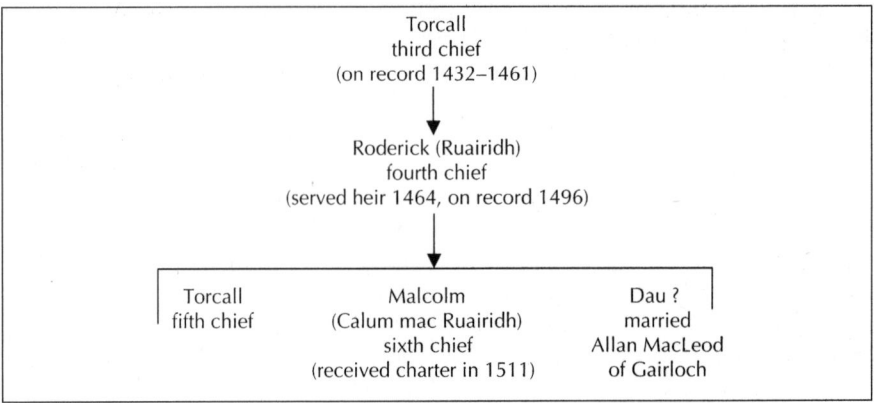

Figure G5. MacLeods of Lewis.

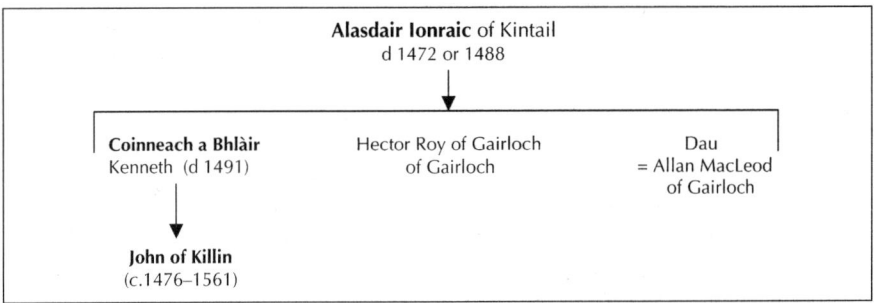

Figure G6. The MacKenzies of Kintail.

is on record in 1496. He was therefore the man whom the tutor tried to dispossess. It is not known how the tutor was related to Ruairidh, the fourth chief. It may be significant that Ruairidh is a name frequently occurring in the MacLeods of Lewis. For that reason, it is possible that Allan MacLeod of Gairloch's father-in-law (if indeed he was named Ruairidh) was not, in fact, a chief of the clan.

Because the MacKenzies of Kintail held their lands from the Crown, they did not support the Lordship of the Isles (see p. 227). It would therefore have been in their interests to have Angus Òg killed. The daughter of the tutor of Lewis is said to have plotted with John MacKenzie. Perhaps the John MacKenzie with whom she plotted was not the Chief of the MacKenzies of Kintail. The MacDonald history was not written until after 1628, so it is also possible that the name John may have been an assumption on the part of the author. The Chief of Kintail until 1491 was Coinneach a Bhlàir. On his death, his brother, Hector Roy, became tutor and was responsible for the administration of the estate and the clan.

The MacLeods of Lewis, however, did support the lordship. Torcall, fifth Chief of Lewis, married Catherine Campbell of Argyll. She is named as his wife in a Crown charter of 1498. Catherine's sister was married to Angus Òg MacDonald. Possibly the strongest claimant to the lordship after his father's death, was Donald Dubh MacDonald, son of Angus Òg. Torcall, fifth of Lewis,

Genealogy of the MacLeods of Gairloch

was a staunch supporter of Donald Dubh's bid to revive the lordship. As a result, the estate of Lewis was forfeited in 1506.

Although dates may be uncertain, there were dealings between the Chiefs of the MacLeods of Lewis and the MacDonald claimants to the Lordship of the Isles. There was a relationship between the MacDonalds of Moidart and some of the MacLeods on Lewis, who were also dealing with the MacKenzies of Kintail. The name Allan appears fairly frequently within the MacDonalds of Moidart and this may be significant.

It is also clear that in the 1460s there was more than one family of MacLeods in Lewis who had aspirations regarding the chieftainship of the clan. Indeed much of the later history of the MacLeods of Lewis shows that internal strife over the chieftainship occupied a great deal of their time and energy.

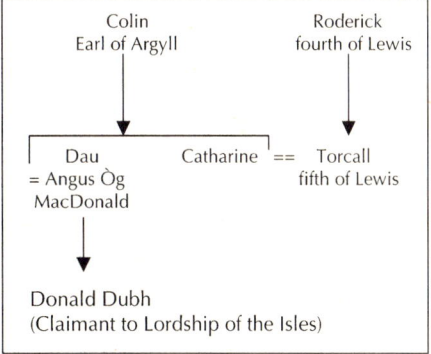

Figure G7. MacLeods of Lewis and MacDonald Claimants to the Lordship.

The supposed enmity between the MacLeods of Gairloch and the MacKenzies of Kintail must also be questioned. There is evidence in the histories of the MacKenzies, as well as those of the MacLeods, that there were many marriages between these two clans. This would be unlikely if they were in a state of almost perpetual war as the histories of the MacLeods imply.

On the death of his brother, Coinneach a Bhlàir, in 1491 Hector Roy MacKenzie took over the administration of the estates as tutor to his nephew, John of Killin. A history of the MacKenzies gives some information about Hector Roy. At that time, Hector Roy

> did all he could to keep his eldest brother's children from the estate. But after some wrangling John the eldest of them, though very young dispossessed him thereof, and made him acknowledge him as his Chief ... Hector after he gave his Nephew the management of his estate had several debates with the Shiellilichallum [Siol GilleChaluim] having purchased legal titles to such parts of the lands of Gairloch as were at that time in their possession. Upon which there followed some skirmishes with the advantage always on Hector's side ...[10]

Gairloch, it seems, was not the only estate that Hector Roy tried to take over.

Hector Roy's second wife was a daughter of Ranald Bayne (or Bàn) MacDonald, Laird of Moidart. Her mother was therefore quite possibly the daughter of Ruairidh Dubh, tutor of Lewis. Hector Roy's grandson, Alasdair Roy, is believed to have married a daughter of Iain na Tuaighe of Raasay and Janet MacKenzie of Kintail.

If the version of events given by the MacKenzie history is accepted, the only one of the MacLeods of Gairloch who survived the massacre at Isay was 'a young

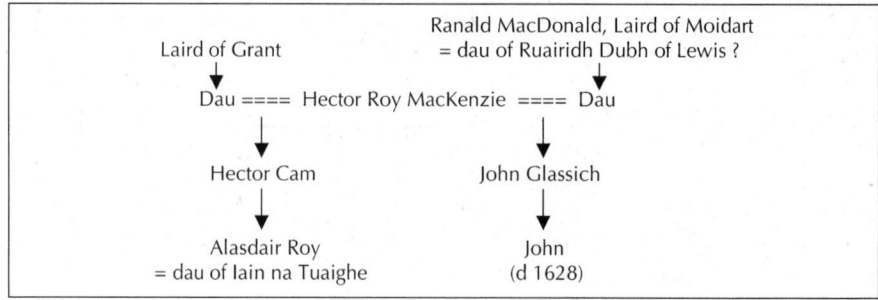

Figure G8. Hector Roy MacKenzie.

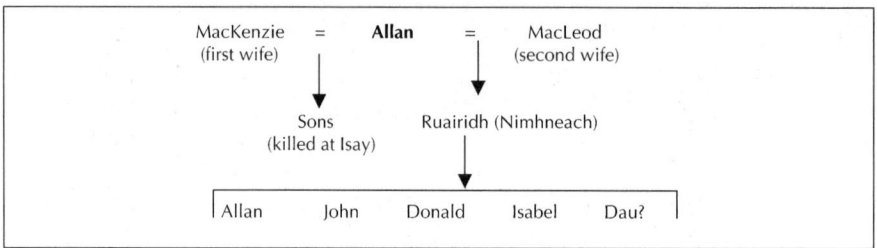

Figure G9. MacLeods of Gairloch.

man', the son of Allan MacLeod and his second wife. His uncle, from Lewis, committed the massacre at Isay, to enable him to take over the lands of Gairloch.

The young man is un-named in the MacKenzie history, but Alexander MacKenzie names him Ruairidh Nimhneach – Ruairidh the Venomous – and declares that he was 'the monster' who committed the massacre at Isay. MacKenzie states that he appears as 'Rory Mac Allan, alias Nevynnauch' in a decree-arbitral between Donald MacDonald, of Sleat and Colin MacKenzie of Kintail dated at Perth, 1 August 1569. In this, Donald MacDonald of Sleat becomes responsible for him, and undertakes that he will stop troubling the Laird of Gairloch's lands. Colin MacKenzie of Kintail undertakes that Torcall Conanach will stop troubling MacDonald's lands. Ruairidh's name, we are told, is also found in a document of 11 November 1586 because he was 'molesting burgesses engaged in the fisheries'. In that, he is described as 'Rory Mac Allan of Lochgair'. Given that Ruairidh was both alive and active in 1586, his date of birth could perhaps be guessed at about 1520.

Both Alexander MacKenzie and Alick Morrison refer to a sister of Ruairidh mac Allan of Gairloch. They state that she was the second wife of Iain na Tuaighe of Raasay. Indeed Alick Morrison states that both a sister and a daughter of Ruairidh mac Allan were Iain na Tuaighe's second wife. The older MacKenzie history, however, makes no mention of her and indicates that Iain na Tuaighe was murdered at Isay, so possibly he was not married to any relative of Ruairidh mac Allan.

Histories of the MacLeods tend to stress the enmity and feuding between them

Genealogy of the MacLeods of Gairloch

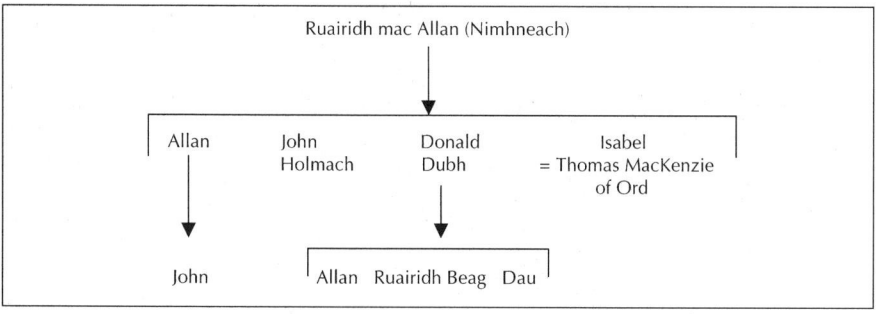

Figure G10. Ruairidh mac Allan of Gairloch.

and the MacKenzies. However, it is worth noting that there were many marriages between these two clans. Allan mac Ruairidh of Gairloch's first wife was a MacKenzie. Ruairidh Nimhneach's daughter, Isabel, married Thomas MacKenzie of Ord, a grandson of one the chiefs of Kintail. The daughter of Ruairidh Nimhneach's son, Allan, also married a MacKenzie. It has already been seen that some of the Raasay MacLeod lairds married MacKenzies.

The MacKenzie history quoted previously tells of other members of the MacLeods of Gairloch. The date given is 1610. There were brothers, Donald Dubh mac Ruairidh, John Holmach mac Ruairidh, and a nephew, John mac Allan mac Ruairidh. Donald Dubh had a daughter. John mac Allan mac Ruairidh was then chief of the MacLeods of Gairloch. Following a skirmish in Glen Torridon, Alexander MacKenzie of Gairloch took John mac Allan mac Ruairidh prisoner. This Alexander MacKenzie of Gairloch was a great-grandson of Hector Roy, who had been so active in the 1490s. In 1610 Alexander's father John, was Laird of the MacKenzie lands in Gairloch. This skirmish is said to have been the final defeat for the MacLeods, following which they lost their lands in Gairloch to the MacKenzies.

Although the MacKenzies at this time were 'at war' with the MacLeods of Gairloch, it appears that it was not always so. The MacKenzie history [11] tells about a feud between themselves and the MacDonalds of Glengarry. This feud was ongoing over many years and was not settled until after the death of Lord Kenneth in 1611. One incident, that probably took place earlier in the seventeenth century, involved John Holmach mac Ruairidh vic (mhic) Allan and his eight-oared boat. We are told that MacKenzie sent Alexander MacKenzie of Achiltie, sixteen gentlemen and eight 'scallag moires', along with John Holmach in his boat to view the coast. As things turned out, they became involved in a skirmish with the enemy. This incident shows that the MacLeods of Gairloch, or some of them at any rate, were at this time working with the MacKenzies.

Alexander MacKenzie, in his *History of the MacKenzies*,[12] tells of a meeting of the privy council held on 20 February 1610. At that meeting a commission was granted to various people, including Kenneth MacKenzie of Kintail, John MacKenzie of Gairloch and Roderick MacKenzie of Redcastle, to apprehend Allan mac Donald Dubh mhic Ruairidh of Culnacnock in Trotternish, Isle of Skye and several others, including Murdo mac Gillechallum, brother of Gillecallum,

Laird of Raasay and also some MacLeods from Lewis. They were Gillecallum mac Ruairidh MacLeod in Lewis, Norman mac Ghillechallum Mhoir and his brother, Ruairidh mac Ghillechallum Mhoir. All these men 'remain unrelaxed from a horning of 18 January 1609'.

There remain many unanswered questions about the MacLeods of Gairloch. As more research is undertaken about the people and events of these times, it must be hoped that more information about them will be revealed.

Notes

1. Alexander MacKenzie, *History of the MacLeods* (1889), pp. 340–90. All quotations from Alexander MacKenzie may be found here.
2. Alick Morrison, *The MacLeods: The Genealogy of a Clan*, Section 5 (1974), pp. 8–13. All quotations from Alick Morrison may be found here.
3. W. Matheson, 'The MacLeods of Lewis', *TGSI*, vol. LI, pp. 320–37.
4. 'Highland Clans and Regiments', ed. J. S. Keltie, F.S.A.S., part 1, p. 74.
5. Although it seems likely that this is in some way relevant to the history of the MacLeods of Gairloch, it is far from clear where or how it fits in.
6. J. MacKenzie, 'Genealogie of Surname of M'Kenzie', written *c.* 1667, *SHS*, Highland Papers, vol. 2, ed J. R. N. MacPhail, p. 20.
7. Old documents, such as this one, use abbreviations that have long since gone out of common usage. The word given here is – y^r – often used to mean 'younger'. However, 'y' could also be used to mean 'th' – giving 'there' or even 'heir'. Usually the meaning is clear within the context of the passage, but in this case there is some doubt as to what exactly is meant.
8. J. MacKenzie, *op. cit.*
9. H. MacDonald, 'History of the MacDonalds', written after 1628, *SHS*, Highland Papers, vol. 1, ed. J. R. N. MacPhail, 1914, p. 51.
10. J. Mackenzie, 'The MacKenzies', *SHS*, Genealogical Collections, vol. 1, ed. J. T. Clark (1900), pp. 69–70.
11. J. MacKenzie, *op. cit.*, pp. 43–4.
12. Alexander MacKenzie, *History of the MacKenzies* (1894), p. 191.

APPENDIX I

Ancient Ruins Still Survive

As the song says, 'Ancient ruins still survive, I'm sure you know a few ...' There are some ancient ruins about, and Raasay has its fair share. A short history of some of those on Raasay is given here.

The Broch (Iron Age)

The Broch stands in Borrodale Woods to the west of the Free Church, surrounded by trees. The trees that were planted very close to it have now grown and it is no longer possible to gain any real impression of the structure, as it might have been. In time, when these trees have been cut, it will be possible for further archaeological work to be carried out on this site leading to better knowledge and understanding of the ruin.

The Raasay Broch is of interest as, unlike others, it is oval in shape. It measures 16.5 m × 13.5 m over the walls. These walls are approximately 4 m thick.

For information, a general description of a broch is given here along with a diagram. This is taken from the *Thesaurus of British Archaeology* by Lesley and Roy Adkins.[1]

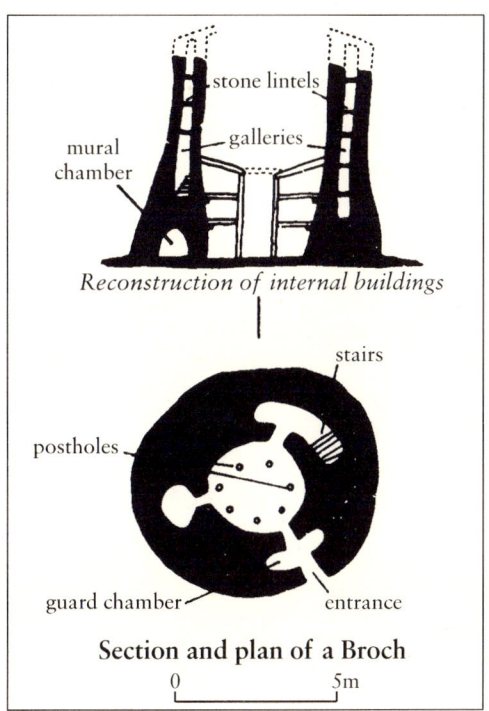

Brochs are found mainly in northern Scotland and the Western and Northern Isles (particularly the Orkneys and Shetlands), singly or in groups. A broch was a circular tower about 10m in internal diameter, with a drystone wall about 5m thick and up to 10m high. The walls had a slight batter on the outer face.

From the first-floor level the wall was usually in two sections about 1m apart, tied together by rows of stone lintels forming superimposed galleries. These were reached by stone staircases. There may have been an upper rampart walk. The ground-floor wall often had galleries and chambers with corbelled roofs. There was usually one entrance to the broch through a narrow passage, often with guard chambers.

Excavations have revealed traces of timber-framed lean-to-huts in the interior. Ledges on the inner wall may have supported an upper floor or gallery. Brochs may have had wooden roofs. They seem to have been built from the second century BC and to have been occupied into the Roman period.

The Dun (Iron Age)

Because brochs are often shown on maps as 'Dun ...' a general description of a dun, from the same source as above, is given.

Plan of a Dun

0   10m

Duns are distributed from south-west Scotland to the Inner Hebrides and northern Scottish mainland. They were fortified homesteads and were circular or oval in plan with drystone walls 3m to 6m thick. They may have been preceded by timber-laced forts.

Galleried duns had walls about 4m thick with an entrance, mural cells, galleries, and stairs, and were similar to brochs. They were about 3m high and up to 20m in internal diameter. There were timber structures in the interior.

Galleried promontory duns had a wall built across the neck of an inland or coastal promontory, the steep sides of which were defended by smaller walls. Larger duns resemble small hillforts, with a thick stone wall enclosing a large area. Some have vitrified timber-laced walls. They were occupied from the late Iron Age to the Roman period. Small forts, duns and brochs in Scotland have been termed the castle complex.

St Moluag's Chapel

The oldest surviving building on Raasay is St Moluag's Chapel, behind Raasay House, at Clachan. It was built in the latter part of the twelfth or early in the thirteenth century, and dedicated to St Moluag, who had been the Bishop of Lismore, where he died in AD 592.

The earliest reference to this church is found in 1501, when Sir Nichol Berchame was granted the parsonage of St Columba's Church in Snizort, together with the its annex of Kilmoluag in Raasay. In 1526, the vicarages of Snizort and Raasay were granted to Donald Monro, following the death of Tormod MacPherson.

In 1549, in his 'Description of the Western Isles of Scotland', Donald Monro said that Raasay had 'one parish church called Kilmoluag'. The next written mention of the church is by Johnson and Boswell in 1773. Johnson says, 'Near the house, at Raasay, is a chapel unroofed and ruinous, which has long been

Ancient Ruins Still Survive

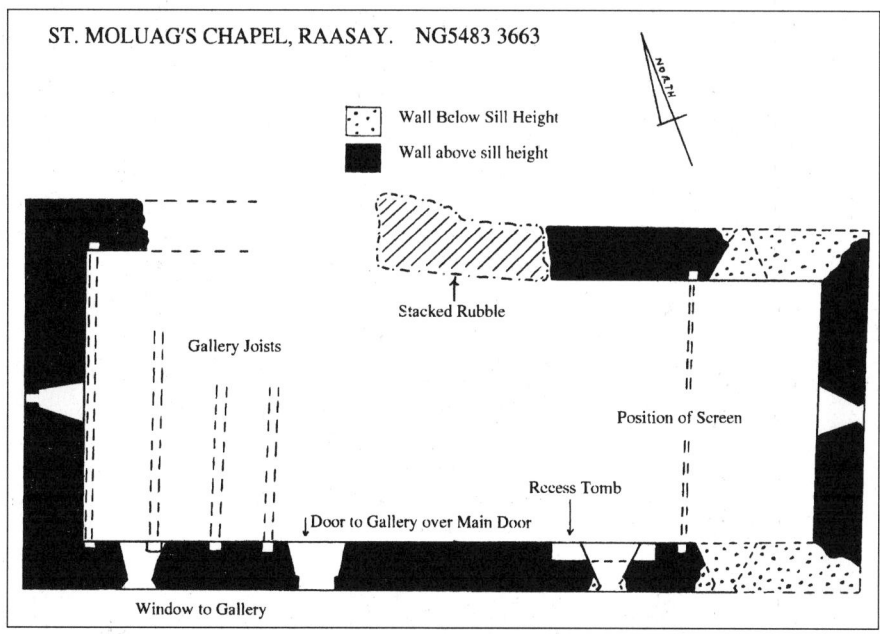

Plan of St Moluag's Chapel by Martin Wildgoose.

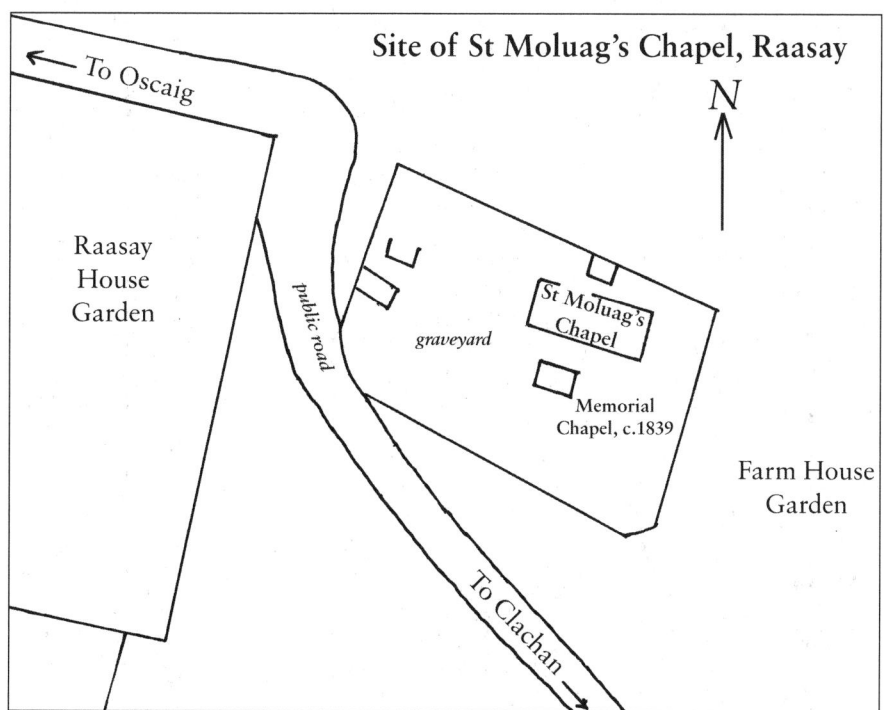

used only as a place of burial.' Boswell makes further observations, but it should be noted that Boswell has a tendency to reversed east and west. He says:

> A little to the west of the house is an old chapel with now no roof upon it. It has never been very curious. I at first imagined it had originally two storeys, from there being holes in the wall as if joists had been there. But Mr Johnson, who is very accurate, found that the holes were not directly opposite to each other in the two walls, and were only defects by the injury of time.

One of these holes held the large human bones of Faobairne MacCuidhein. Boswell continues:

> This chapel appears to have been a good deal filled up with earth. On the floor of it are several gravestones, but without any legible inscriptions. A little to the east of it, I suppose about twelve feet, is a ruin of a burying-place of another tribe of the MacLeods (for there were several in the island), and in the space between the two were some recent graves. On the south of the chapel is the family burying-place. Above the door on the east end of it is a small bust or image of the Virgin Mary, carved upon a stone which makes part of the wall; and to the south of the family burying-place is a smaller one said to be for another tribe. All these ruins are unroofed and full of nettles and other weeds, and look like one cluster at small distance. As they are now in a grove, they have somewhat of a venerable air; at least they affect the mind with pious awe to a certain degree.

In 1786, John Knox commented, 'Immediately behind the house of Raasay are the ruins of an ancient chapel, now used as the family burying place.'

In June 1921, Peter B. Nicolson wrote a description of St Moluag's Chapel.[2] It is not known whether this was done purely from his own research, or whether it was copied from a previous work. He says:

> The ruins of this chapel are situated at an elevation of 100 feet above sea level in a small burial ground about one hundred yards north-east of Raasay House. Both gables and the larger portion of the south wall remain to their original height, but the north wall is now considerably broken down. The ruin has a number of interesting features, details of which are to some extent obscured by obvious changes of ground level, both in the internal and external surroundings. The chapel is roofless and has been orientated north-west and south-east. It measures externally fifty two feet long, twenty-four and a half feet wide at the north-west gable and twenty-one feet wide at the south-east gable.
>
> The walls are three feet thick and there is evidence, especially on the south wall, of structural alterations at different periods. The original door, two feet eight inches wide with chamfered jambs and lintel, was placed sixteen and a half feet from the west end of the south wall, but owing to the configuration of the ground, it now shows only to a height of three feet four inches. It appears to have been built up and substituted by another doorway, traces of which can still be detected in the dilapidated wall on the north.

Immediately above the original doorway, an entrance to a gallery, which was probably reached by an outside wooden stair, has been inserted, but this entrance has also been subsequently built up, and the interior of the chapel afterwards roughly plastered. On the same wall, but towards the east end, there are a round-headed window, splayed internally, and indications of a second window of like construction in a dilapidated portion adjoining the eastern gable. A similar window, three feet five inches in height and ten and a half inches wide, occurs on the south-east gable. This window is chamfered on the outside and splayed internally. There has apparently been another window in the east end of the north wall, but little remains to give any idea of its character.

The western gable has been lit by three apertures, one of which is not now apparent externally. The two others are of lancet form, with the heads cut out of one stone. These lancet windows are chamfered on the outside and all three are splayed internally. The western gable is intaken ten inches to one foot at ten and a half feet above the present interior level and remaining joist holes indicate that there was a gallery at this end. Similar joist holes in the north and south walls at nine feet from the east gable possibly indicate provision for a screen.

Midway in the interior, between the two south wall windows, the upper portion of the tomb recess shows to a height of two feet above the existing internal level.

Lying loose at the foot of a grave in the burial ground is a small cross-slab of red sandstone measuring fifteen and a half, by six and a quarter, by one and a quarter inches. It bears, on the rounded and somewhat mutilated upper portion, the design in low relief of a cross-head with semicircular hollow angles and arms of equal length, connected at their extremities by a ring of glory.

17 June 1921
Peter Bethune Nicolson

Brochel Castle

Brochel Castle is on the north-east coast of the island. It was built during the fifteenth century, with possibly two phases of construction. Both its position and its construction show that its main purpose was defensive. The MacLeods of Raasay lived in it until the time of Iain Garbh. It is believed that he died about 1671. Most of the castle's history is therefore lost in the mists of time, and we are left with only a handful of references to it through the centuries.

The first of these is by Dean Monro who, in 1549, mentions the 'castle of Brochel' and says that it has a 'fair orchard'. One should not expect fruit trees, however, as this refers to a garden, rather than a modern orchard. To the north of the castle ruins, an archaeological survey found an area that had been enclosed within a turf dyke. This may be the castle garden, spoken of by Dean Monro. Within the enclosure are some ruins. The Ordnance Survey map shows 'Chapel, remains of', which may refer to this ruin. Although no other reference to this chapel has been found, it was often the case that castles, such as Brochel, had their own private chapel.

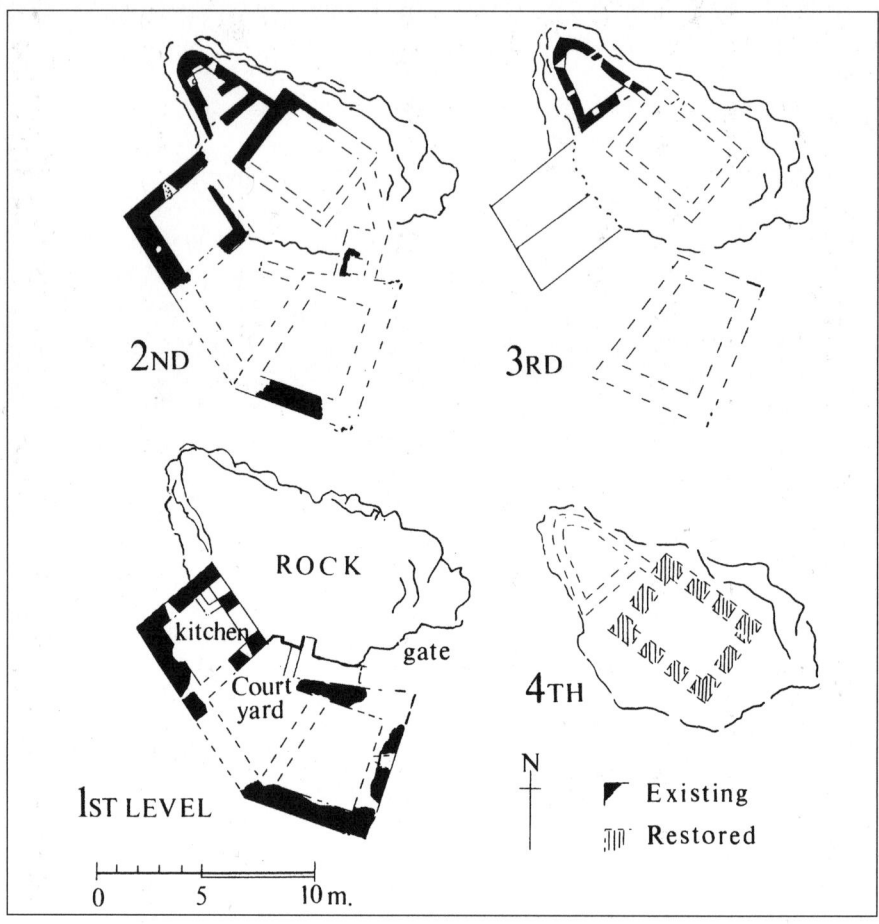

Brochel Castle from *Medieval Castles of Skye and Lochalsh*, R. Miket and D. Roberts. Reproduced by permission of Roger Miket.

James VI tried to bring the Highlands under central control. The more control he had, the greater were the potential revenues for the Crown. In this connection, a survey of the islands' revenue and fighting power was compiled between 1577 and 1595. This refers to 'ane strong little castell in this ile, biggit on the heid of ane heich craig, and is calleit Prokill'. There can be no doubt that Brochel was a strong little castle, built on the head of a high crag.

The MacLeods of Raasay were still living in Brochel when Margaret, a sister of Iain Garbh, married Calum Nicolson of Scorrybreac. A song in celebration of this marriage mentions Brochel.

Doilleir dorch' air oidhche reòta   Dim and dark on a frosty night
Chaidh do bhàt thar Rubha Rònaidh   Your boat went past Rona Point

Dol troimh na caoil a-null a Bhròchaill   Going through the kyles over to Brochel
Dh' amharc air maighdeann an òr fhuilt   To see the gold haired maiden.

About 1695 Martin Martin refers to 'an artificial fort, three stories high, called Castle Vreokle'. By this time, however, Brochel had probably been abandoned. The popular laird, Iain Garbh had died some time before. In 1692, Alasdair MacLeod took possession of the estate, after a legal dispute which had lasted for four years. He, it seems, did not live at Brochel.

In 1773, possibly a hundred years after it had last been inhabited, James Boswell wrote about Brochel castle in some detail. He said:

> The old castle is situated upon a rock very near the sea. The rock is not one mass of stone, but a concretion of pebbles and earth; but so firm that it does not appear to have mouldered. I perceived no pieces of it fallen off. The entry was by a steep stair from the quarter next the sea, of which stair only three or four steps are remaining, all at the top of it. Above them the castle projects, and there is an opening in the wall from which hot water or stones could be thrown upon an invader. Upon entering the gate or door, there was what I never saw before: a sentry box or alcove in the wall on your right hand. The man placed there could only watch in case of noise. He could see nothing. The next advance was to a court or close as it was called, in the centre of four towers, and open above just like any other court of an old castle in the square form. Only that this seemed extraordinary, as you came to it after ascending a stair and entering a gate: but as Mr Johnson observed, it was just an ordinary court, with the difference that the rock here was as the ground in other. The court here was very small. There was a fine well – just a spring in the rock – but it was now filled up with rubbish. One could distinguish tolerably that there had been four towers, but time and storms had left little but ruinous fragments: pieces of wall, pieces of stairs, a part of the battlement to the sea.
>
> There was one small room in one of the towers quite entire. It was a little confined triangular place, vaulted as in the ancient manner. In a corner of it was a square freestone in which was cut an exact circular opening such as in every temple of Cloacina, and from it there appears a clear communication to the bottom, that is to say anything will be carried by the outside of the rock to the bottom. They call this room the nursery, and say the hole was for the children. But I take it to have been the necessary-house of the castle. It was much to find such a convenience in an old tower. I did not imagine that the invention had been introduced into Scotland till in very modern days, from our connexion with England. But it seems we have forgotten something of civilized life that our ancestors knew.

In June 1921, Peter B. Nicolson wrote out a description of Brochel. Whether this was written from personal observation or perhaps copied from an earlier source is not known. He wrote:

> This eyrie-like structure occupies the whole of the summit of an isolated mass of agglomerate Torridon grit and sandstone conspicuously placed in a small crescentic bay that breaks the line of precipitous cliffs forming the northern part of the east coast of the Island of Raasay. A plantation of birch trees

straggles round the face of the brae behind and follows the curve of the bay to the sea face on either side. To the north the view is closed by the rising ground but there is a clear outlook to the Ross-shire coast in front and down the Inner Sound.

Rising from a slight slope the pinnacle of rock all round stands about fifty feet above the terrain though the summit is in two levels, that on the east side being twenty feet above the other. On both levels there are buildings.

The entrance is on the east face and is approached up a rather steep narrow ridge. On the right the bare rock rises to the higher level, on the left the lower level carries the corner of the building on this side. The approach is thus narrowed and there is evidence that originally there was some kind of overbuilding outside the present doorway. The walling on both sides was apparently continued outwards with a chamber above providing a passage roofed with slabs of which only the inner end now exists. Another chamber would seem to have been contrived over this surviving portion of the lintelled passage and beyond this on the level a narrow open way continues between the rocky sides which have been faced with stone for eleven feet or so. In this alley are several recesses large and small. The entrance as a whole is in a tumbled-down condition. Much of the building, having been but a skin on the rock face on either side, has disappeared. The entrance corridor opens upon the middle one of three apartments which occupy the lower level and are angled upon plan to follow the ground. The walls of this middle apartment have almost wholly disappeared. On the short north eastern face the wall is again but a facing on the rock, and then only as high as where the rock overhangs. At the north corner are recesses. The apartment to the east has been about seventeen × eleven or twelve feet, but only one wall and portions of the other two are left. Of the western apartment more remains, and, as laid out, this forms almost a square of eleven feet; but at the north corner what has been the stair projects inwards, while the greater part of the rest of the north east face is occupied by a five feet recess with a slab lintel, the back of which is bare rock. In the north-western wall, on the upper floor, is a narrow window opening or slit splayed inwards; one jamb of which is a single stone, while the other is built up of small stones. Another similar slit in the south-west corner, completes the exceedingly meagre lighting of this apartment, which, like the other, must have had a room over.

The higher level can now be reached only by scrambling up, and of the battlemented tower of two stories which according to William Daniel's view of 1819, occupied the greater part of it, only some indications of the foundations remain. But on the spur of rock projecting to the north-west still stands a small triangular building which adjoined the tower and which on the lower floor contains a couple of narrow through apartments of indeterminate purpose, while the upper floor is a single chamber. In the inner of the lower rooms on the western wall is a garderobe with an external chute. The northern end of the wall of this structure butted against the tower wall. This wing too had an upper floor, lighted by three slits, one of which has been built up, while the lower floor has been lighted by a single slit in the north-east wall. At the apex of the triangle the upper part of the corner is built out on corbels to overhang the tower. About twelve feet high of the building remains with on one face some indication of the parapet in slight projection on a continuous corbel coivise. On the south-western face of the lower building are six of the quarter-round corbels that supported the parapet, part of the lower courses of which is in position near the corner. These are of very small stones and there is no sign of an embrasure but according to the 1819 view the embrasures on the tower, and so no doubt here also, were few – two on a face – and at a rather higher level than the fragment which remains.

The building is in roughly coursed blocks of sandstone and basalt of all shapes and sizes, imbedded in plentiful mortar of shell lime and gravel and is in a very bad state. The walls are nowhere more than 4 feet thick. It may be noted that, in the Daniel picture what looks like an approach and entrance to the right on the lower level cannot have been intended to suggest such as there is no indication of anything of the kind, and, where a door might be expected to exist, there is really a small chute from the interior.

17 June 1921
Peter Bethune Nicolson

Raasay House

In his description of the island in 1549, Dean Monro mentions the building at Clachan. Like Brochel, he describes it as a castle with a garden. Although Monro makes no distinction between these two castles, the one at Clachan does not appear to have been built for defensive reasons as it is not mentioned in the official description written between 1577 and 1595.

In 1695, however, Martin Martin describes it as 'a little tower surrounded by lesser houses'. By then, we are told, the laird had his seat at Clachan, confirming that Brochel was no longer occupied. Martin also mentions 'an orchard with several sorts of berries, pot herbs etc.' at Clachan.

Prior to 1745, possibly as early as 1726 when Malcolm MacLeod of Raasay is known to have mortgaged the lands of Rona and Screapadal, a new building was erected at Clachan. Stone from the older house, probably Martin's 'little tower', was re-used at this time. A cobbled yard, below the present ground level, has been found in the garden of Raasay House. The new building was, therefore, in front of the site of the older one.

In 1746 this new house was burnt by government troops. Boswell says that all but the walls were 'consumed with fire'. Before setting it alight, however, they carefully took out the oak-framed windows, which were put on board a ship and taken to Leith to be sold. When the ship docked at Leith, James MacDonald, a relative of the MacLeods of Raasay, bought the windows and returned them to Raasay.

Rebuilding work began in 1747 and was carried out with some urgency, as John MacLeod, the laird, was obliged to stay elsewhere until it was completed. For at least part of the time, he was with his in-laws in Totaroam, Trotternish. There are signs that this work was carried out quickly, with quality suffering in the process.

Appendix 1

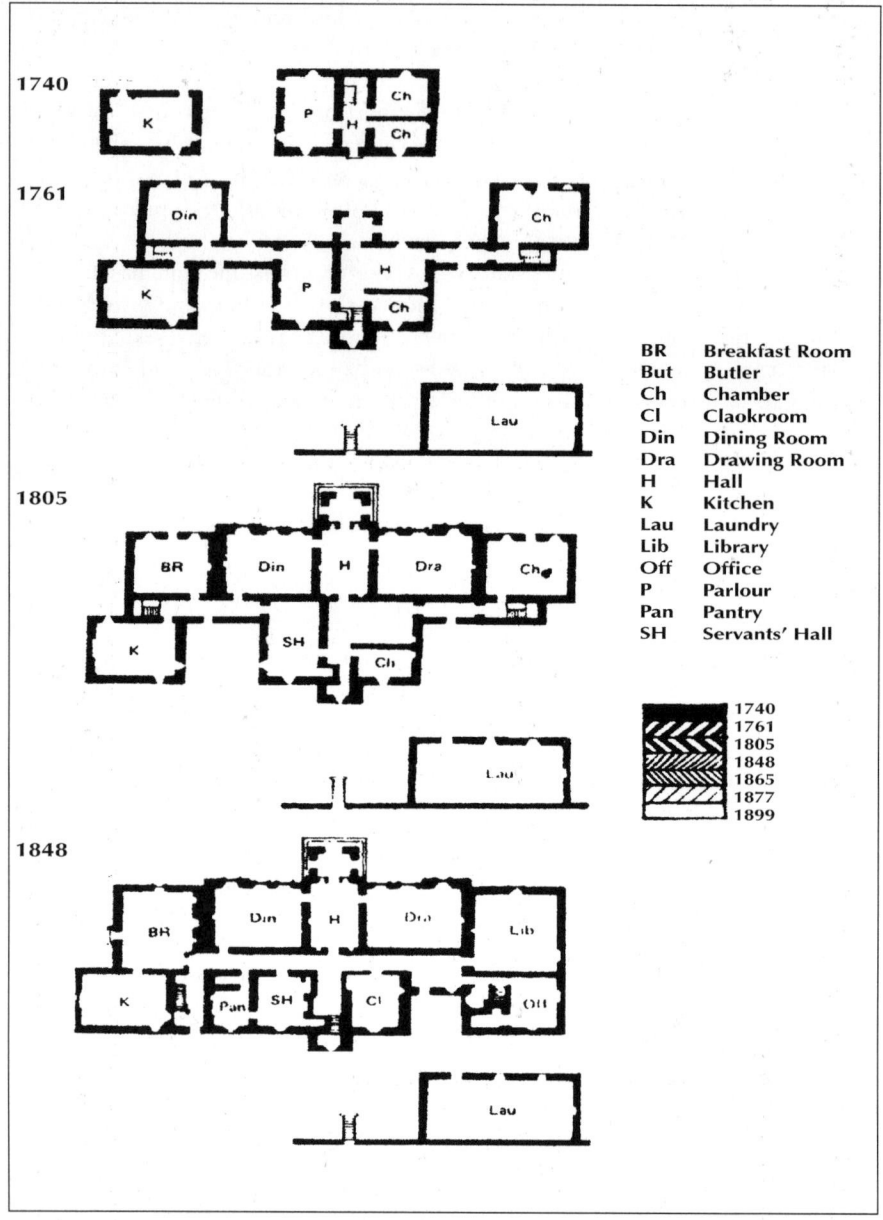

The development of Raasay House from plans by David Roberts. Reproduced here with the kind permission of Mrs Marion Roberts.

Above: Plans of Raasay House showing its development from 1740.

Despite the financial problems of the MacLeods, new building work to Raasay House was begun almost immediately, and by about 1761 the house had almost doubled in size. In 1786, John Knox commented, 'The house of Raasay is

Ancient Ruins Still Survive

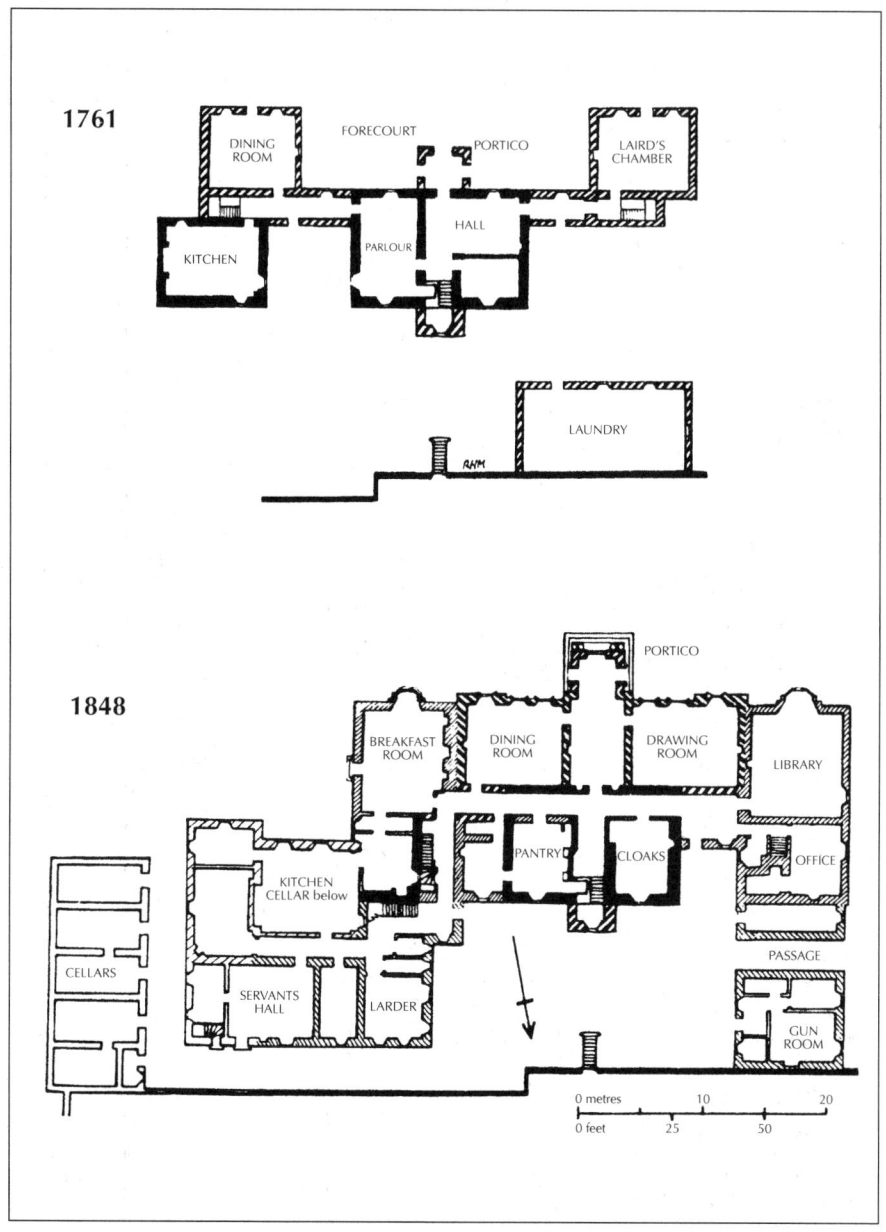

As the house might have been in 1761 (upper), with pavilions set in antis and conjectural portico; and in 1980 (lower), showing the Victorian additions of wings and servants' quarters.

pleasantly situated near the south-west end of the island, which is the most level part of it. It has an extensive and excellent garden and is surrounded with forest trees of considerable magnitude.'

Further extensions were made by James, the next laird, either at the end of the eighteenth or early in the nineteenth century. In 1796 he had a loan of £7 700, probably to finance the works. A new building, to the front of the old house, and other renovation work was carried out. This was the last of the alterations carried out by the MacLeods.

After buying the estate in 1846, George Rainy made alterations and additions to it. His son, George Haygarth Rainy, added the upper floor of the west wing in the 1860s.

Further alterations and a large addition for servants' quarters was made by the Woods after they bought the estate in 1876. After Mr Wood died in 1886, Mrs Wood let Raasay House along with the sporting rights. She and the family lived in Suisnish House while the main house was let.

In 1911 the estate was sold to William Baird & Co. Ltd. They too let Raasay House to a tenant, who also held the Home Farm, Sheep Farm and sporting rights until Bairds sold the greater part of the estate.

In 1923 the Board of Agriculture for Scotland took over the estate. Raasay House was let annually until, in 1937, Mrs Davidson took a twenty-year lease on it to run a 'tourist and sporting hotel'. When she left Raasay in 1960, the hotel closed.

It may be assumed that while Mrs Wood owned the estate, Raasay House was well maintained. It is unlikely that anything more than was absolutely necessary was spent on it between 1911 and 1960. Thus by the time Dr John Green bought it from the Department of Agriculture and Fisheries in 1961, it required extensive refurbishment.

It is interesting to note that Raasay House had been newly built prior to 1745 (possibly as early as the late 1720s). John MacLeod rebuilt it in 1747, and then carried out further alterations, finishing the work possibly about 1761. It was further enlarged and refurbished in the late 1790s. George Rainy modernised the house again in 1848, as did Mr Wood in 1876. Thus Raasay House had had money poured into modernisation and extensions no fewer than five times in the period c.1730–1880, 150 years. During that time, it must be assumed, that any maintenance require would have been speedily executed. Little wonder then, that come 1961, after a period of sixty years with very little maintenance, Raasay House required major refurbishment.

Bought by the Highlands and Islands Development Board from Dr Green in 1979, the greater part of the house is now leased to Raasay Outdoor Centre and is once again the base of the major employer on the island.

Notes

1. L. and R. Adkins, *Thesaurus of British Archaeology* (David & Charles, 1982).
2. Many thanks to Isobel MacLean, Oscaig, for Peter Nicolson's description of St Moluag's Chapel and of Brochel Castle.

APPENDIX 2

Orain Ratharsair
Songs of Raasay

There are three songs given here in the original Gaelic with an English 'translation'. They have been taken from a paper written by Dr Somhairle MacLean for the Gaelic Society of Inverness. As with any translation from an old language, such as Gaelic, the English version can give only some idea of the thoughts and sentiments express in the original. It is also relevant that these songs were composed more than three centuries ago and Gaelic words, in common with all living languages, have changed with time. Many thanks to Miss Mary Gillies, Oscaig and Inverness, for the English version and also to Mr D. R. MacDonald, Braes, Portree for his comments.

Sgoirebreac

It is said that Margaret MacLeod, a sister of Iain Garbh of Raasay, married Calum Nicolson, son and heir of Donald Nicolson, the then chief of the Nicolsons of Scorrybreac. Somhairle's grandmother, Mary MacLean (nee Matheson), and his Aunt Peggie sang this song which could be the celebration of such a marriage.

As with all of these very old songs, there were variants. Dr John MacInnes noted some other lines of this song in 1955, from Mrs Kate Beaton, Woodend, Portree. Dr MacInnes notes:

> I have separated the sections as shown but it was not clear to me where the names of 'Mr John and Mr Donald' were meant to fit. There can be little doubt, however, that these two are Nicolsons of the Sgorabreac family. They only occur in Mrs Beaton's text.

Sgoirebreac

(From Dr Sam MacLean, 'Some Raasay Traditions', *TGSI*, vol. XLIX, pp. 387–8)

Ciad soraidh bhuam fhìn gu m' eòlas
Gu Sgoirebreac am bi' chòisir

ù hoireann ó hì rì oho
ù hoireann ó hì riri rì u
ì hoireann ó hì rì oho

Gu talla farsaing Chlann Dhòmhnaill
Gu taigh mór an ùrlair chòmhnaird

Far am faighte fion ri òl ann
A cupan donna bheòil bhòidhich

mìosairean 's truinnsearan feòdair
's amar bruithidh an eòrna

Deoch cho làidir 's thig o 'n Olaind

'S b' aithne dhomh fhìn beus bu dual dut
'S beus dhe d' bheus bhith suirghe ghruagach

'S ag cur nan geall, 's ann leat bu bhuadhar

'S gheibhte siod an taigh an uasail
Bhith 'g òl fion á pìosan fuara

'N taigh mór farsaing 's urlar sguabte
Ruighleadh ubhal sìos is suas air

'S gheibhte siod an taigh mo leannain
Muc 'ga sgrìobadh 's mart 'ga feannadh

'S coinnleir òir air bhòrdaibh geala

Doilleir dorch' air oidhche reòta
Chaidh do bhàt thar Rubha Rònaidh

Dol troimh na caoil a-null a Bhròchaill
Dh' amharc air maighdeann an òr fhuilt

'S fhuair thu 'chéile 's cha b' i 'n òinid
Cha b' i 'n amaid (ainnis), cha b' i 'n òinnseach

Nighean fir á Caisteal Bhrochaill
A Ratharsair mhóir nan Leòdach
Tìr nan gaisgeach air an òrlaich
Iain mór is Iain Og dhiubh
A shiol Torcuill thig á Leódhas

Scorrybreac

A hundred blessings from me to my homeland
To Scorrybreac where there is festivity

Chorus

To the spacious hall of the children of Donald (Nicolson)
To the big house of the smooth floor

Where wine can be found to drink
From brown cups with lovely lips

Pewter dishes and plates
And a trough to boil barley

Drink as strong as comes from Holland

And I knew that one of your inherent traits
was to woo young women

And in betting you were successful

And in the house of the noble man
Wine would be drunk from cold, silver cups

In the big wide house with swept floor
An apple would roll up and down on it

And you would get that in my sweetheart's house
A pig being scraped and a cow being skinned

And a golden candlestick on white tables

Dim and dark on a frosty night
Your boat went past Rona Point

Going through the kyles over to Brochel
To see the gold haired maiden

And you found a wife and she was not a foolish woman
She was not a silly woman, she was not a stupid woman

Daughter of the man of Brochel Castle
From great Raasay of the MacLeods
Land of heroes on the battle-field
Big John and Young John descended from them
From Siol Thorcaill from Lewis

Further lines were given by Mrs Kate Beaton, Woodend, Portree in 1955.
(From Dr John MacInnes – Gleanings From Raasay Tradition – *TGSI*, vol. LVI,
pp. 15–16)

>Ceud soraidh bhuam fhìn go m'eòlas
>Go Sgorabreac am bi a' chòisir
>Far an dean am marcraich tòirleim
>Chan ionann sin is mar dh'éirich dhomh-sa
>Mi am bothan beag air dhroch còmhdhail
>Bidh siod aig Calum mac Dhòmhnaill
>Ciste nan iuchraichean bòidheach
>Dhe an umha dhe an airgead dhe an òr ann
>An taigh-mór an ùrlair chòmhnaird
>Le seuraichean 'gan cur an ordugh

&c.

>Iain Mór is Iain Og dhiubh
>Bu dhiubh Sileas agus Seònaid
>Is Alasdair am mac a b'òige

&c.

Maighstir Iain is Maighstir Dòmhnall

Lines from Mrs Kate Beaton, collected by Dr John MacInnes in 1955

> A hundred blessings from me to my homeland
> To Scorrybreac where there is festivity
> Where the horsemen leap vigorously
> Not like what has happened to me
> I am in a small bothy in a distressed state
> Calum son of Donald will have
> The chest of the lovely keys
> Of brass, of silver, of gold there
> In the big house of the smooth floor
> With chairs put in order

Big John and Young John descended from them
From them Sileas and Seonaid
And Alasdair the youngest son

Mr John and Mr Donald

Iain Garbh of Raasay drowned in the Minch when returning from Lewis at Easter 1671. Some traditions say that his wet-nurse, a witch, caused his death. She is believed to have made this famous lament. This was the version sung by Somhairle's grandmother and Aunt Peggie.

'S mi 'nam Shuidh' air an Fhaoilinn

(From Dr Sam MacLean, 'Some Raasay Traditions', *TGSI*, vol. XLIX, p. 385.) The third and fourth lines of each verse are the first two lines of the next verse.

'S mi 'nam shuidh' air an fhaoilinn
'S mi gun fhaoilte gun fhuran
Cha thog me fonn aotrom
O Dhi-h-aoine mo dhunaidh

Hì leò:
Hìl ó ro hó:
Hìl ó ro bha hó
Hìl ó ho robhan hìl leò

On a chailleadh am bàta
Is a bhàthadh an curaidh

Siod na fir a bha làidir
Ged a shàraich a' mhuir iad

Gille Calum a b' òige
'S Iain mór, mo sgeul duilich

Ann an clachan gun tràghadh
Tha mo ghràdh-sa air uirigh

Thu gun bhann air do léinidh
'S i gun fheum air a cumadh

Thu gun shìod air do chluasaig
Air lic uaine na tuinne
(or Air leacan fuaraidh na tuinne)

Tha do chlaidheamh 'na dhùblan
'S e fo dhrùdhadh nan uinneag

Có 's urrainn a ghiùlan
No rùisgeas e tuilleadh

Tha do mhìol-chion air iallaibh
'S iad gun triall thun a' mhunaidh

Tha do choinnl' air an smùradh
'S tu gun dùil ri bhi tilleadh.

And I sitting above the shore
And I without cheer, without welcoming joy
I will not raise a lightsome air
Since Friday of my woe.

Chorus

Since the boat was lost
And the hero was drowned

Those were the strong men
Though the sea overpowered them

GilleChaluim the youngest
And Iain Mòr, my sad tale

In a burying place without an ebbing
My beloved is on his couch

You are without a band on your shirt
And it without need for shape

You are without silk on your pillow
On the green slabs under the waves

Your sword is in its scabbard
Soaked by the leaking windows

Who is able to wield it
Or unsheath it evermore

Your hounds are on leashes
And they have not travelled to the hills

Your candle is snuffed out
Without hope of your return

This is another of the many laments that were composed for Iain Garbh. The alternative first two lines were how Somhairle's uncle, Alasdair MacLean, began the song.

'S mi 'nam Shuidh' air an Tulaich

(From Dr Sam MacLean, 'Some Raasay Traditions', *TGSI*, vol. XLIX, p. 386.

'S mi 'nam shuidh' air an tulaich
'S mi ri feitheamh na fàire
Leis an luasgan th' air m' aigne
Chan eil an cadal 'na thàmh dhomh

'S na hé ho
'S na hì rirì
'S na hì u bhì
'S gun thu thighinn fallain i ó

Fhir mhóir o Shiol Torcuill
'S e do chorp a bha làidir
'N am bhith caitheamh a' chuspair
Cha b'e uchdag a' gharlaoich

Tha na staimh dhut 'nan lainmir
Ann an clachan gun tràghadh
T' fhaotainn marbh air a' charraig
Mar ri Calum do bhràthair
(or Mar ri mac Muire Bàine)

Tha a' ghàir-thonn 'gad luasgadh
Is 'gad bhualadh ri stalla
'S tha do ghàirdean gun tuairmse
Ge bu chruaidh e na 'n darach

An alternative first two lines are

'Seal a mach an e 'n là e
'S mi ri feitheamh na fàire

And I sitting on the hillock
And I awaiting the dawning
With the upheaval that's on my spirit
Sleep is not a rest for me

Chorus

Big man of Siol Thorcaill
It's your body that was strong
When it came to shooting at a mark
You did not pant like a weakling

The seaweed is a brightness for you
In the burial ground without ebb
Finding you dead on the rock
Along with Calum your brother
(or with the son of Fair Mary)

The turbulent waves are tossing you
And knocking you against the rocks
And your arm is without co-ordination
Though it was harder than oak

An alternative first two lines are

Look out to see if it is daylight
And me awaiting the dawn

Raasay by Neil Nicolson. Thanks to Mrs Isobel MacLean, Oscaig, for the following poem. It is believed to have been composed by Neil Nicolson, a son of Peter Nicolson. Peter had the shop at Mill Place, Raasay, after he moved from Fearns. Neil lived for a time at the Orchard Cottage.

Raasay

I dream of an island so wondrously fair,
Where birds greet the dawn with a rapturous air,
And the sun's last rays weave a carpet of gold,
Adorning all nature; God's love to unfold,
Such is my heritage, I'll tarry no more,
But haste to my kinsfolk, on sweet Raasay's shore.

Island of youthful days,
Sweet Isle of bardic lays,
Lulled by the lap of waves,
Kissed by the sun.
Woodlands e'er fresh and green,
Brooklets and mountain stream,
Nectar of exile's dream,
When day is done.

Speed my course swiftly in tempest and lashing wave,
Or calm sea that mirrors the hill and the crag,
Slack not the sail till we reach all my heart doth crave,
Where dwells the heron, the eagle and stag.

Neil Nicolson

Some details of this accident can be found in Chapter 7. It is believed that W. Geddes, Aberdeen, translated this poem from the original Gaelic. It is not known, however, who he/she was. Thanks to Norrie Gillies for a copy of this poem. It is given here as found.

In memory of JOHN NICOLSON and MURDO GILLIES and a lad (ANGUS GILLIES) the son of John Gillies, the crew of the fishing boat of Torran, Raasay, which was lost, and the above named fishermen, in the Sound of Raasay, off Skye, while returning home from Portree, on Saturday, 7 February 1885.

> Oh! Raasay, tell to me the cause
> Of this sorrow all around,
> Where joy was wont at early morn
> Alas now grief is found.
>
> On Raasay the gloom of sorrow rests,
> While eyes with tears down flow,
> To part with those we dearly loved,
> Our hearts do rend with woe.
>
> That morn was hailed by willing hands,
> And hearts so brave and free;
> The sails were set, they make the shore,
> Arriving at Portree.
>
> While there they stayed a few short hours,
> For soon their work was o'er;
> The sails were set, they steered for home,
> But never reached the shore.
>
> How little did we think last time
> We parted on the shore
> When all seemed well, God's speed to them,
> But now their journey's o'er.
>
> How sad to think, no eye was near,
> No helping hand to save,
> But in the swelling seas they sank,
> Beneath the stormy wave.
>
> Yet though the ocean be their grave,
> Till Jesus come again,
> When Victory shall be conqueror,
> The power of death be slain.

Now hushed for ever is their voice
   They're now by death set free;
Nor can we see their smiling face,
   Oft filled our hearts with glee.

Their wives and children left to mourn,
   O Lord them shield while here:
May they, in faith, look up to Thee,
   And to Thy throne draw near.

Then let us live, O Lord, for Thee,
   To love Thee more and more;
Then we shall meet no more to part,
   But live for evermore.

W. Geddes, Aberdeen

Although better known for his novels, Neil Munro also wrote poetry relating to the First World War. This lament is for 'Allan Ian Og Macleod of Raasay' who died at the Battle of Loos (June 1915) while serving with an English regiment.

Lament for Macleod of Raasay

Allan Ian Og Macleod of Raasay,
Treasure of mine, lies yonder dead in Loos,
His body unadorned by Highland raiment,
Trammelled, for glorious hours, in Saxon trews.
Never man before of all his kindred
Went so apparelled to the burial knowe,
But with the pleated tartan for his shrouding,
The bonnet on his brow.

My grief! that Allan should depart so sadly,
When no wild mountain pipe his bosom wrung,
With no one of his race beside his shoulder,
Who knew his history and spoke his tongue.
Ah! lonely death and drear for darling Allan!
Before his ghost had taken wings and gone,
Loud would he cry in Gaelic to his gallants,
'Children of storm, press on!'

Beside him, when he fell there in his beauty,
Macleods of all the islands should have died;
Brave hearts his English! – but they could not fathom
To what old deeps the voice of Allan cried,
When in that strange French countryside, war-battered,
Far from the creeks of home and hills of heath,
A boy, he kept the old tryst of his people
With the dark girl Death.

O Allan Ian Og! O Allan aluinn!
Sore is my heart remembering the past,
And you of Raasay's ancient gentle children
The farthest-wandered, kindliest and last.
It should have been the brave dead of the islands
That heard ring o'er their tombs your battle-cry,
To shake them from their sleep again, and quicken
Peaks of Torridon and Skye!

> Gone in the mist the brave Macleods of Raasay,
> Far furth from fortune, sundered from their lands
> And now the last grey stone of castle Raasay
> Lies desolate and levelled with the sands;
> But pluck the old isle from its roots deep planted
> Where tides cry coronach round the Hebrides,
> And it will bleed of the Macleods lamented,
> Their loves and memories!
>
> *Neil Munro*

It is now believed that 'Allan Ian Og Macleod of Raasay' was an invention, based in part on Captain John Lockhart Wood (1871–1915) of the 18th Hussars. His father had bought the Raasay estate in 1876. Captain Wood's mother sold the Raasay estate in 1911. It may also be significant that Neil Munro's own son, Hugh, was killed in September 1915 at the Somme. This information is taken from 'Neil Munro and 'the last of the Raasay MacLeods' – Unravelling a Literary Mystery' by Donald Gillies (*Para Graphs*, 11, 2002).

If the name is indeed fictitious, it is curious that the name 'Allan' was chosen. If, as suspected, the MacLeods of Raasay were descended from the MacLeods of Gairloch, the name 'Allan' is significant. The first of the Gairloch MacLeods, for whom any substantive information exists, was Allan MacLeod who lived about the end of the fifteenth century. For more information, see Part II – Genealogy.

APPENDIX 3

Some place-names of Raasay and Rona

The following lists give some idea of the variety of place-names that exist within a small area. Also included is one version of 'The Wells of Raasay'. There may be others. Sources of clean water that were unlikely to dry up, even if the weather was dry for a time, were important.

Tobraichean Ratharsair (The Wells of Raasay)

Tobar Mòr Shuidhisnis 'Suil na Mnatha
Struthan Lag a'chrò anns an Fearna
Tobar na Creachainn an Òscaig
Tobar an Dòmhnaich's a Ghleann
Tobar an Fiar air Thobhtagan
Tobar a'Bhiorain ann an Glac nan Curran
Cuairneag Hallaig
Tobar Sìle Mhaoir – Ard na Bràthan
Tobar Sheagarraidh.

CLACHAN TO OSCAIG
1. *Ard na Bràthan* — Headland of the Quern Stones
2. *An Tigh Còinneach* — Moss House
3. *Bealach na Cobh-Laraich* — Pass (of the victory battleground ?)
4. *Creagan Beaga* — Small Rocks
5. *Aird Ghiuthais* — Point of the Pines
6. *Rudha na Fainge* — Point of the Fank (North point of Aird Ghiuthais)
7. *Creag na Cailleach* — Old Woman's Rock
8. *An Cùil* — The Back
9. *Cùil nam Paircean* — The Back of the Parks
10. *Allt a' Roller (burn at south cattle grid at Oscaig)*
11. *Cairidh Làthach* — Silted Fish-trap (a sea-wall enclosure)

OSCAIG TO HOLOMAN
12. *Allt na Mòine* — Burn of the Peat
13. *Na Stacannan* — The Stacks
14. *Bruach na Stacannan* — Brae of the Stacks
15. *Allt Thomais* — Thomas's Burn

HOLOMAN TO BALACHUIRN
16. *Bad a'Choill* — Clump of Wood
17. *An Iar Ghabhail* — The Western Approaches
18. *Am Bealach Fiaraidh* — Crooked Pass

19. Cul a'Bhealaich — Back of the Pass
20. Bealach a'Mhaoirich — Pass of the Shellfish

BALACHUIRN
21. An Gleannan — The Little Glen
22. Am Punnd — The Pound (as in impound)
23. A'Chreag Bheag — Little Rock
24. Druim an t-seanna Bhaile — The Back (or Ridge) of the Old Township
25. An Cnoc Mòr — Big Hill
26. A'Bhuaile — The Fold
27. Glac a'Chapuil — Hollow of the Horse
28. Achadh nan Caorach — Field of the Sheep
29. Loch a'Roid — Loch of the Bogmyrtle
30. Loch Cròdain — Loch of the Gurnet
31. Sgeir nam Bodach — Rock of the Old Men
32. Loch Eadar da Bhaille — The Loch between Two Villages

BALMEANACH TO GLAM
33. A'laprach Bhuidhe — The Yellow Swamp
34. An Drochaid Mhòr — Big Bridge
35. Gob Eadar da Abhainn — Point between Two Rivers
36. Pol a'Bhainne — Moss of the Milk
37. Na Lianagan Gorma — Green Meadows
38. Pairce nan Each — Horse Park
39. A'Sgàlan — (Scales or Trough ?)
40. An Sgéithe Bhàn — White Promontory
41. Sléitbheinn — Moor or Hill
42. An Coire Beag — Little Corry
43. An Spinnein — The Pinnacle (?)

GLAM NORTHWARDS
44. A'Ghearradh Mhòine — Peat Cutting
45. Bothag nan Deargadan — Fleas Bothy
46. An Carn Mòr — Big Cairn
47. Am Bealach Ruadh — Red Pass
48. Lianag Fir Oscaig — Meadow of the Oscaig Men
49. Cnoc nan Uan — Lambs' hill
50. Crudha an Eich — Horse shoe (a bend in the road)
51. Loch an Leanna — Beer Loch (there was a still there)
52. Lon a'Strath — Bog of the Strath

EAST SIDE
53. Ratharsair Bheag — Little Raasay
54. Achadh Àth — Field of the Kiln
55. Bealach na Coinneal — Pass of the Candle
56. An Tòr — The Heap
57. A'Chreag — The Rock.

SOME OTHER NAMES
58. Coille Mhòr — Big Wood
59. Sgeir Choinneach — Kenneth's Rock

60.	Sgeir a Mheallan	Rock of the Lump (Meallan – hillock or lump)
61.	Geodha na Caluman	Creek of Pigeons
62.	Baile nan Cipean	Tether-peg Township
63.	Ceann nan Cnoc	End of the Hill
64.	Lag gun Daoine	Hollow without People
65.	Uamha Mhòr	Big Cave (no longer there – south of Suisnish House)
66.	Glac Dhorcha	Dark Hollow
67.	Glac na Curran	Hollow of the Carrots
68.	Allt na Bothaig	Burn of the Hut
69.	Faolin Eighre	The Raised Beach at Eyre
70.	Tota Clann Iain Mòr	Ruin of the family of Iain Mòr MacSween
71.	Corran Eighre	Eyre Point
72.	The Stable	at Hallaig
73.	Gleanan Eighre	The Little Glen of Eyre
74.	Geodha Riabhaig	Chasm of the Hedge Sparrow
75.	Guala na Marbh	The Shoulder of the Dead
76.	Lonbàn	Fair Field

Place-names from Charlie MacLeod

Place-names of Torran

WEST SIDE – COASTAL NAMES FROM FLADDA HARBOUR SOUTHWARDS

1.	Carn nam Meann	Cairn of the Kids
2.	Allt Mòr	Big Burn
3.	Allt Beag	Small Burn
4.	Lag Mòr	Big Hollow
5.	Cùl Phort	Black Port
6.	Coille Bheag	Small Wood
7.	Na Trì Gheòdhaidhean	The Three Creeks
8.	Am Fraoch Eilean	Heather Island
9.	Rudh nan Spor	Quartz Point
	(usually known as Gob na h-Àirde: spor means quartz)	

TURNING INTO LOCH ARNISH

10.	Rudh na Cruaiche Mona	Peatstack Point
11.	Camus na Feannag	Crows Inlet
12.	Sgeir Chamus na Feannag	Sea Rock of Crows Inlet
13.	Geòdha Chalum mac Ruairidh	Creek of Malcolm son of Roderick
14.	Geòdha na Caillich	Old Woman's Creek
15.	Eilean an t-Sluichd Bhig	Island of the Small Hollow
16.	An Slochd Beag	The Small Hollow
17.	Port an Torrain	Port of Torran
18.	Sgeir an Doire Dhuibh	Sea Rock of the Black Grove (Black Hollow)
19.	Geòdha na Poite	Pot Creek
20.	Iochdar na Losaid	Lower Losaid (Baking Trough)
21.	Geòdha a Ghrianain	Sunny Creek
22.	Eilean Geò' a Ghrianain	Island of Sunny Creek

23. *Lamarig an Leòdhasich* — Lewisman's Landing
24. *Ceann a Ghàraidh (Boundary)* — End of Dyke

EAST SIDE SOUTHWARDS FROM UMACHAN
25. *Lochan na Faochag* — Pool of the Whelks
26. *A Chreag Gharbh* — Rough Rock
27. *Geòdha Meall a Gheòidh* — Goose Hill Creek
28. *Lamarig Clann 'ic Ailean* — Landing-place of Allan's Children
29. *Meall an Doire Mholaich* — Hill of the Hairy Hollow
30. *Eiginn Allt* — Burn of Distress

PATCHES OF ARABLE LAND ABOUT TORRAN, FROM THE MISSION BUILDING NORTHWARDS
31. *Am Budha Roide* — Bog Myrtle Hollow
32. *Culduibh (behind Nicolson's house)* — Black Background
33. *An Losaid* — Baking Trough
34. *Gead a Ghrianain* — Sunny Rig
35. *Lòn Dubh* — Black Ground
36. *Lòn na buaile* — Ground of the (Cattle) Fold
37. *Lòn Liath (east of the footpath, above cliff)* — Grey Ground
38. *A Ghead Chruaidh* — The Hard Rig
39. *Buaile a Phuirt* — (Cattle) Fold of the Port
40. *A Ghlac Mhòr* — The Big Glen

The last two are north of Port an Torrain. There was also some arable land in Àird which was cultivated until about 1936.

INLAND NAMES
41. *Meall an Torrain* — Torran Hill (Meall is actually 'Lump')
42. *Creag an Rùd* — Rock of the Ram
43. *Meall Dearg* — Red Hill
44. *Guala an Lochain* — Shoulder of the Pool
45. *Clais a Ghuail* — Coal Ditch
46. *An Leac Bhàn* — White Slab
47. *Meall an Dabhaidh* — Scorched Hill
48. *An t-Easan Dubh* — Little Black Waterfall
49. *An Carn Mòr* — Big Cairn
50. *Creag nan Speirag* — Rock of the Sparrow-hawks
51. *Lag an Eich Bhuidhe* — Hollow of the Yellow Horse

The last three are above Torran School.

52. *Cnoc a Ghrianain* — Sunny Hill
53. *Cul a Ghrianain* — Sunny Background
54. *An Cladh* — The Cemetery
55. *An Cnoc Eòrna (above the Mission House)* — Barley Hill

ON TORRAN MOOR
56. *Na Feath Lochain* — The Calm Pools
57. *Bealach an t-Slugain* — Gap of the Gullet
58. *Faire an Da Mhuir* — Sight of Two Seas

Some place-names of Raasay and Rona

59. Glac an Sgiamhaich — Glen of the Wildcat

Place-names of North Arnish

EAST SIDE, SOUTHWARDS FROM EIGINN ALLT

60. Totaichean Tigh Ailean Bhig — Ruins of Little Allan's House
61. An Drip — (Meaning is unknown)
62. Ministeir Dubh na Drip — Black Minister of 'Drip' (actually a black stone)
63. A Chreag Mhàsach — Rock with a prominent base or bottom
64. Na h-Uird Bhàirnich — The Limpet Hammers
65. Rudha Slochdag an Innil — unknown
66. Sgeir an Fheadain Ghairbh — Rock of the Rough Chanter
67. An Feadan Garbh — The Rough Chanter
68. Am Feadan Mìn (Boundary with South Arnish) — The Fine Chanter

(In each case the 'Chanter' is a long, steep gorge)

NORTH ARNISH MOOR, FROM TORRAN MOOR SOUTHWARDS

69. Loch nan Dubhan — Loch of the Hooks
70. A Chlach Tholltach — Tunnelled Stone. Several boulders with a passage between.
71. Sgardan Nic Mhannain — Miss Buchanan's Ledge
72. Loch Airigh na h-aonaich — Loch of the Moorland Shieling
73. Loch ann an Creithal — Loch in a Cradle
74. Meall na Bruthaich — Hill of the Slope
75. Buaile' Bhudha — Fold of the Flat Ground
76. Clach a Scuinn — unknown

STARTING FROM THE BOUNDARY BELOW TORRAN SCHOOL

77. An Staca Buidhe — The Yellow Stack
78. Port Arnis — Port Arnish
79. Gob na Saorach — Point of the Whinstone Dyke

(Geological dykes or veins are common in North Raasay)

80. Talamh a Chladaidh — Shore Ground

FURTHER INLAND AND AROUND THE CROFTS

81. Am Budha Cruinn (behind the school) — The Round Flat Ground
82. Glàm na Crìche — Boundary Plain
83. An Leac Riabhach — The Brindled Slab
84. A Chist Uisge — The Water Chest
85. Guala nam Ploc — Shoulder of the Turfs
86. An t-Allt Nigheadh — Washing Burn
87. An Tulchan — The Knoll
88. An t-Iomaire Rainnich — Bracken Rig
89. Lòn Dubh — Black Ground
90. An Tota Bhreac — The Speckled Ruin
91. Lag Arnis — Arnish Hollow
92. Cnoc na h-Uinnseann — Hill of the Ash Trees
93. An Àtha Bheag — The Little Kiln

94. Uchd na Saorach   The Hump of the Natural Dyke

Place-names of South Arnish

EASTERN SHORE SOUTHWARDS FROM NORTH ARNISH BOUNDARY
95. Chreag Ghaineamhich   Sandy Rock
96. A Ghobhar (sea rock)   The Goat
97. Bhannsgail   unknown
98. Geòdha na Bà Doinne   Creek of the Brown Cow
99. Creag Nèill   Neil's Rock
100. Rugha Chreag na Gaoithe   Point of the Windy Rock
101. Uirigh nam Fiadh   Ledge of the Deer
102. Rudha Phuill Bhric   Point of the Speckled Pool
103. Camus Bàn (end of the stone dyke) White Inlet
104. Chlach Uaine   Green Stone
105. Camus Crithionn   Aspen Inlet
106. Rudh Aird Ghlaisean   Grey Promontory
107. Camus a Mhaide   Inlet of the Wooden Beam
108. Port a Mheirlich (boundary fence). Thief's Port

WEST SIDE OF LOCH ARNISH, FROM BOUNDARY FENCE SOUTHWARDS
109. Geòdha nan Cat   Creek of the Cats
110. Camus Beag   Little Inlet
111. Geòdha an Eilean Dhuibh   Black Island Creek
112. An t-Eilean Dubh   Black Island
113. Uirigh na Bà Ìridh   Ledge of the Sable Cow
114. Gob an Rudha   Promontory Point
115. Camus a Bhudh-allt   Flat Burn Inlet
116. Rudha Crithionn   Aspen Point
117. An Tairbairt   Tarbert
118. Sgeirean Ian 'ic Dhonnchaidh   Sea Rocks of John son of Duncan
119. An s-Stroin Ruadh   Rust-coloured Point
120. Creag an Tairbh   Bull Rock
121. Port an Alltain   Port of the Streamlet
122. Eilean Leathad Charrain (boundary Island of Scurvy-grass Slope
     fence)

INLAND NAMES FROM NORTH BOUNDARY ON THE EAST SIDE
123. Cnoc na h-Airigh   Shieling Hill
124. Na h-Achaidhean   The Fields
125. Bealach nan Achaidhean   Gap of the Fields
126. Creag na Gaoithe   Windy Rock
127. Meall Meadhonach   Middle Hill
128. Glac an t-Sithean Mhòir   Big Hill Valley
129. An Sithean Mòr   Big Hill
130. Glac an Fhuchdadair (stone dyke Fuller's Valley
     right through)
131. Chreag Bhàn   Fair Rock
132. Glac a Chamuis Chrithionn   Valley of Aspen Inlet
133. Creag na Caillich   Old Woman's Rock

134.	An Doire Mòr	The Great Hollow
135.	An Lòn Còmhnard	The Flat Ground

WESTWARDS FROM THE SOUTH-EAST BOUNDARY FENCE

136.	Loch nan Oitir	Loch of the Reefs
137.	Loch Beag	Little Loch
138.	Lòn Cruinn (above land formerly cultivated at Port an Alltain)	Round Ground
139.	Lòn an Ear	East Ground
140.	Lòn an Iar (last two are peatland)	West Ground
141.	Torr nan Aighean	Mound of the Hinds
142.	Bealach Doire Polaig	Gap of the Hollow of the Pits
143.	Lòn Fearna (near Tarbert)	Alder Flat
144.	Chromleachd	Slope of Slabs
145.	Am Bealach Lachdunn	Swarthy Gap

AROUND THE SOUTH ARNISH CROFTS

146.	An Camus Beag (a patch of arable land above Camus Beag)	
147.	Cnoc is Doire	Hill and Grove
148.	Buaile Bhuntata	Potato Ground
149.	An Riasg	Dirk-grass Ground
150.	Cnoc an Rudhain Duibh	Black Heap Hill
151.	Cnoc Talamh Iain Bhain	Hill of Fair John's Ground
152.	Talamh Alasdair Dhòmhnuil	Alexander son of Donald's Ground
153.	Glac na Fainge	Fank Valley
154.	Cnoc an t-Sithean	Hill of the Knoll
155.	Ghuala Bhuidhe	Yellow Shoulder
156.	Bealach na Buaile Bhuntata	Gap of the Potato Plot

Place-names from Duncan Macswan of Rona to Dualchas Museum

Place-names of Rona, principally coast names, in a circuit of the island from Caol Ronaidh, beginning in the south-east and sailing north round the island, going south, taking in the place-names of the west side to Eilean Phladaigh.

Caol Ronaidh, including

1.	Eilean Taighe	Isle of the House
2.	Eilean an Fhraoich	Heather Isle
3.	Sgeir nan Eun	Bird Rock
4.	An Garbh Eilean	Rough Island
5.	Doire na Guailla	Grove of the Shoulder
6.	Rubha an Eireannaich	Irishman's Point
7.	An Doire Seilach	Grove of Willows
8.	Tairbeart	Narrows (of land)
9.	Meall Dearg	Red Blunt Hill
10.	Acarsaid Iain 'ic Dhonnchaidh	Ian son of Duncan's Harbour
11.	Sgeir nan Gobhar	Goat Rock
12.	A' Chaoidh	Weeping

13.	Uamh an Fhuamhair	Cave of (the ?) Giant – Kirk Cave
14.	Port a Creadha	Port of Clay
15.	An Geodha Uisge	The Water Harbour
16.	Creag na h-Eigheach	Rock of the Shouting
17.	Port Doire nan Earb	Port of Roe-deer Grove
18.	Geodha an Taighe Dhuibh	Harbour of the Black House (possibly a still)
19.	Creag a Ghaisidh Dhuibh	Rock of the Black Torrent ?
20.	Geodha an Uillt	Harbour of the Burn
21.	Sgeir an Dunain	Castle Rock
22.	Eilean an Dunain	Castle Island
23.	Carn Gorm	Blue Cairn
24.	Creag a' Phruis	Rock of the Priest ?
25.	Geodha an Taileir	Tailor's Harbour
26.	Port a' Gharbh Ghaineimh	Port of Rough Sand
27.	A' Chuil	The Nook or Corner
28.	A' Chreag Ghairnmhich	Rock of Sand
29.	An Acarsaid Fhalach	Concealed Harbour
30.	Geodha Bolaig	?
31.	An Dunan Odhar	Brown Castle or Heap
32.	Doireachan Dubha	Black Groves
33.	Geodha na Maighdinn	Harbour of the Maiden
34.	Am Braidhig	?
35.	Rubha na Cloiche Fluiche	Point of the Wet Stone
36.	Meall na Làthaich	Hill of the Silt (above a nearby swamp)
37.	An Dreathan Donn	The Brown Wren
38.	An Roinn (where the lighthouse is)	Point
39.	Geodha an Rudha	Harbour of the Point
40.	Na Gamhnaichean	Sandy Rock
41.	Camus na Beiste	Bay of the Beast (otter ?)
42.	Cladh Nighean Righ na Greige	Danish Princess's Grave
43.	Camus na h-Athann Moire	Bay of the Big Ford ? (could be Big Kiln)
44.	Eilean Dubh nam Meann	Black Isle of the Young Roe
45.	Sgeir nan Stearnan	Rock of the Terns
46.	Sgeir na h-Iolaire	Rock of the Eagle
47.	An Rubha Dearg	Red Point
48.	An Seolaidair	The Sailor
49.	Carn Iain Ghairbh	Ian's Rough Cairn
50.	Sgeir Bhuidhe na Roinne	Yellow Rock of Peninsula
51.	Creag nan Sgarbh	Cormorant Rock
52.	An Sgeir-Thraghad	Rock that Ebbs
53.	Camus an Daimh	Bay of the Stag
54.	Sgeir nan Faoileag	Seagull Rock
55.	Eilean Chaluim Mhoir	Big Calum's Rock
56.	Ob an Dreallaire	Bay of the Loiterer
57.	Meall Talamh Anna	Hill of Anne's Ground
58.	An Roinn	The Peninsula
59.	An Sithean Uaine	Green Knowe
60.	Loch Bhraighig	Loch of the Summit
61.	An Aird Sheilich	Willow Point
62.	An Aird Dubh	Black Cliff

Some place-names of Raasay and Rona

63.	An Dreallaire	The Loiterer
64.	Ob an Roinn	Peninsula Bay
65.	An t-Ob Lobhte	The Bay of the Rottenness (putrid or smelling)
66.	Bord Cruinn	Circular Table
67.	An t-Ob Gainmich	Sandy Bay
68.	Eilean na h-Athann	Isle of the Ford
69.	Acarsaid Bhlarain	Harbour of the Plain
70.	Stroin a' Bhocaich	Sharp Point of Kids
71.	Ob a'Bhocain	Bay of Kids
72.	Rubha an Sgath Mhoire	Point of the Big Wing
73.	Port an Fhearainn	Port of the Men
74.	Port na Ba Brice	Port of Speckled Cow
75.	Ob nam Fiasgan	Bay of the Mussel
76.	Rubha na Laire Baine	Point of the White Mare
77.	Port an Fhuinn	Port of the Soil
78.	Sloc an Dobhar-Chu	Hollow of the Mythical Otter
79.	Sgur nam Boc	Rough Peak of the He-Goat
80.	A' Ghlaic Chuilinn	Holly Dale
81.	Geodha na Comhla	Harbour of the Company
82.	Eilean nan Lion	Island of the Nets
83.	Sgeir Garradh na Cairidh	Rock of the Dyke (Cuddy Trap ?)
84.	An Acarsaid Thioram	Dry Harbour
85.	Geodha Riabhaig	Cove of the Lark
86.	Geodha Caitriona	Catriona's Creek
87.	Meall Dearg	Blunt Red Peak
88.	Gob a' Mhill	Lumpy Beak
89.	Doire nan Diosgan	Grove of the Creaking
90.	An Acarsaid Mhor	Big Harbour
91.	Tigh Rhonaidh	The House of Rona
92.	An Garbh Eilean	Rough Island
93.	Geodha na Cuileag	Creek of Flies
94.	An Dubh-Chamus	Black Bay
95.	Port an Teampul	(Chapel, and burial ground of the Grahams)

APPENDIX 4

Document Sources

Most of these documents are given in Latin, with an English translation, by Richard Sharpe in his book *Raasay: a Study in Island History: Documents and Sources, People and Places*, where they will be found on the pages indicated.

Crown Charter of 1511

The estate of Lewis had been forfeited in 1506 because Torcall, chief at that time, had strongly supported a bid to revive the Lordship of the Isles. A Crown charter of 1511, granted by James IV, restored the lands of Lewis to the MacLeods. However, the estate was not restored to Torcall, but to his younger brother, Calum MacLeod. The Latin charter, and its translation, is as given by Richard Sharpe, *Documents and Sources*, p. 64:

Apud Edinburgh, 29 Jun.
REX concessit et pro bono servitio quitteclamavit MALCOLMO MAKCLODE filio et heredi quondam Rory Makcolde de Lewis, et heredibus dicti Malc., – terras et castrum de Lewis et Wattirnes, infra dominium Insularum: terras de Assent, infra comitatum de Sutherland, et terras de Coidgeaich, infra vic. Rossie, vic. Invernys: cum fortaliciis, domibus, edificis, lacubus, piscationibus, advocatione et donatione ecclesiarum et capellaniarum, una cum molendinis annexis etc:- quequidem in manibus regis ratione forisfacturae, nonintroitus seu alias extiterunt: – et quas rex incorporavit in unam liberam baroniam et dominium de Lewis et castrum de Stornochway voluit principale messuagium fore earundem: REDDEND: regi servitium debitum et consuetum: salva comiti de Sutherland superioritate terrarum de Assent si de eo prius tenebantur. TEST.

At Edinburgh, 29 June 1511
The KING has granted and in return for loyal services has released to Calum MacLeod, son and heir of the late Ruairidh MacLeod of Lewis, and to the heirs of the said Calum, all claim on the lands and castle of Lewis and Vaternish, in the Lordship of the Isles: the lands of Assynt in the County of Sutherland, and the lands of Coigeach, part in Ross and part in Inverness, together with the fortalices, houses and buildings, lochs and fisheries, the advowson and presentment of churches and chapels, and also the attached mills etc. These lands came into the King's hands by reason of forfeiture, nonentry or other means. The King has conjoined them into one free barony and Lordship of Lewis, and has wished that the castle of Stornoway be the principal seat of the same. Due in return: the accustomed service owed to the King, and greeting to the Earl of Sutherland, as superior of the lands of Assynt, formerly held of him. Witnessed etc.

This charter of 1511 describes the lands of the MacLeods of Lewis as – the lands of Lewis, Waternish (Skye), Assynt and Coigeach. The king has also created these lands into 'one free barony and Lordship of Lewis'.

According to Alexander MacKenzie, Calum MacLeod of Lewis granted Raasay to his second son, Calum Garbh, early in the sixteenth century. If that were so, it might be expected that the charter would have included Raasay in the list of lands belonging to MacLeod of Lewis. However, there is no mention of Raasay, or any other part of the Raasay estate.

Crown Charter of 1572

Ruairidh Chaluim, Roderick MacLeod, was Chief of the MacLeods of Lewis by the 1530s. His first wife was Janet MacKenzie of Kintail. Ruairidh claimed that she had had an adulterous relationship with Hugh (sometimes referred to as Hucheon) Morrison, the brieve of Lewis. Consequently, Ruairidh Chaluim disowned and disinherited their son, Torcall, claiming that Torcall was not his son. Torcall is usually referred to as Torcall Conanach, because he had been brought up by his mother's people in Strathconon. He fought for his inheritance, backed by the MacKenzies.

Torcall Conanach had held Ruairidh Chaluim prisoner for four years, releasing him only when he agreed that Torcall should be named as his heir. The charter of 1572 names Torcall Conanach as Ruairidh Chaluim's heir. It may be noted that on 2 June 1572 Ruairidh Chaluim made an official declaration telling of his ill-treatment by Torcall and revoking his agreement to this charter on the grounds that he had been in fear of his life at the time. The charter in Latin and with translation, is as given by Richard Sharpe, pp. 67–8:

Apud Leith, 14 Feb.
Rex etc concessit TORQUILIO MAKCLOYD, filio et heredi apparenti Rodorici M. de Lewis, – terras et baroniam de Assynt, cum maneriis, turribus, fortaliciis, molendinis, piscariis, tenentibus etc., advocatione ecclesiarum et capellaniarum, [terras et baroniam de Cogeach, cum manerie, turre, fortalicio, molendinis, piscarris, tenentibus etc. advocatione ecclesiarum et capellaniarum earundem], in comitatu de Ros, vic Invernes; terras, insulam et baroniam de Lewis, cum castro, turre, fortalicio, manerie, molendinis, piscariis, tenentibus etc. advocatione ecclesiarum et capellaniarum earundem, terras et insulam de Watternes, cum manerie, piscaria, toftis, croftis vic Invernes: quas dictus Rod. apud Striveling personaliter resignavit. TENEND. dicto Tor. et heredibus masculis ejus de corpore legit. procreatis, quibus deficientibus. Gillicalmo vic Gillecallum Garwe M'Cloid de Raisay et heredibus etc. quibus def. propinquioribus et legitimis heredibus masculis dicti Torq. quibuscunque, arma et cognomen de M'Cloyd gerentibus et assignatis, in libera baronia de Lewis, ut prius unitas. RESERVATO libero tenemento dicto Rod. PROVISO quod dicti Rod. et Tor. regi fideles et obedientes remanerent, et nullum proditionis et lese majestatis crimen facerent aut attemptarent. TEST.

At Leith, 14 February 1572
The KING etc. has granted to Torquil MacLeod, son and heir apparent of Ruairidh MacLeod of Lewis – the lands and barony of Assynt, together with the manors, towers, fortalices, mills, fishings, teinds etc. the advowson of churches and chapels, the lands and barony of Coigeach, with the manor, tower, fortalice, mills, fishings, teinds and advowson of the churches and chapels of the same, in the County of Ross and part in Inverness; the lands, island and barony of Lewis, together with the castle, tower, fortalice, manor, mills, fishings, teinds etc. advowson of the churches and chapels of the same, the lands and island of Vaternish, together with the manor, fishing, tofts, crofts, in the County of Inverness; all of which the said Ruairidh personally resigned at Stirling. To be held by the said Torquil, and the legitimate male heirs of his body; or in the absence of such, by the nearest legitimate male heirs whatsoever of the said Torquil, bearing the arms and name of MacLeod, and his assignees, in the free barony of Lewis as previously united. The freehold to be retained by the said Ruairidh. With the proviso that the said Ruairidh and Torquil remain faithful and obedient to the King, and neither perform nor attempt betrayal or treason. Witness, etc. ...

The lands of Lewis are named here as – Assynt, Coigeach, Lewis and Waternish. These are the same lands as given in the 1511 charter. Once again Raasay is not mentioned.

That part of the original charter, relating to the MacLeods of Raasay has not been translated into English. It says, 'quibus deficientibus. Gillicalmo vic Gillecallum Garwe M'Cloid de Raisay et heredibus etc.' This has been translated by Mr Sellar as – 'whom failing Calum son of Calum Garbh MacLeod of Raasay and his heirs etc.' In 1572, therefore, the Laird of Raasay was Calum, son of Calum Garbh. He was quite possibly known as Calum Òg (Young Calum) to distinguish him from his father. Histories of the MacKenzies of Kintail refer to him as such.

Mr Sellar also comments:

> It is interesting to note that Torcall Conanach places Calum of Raasay and his heirs immediately after the heirs male of his own body, and before his own other nearest and legitimate heirs male (this would include his half-brothers).

Crown Charter of 1596

The first Crown charter to the MacLeod lairds of Raasay was granted by James VI in 1596. Again, this is quoted as given by Richard Sharpe, p. 73:

Apud Falkland, 20 Jul.
REX ad feudifirmam dimisit MALCOLMO M'GILLICHALLUM filio et apparenti heredi Malcolmi Macallester V'Gillichallum de Rasay, heredibus ejus et assignatis quibuscumque – terras de Rarsay, viz. Claichane, Oscaig, Inverweig, Claim, Madniso, Brewquhill, Awirnis cum insulis de Pladda et Ronehae, Screbiddill, Hallaig, Auldali, Livast, Nefuernyn, Laggan, Atthro, Satir, Ire, Suisnis, Inverarois, Toradoill et Ramsdall, extenden. ad 8 mercat. antiqui extentus,

necnon terras de Ire in Troueternes, Totua, Caraboist, Unresalider et Unisuisod, extenden. ad 3 mercat., et in toto ad 11 mercat. ant. ext., cum fortaliciis, molendinis, silvis, piscationibus, tenentibus etc., advocatione ecclesiarum et capellaniarum ecclesiarum de Kilmaluak in Rasay et Sneissort in Trouternes (per dictum Malc. seniorem et ejus tenentes occupatas), in episcopatu Insularum, vic Invernes;- que fuerunt dicti Malc. senioris, ejus patris, avi et predecessorum, tanquam antiquorum feudifirmariorum et nativorum tenentium de episcopis Insularum; et regi devenerunt per actum annexationis:- REDDEND. annuatim 24 merc et 30 sol. 4 den. nove augmentationis, viz. 12½ merc. ad festum Penthescostis et 12½ merc. ad festum S. Martini; et attendendo super regem et regis locumtenentes quandocumque ad dictas insulas repararent, sicuti ad dictos episcopos obligati erant. TEST etc.

At Falkland, 20 Jul.
The KING has granted as fee farm to Calum MacGillichaluim, son and heir apparent of Calum MacAlasdair MacGillichaluim of Raasay, his heirs and assignees whatsoever – the lands of Raasay, namely, Clachan, Oskaig [etc.], extending to 8 merklands of Old Extent, besides the lands of Eyre, in Trotternish, [etc.] extending to 3 merklands, the total 11 merklands of Old Extent, together with the fortalices, mills, woods, teinds, etc. advowson of the churches and chapels of the parishes of Kilmoluag in Raasay and Snizort in Trotternish (occupied by the said elder Calum and his tenants), in the diocese of the Isles, Inverness-shire. They have belonged to the said elder Calum, his father, grandfather and his predecessors, since time immemorial fee-holders and tenants of the bishop of the Isles. The lands came to the King by the Act of Annexation. Due in return: 24 merks annually and 30s. 4d. of new augmentation, payable 12½ merks at Whitsuntide and 12½ merks at Martinmas, and attendance on the king and his representatives, whenever they visit the said islands, just as they owed to the said bishops. Witness etc. ...

This charter names the Laird of Raasay in 1596 as Calum MacGilleChaluim, son of Calum, son of Alasdair. The next word, V'Gillichallum, could mean 'son of Calum'. It may however mean 'MacGilleChaluim' in the sense of 'MacLeod of Raasay'. Mr Sellar says that 'we cannot say for certain that the father of Alasdair was Calum, although this seems quite likely'. The recipient was therefore Calum Òg, son of Calum Garbh, the same man as was named in 1572.

Calum Òg is described here as 'filio et apparenti heredi' of Calum Garbh. This has been translated as 'son and heir apparent' of Calum Garbh, suggesting that the charter was made in favour of the eldest son of the laird at the time. It implies that his father was still alive. If the phrase was instead translated as 'apparent heir',[1] implying that his father, Calum Garbh, was dead, it make more sense.

There seems to be no good reason to alter the order of words in the original Latin. It can be seen that in the crown charter of 1572, Torcall Conanach was named as 'filio et heredi apparenti Rodorici ...'. This was translated as 'son and heir apparent of Ruairidh ...'. In that case Ruairidh Chaluim was alive, and the charter took account of that by granting him freehold of the lands.

It was usual that when a landowner, who held his lands from the Crown, died, his heir had to prove his right to inherit his ancestor's lands. This was done by means of a 'Retour', also known as 'service of Heirs'.[2] Because the MacLeods had not, until 1596, held their lands from the Crown, there had been no retours concerning their lands. The granting of this charter had to rectify this. Therefore, Calum Òg is named as 'apparent heir' of his father, Calum Garbh. Calum Garbh's father and possibly his grandfather are also named.

The lands granted in this charter amount to eleven merklands in total — the eight of Raasay and three in the parish of Snizort, Skye. The charter makes it clear that these lands, in the past, had been held as a 'unit', and that they continue to be so. The MacLeods held both parts of the estate until their financial problems forced them to sell up in the 1840s. Not until then were the Raasay and Skye parts of the estate separated.

This charter was the first Crown charter to the MacLeods of Raasay. It explains why this was so. Previously, the Crown had not held these lands. Until the Act of Annexation of 1587, they had been held by the Church. That Act had transferred ownership of all lands, previously held by the Church, to the Crown. The MacLeods 'since time immemorial' had held the lands as 'fee-holders and tenants' of the Bishop of the Isles, who was the Church's representative.

Retour of 1630

This is mentioned, but not quoted in full by Sharpe (page 76). It is taken from the copy of the retours held by the Highland Council Library in Inverness.

> Jul. 31.1630
> ALEXANDER M'LEANE, haeres Donaldi M'Leane Ferquhardi Hectoris filii, patris, – in terris de Rarsay, viz. Clachan Oistage, Innerwig, Clam, Maenes, Browkill, Awoynes cum insula Phladda, Ronaha, Skrebidell, Halleg et Larg, Lebost, Naseiring, Lagan, Achositore, Ire, Swysnes, Inneraros, Borradaill, Ramisdill; – Terris de Ire in Trouternes, Tuych, Tarrabost, Wgysadder, extendentibus in Rarsay ad 8 mercatas terrarum, et in Trouternes ad 3 mercatas, infra dominium insularum – E.24m[erks].

In this retour Alexander MacLean (son of Donald, son of Farquhar, son of Hector) is served heir to his father Donald, in the eight merklands of Raasay and the three merklands of Trotternish.

Quite apart from the fact that Alexander MacLean was served heir to his father while the MacLeods were in possession of the estate, this retour is of interest as it names the townships of Raasay.

A 'History of the Clan Tarlach O'Bui' by an unknown author – an 'Associate of the Family' – was published in 1864, and gives (on page 79) details of an instrument of sasine which followed from this retour. This tells that one of the 'witnesses to the delivery of earth and stone' in the various islands was 'John M'Gillichallum in Barsay'.

It is known that the Laird of Raasay in the 1630s was Alasdair, so it must be assumed that John MacGilleChaluim, the witness, was a relative of his.

Retour of 1688

On the death of Alasdair MacLeod in 1688, his two daughters, Seonaid and Sileas, were served joint heirs to him. As before, this can be found in Sharpe (pages 76–77), although, in this case, only part of the original has been translated into English.

> Janeta et Aegidia M'Leods alias M'Alaster vic Gillichallum haeredes lineae conquestus et provisionis Alexandri M'Leod alias M'Alaster vic Gillichallum de Rasay, patris, – qui fuit filius et haeres quondam Alexandri M'Leod alias M'Gillichallum, avi dictarum Janetae et Igidiae M'Leods alias M'Alaster vic Gillicallum, qui fuit filius et haeres Malcolumbi M'Leod alias M'Gillichallum de Rasay, proavi dictarum Janetae, et Igidiae M'Leods alias M'Alaster vic Gillicallum de Rasay; in omnibus terris et insulis de Rasay, et Snisort et Trotternish, comprehendentibus villas, terras, insulas, lie grassings, Kilmiluach, Ausach, Balliechurne, Balliemeanoch, Invervig, Glam, Moisnes, Crochill cum pertinentiis de Sciepadeall, Hallag, Leaghk, Kamorick, Lieboast, Slagadine, Slachro, Fearne, Stair, Ire, Shuashnesmore, Shuashnesbeg, Inneraross, Broradell, Glen, et Kylehan:- duabus insulis quae vulgo Rona et Fladda appellantur; – oppidis, terris, lie grassings de Ire, Cott (i.e. Tott), Carabost, Glengrast, Ugisarder, Knockshint, Penniemore, et Pennie-Cappan, in patria vel baronia de Trouternish; – caeteris villis, terris, insulis, et aliis de Fortune-Rasaye in parochia de Snisort. – E.26m. 3s. 4d. feudifirmae.

> Janet and Giles (or Julia) MacLeod, otherwise MacAlasdair MacGillichaluim, heirs of line, conquest and provision of Alexander MacLeod, otherwise MacAlasdair MacGillichaluim of Raasay, their father, who was son and heir of the late Alexander MacLeod alias MacGillichaluim, grandfather of the said Janet and Giles MacLeod otherwise MacAlasdair MacGillichaluim, who was son and heir of Calum MacLeod otherwise MacGillichaluim of Raasay, great grandfather of the said Janet and Giles MacLeod otherwise MacAlasdair MacGillichaluim of Raasay, including those in Snizort and Trotternish, comprising the townships, lands, islands and grazings of Kilmoluag etc. with the two islands commonly called Rona and Fladda, and the towns, lands and grazings of Eyre, Tote etc.

A retour was necessary to prove the right of the heir, or in this case heiresses, to inherit the lands of their ancestor, in this case their father. It is strange that the document uses 'mac', meaning 'son of', rather than 'nighean', meaning 'daughter of'. We are told that Seonaid and Sileas were the daughters of Alasdair (or Alexander); that their grandfather was also named Alasdair, and that their great-grandfather was named Calum.

Alexander MacKenzie firmly believed that the retour also names the ladies' great-great grandfather. Possibly this is due to the fact that instead of saying simply 'Janet and Giles MacLeod' the document says 'Janet and Giles MacLeod otherwise MacAlasdair MacGillichaluim' and it gives that whole mouthful each time they are mentioned. MacKenzie has, it would seem, taken the final rendition of 'otherwise MacAlasdair MacGillechaluim' to refer to their great-grandfather rather than themselves.

So the retour goes as far back as the ladies' great-grandfather, Calum, and no further. There was no need for it to do so. It was unusual for a retour to indicate, or prove, more than one relationship, usually with the father. Unlike all the other Inverness-shire retours of this period, this retour traces the ladies' ancestors back as far as Calum Òg, their great-grandfather. It had no need to go further than that as he had received a Crown charter in 1596, which had established his right to inherit the estate.

On the other hand, it is strange that this retour had to go as far back as Calum Òg. Alexander MacKenzie states that the two lairds immediately after Calum Òg, both named Alexander, were served heir respectively on 18 February 1617 and 20 August 1643. Although Alick Morrison gives only the date, February 1617, he lists both Alexanders in his genealogy. Iain Garbh was said to have been served heir on 22 September 1648. Neither of the Alexanders nor Iain Garbh are found in the copy of the retours for Inverness-shire, held in the Highland Council Library in Inverness. The original 'services of Heirs' in Edinburgh has not been checked. That the retour of 1688 had to go back to Calum Òg, might suggest that there was some problem with the retours of 1617, 1643 and 1648.

Alexander MacKenzie, followed by Alick Morrison, states that Seonaid and Sileas were sisters of Iain Garbh and Alasdair. The retour, however, has them served as heiresses of their father. That is one reason for suggesting that they were nieces, not sisters of Iain Garbh. Another reason is that Iain Garbh's sister, Margaret, who married Calum Nicolson of Scorrybreac is not named in the retour. If two sisters were allowed to inherit the estate, why not have all three?

Thus it seems more likely that Seonaid and Sileas were daughters of Alasdair and nieces of Iain Garbh.

Notes

1. Mr Sellar has indicated that he would agree with this translation.
2. Cecil Sinclair, *Tracing Your Scottish Ancestors* (revised edn, 1990), p. 46.

APPENDIX 5

List of Lairds/Owners of Raasay and Rona

Until the 1587 Act of Annexation, which transferred ownership of all Church lands to the Crown, the lands of Raasay and Rona were owned by the Church. They were held by the Bishop of the Isles as representative of the Church.

From sometime in the fifteenth century, the MacLeods of Raasay held these lands as tenants of the Bishop of the Isles. Prior to that, according to tradition, Raasay and Rona had been held by MacSweens. Quite possibly they too had been tenants of the bishop.

The MacLeod Lairds of Raasay

1. Father of Alasdair, quite possibly named Calum, is the earliest MacLeod laird mentioned, but it may be that his predecessors also held Raasay.
2. Alasdair
3. Calum Garbh may have become laird in the 1540s. He died before May 1570.
4. Calum Òg was laird by 1572.
5. Alasdair became laird in 1617
6. Iain Garbh became laird in 1648. Drowned 1671.
7. Alasdair, brother of Iain Garbh, had died by 1688.
8. Sileas and Seonaid, daughters of Alasdair, were served heirs in 1688. They resigned their rights in 1692 to their cousin, Alasdair.
9. Alasdair (1692 – date not known)
10. Malcolm of the '45 (laird by 1726–1745)
11. John (1745–1786)
12. James (1786–1824)
13. John (1824–1843). The last of the MacLeod lairds.

1843–1846	Creditors of John MacLeod.
1846–1863	George Rainy (Senior)
1863–1872	George Haygarth Rainy (did not come of age until 1866)
1872–1874	George G. MacKay
1874–1876	William James Armitage

1876–1911   Edward Herbert Wood (died 1886, but estate then run by his widow).

1911–1923   William Baird & Co. Ltd, Ironmasters of Coatbridge. They sold the bulk of the estate in 1923, but retained mineral rights and those areas that would be required to restart mining operations.

1923–   Board of Agriculture for Scotland, later became the Department of Agriculture & Fisheries for Scotland, and is now Scottish Executive Environment & Rural Affairs Department, took over the bulk of the estate.

Kings of Man/MacLeods/Lords of the Isles

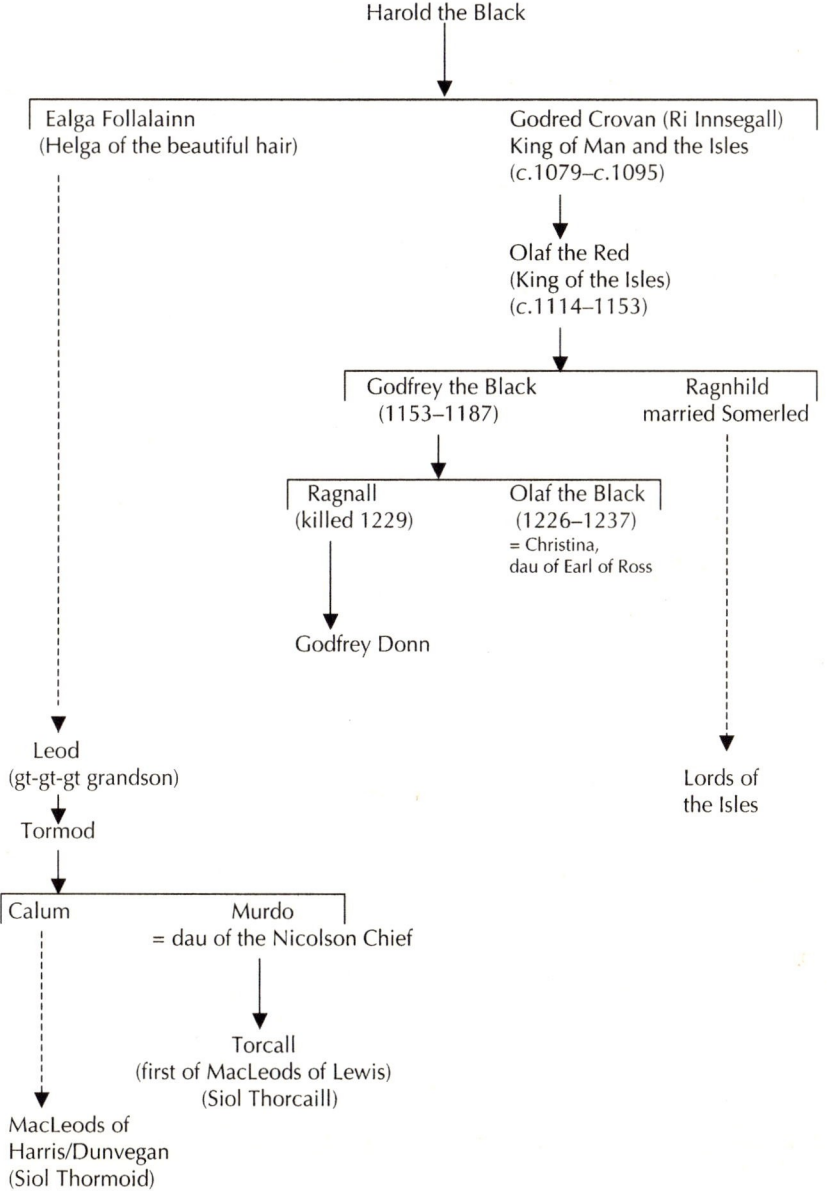

Note: Based on W.D.H. Sellar, 'The Ancestry of the MacLeods Reconsidered', *TGSI*, vol. LX.

MacLeods of Lewis

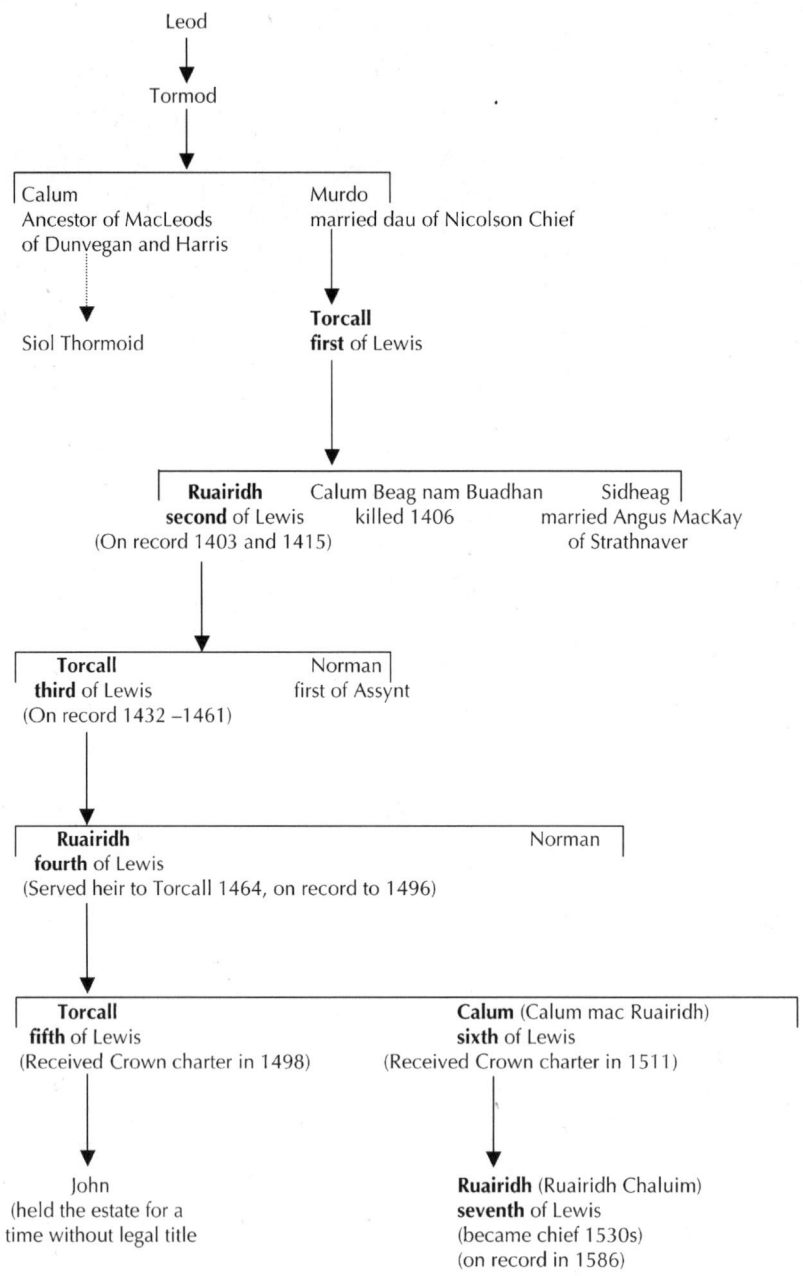

MacLeods of Raasay
based on Alexander MacKenzie 1889

Malcolm MacLeod of Lewis
(Received charter for Lewis 1511)

- Roderick (Ruairidh Chaluim) of Lewis
  = Janet MacKenzie*
- Calum Garbh
  second son: succeeded to Raasay early 1500s
  I of Raasay

From Roderick:
- Alasdair
  II of Raasay
  named in retour of 1688

From Calum Garbh (I of Raasay):
- John (Iain na Tuaighe)
  = 1 Janet MacKenzie*
  = 2 dau of Allan mac Ruairidh of Gairloch
  = 3? name not given

From Alasdair (II of Raasay):
- Calum Garbh **III of Raasay** d 1611
- other sons killed at Isay 1568

From John (Iain na Tuaighe):
- Sons killed at Isay 1568
- Dau
- Sons
- John killed 1597 at Conon market

From Calum Garbh (III of Raasay):
- Murdo illegitimate
- Calum Òg eldest son killed 1611
- Alexander **IV of Raasay** (minor in 1611: served heir 1617)
  = dau of John MacLeod of Drynoch, Skye
  (widow = 2 Thomas Graham & =3 Alexander MacKenzie)

From Alexander IV of Raasay:
- Alexander **V of Raasay** (served heir 1643)
  = Sibella MacKenzie of Applecross
- John

From Alexander V of Raasay:
- John Garbh **VI of Raasay** (served heir 1648)
  = Janet MacLeod dau of Sir Ruairidh Mòr
- Janet = Duncan MacRae of Inverinate
- Giles (unm)

From John:
- Alexander **VII of Raasay** (charter 1692)
  = Catherine MacLeod

From Alexander VII of Raasay:
- Malcolm (of the '45) **VIII of Raasay**
  1713 = 1 Mary MacKenzie of Applecross
  (1748 = 2 Janet MacLeod)
- John I of Rigg

From Malcolm VIII of Raasay:
- John **IX of Raasay** = Jane MacQueen
- Dr Murdo of Eyre, Snizort
- Norman
- Janet

From John I of Rigg:
- Capt. Malcolm of the '45 b 1711, unm.
- Norman II of Rigg

From John IX of Raasay:
- James **X of Raasay**
- John died young
- Malcolm Unm
- 10 girls all married

From Norman II of Rigg:
- Norman of Camustinavaig
- John of Ollach

From James X of Raasay:
- John **XI of Raasay**
- James
- Loudon
- Francis
- Hannah Elizabeth

From John of Ollach:
- Norman of Scalpay

MacLeods of Raasay
based on Alick Morrison 1974

Calum Garbh, **I of Raasay**
Second son of Malcolm of Lewis: received Raasay, Rona, Coigeach and Gairloch c.1510
(neither history nor tradition has much to say about him)

Alasdair **II of Raasay** (nothing known of this chief) — John (Iain na Tuaighe) (details as given by A. MacKenzie)

Sons killed at Isay 1568 — Calum **III of Raasay** (youngest son: survived Isay, fostered away from home) (named in charter 1596: raids to Caithness and Torridon: d 1610)

Calum Òg **IV of Raasay** d 1611 Clachan — Alasdair **V of Raasay** served heir 1617 — John, Raids on Caithness and Torridon, killed on one of them — Dau = Hector MacKenzie — Murdo illegitimate

Alexander **VI of Raasay** = Sibella MacKenzie — John I of Rigg (nothing known of him) — MacLeods of Marishadder

Iain Garbh **VII of Raasay** d 1671 = Janet MacLeod — Alasdair **VIII of Raasay** d1688 — Janet, Julia Served heirs 1688 — John II of Rigg — Murdo I of Glen

Alexander **IX of Raasay** = Catherine MacLeod — John III of Rigg — Murdo Tacksman of Brae in 1745

Malcolm (of the '45) **X of Raasay** =1 Mary MacKenzie — Norman IV of Rigg d 1752 — Capt Malcolm of the '45 b 1711 = Catherine MacQueen

John **XI of Raasay** = Jane MacQueen — Dr Murdo of Eyre, Snizort — John of Ollach — Norman of Camustinavaig — William

James **XII of Raasay** — Norman of Scalpay — Archibald North Uist — Norman — John

John **XIII of Raasay** — James — Loudoun — Francis

Gaelic/English Equivalents

During the nineteenth century personal names on official documents (such as the census) had to be in English. Thus English names, which sounded vaguely similar, were attributed to many Gaelic names. Most of these may be termed 'equivalents' rather than 'translations'.

Gaelic	English	Gaelic	English
Ailean	Allan, Alan	Seumas	James
Alasdair	Alexander, Alister, Alastair (and all other variations)	Sìle, Sileas	Sheila, Julia
		Sìne, Sìneag	Jane
		Somhairle	Samuel
Anna	Anne	Teàrlach	Charles
Aonghas	Angus	Torcall	Torquil
Beileag	Bella, Isabel, Isabella	Tormod	Norman
Beitidh	Betty	Uilleam	William
Calum	Malcolm	achadh	field
Catriona	Catherine	bàn	fair-haired
Ceit, Ceiteag	Kate, Catherine	beag	small, younger
Coinneach	Kenneth	cam	blind in one eye
Dòmhnall	Donald	clann	clan, children
Donnchadh	Duncan	dearg	scarlet, crimson
Eachann	Hector	donn	brown
Fionnlagh	Finlay	dubh	black
Iain	John	eilean	island
Mairearad	Margaret	fada	long
Màiri	Mary	gille	young man, servant man
Murchadh	Murdo		
Niall	Neil	laimrig	landing place
Pàdraig	Peter, Patrick	liath	grey, blue grey (hair)
Raghnall	Ronald, Ranald	mac	son of
Raghnaid	Rachel	mòr	big, older
Ruairidh	Roderick	nighean	daughter of
Seasaidh, Seasag	Jessie	òg	young, younger
		ruadh	red-haired
Seonag	Johan	saighdear	soldier
Seònaid	Janet	taigh	house
Seonaidh	Johnnie, John	tàillear	tailor

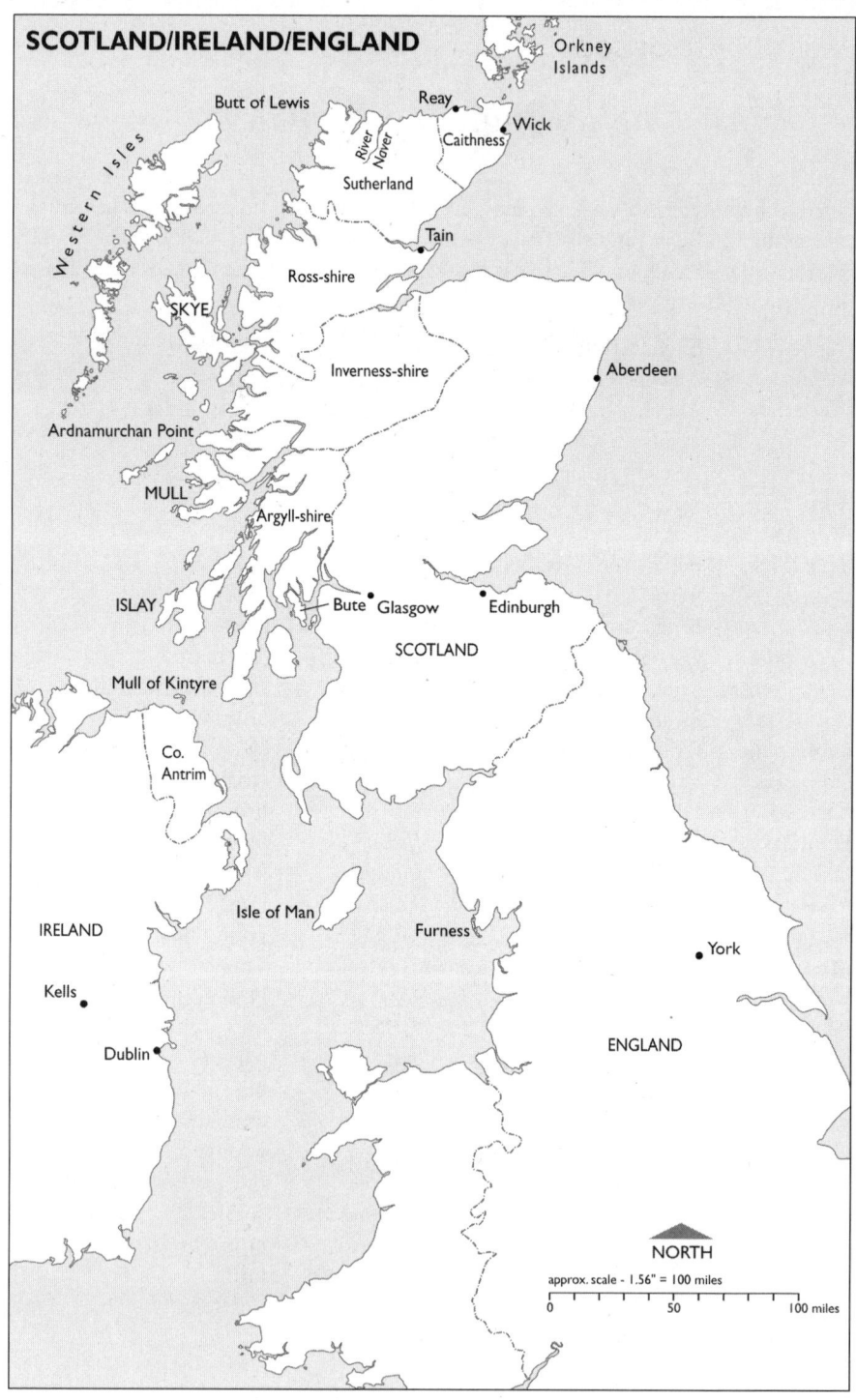

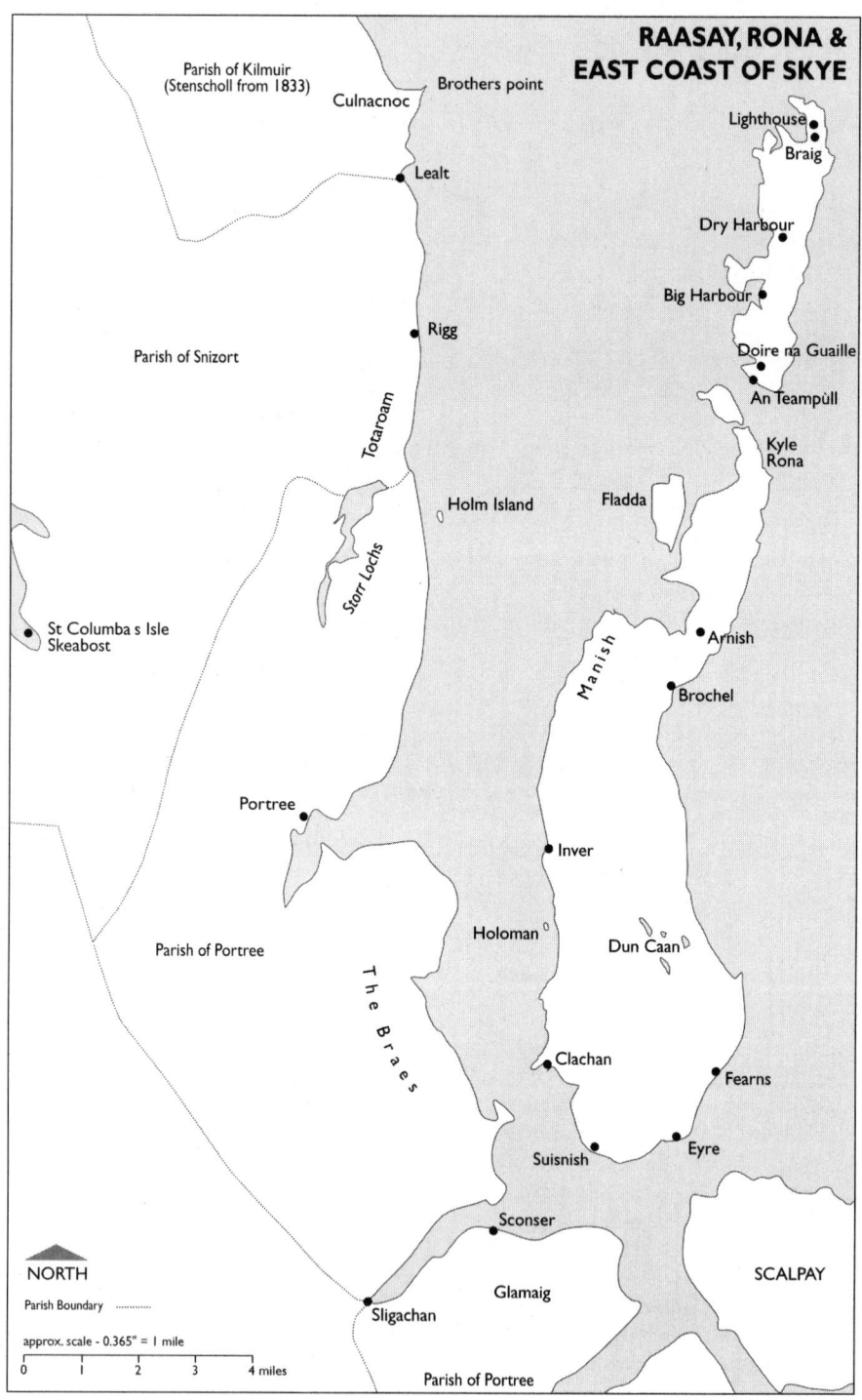

Select Bibliography

An Associate of the Family, *History of the Clan Tarlach O'Bui* (1864)
Cameron, E. A., *Land for the People: The British Government and the Scottish Highlands c.1880–1925*, Scottish Historical Review Monograph (1996)
Cowan, E. J. and McDonald, R. A. (eds), *Alba: Celtic Scotland in the Medieval Era* (2000)
Downie, Sir A. M. and MacKinnon, A.D., *Genealogical Account of the Family of MacKinnon* (1883)
Dodgshon, R. A., *From Chiefs to Landlords c1493–1820* (1998)
Draper, L. and P., *The Raasay Iron Mine 1912–1942* (1990)
Fraser, William, *The Earls of Cromartie*, vol. 1 and vol. 2 (MDCCCLXVI)
Fraser, Master James, 'The Wardlaw Manuscript', *SHS*, vol. XLVII, ed. W. MacKay (1905)
Grant, I. F., *History of the Clan MacLeod* (1959; 1981 edn)
Keltie, J. S. (ed), *Highland Clans and Regiments*
Johnston, G. H., *The Heraldry of the Campbells* (1977)
Knox, J., *The Highlands and Hebrides in 1786–1787* (Reprint 1975)
Livingstone, A. and Aikman, C. W. H. and Hart, B. S. (eds), *Muster Roll of Prince Charles Edward Stuart's Army 1745–46* (1984; reprinted 1985)
MacAulay, Rev. M., *Aspects of the Religious History of Lewis* (Inverness)
MacDonald, D., Lewis, *A History of the Island* (1983)
MacDonald, Hugh, 'History of the MacDonalds', *SHS*, Highland Papers, vol. I, ed. J. R. N. MacPhail (1914)
McDonald, R. A., *The Kingdom of the Isles: Scotland's Western Seaboard c1100–c1336* (Scottish Historical Review Monographs Series, 1997)
MacInnes, Dr J., 'Gleanings from Raasay Tradition', *TGSI*, vol. LVI
MacKay, J. G., 'Social Life in Skye from Legend and Story', Parts 1 and 2, *TGSI*, vol. XXIX
McKay, N. T., 'Angus MacKay (1812–1859) and his Contribution to Highland Music', *TSGI*, vol. LV
MacKay, W., *Urquhart and Glenmoriston: Olden Times in a Highland Parish* (1893)
MacKenzie, A., *The Prophecies of the Brahan Seer, 1877* (Foreword, Commentary and Conclusion by Elizabeth Sutherland (1977; reprinted 1984)
MacKenzie, A., *History of the MacLeods* (1889)
MacKenzie, A., *History of the MacKenzies* (1894; reprinted 1998)
MacKenzie, H. H., *The MacLeans of Boreray* (1946)
MacKenzie, John of Applecross, 'Genealogie of Surname of M'Kenzie', *SHS*, Highland Papers, vol. II, ed. J. R. N. MacPhail (1916)
MacKenzie, John of Applecross, 'The MacKenzies', *SHS*, Genealogical Collections, vol. I, ed. J. T. Clark (1900)
MacKenzie, W., *Old Skye Tales* (1930; ed. and amalgamated by Dr A. MacLean, 1995)
MacKintosh of MacKintosh, M., *The History of the Clan MacKintosh and the Clan Chattan* (1892)
MacLean-Bristol, N., *Warriors and Priests: The History of the Clan MacLean* (1995)

MacLean, Dr. S., 'Some Raasay Traditions', *TGSI*, vol. XLIX
MacLeod, J. L., *The Second Disruption* (2000)
MacRae, Rev. A., *History of the Clan MacRae* (1899)
Matheson, W., The MacLeods of Lewis, *TGSI*, vol. LI
Miket, R. and Roberts, D. L., *The Mediaeval Castles of Skye and Lochalsh* (1990)
Monro, Dean Donald, *The Western Isles of Scotland: 1549*, ed. R. W. Munro (1961)
Morrison, A., The MacLeods: *The Genealogy of a Clan: Section 4* (1974)
Morrison, A., The MacLeods: *The Genealogy of a Clan: Section 5* (1974)
Nicolson, A., *History of Skye* (1930; revised and ed. by Dr A MacLean, 1995)
Sellar, W. D. H., BA, LLB, 'Marriage, Divorce & Concubinage in Gaelic Scotland', *TGSI*, vol. LI
Sellar, W. D. H., 'The Ancestry of the MacLeods Reconsidered', *TGSI*, vol. LX
Sharpe, R., *Raasay: A Study in Island History* (1977)
Sharpe, R., *Raasay: A Study in Island History: Documents and Sources* (1978)
Shaw, F. J., *The Northern and Western Islands: Their Economy and Society in the Seventeenth Century* (1980)
Sinclair, C., *Tracing Your Scottish Ancestors* (1990; revised edn, 1997)
Warrand, D., *Some MacKenzie Pedigrees* (1965)
Watt, D. E. R., 'Bishops in the Isles before 1203', *The Innes Review*, vol. 45, no. 2 (1994)
Williams, R., *The Lords of the Isles: The Clan Donald and the early Kingdom of the Scots* (1984)
Not Known, 'The Manuscript History of Craignish', *SHS*, 3rd series, vol. IV
MacKintosh Muniments

Index

Act of Annexation 1587 12, 31–32, 190, 207, 269–270
American War of Independence 68
Anderson, Thomas, agricultural manager 95, 110
archaeology (evidence, sites, surveys etc.) 1, 7–8, 17–18, 26, 235
Ardnamurchan – raid 20–21, 189–190
Armitage, William James (1874–1876) 119–120

Baintighearna Dhubh Oscaig, Seonaid MacLeod 59–60, 65, 71, 214–215
Baird, William & Co. Ltd, Ironmasters (1911–1923) 160–166, 167, 171–172, 174
barrilla 75–76
Barron, Mr, estate manager 159
barter system 33, 48, 50
Battery at Clachan, Raasay 75
Baynes of Tulloch 35, 39–40, 208
Bethune, John, miller 113
birlinn & galley (traditional boats) 19–20, 25–27, 33, 38, 40, 45–46, 61–62
Bishop(s) of the Isles 11–15, 23, 30, 37–38, 42, 190, 192, 207–208, 210
Board of Agriculture for Scotland (BoAS) 159–160, 162–169, 171, 242
Board of Trustees for Manufacturers & Fisheries 68
Boswell, James – see *Johnson, Dr Samuel & Boswell, James*
Brahan Seer, Coinneach Odhar 61, 92–93
British Fisheries Society 66–68
British Navy 66
broch 8–9, 231–232
Brochel Castle, history of 235–239
Brochel Castle, money to build 19–20, 194
Brown, William, sheep farm manager 121
Bunning, Thomas, butler 95–97, 100, 102–103, 109, 111, 114, 117
Burns, Dr 160
Bute, Isle of 13, 15, 122

Caithness – raid 31
Calum's Road 181
Campbell, Alexander, Rev., teacher & minister of Portree 69, 72, 88
Campbell, Duncan, ground officer 95, 97, 100, 102
Campbells of Ardkinglass 20, 194–195
Campbells of Argyll 226–227
Campbells of Calder (Cawdor) 24, 203–204, 206
Campbells of Craignish 20
Campbells of Craignish, Marion 20, 194–197, 200, 209
Canada, Cape Breton & Prince Edward Island 76–77, 79, 87–88, 90
car ferry 1, 175–178, 181–183
car ferry, *Canna, Eigg* 176
cash/market economy 48–50, 72, 74
casualties 33, 48
cattle, black 48, 63, 70, 77–79, 85–86
caves 7, 49
Church, early Church in the Isles 9–17
Church, Established Church of Scotland 80, 88–89, 96
Church, Free Church of Scotland 89, 95–96, 112, 114, 139–140 (NC), 156, 159, 171
Church, Free Presbyterian Church of Scotland 156, 159, 171
clearances 89–90, 89–90, 100, 104, 106–108
Commission for Annexed Estates 65–66, 76
commission(s) of fire & sword 27, 31, 223
Common Grazings Act 1908 159
Congested Districts (Scotland) Act 1897 (including Board) 156–157, 159
corn laws 98
cottars 49, 57, 70–72
Coysh, Thomas, head gardener 121
Crofter Holdings (Scotland) Act of 1886 142, 144, 155
Crofters' Commission 142–143, 156, 159

Crofters' Common Grazing Regulations Act of 1892 156
Crown Charter of 1511 (Lewis) 23, 190, 201, 266–267
Crown Charter of 1572 (Lewis) 30, 190–191, 201, 207, 267–268
Crown Charter of 1596 (Raasay) 31–33, 190, 192, 199, 207, 268–270

Dàl Riata 9
Davidson, Mrs C. 169, 174–175, 242
Deer Forest Commission 146–151, 153–155
denounced as a rebel/as rebels 31, 35, 207
Department of Agriculture & Fisheries (DAFS) 171, 173–176, 182–183
destitution 79, 97, 99, 144–145
Diabaig, raid 39
drowning accidents 81, 84, 109, 111–112, 114, 122–123, 253–254
dun 9, 232
Dundee Advertiser 164

Earl(s) & Earldom of Ross 12–13, 15, 27
Earl(s) of Seaforth 41–42, 45, 61
emigrant ship to Canada, *Polly* 76
emigrant ships to Australia, *Borneuf, Edward Johnstone, Georgiana, Medina, Ticonderoga, Typhoon* 103
emigrant ships to Australia, *Ontario* 101, 103
emigration/emigrants 56, 65, 74, 76–77, 79, 86–88, 90, 101–104, 144
employment/employed 72, 79, 86, 95, 109, 113, 116, 120, 130, 146, 157, 168–169, 173, 181–182

factors on Raasay 88–90, 101, 216
fairs 50, 72
Faobairne MacCuidhein 16, 69
Ferguson, Captain of the *Furnace* 52, 54–55, 57
Fernaig Manuscript 211
Fife Adventurers 36
Finlayson, Alexander, Clachan 114
fishery cruiser, *Mina* 166
fishing/fisheries 30–31, 49, 66–68, 72–74, 77–79, 109, 122, 144
fishing boats, *Helen, Hero, Janet, Swan* 122

fishing busses 66–67, 72, 78
Fladda, proposed slate quarry 124
Forestry Commission 168, 173
forests, including trees, woods etc. 25–26, 33, 63, 67, 71, 77–78
forests, sale of timber 71, 114, 168–169
forfeiture of estates 27, 65, 227, 266
Forward 165
fosterage 17, 24, 34–35, 48
freestone 63, 67, 71, 77
French invasion, threat of 75
Furness Abbey, Lancashire 12–13

Gaelic Schools Society (GSS) 83–84
Gairloch, massacre 205, 222–224
Galbraith, Angus, Rev., FC minister 100 (NC), 114, 116, 118–120 (NC), 123–141 (NC), 145
German Prisoners of War 161–162
Gillies, Alexander, Doire Dubh 149 (DFC)
Gillies, Alexander, Umachan 150 (DFC)
Gillies, Angus, Umachan 123, 253
Gillies, Calum, Torran 111–112, 123
Gillies, Donald, Fladda 111–112
Gillies, John, Doire Dubh & Torran 127
Gillies, John, Fladda 111–112
Gillies, John, Fladda & Balachuirn 127, 134 (NC)
Gillies, John, Seonaidh Iain Dhòmhnaill 88
Gillies, John, Torran 149–150 (DFC)
Gillies, John, Umachan 108 (NC), 135 (NC)
Gillies, Kenneth, Doire Dubh & Torran 127
Gillies, Murdo, Torran 123, 253
Gillies, Norman, Torran, Eilean Taigh & Oscaig 107 (DFC), 116, 120 (DFC), 153 (DFC)
Gillies, Ronald, Fladda 149 (DFC)
Glam Hill Farm 124–125
Government survey of the islands (1577–1595) 26, 30, 236, 239
Graham, James, Doire na Guaille 170
Green, Dr John of Sussex 174–181, 183, 242
Greenock Telegraph 164–165
gulf between the laird and the people 65, 74

Hands, James, head gamekeeper 121

Heron, Robert (*General View* ... 1794) 69
Highland Destitution Relief Board & Committee 97–99
Highland Land League (HLL) 164–165
Highland Rifle Volunteers 115
Highlands & Islands Development Board (HIDB) 175–181, 183, 242
Highlands & Islands Emigration Society (HIES) 101, 103
Home Farm 63, 70, 110, 122, 160, 166, 174, 181

Inverness Courier 120–121
Ireland 9–10, 27
Isay, Waternish, Skye, massacre 24, 191, 201–206, 224, 227–228

Johnson, Dr Samuel & Boswell, James (visit in 1773) 59–64

kelp 73, 75–76, 78–79, 91
Kennedy, Hector, Rev., FC minister 159, 171
Kings of Man & the Isles 12–13, 275
Kippin, James, Rev., FC minister 96, 112, 114
Knox, John (*Tour* ... 1786) 67

land raid, Raasay 164–167
land raids 163
Land Settlement (Scotland) Act 1919 162–163
lighthouse, Rona 138, 145
lime/limestone 63, 67, 69, 77
Lord(s) & Lordship of the Isles 14–15, 23, 27, 225–227, 275
Loudoun, Lord and Earl of 52, 55–56, 215–216

M'Neill Commission of 1851 97–100
MacBeath, John, teacher 145
MacCrimmon Pipers of Dunvegan 46, 69
MacDonald, Archibald, Rev., FC minister 171
MacDonald, Flora (of the '45) 53, 55
MacDonald, Harry, Portree, factor for Raasay 101–102, 107–108, 114–116
MacDonald, J (*General view* ... 1811) 77–79, 149
MacDonald, John, Rev., FC minister 159
MacDonalds of Duntulm 41, 45–46
MacDonalds of Glengarry 38, 229
MacDonalds of Moidart 225–227
MacDonalds of Sleat 19, 51–52, 195, 228
MacDougall, William Stewart, Rev., FC minister 96, 112
MacFarlane, Alexander, teacher 113, 116, 145, 156
MacFarlane, Donald, Rev., FC & FPC minister 156, 159
MacGilleChaluim, origin of the name 193–194
MacInnes, Alexander, Clachan (coachman) 121
MacInnes, Mary Ann, teacher 170–171
MacKay Pipers of Gairloch 69
MacKay Pipers of Raasay 69, 82–83, 217
MacKay, George G (1872–1874) 118–119
MacKay, Roderick, Dry Harbour 136–137 (NC)
MacKays of Strathnaver 193–194, 220–222
MacKenzie, Ewen, teacher 145
MacKenzie, Kenneth, Janet & Catharine, Big Harbour 81
MacKenzie, Malcolm, Torran 111–112
MacKenzie, Murdo, Balmeanach 128, 150–151 (DFC), 153 (DFC)
MacKenzie, Royston, sheep farmer 104, 106, 108, 113–114, 116, 120
MacKenzies of Applecross, Isabella/Sibella 41, 209
MacKenzies of Applecross, Mary 50–51, 213–214
MacKenzies of Delvine, John 60
MacKenzies of Gairloch 39–40, 208, 229
MacKenzies of Kintail 38–39, 41, 44, 201, 208, 222, 226–228
MacKenzies of Kintail, Isobel 28–29, 196, 202
MacKenzies of Kintail, Janet 29–30, 197–199
MacKenzies of Kintail, Kenneth, later Lord Kintail 36–38
MacKenzies of Kintail, Roderick, Tutor of Kintail 36–37
MacKinnon, Catherine, teacher 170–171
MacKinnon, James, teacher 169–170
MacKinnons of Strath 41, 213–214
MacKintosh, James of Stroine 196

MacLean, Catherine & Isabella, Eilean Taigh 148
MacLean, John, gamekeeper 145
MacLean, John, Oscaig 114–115 (DFC), 125–127 (NC), 153 (DFC)
MacLean, Kate, Oscaig 128
MacLean, Norman, Balachuirn 131 (NC)
MacLeans of Boreray 19
MacLeans of Dochgarroch 22–23, 28, 38, 41–42, 44
MacLeans of Duart 41
MacLeans of Duart, Janet 36–37
MacLeans of Muck, Flora Ann 75
MacLeans, Clann Theàrlaich 28, 41
MacLennan, Alexander, Fladda 107 (NC), 116 (NC), 134 (NC)
MacLennan, Alexander, missionary 145
MacLennan, Alexander, Umachan 135
MacLennan, Donald, Umachan & Kyle Rona 135
MacLennan, Finlay, Fladda 146
MacLennan, Murdo, Fladda 135
MacLennan, Ronald, Kyle Rona & Doire na Guaille 116–117, 145, 147–148 (DFC)
MacLeod, Alasdair, North Arnish 133 (NC)
MacLeod, Alexander, Dry Harbour 145
MacLeod, Allan, Dry Harbour 119
MacLeod, Angus, Fladda 111–112
MacLeod, Bella, Beileag an Achaidh 193
MacLeod, Catherine, teacher 170
MacLeod, Charles, Arnish 133 (NC)
MacLeod, Donald, Balmeanach 128
MacLeod, Donald, Kyle Rona 101 (NC), 107 (NC), 135–136 (NC)
MacLeod, Donald, Manish & Arnish 106
MacLeod, Ewen Thorcaill 37
MacLeod, Hannah, Arnish 101
MacLeod, Hector, Brae 128
MacLeod, John Malcolm, the Shoemaker 193
MacLeod, John, Arnish 101
MacLeod, John, Balmeanach 59
MacLeod, John, Brae 128, 150 (DFC)
MacLeod, John, teacher, Dry Harbour & Torran 109, 112–113, 116, 145
MacLeod, Margaret, Arnish 101
MacLeod, Murdo, Clachan 114

MacLeod, Murdo, Dry Harbour 122–123
MacLeod, Neil, Braig 138 (NC), 147
MacLeod, Neil, teacher 116, 145
MacLeod, Norman, Fladda 111–112
MacLeod, Norman, Mill Place 146
MacLeod, Roderick, Dry Harbour 122–123
MacLeod, Torcall, Fladda 122
MacLeod, Torcall, Umachan 113
MacLeod, William, Dry Harbour 122
MacLeods, origins of the clan 188, 275
MacLeods, written histories of the clan 187–188
MacLeods in Lewis 39, 230
MacLeods of Bernera, Catherine 50–51, 213
MacLeods of Bernera, Donald, (*The Old Trojan*) 52
MacLeods of Bharcasaig, Mary 218
MacLeods of Colbecks 214
MacLeods of Dunvegan 36–37, 41, 45–46, 52, 64, 201
MacLeods of Dunvegan, Dame Flora MacLeod of MacLeod 216–217
MacLeods of Dunvegan, Janet 209
MacLeods of Gairloch 19, 38–39, 44
MacLeods of Gairloch, John Holmach 38–39
MacLeods of Lewis 23–24, 44, 189, 225–227, 276
MacLeods of Lewis, disputed succession 29–30, 190
MacLeods of Lewis, downfall of 35–36
MacLeods of Lewis, forfeiture of estate 23, 226–227
MacLeods of Lewis, internal conflict 23–24
MacLeods of Lewis, Calum Beag nam Buadhan 193–194, 221
MacLeods of Lewis, Ruairidh Chaluim 27, 189–190, 197–199, 214
MacLeods of Lewis, Torcall Conanach 29–30, 190–191, 197–198, 207
MacLeods of Lewis, Torcall Dubh 36–37, 45, 90
MacLeods of Lewis, Torcall Oighre 30
MacLeods of Raasay, after 1843 218–219
MacLeods of Raasay, descent as given in previous histories 189–190, 197, 277–278

MacLeods of Raasay, financial problems 84–86, 91–92
MacLeods of Raasay, *Lament for Allan Ian Og* 255–256
MacLeods of Raasay, MacLeods of Glen 70, 212, 278
MacLeods of Raasay, MacLeods of Marrishadder 39, 278
MacLeods of Raasay, Alasdair (1617–c. 1648) 41, 44, 208–209
MacLeods of Raasay, Alasdair (1692–c. 1726) 47–48, 50–51, 211–213
MacLeods of Raasay, Alasdair, bro. of Iain Garbh 46–47, 210
MacLeods of Raasay, Alexander, son of Malcolm & Seonaid 80, 215
MacLeods of Raasay, Calum Garbh (?–c. 1570) 24–25, 28–29, 189–192, 206–209
MacLeods of Raasay, Calum Òg (c. 1570–1611) 29–32, 37–38, 40–41, 191–192, 196, 207–2098
MacLeods of Raasay, Flora, sister of James 56, 65
MacLeods of Raasay, Iain Garbh (c. 1648–c. 1671) 45–47, 194–196, 209–212, 248–251
MacLeods of Raasay, Iain na Tuaighe 22, 195–202
MacLeods of Raasay, James (1786–1824) 68–84, 217
MacLeods of Raasay, John (1745–1786) 51–53, 55, 59–61, 215–217
MacLeods of Raasay, John (1824–1843) 75, 84–93, 217–218
MacLeods of Raasay, John, bro. of Calum Òg 35, 207
MacLeods of Raasay, Malcolm (c. 1726–1745) 50–61, 213–215
MacLeods of Raasay, Malcolm of Eyre or Brae, Captain 51–58, 61, 64, 69, 212–213
MacLeods of Raasay, Malcolm, Rev., son of Malcolm & Seonaid 215
MacLeods of Raasay, Margaret, sister of Iain Garbh 44–45, 209, 211–212, 243
MacLeods of Raasay, Mary, dau. of James & Mary Reid 75, 217
MacLeods of Raasay, Murdo of Brae 54, 57
MacLeods of Raasay, Murdo, bro. of Calum Òg 207–208
MacLeods of Raasay, Murdo, Dr, of Eyre, Snizort 52–55, 213–214
MacLeods of Raasay, Roderick, Maighistir Ruairidh 215
MacLeods of Raasay, Seonaid (1688–1692) 47, 210–212
MacLeods of Raasay, Sileas (1688–1692) 47, 210–212
MacLeods of Talisker, John 54–55, 64
MacMillan, Alexander, teacher 84, 112
MacMillan, Daniel, Oscaig 113
MacMillan, John, Clachan 116, 121, 146
MacQueen, Malcolm, smith 109
MacQueens of Totaroam, Jane 60, 62, 215–217
MacRae, Alexander, Hallaig 106
MacRae, Annie, teacher 169
MacRae, Christopher, Rona 122–123
MacRae, Donald, Balachuirn 107 (DFC), 150–151 (DFC)
MacRae, Farquhar, Castle 104, 148
MacRae, Kenneth, Big Harbour 81
MacRaes of Inverinate, Duncan, Donnchadh nam Piòs 47, 211
MacSwan, Alexander, Dry Harbour 148 (DFC)
MacSween, Donald, Clachan 121
MacSween, Iain Mòr, Doire Domhain 104, 148
MacSweens of Raasay 17–18
Man, Isle of 12–15
marriage, Celtic laws of 28–29
Martin, Martin (*A Description* . . . c. 1695) 49, 62
Matheson, Duncan, Oscaig 110, 122, 143
Matheson, Thomas, ploughman 95
mill, Raasay 63, 70, 151
millstones 71, 77
Minty, William, head gardener 145
Monro, Donald (*Description* . . . 1549) 22–23, 25–26
Montgomery, John Roy, servant of Captain Malcolm 54
Morrison, Murdo, Rev., FPC minister 159
Munro, David, mining engineer 160, 166
Munro, John, missionary 130–131 (NC), 138–139 (NC), 145
Murchison, Isabella, Screapadal 106

Napier Commission 123–142, 157
Nicolson, Alexander, Dry Harbour 145
Nicolson, Alexander, teacher 116, 158
Nicolson, Anne, Dry Harbour 148
Nicolson, Donald, Dry Harbour 145
Nicolson, Donald, servant of Captain Malcolm 54, 56
Nicolson, Ewen, Doire na Guaille 122
Nicolson, John, Doire na Guaille 137–138 (NC)
Nicolson, John, Torran 122–123, 253
Nicolson, Murdo, Dry Harbour 145
Nicolson, Murdo, Torran 133 (NC)
Nicolson, Norman, Arnish 116
Nicolson, Peter 113, 146, 173, 252
Nicolson, Ronald, Doire na Guaille 146–147 (DFC)
Nicolsons of Scorrybreac 44–45, 209, 243
North of Scotland Hydro Electric Board 173

Old Parish Records (OPR) 80, 93
Old Statistical Account (OSA) 69–73
Ordnance Survey name books 158–159
Oscaig Township, creation of 125–127
Otter, Captain, nautical survey *c.* 1851 81

Park, Abraham, teacher 113
peat 33, 50, 63, 109, 128, 137
Picts/Pictish 9, 11
pier, new pier at Suisnish, Raasay 160
pier, old pier at Clachan, Raasay 110–111, 174–175,
poor fund 72
population on Raasay 34, 63, 67, 71, 77, 80–81, 90, 96–98, 108, 176, 181–182
Post Office 72, 113–114, 158
privy council 39, 207, 229

Raasay, ownership of the estate 190–191
Raasay estate, management 1830s and 1840s 89–92
Raasay House, the history of 239–242
Raasay Outdoor Centre 181–182, 242
raiding & feuding 27, 57, 74
Rainy, estate rules 100–101
Rainy, George 95–114
Rainy, George Haygarth 114–117, 158
Rainy, Robert, Rev. 112, 139
Rainy's yacht, *Falcon* 110

Rankin, William, cashier 160
Rawnsley, Mr, tenant of sporting estate 160, 165
rebellion of 1745 51–58
Regional Council, Roads Department 173
Rennie, John, gardener 95, 110, 113–114
rent per township 86–87, 119, 143
retour of 1630 270
retour of 1688 47–48, 210, 271–272
Ross, Elizabeth 82, 216–217
Ross, James, factor 118–120 (DFC), 123–141 (NC), 153–155 (DFC)
Royal burghs 30, 49, 67
run-rig 33–34, 70–71, 76, 91

salt/salt laws 73, 78–79
Scalpay, Isle of 41, 177
schools 78, 83–84, 109, 112–113, 145, 158, 161, 169–171
Scotti 9
Scottish Land Court (SLC) 159–160, 163–164
Scottish Society for the Propagation of Christian Knowledge (SSPCK) 83–84, 109, 112
sculptured slabs 15, 17
sea fight at Clachan 39–41, 208
sheep club stocks 156, 167
sheep farm/farming 79, 89, 104, 108, 148, 160
shop 72, 173
Small Landholders (Scotland) Act 1911 159–160, 162
smallpox 71, 113
soumming 50, 63
St Columba 10–15
St Moluag 11, 15–17
St Moluag's chapel, description of 232–235
Statutes of Iona 41–42, 48, 57
steamers of the nineteenth century, *Chevalier, Clansman, Cygnet, Dolphin, Duntroon, Islay, Marquis of Stafford, Mary Jane* 96, 102–103, 109–110
steamers of the twentieth century, *Loch Arkaig, Loch Nevis* 173, 175–176
Stewart, Alexander, estate manager 121
stock held by tenants and cottars in 1851 105–106

Storab 8, 57, 128
strike by mine workers 162
Stuart, Charles Edward, Bonnie Prince Charlie 51–54, 56
surnames 21–22, 222
symbol stones 11

tacks/tacksmen 48–49, 57, 65, 69–70, 74, 79, 86, 89–90
Tallach, Miss Margaret, teacher 161, 169
teinds 23, 31
townships 32–33, 42, 47–48
trades, encouragement of 66
Treaty of Perth 1266 13

typhoid 102–103

Union of the Parliaments 49
Urquhart, James, teacher 109, 113, 116

Vikings 10–11

Wardlaw Manuscript 46, 210
West Highland Free Press 166, 174–180
witchcraft 45–46
Wood, Mrs Evelyn (1886–1911) 142–160
Wood, Edward Herbert (1876–1886) 120–142
Wood's schooner, *Rona* 122, 143